EUROPEAN SECURITY BEYOND THE YEAR 2000

EUROPEAN SECURITY BEYOND THE YEAR 2000

Edited by
Robert Rudney
and Luc Reychler

PRAEGER

New York
Westport, Connecticut
London

Library of Congress Cataloging-in-Publication Data

European security beyond the year 2000.

Includes index.
1. Europe—Defenses. 2. North Atlantic Treaty
Organization. I. Rudney, Robert. II. Reychler, Luc.
UA646.E9253 1988   355'.03304   87-12494
ISBN 0-275-92625-7 (alk. paper)

Library of Congress Catalog Card Number: 87-12494
ISBN: 0-275-92625-7

First published in 1988

Praeger Publishers, One Madison Avenue, New York, NY 10010
A division of Greenwood Press, Inc.

Printed in the United States of America

The paper used in this book complies with the
Permanent Paper Standard issued by the National
Information Standards Organization (Z39.48-1984).

10 9 8 7 6 5 4 3 2 1

323418

Contents

Preface

This book is the end product of a multi-year project on European security and defense thinking, undertaken by the Division of International Relations, University of Leuven (Louvain), Belgium. In the course of this project, we surveyed the research sector and published our results in the <u>Directory Guide of European Security and Defense Research</u>. Our project report comprimising country-by-country analyses was subsequently published as <u>In Search of European Security : An Assessment of the European Security and Defense Research Sector</u>. We are grateful to the Ford and Rockefeller Foundations, the Defense Studies Center (Brussels), and NATO for providing funding support for this work.

The next logical step was to ask where Europe was headed in the long-term future. One area in which European scholars can make a valuable contribution is in the formulation of long-range thinking and forecasting, providing a 20- or 30-year perspective for political leaders and policy-makers operating in six-to 18-month time frames. To this end, we commissioned prospective papers from experts in the 18 major non-Communist countries with the objective of evaluating future scenarios for security policies. For the United Kingdom, France, and the Federal Republic of Germany, we asked for two assessments each. The contributors were requested to define their countries' long-term threat perceptions, to evaluate the official security policies designed to cope with these threats, to assess whether these policies commanded a sufficient public and elite consensus, and to make prescriptions for improving security policies over the next thirty years. Prediction is admittedly a perilous undertaking, but it is the role of the policy analyst to provide guidelines and caution signs for future years.

We would like to thank each of our contributors for his support and interest in this project. From this work, we hope to stimulate an increased awareness of common security interests among Europeans with the ultimate goal of forging a stronger European consciousness and identity in this critical policy area. In the last chapter, we advance a series of recommendations for constructing a viable, forward-looking security policy for the beginning of the twenty-first century. Today, Europeans find themselves equidistant in time between the years 1973-74, whose tumultuous events greatly shaped Europe's present security environment, and the year 2000, symbol of a new departure, of new possibilities. It is not too early to begin thinking about the configuration of a security system in the next century.

This study was done under the auspices of the Division of International Relations in the Department of Political Science at Leuven. We would like to thank all of our associates at Leuven for their help and encouragement. We would also like to thank Joëlle and Ilse for tolerating so many arcane discussions of bombs and missiles with such good humor. Ronny Van Ermen did an excellent job of word-processing.

The authors take full responsibility for the contents of this book. We would appreciate any comments or reactions of readers.

EUROPEAN SECURITY BEYOND THE YEAR 2000

Introduction: What Future for Europe?

Robert Rudney

A specter is haunting Europe: the specter of Europe. The long-term process of reconciliation, reconstruction, integration, and ultimate unification of the Western European peoples constitutes one of the major turning points in twentieth-century history. It is a success story unimaginable in 1815 or 1871 or 1918, and barely conceivable in 1945. The progress achieved by the now twelve European Community member states in the political, economic and social spheres is indeed impressive, despite the perennial quarrels. A governing system, based on intensive consultation among partners, has asserted itself, and an institutional superstructure, situated in Brussels, is assuming more and more of the powers of administration. The European Parliament, elected by universal suffrage, is also demanding a larger role in policymaking. Most important, Europeans have begun to think European; this sense of identity has been transmitted to the postwar generation, which has been brought up with the European ideal. From this standpoint, the movement toward European unification seems ineluctable.

Why, then, is there such a prevalent feeling of pessimism, even fatalism, in Western Europe today ? Many reasons can be offered for this psychological downturn. The lingering economic crisis, the ensuing political paralysis, the constant disputes over agricultural policy and the equitable division of financial burdens, the inevitable weight of bureaucracy in Brussels, the threat of technological retardation all partly explain why present-day Europe lacks confidence and vitality. Another element is one of security. Over the past decade, Europeans have begun to question the basis of the transatlantic security system that has been essential to political integration and economic recovery. They feel themselves more menaced (due to a perceived Soviet threat and other factors of global instability) and less protected (due to strained relations with the United States). This growing sense of insecurity extends to neutral countries as well. For almost four decades, non-Communist Europe has enjoyed all the advantages of armed, nuclear peace and very few of the inconveniences. All the Western European countries, neutral states included, have constructed their postwar social welfare systems on the assumption that their defense expenditures would remain at relatively moderate levels. Moreover, detente, enshrined in the Helsinki accords of 1975, appeared to inaugurate a period of negotiation, accommodation, and relaxation of tensions with the superpower to the east and its Eastern European allies.

All of these factors have altered dramatically over the past decade. Europe now stands at a crossroads; the present ad hoc approach to political and economic integration does not work very well anymore, and the postwar system of security dependencies is fragile and outdated. One prevalent reaction to these circumstances has been the short-sighted protection of the national, particularist advantages to the detriment of the common interest. But Western Europe can no longer function as an economic superpower, a political schizophrenic, and a military vassal. One of the principal obstacles blocking European progress has been the constant inability to conceive of long-range future trends, especially with respect to security and defense. For the European NATO members, a fundamental reassessment of their security policies has led them to question U.S. strategic guarantees and the entire Atlantic system. For the neutrals, such an analysis raises serious challenges to their previously comfortable security assumptions. These attitudes, however, disregard the dynamic nature of the international system. Consequently, in moments of crisis, the policy of Europe has been largely fragmented and reactive, responding to threats rather than taking steps to solve security problems. This is a nonpolicy.

The following essays represent a collaborative effort on the part of specialists from eighteen countries of non-Communist Europe to evaluate long-term future scenarios within the European security environment; All of the contibutors come from independent or university-related research centers.[1] It is primarily by means of independent research, networking, and scholarly interchange that a distinctly European consciousness on security and defense issues can evolve. The first step is to increase communication and cooperation between researchers and research organizations. Frequently, European researchers maintain closer contacts with their U.S. counterparts than with each other. What we intend to present here is a comprehensive, country-by-country security assessment, followed by an examination of the overall prospects for greater European cooperation and a step-by-step agenda for encouraging increased European self-reliance in security and defense.[2] We have asked each contributor to analyze threat perceptions on a national basis, to assess official security policies and alternative future strategies, and to prescribe an optimal strategy for the next 30 years, combining military and economic credibility with public support.

Most of the contributors believe that present security arrangements will survive more or less intact until the end of the century. Very few of these observers predict any serious movement toward European political integration and/or a structural reform in defense. They tend to extrapolate from past trends and posit an extension of the politics of "muddling through." Nearly all contributors foresee a continuation of the existing "economy of limits" and predict difficult trade-offs between defense and social expenditures. No one really foresees a new period of economic prosperity with expanding resources for all concerned. One aspect of a continuing economy of limits is the perceived infeasibility of alternative strategies or a significant increase in defense appropriations (ergo responsibilities). There is too much invested in the present system, and the political risks of any major transformation of policy are seen as too great. These views reflect prevailing attitudes in European countries and not necessarily the personal predilections of the contributors.

What these papers demonstrate is not so much a sense of "Europessimism," but rather a pervasive aura of "Euroskepticism," of policy drift with no guiding objectives.

There appears to be little faith in new initiatives to organize European defense more effectively and efficiently. Among NATO countries, there is an ongoing insistence on a dependency relationship with the United States, a relationship which the United States cannot and will not sustain in its present form for the indefinite future. Among neutral states, there is a complacent satisfaction with the status quo, even though long-term external dangers are recognized and political and economic dependencies are acknowledged. There is some expectation of moderately improved relations with the East, but nothing on the scale of the late 1960s and early 1970s. Last, there is a psychological element, a "little Europe" mentality, produced largely by the shrinking of Europe with the loss of empires and by the psychological hangover of the European civil wars (1914-1945). Europeans have become introspective, and the economic dislocations of the past fifteen years have accelerated this tendency. Unfortunately, the world outside is changing rapidly. Most European governments appear to be waiting on external circumstances to force policy decisions. What may be required to reawaken Europe is the shock of a major global crisis. But then it may be too late.

The authors assembled here are very much aware of the shortcomings of their national security policies and of the strategic vulnerability of a divided continent. The lack of physical space (Europe's geographic position as a densely populated peninsula extending westward from the Asian land mass) has significantly reinforced the idea of interdependence (and shared external dependencies) among European nations. This impression of physical exposure is all the more apparent when modern weapons technologies, both nuclear and non-nuclear, are assessed. As the region with the highest concentration of advanced armament, Europe necessarily becomes the most likely battlefield for World War III. All of the European countries are conscious of the inherent dangers in ·the continued division of the continent into two hostile alliance systems. From the European perspective, detente between East and West is not so much a policy option as it is a policy requirement. In the same way, a sufficient national defense effort is deemed essential for the very preservation of the national existence.

The past several years have seen a remarkable growth in the number and quality of European research institutions dedicated to the study of these complex problems. Because of the diverse political sensitivities involved in security issues, it is extremely difficult for European governments and intergovernmental organizations to carry out a security assessment of this scope and direction. But independent and university-related institutions have the autonomy, expertise, and flexibility to engage in a thorough examination of problems of these dimensions. Lately, there are encouraging signs of what might be called a European "proto-consciousness" on security and defense issues. The expanding research sector testifies to a realization on the national level of the need for more detached, objective analysis. Channels of communication and collaboration are opening up between specialists in different countries who seek to transcend limited national perspectives and to develop a more profound European identification of interests in these vital areas. Practically all the conceptual framework defining the transatlantic security relationship was formulated in the United States, and it could be claimed that the field of international relations has been almost exclusively a U.S. social science (though influenced appreciably by European emigrés). Today, however, the Europeans themselves must define their security requirements and capabilities more rigorously and communicate these perspectives to each other. External upheavals, coupled with economic stringencies and the growing restiveness of the European public and political elites, have exposed all the pitfalls of the traditional policy of "muddling through" and waiting on events.

THREAT PERCEPTIONS

The primary threat perception derives, not surprisingly, from the Soviet Union. But there are conceptual nuances to the appreciation of this danger. In his chapter on Belgium, Steven Dierckx develops a useful typology of schools of thought in this area. He distinguishes between adherents of "separate" security (that is, "a scarce resource of fixed quantity : the more security 'they' have, the less security 'we' have") and adherents of "common" security (that is, "a resource of variable quantity: cooperative measures will enhance the security of both sides"). Those advocates of "separate" security perceive the Soviet Union as "an expansionistic, but opportunistic actor." Dierckx divides this school into two subparadigms : the "Atlanticists," who see the dissolution of Atlantic solidarity as the "most threatening" result of the Soviet challenge, and the "Federalists," who see fundamentally divergent interests between the United States and its European allies and propose greater European independence in the domain of defense. By contrast, the common security advocates perceive the primary threat coming from tensions between the alliance blocs and the ensuing arms race (which appears to them to be escalating out of control). According to this view, "Western Europe is not only a nuclear hostage of the Soviet Union, but is also a military (and secondary) pawn on the American chess-board." Dierckx further distinguishes between moderates and radicals in this school, the latter distrusting U.S. policy as inherently more destabilizing than Soviet policy.

This typology is valuable in classifying the threat perceptions of the contributors to this book. All of the contributors from NATO countries subscribe more or less to the separate security paradigm. On the other hand, authors from neutral countries reflect more of a common security approach. This breakdown is predictable, since contributors were selected in part because their expert views were largely representative of the prevailing security consensus in their countries. In this way, NATO members perceive a real, tangible threat from the Soviet Union, while neutral states tend more to fear political-military instabilities derived from the alliance systems and the arms race dynamic. Both groupings mention vulnerabilities due to external dependency on energy, food and raw material supplies. The authors from NATO southern countries are generally more responsive to potential threats from political and social upheaval in the Third World. Interestingly enough, no contributor cites any long-term threat coming from the resurgence of fundamentalist Islam in the Middle East/Mediterranean area. Their concerns are principally directed toward specific menaces, such as possible Libyan support of terrorism and insurgencies in the region, the possible threat by Morocco to Spanish possessions (Antonio Sánchez-Gijón), Italian sensitivity regarding U.S. antiterrorist operations (Virgilio Ilari), and Kurdish separatism (Ersin Onulduran).

The general tendency among authors from NATO countries is to perceive the Soviet Union as "a 'normal great power' pursuing its interests in the way great powers do and in ways which often conflict with Western interests". (Faurby, chapter 10). From this standpoint, the principal Soviet threat is not one of overt aggression, but rather one of calculating opportunism. The real danger is not so much a blitzkrieg attack on Western Europe, in which the Soviet Union would be taking enormous risks of unleashing a full-scale nuclear war. On the contrary, Reimund Seidelmann notes, the political elites have concluded that "the Soviet Union is saturated in Europe, pursues an overall defensive posture, and does not intend to use direct military threat in the foreseeable future." The danger that preoccupies Europeans is rather the possibility of misperceptions or miscalculations leading to conflict and escalating to total war. Historically speaking, the 1914 analogy has precedence over the 1939 analogy in their view. In addition, there is apprehension among some contributors over the potential consequences of an "indirect" strategy perpetrated by the Soviets with the objective of decoupling the United States from Europe. To observers like Michel Makinsky, recent events (notably the Afghanistan invasion and the Polish coup) have demonstrated that the Soviets are not willing to abide by "the rules of the game," as established in the detente process. In this perspective, Soviet propaganda has exploited the antimissile movement to drive a wedge between the United States and its European allies. The ultimate goal is to neutralize or "Finlandize" Western Europe. The Soviets also allegedly capitalize on Third World instability to undermine Western political-strategic positions. Their rapidly expanding navy is seen as a symbol of this capability to project power around the globe.

Consequently, while the authors from NATO countries do not perceive the Soviet Union as an ideologically driven power bent on world domination, they differ on the nature and extent of the threat (especially outside of Europe). There is a realization of the risk that a regional conflict (most likely in the Middle East) could expand into a superpower confrontation and spill over into a war in Europe. Some of these observers also see a serious threat of a deteriorating crisis situation in Eastern Europe ultimately provoking the Soviets to attack the West. But as the true intentions of Soviet policy will probably never be known, it is not all that fruitful to speculate on their raison d'être. The most effective response, it is agreed, is to maintain some sort of perceived balance in military capabilities and commitments. Baard Bredrup Knudsen writes that "whether it is 'defensive' or 'offensive,' whether it is purely a reflection of the desire to equal the United States as a superpower, or whether there are underlying or concrete plans for a continued expansion of the Soviet sphere of influence in Europe, if necessary through military means - is of secondary importance. What the Soviets themselves refer to as the 'correlation of forces' inherently produces its own logic with politically real consequences." According to Dierckx's typology, all the authors from NATO states subscribe to the Atlanticist paradigm in that they view a continued U.S. commitment to Europe as absolutely necessary to its security. Some of them do reveal long-term Federalist predilections (with Europe taking on an increasing share of the defense burden), but no contributor goes so far as to advocate an eventual transatlantic divorce. This may be seen as a measure of the underlying political consensus in these countries.

The contributors from the neutral countries are less preoccupied with the Soviet threat and more concerned with encouraging stabilizing elements within regional, European, and global strategic environments. Their objective is to maintain a balance and, even more important, to alleviate the sources of conflict in Europe. As advocates of the "common" security paradigm, the neutrals see all actors benefiting from measures to preserve peace and slow down (or stop) the arms race. Unto Vesa, for one, contends that there is no official Finnish threat perception "aimed at a certain state or group of states." Instead, the Finns view with alarm the impressive advances in military (especially nuclear) technology that are undermining, in their perspective, the process of East-West detente. In similar terms, Daniel Frei depicts the actual European security situation as one of "relative peace," which is "presently maintained by the balance of terror only, a delicate balance prone to destabilization by technological breakthroughs, the arms race, and irrational actions." Neutral countries tend to fear that they will be brought into a conflict through indirect developments. In Heinz Gärtner's analysis, for instance, Austria might be occupied in order to serve as a "launching pad" or "transit point" for a major attack. Bo Huldt, Frei and Gärtner stress the risk of economic vulnerability (interruption of international trade and access to raw materials), which could compromise neutralist policy or encourage political-military blackmail on the part of an outside power. Moreover, Huldt points to the dependencies and enormous expense involved in maintaining a credible military deterrent. At times, neutralist threat perceptions appear purposely vague, as in the Finnish rationalization of the Friendship, Cooperation and Mutual Assistance (FCMA) Treaty with the USSR. In the Irish case, as Patrick Keatinge observes, there is no external threat perception, given the Irish geographic situation, traditional insularity, and obsession with the situation in Ulster. Unlike the other four states, Ireland is not a frontline neutral and does not perceive an immediate threat from the bloc system. The common security paradigm is shared by an increasing number of opposition parties in NATO countries, especially the "Scandilux" states, with strong ties between socialist parties. These opposition parties (not to mention the German Social Democrats and British Labour) could well come to power over the next decade and totally transform the security policy landscape. The arrival in power of one such party could exert a domino effect on the political scene in the other countries.

As for the levels of potential conflict, Ken Booth lists : (1) nuclear war between the superpowers; (2) a war in Europe between NATO and the Warsaw Pact; (3) conflicts outside Europe; and (4) domestic security problems. All contributors agree that the chance of a total nuclear war is extremely slim (and could be triggered only by accident or miscalculation). These conflict scenarios are interrelated, as a crisis outside of Europe could well induce an interbloc war, and both these eventualities could spark a superpower nuclear confrontation. This concept of an "escalation ladder" is generally accepted by contributors from both NATO and neutral countries.

The authors' threat perceptions can also be divided according to their geographic situations, that is, Northern, Central, or Southern Europe. The Northern European commentators (both NATO and neutral) share a common concern about their previously peaceful region evolving into an area of increasing superpower competition and stress the growing vulnerability of small states caught up in a global power struggle. In Southern Europe there is less a communal security consciousness and more interstate rivalry (Greece-Turkey and, to a much lesser extent, Portugal-Spain). As the southern countries are generally poorer and more exposed to Third World upheavals, they reflect a stronger sense of economic vulnerabilities and potential threats emanating from the Mediterranean-Red Sea-Persian Gulf region. Their detached situation vis-à-vis the Soviet Union (except for Turkey) gives them some strategic breathing space, but their economic weakness and dependency relationship with the United States (sealed in military base accords) restrict their freedom of action. Alvaro Vasconcelos, for example, conveys Portuguese disillusionment with "the disproportion between the importance of facilities granted to NATO allies and the means of the Portuguese armed forces."

Within the central layer of states, one has first to differentiate between the two nuclear countries (France and Britain) with great power status at the United Nations and worldwide commitments, and the nonnuclear countries, whose security perspective is limited to Europe. In this area, it could be claimed that the Federal Republic of Germany (FRG) is the biggest of the small powers, with strong dependency relationships, a distinctly defensive (and reactive) military posture, and an intense fear of being transformed into the logical battlefield for World War III. Both Frei and Gärtner stress their neutral countries' highly dependent (i.e., small and landlocked) status, the defensive nature of their military forces, and the realization that Switzerland and Austria occupy a dangerous position in the event of East-West conflict. The intense debate (and many delays) over the Cruise missile deployment in Belgium and the Netherlands reflects their highly vulnerable, highly dependent self-images. Only Ireland, because of its geographic isolation, perceives itself (according to Keatinge) to be remote from the vagaries of interbloc conflict.

Britain and France share many similarities in that they both have medium-sized (and growing) nuclear arsenals consuming a large share of their defense budget, global strategic considerations (owing to their former status as world empires), and ambivalent attitudes toward the threat in Central Europe. Christopher Coker points to arguments within the British government between those who favor a maritime strategy and those who perceive basic security interests depending on continued maintenance of the British Army of the Rhine. Both Makinsky and Nicole Gnesotto emphasize the continued tension between the strategic assumptions sustaining the independent French nuclear deterrent and the perceived need to increase cooperation with European allies (especially the FRG). This last imperative is felt more deeply in France than in Britain, mainly for geographic reasons.

Historical factors have also shaped European threat perceptions. Contributors from Norway, Denmark, the Netherlands, and Belgium all state that the experience of neutrality during the interwar period and the shock of the German invasion and occupation convinced their ruling elites that some system of collective security was essential in the postwar era. The two defeated enemies, Germany and Italy, became members of the Atlantic Alliance in part to accelerate their own integration into Europe and acceptance into the world community. On the other hand, French suspicions of NATO can be traced to their futile efforts to build a collective security system in the interwar period and to their own pretensions as a great (i.e., independent) power after 1945. In the Gaullist vision, France was to serve as a balancer and intermediary between the "Anglo-Saxon" and Soviet powers and as the driving force behind the liberation of Europe from the bloc system. As for Britain, the disastrous victory of 1945, the loss of empire, and the rise of the U.S. colossus were all factors in the country's geopolitical and economic decline and acceptance of the principal secondary role in the new alliance system.

On the other hand, both Spain and Portugal were officially neutral in World War II. Portugal, like Iceland, did grant the Allies base rights, and both countries were subsequently integrated into the Atlantic system (as Vasconcelos and Gunnarsson show). For Franco, as for the postwar West German and Italian regimes, membership in the Western alliance would have served as a political legitimizing factor. Unlike the FRG and Italy, Spain has no direct threat perception of the Soviet Union and, in fact, fought its last declared war with the United States in 1898. Sánchez-Gijón relates how leftist hostility toward NATO membership is tied to U.S. support for Franco's dictatorship. Greece and Turkey, though historic enemies, were brought into the Atlantic system largely because of the U.S. threat perceptions, as expressed in the Truman Doctrine of 1947. Their potentially explosive dispute, centering around control of Cyprus and Aegean air and maritime space, clouds NATO planning in the Mediterranean. Both countries' perceptions of the Soviet threat are tempered by the intense, centuries-old suspicions and antagonisms toward each other. This is the one spot in Europe where actual war could break out between erstwhile allies.

Two neutral countries, Switzerland and Sweden, have historical traditions of international neutrality and were able to preserve this status during World War II. Two other neutrals, Finland and Austria, had their status dictated to them by international agreement; the bilateral FCMA Treaty and the multilateral State Treaty literally defined defense posture (and thus threat analysis) for the Finns and Austrians, respectively. The other neutral country, Ireland, maintained this status partially because of its historical antagonism toward NATO member Britain; Irish neutrality poses an institutional problem for projects to increase European defense cooperation as it is the only EC member not in the Atlantic Alliance.

There is also a domestic aspect to threat perceptions. First, the painful, long-term economic crisis that Europe has endured over the past fifteen years has had a profound effect on the way Europeans view their defense efforts. Most commentators insist that there will be strict financial limitations to the expansion of defense budgets over the next several years. Nearly all polling data reveal that economic problems (notably unemployment) far exceed defense issues in the public's policy priorities. Moreover, the rapidly escalating costs of modern weapon systems have put a procurement "squeeze" on all the military establishments. Thus the amount of money available for defense purposes will increase marginally (in most cases), but the projected costs for defense are expected to skyrocket. All these countries face a defense budget gap between what is deemed essential for national security and what is affordable. Social welfare expenditures have also suffered from huge deficits, but these benefits are, for the most part, untouchable. Social security precedes national security, from the point of view of most Europeans. These economic constraints constitute one more argument for European cooperation in defense, especially in the rationalization of defense industries.

Booth sees the possibility of violent action resulting from the economic crisis and points to the trauma of the British miners' strike as an indicator of this potential for future violence. The two German contributors (Seidelmann and Brauch) stress the need for economic growth and welfare structures to ensure political stability and legitimacy. In all countries, the preservation of the social security system is a necessary condition for maintaining the political consensus supporting the defense effort. Any severe cut in social expenditures (to the benefit of defense) would encounter major public resistance and would entail political suicide for the parties and individuals in power. Only in the context of a serious international crisis situation would such a reallocation of resources be thinkable. A few contributors also mention the long-term threat of Europe falling behind in the high technology race. In his chapter on Sweden, Huldt cites environmental menaces, in particular the consequences of the Chernobyl disaster and the future of the nuclear power industry.

There is the additional problem of internal destabilization, largely through provocation by terrorist activities. These terrorist campaigns have ethnic and religious, as well as political origins, and often traverse international boundaries. The objectives of politically oriented terrorist groups are not so much to seize power, but to point up the vulnerability of society and the impotence of the government in power and to incite a crackdown by public authorities which would, in theory, radicalize a larger portion of the population. In Italy, the FRG, France, and Belgium, these fringe groups have been mostly broken up, but terrorist activities still pose a serious problem. The international nature of political terrorism (what the media has labeled "Euroterrorism") has been recognized, and European cooperation in this area has increased appreciably, especially in the wake of the U.S. bombing of Libya in March - April 1986.

Terrorism can also take the form of religious or ethnic agitation. The situation in Northern Ireland has been described by Keatinge as "a transnational threat posed by extremist nationalists, such as the Provisional Irish Republican Army (PIRA)." Both Coker and Booth point to the British military success in curbing terrorist activities, but also to the inability of the parties involved to reach a political settlement. The Hillsborough agreement signed in November 1985 may represent a first step in negotiating a long-term compromise, but, thus far, it has resulted only in a further radicalization of the Protestant population. As Coker notes, a Catholic voting majority (projected for 2006) may bring about ultimate union, "and Dublin will have to deal with the problems that will undoubtedly come from a discontented Protestant minority."

Spain also faces a critical terrorist challenge, primarily from the Basque extremists of the ETA militar. As Sánchez-Gijón observes, the process of devolution of powers seems to have satisfied Catalan separatists, and the main Basque political movements have agreed to form a regional government. The problem has taken on international dimensions, since the ETA militar has used the French sanctuary as a hide-out and staging ground, though the French have recently tightened border control. It is hoped that the progressive integration of the Basque parties into the governmental process will succeed in defusing the terrorist threat.

A number of contributors (notably Makinsky) mention the international link between terrorist organizations and finger Col. Khadaffi as the chief instigator behind this network. Makinsky sees these terrorist activities as part of the "indirect" or "oblique" strategy of destabilization perpetrated by the Soviet Union. Both Vasconcelos and Ilari also cite destabilization techniques utilized by Communist parties, in close association with the Soviet Union.

Another important factor with both domestic and international overtones is the future of European overseas territories, the last remnants of global empires. The Falklands War of 1982 drove home to the British the fact that worldwide possessions, no matter how small or seemingly insignificant, carried with them security risks, responsibilities, and ultimately costs in men and equipment. On the other hand, the Spanish - British dispute over Gibraltar was mitigated by the agreement to negotiate and to reopen the border (closed by Spain since 1969). Spain has also security concerns for the enclave cities of Ceuta and Melilla (threatened by Morocco) and the Canary Islands (menaced by a small separatist movement). Minor separatist movements are also active in the Portuguese possessions of the Azores and Madeira. For his part, Makinsky criticizes the previous French Socialist government's laxness over the threats of insurrection in the overseas departments, particularly New Caledonia and Guadeloupe. In a different region, Denmark (according to Faurby) may, in the future find itself estranged from its strategically located territories of Greenland and the Faroe Islands. The important point here is that these overseas possessions require defense commitments and could conceivably embroil NATO allies in conflicts, like the Falklands War, where there are no clear-cut Western interests involved.

Another potential threat mentioned by a few authors is the huge influx of immigrant workers entering Europe from the Third World. The racially motivated riots in Britain in 1985 were perhaps an augur for other European countries. The immigrant populations have suffered most of all from the economic crisis, and their growing presence has begun to provoke a "white backlash," best illustrated by the stunning success of the xenophobic National Front in the 1986 French legislative elections. The issue of immigrant populations also underlines the demographic decline of most European countries (although the potential for danger here was mentioned only by Brauch, Gnesotto and Sánchez-Gijón). The falling birthrate statistics mean a critical manpower shortage for NATO, which in the FRG has already resulted in the extension of compulsory military service to 18 months. This development is bound to have major implications for future conventional deterrence strategies (as Brauch demonstrates).

The phenomenon of terrorism is also associated with the question of civilian control of the military, principally in the southern countries. The February 1981 coup attempt in Spain was directly related to the military insistence that the civilian government could not deal effectively with the terrorist threat. Similarly, the Turkish army's seizure of power in 1980 arose from the undeniably deteriorating situation of domestic security, with daily terrorist killings and bombings. The civilian republican governments in Portugal and Greece have also had to deal with problems of the military's role in politics, which has historically been important in both cases. These internal considerations permeate all aspects of security and defense policy, especially in the newly democratic regimes.

Security issues can also be manipulated for domestic political ends, most evidently in the Euromissile debates. As Siccama emphasizes for the Netherlands, the Cruise missile deployment has been used by political parties to mobilize electoral support and by political figures to further career ambitions. In Denmark, the fragile center-right coalition has been regularly embarrassed by being put in the minority for motions on security issues introduced by the left-wing opposition parties. One element in the Spanish NATO referendum campaign was the manipulation of anti-U.S. sentiments, associated with Washington's support of Franco. In all these controversies, it is difficult to determine exactly where domestic considerations terminate and external considerations begin. Nevertheless, domestic political factors now impinge on the formulation of security and defense policy, to a degree unparalleled since World War II, and these factors color the way nations perceive threats. It is generally agreed that security and defense policy has undergone a politicization process, marked by a heightened consciousness and changing attitudes among the political elites, rather than a democratization process that would entail a grass-roots transformation of popular perceptions. This contention is borne out by polling data and results of recent elections. In any event, political calculations now pervade the security and defense debate to an unprecedented degree.

Finally, a number of contributors note the lack of a "strategic culture" (Ilari, chapter 14) to provide objective analysis of complex security issues and to coordinate policymaking between the various ministries involved in the process. Accurate threat perceptions are only possible when governments have the conceptual resources and the information available to evaluate the global power balance and to assess realistic policy alternatives. Democratic governments have to convince public opinion leaders that official policies conform to dominant national values and contribute to the realization of these values (what we call the normative legitimacy of security policy). In addition, these governments have to convince public opinion leaders that it has enough insight into the changing international environment to realize its aims most effectively with the means at hand (i.e., the cognitive legitimacy of security policy). Both of these elements of security policy have to be based on a precise reading of short-term and long-term menaces.

POLICIES AND PRESCRIPTIONS

In December 1967, the NATO Council of Ministers approved a report on "The Future Tasks of the Alliance," drawn up by a committee headed by the Belgian Foreign Minister, Pierre Harmel. The Harmel report (often described as the "Harmel Doctrine") outlined two main functions for the Alliance : to "maintain as necessary a suitable military capability to assure the balance of forces" and "to pursue the search for the progress towards a more stable relationship in which the underlying political issues can be solved."[3] In the long run, according to Harmel, "the ultimate political purpose of the Alliance is to achieve a just and lasting peaceful order in Europe accompanied by appropriate security guarantees." From this perspective, the allies should consult on and coordinate their detente policies to maximize success in negotiations with the Soviet Union and Eastern Europe. Most importantly, Harmel insisted that "military security and a policy of detente are not contradictory but complementary."

Over the past 20 years, the percepts laid out by Harmel have become the core of Atlantic solidarity as envisioned by the European member states. His report was issued at another moment of ephemeral crisis in NATO, precipitated by the French military withdrawal, the inauguration of West German Ostpolitik, the failure of the multilateral nuclear force (MLF) proposal, the debate over the Vietnam War, and the formulation of the "flexible response" strategy. The purpose behind his study was to give a political/diplomatic dimension to a basically military alliance and to pave the way for disarmament and "practical" arms control measures in a European framework. The high degree of cooperation among NATO states in the Conference on Security and Cooperation in Europe (CSCE) and Mutual and Balanced Force Reduction (MBFR) negotiations, for example, are testament to the judiciousness of this reorientation. From 1967 on, NATO, for the Europeans, evolved into an instrument for building bridges to the East as well for ensuring their own communal self-protection. In this light, the "double-track" decision of December 1979 appears as an element of continuity in Alliance policy. To the European member countries, the declaration of intention to negotiate on the reduction of intermediate nuclear forces was as important as (if not more important than) the agreement to deploy Pershing II and Cruise missiles. Yet the heated controversy that erupted over this decision represented the most dangerous challenge to the Harmel consensus and indicated the necessity to restate (and update) Alliance policy priorities.

A number of NATO contributors to this book cite the Harmel report as the foundation for official security policy in their countries. Nearly all of these commentators would agree that the preservation of the NATO military deterrent and the promotion of detente and arms control are the two major tasks for the Alliance. The long-range policy objective, in their view, remains precisely "a just and lasting peaceful order in Europe accompanied by appropriate security guarantees." This goal is shared by the neutral countries, as reflected in the chapters that follow. The requirement for a sufficient defense, coupled with an active search for political tension-reduction measures in Europe, constitutes the basis for security policy in Austria, Finland, Sweden, and Switzerland. Only Ireland (as Keatinge notes) still profits from "the relatively 'insulated' geostrategic position of the state," a minimalist external security and defense posture; even here, Dublin's participation in the European Political Cooperation (EPC) and CSCE processes has increased awareness of the pressing issues in this area. Relations between the Alliance systems have largely shaped neutralist policies, since these nations can no longer afford to ignore strategic realities (even while proclaiming their nonalignment).

The exposed position of the Federal Republic of Germany (FRG) and its commitment to ultimate German reunification have transformed the Bonn government into the strongest proponent of the Harmel formula. Although they offer quite different future policy prescriptions, both Seidelmann and Brauch emphasize the essentially defensive structure and mission of the FRG's military forces and the permanent engagement of the FRG in a political dialogue with the East. As Harmel observed, the future of Europe will be largely determined by the future of Germany. This perennial question has immense ramifications for the security policies of Northern and Central Europe--NATO, Warsaw Pact, and neutral states alike. It is noteworthy that neither West German contributor presents a specific plan for political reunification over the next three decades. Rather, they perceive movement in this direction as a result of incrementalist steps toward solving East-West disputes (and thus they reflect the prevailing consensus in the FRG). The Finlandization option is largely discounted.

All the contributors from NATO countries expect continued support for membership in the Alliance. Similarly, the writers from neutral states see strong backing for the present non-aligned status. The NATO connection for the southern states represents a legitimizing factor domestically; Ilari, for instance, calls Italy's adherence to the North Atlantic Treaty one of the three pillars of the Republic (the others are the Constitution and the Concordat with the Holy See). Sánchez-Gijón and Vasconcelos see NATO membership as part of their countries' commitment to European integration. Both the Greek and Turkish contributors imply that Alliance participation will remain a factor in their own "cold war", in this way exploiting the most effective institutional means of leverage the United States. Interestingly, the countries on the geographic periphery of Europe, Greece, Turkey, Norway, and Iceland, interpret their Alliance vocation more in terms of bilateral relations with the superpower ally. Knudsen writes that Norway has always perceived itself as primarily an Atlantic (and secondarily a European) country, and Gunnarsson remarks that Iceland's European identity has never been strong. These two countries (and Turkey) are the only NATO European allies not in the EC, and Norway and Turkey are the only allies with borders on the Soviet Union. To a lesser extent, Britain's postwar insistence on a special relationship with the United States reflects its geographic separation from the continent. Both Spain and Portugal have a recent history of isolation from European political developments. Yet the contributors from all these countries foresee European linkages becoming stronger in future years. As in most other European countries, their governments are, however, waiting on external events to force painful policy choices.

The public security and defense consensus in NATO countries appears to have survived the crisis in transatlantic relations. As numerous specialists have noted, these countries underwent a significant politicization of elite opinion in this area, rather than a full-scale democratization of the public debate .[4] Recent election and referendum results and polling data demonstrate that the public consensus behind NATO is still strong, but that political elites have been split by the Intermediate Nuclear Force (INF) decision and other transatlantic polemics. Nonetheless, there is a realization that the consensus may come apart in future years if the supporting principles behind these policies undergo constant challenges by an articulate and influential opposition (quite often including the major party out of power). As a consequence, European governments will be less and less amenable to new defense commitments within the Atlantic system. Traditionally, the public has been more concerned with domestic issues (particularly the economy and unemployment), and defense expenditures, barring an unforeseen crisis, will remain a low public priority.

As Siccama writes, "a reasonable degree of confidence in the U.S. has . . . replaced the unlimited confidence of the 1950s and early 1960s." The greater public realism is reflected in other NATO member states. Coker contends that the more hardline U.S. tone toward the Soviet Union may even increase public confidence that the United States will live up to its commitments to its allies (in event of attack). The perceptions of the threat posed by the Soviet Union have generally maintained themselves in public opinion and (in some cases) they have intensified in the wake of developments in Afghanistan and Poland and maritime intrusions into Scandinavia. Dutch polls show that the public in the Netherlands prefers the existing NATO system of security to any of the alternatives (including "Europeanization" of defense and rapprochement with the Soviet Union). While these samplings reflect a strong suspicion of structural change in the system, they also indicate a desire for a greater European voice in Alliance defense policy. It could be claimed that most Europeans in NATO states are satisfied with the security system at present, but would like to see it more responsive to the growing European role in the world.

All five neutralist countries have a strong public and elite consensus backing official security policy. The debate is centered more on the mechanics and costs of this policy, and the need to pursue an activist foreign policy to complement the national defense effort. The firm Swiss public support behind the principle of general (territorial) defense is often cited by advocates of this doctrine in NATO countries. A broad consensus exists in Sweden, Finland, and Austria as well. However, Huldt fears that the economic costs of maintaining a strong welfare and defense system may seriously strain the Swedish social fabric in future years. In Finland, as Vesa shows, the population believes that the FCMA Treaty has had a positive impact on Finland's international status; at the same time, Finns overwhelmingly support a strong national defense and armed resistance to an external attack. Interestingly, the public support for such a defense effort drops by almost half in scenarios where nuclear weapons are used. In this view, nuclear war continues to be "unthinkable." Although they strongly endorse a national defense, the Austrian public, according to Gärtner, is skeptical of their armed forces' ability to repulse a direct military attack. Rather, they put their faith (as do the Finns) in an activist foreign policy designed to defuse potential conflict situations. Irish neutrality is also overwhelmingly endorsed by public opinion, and one poll mentioned by Keatinge found that 77 percent preferred neutrality in the event of a superpower conflict. As in the other neutral countries, the security debate focuses on how activist a foreign policy is necessary to protect the country's neutral status.

The NATO commentators generally agree that Europe needs a greater voice in the Alliance. No one wants to sever the U.S. connection, especially the nuclear guarantees, but there is little European realization of the seriousness of the U.S. reappraisal of its Atlantic commitments. Knudsen quotes the former Norwegian Foreign Minister in a refreshingly candid statement : "The logical solution ought to be that a potential American withdrawal takes place simultaneously with a larger Western

European role for the defense of Western Europe. The American forces have been in Europe for 40 years. One cannot take for granted that they will stay for another 40 years."

The problem has been to define the institutional framework for such a heightened European role. The European Community has been reticent about taking on security responsibilities, and the Western European Union (WEU) remains a forum without a mission. There appears to be a broad consensus that a European security identity should assert itself within the existing structure of NATO, but the mechanics of such self-assertion have yet to be worked out. The most promising strategy revolves around greater Franco-German cooperation and consultation. Makinsky and Gnesotto cite the support among the French political elites for stronger security ties to the FRG, and Seidelmann explores the options of French nuclear guarantees covering West German territory. The French-German dilemma, however, is that the French still exhibit qualms over compromising their independent deterrent and autonomy of decision-making, whereas the West Germans habitually want to increase the U.S. and French linkages simultaneously. If the French-German duo is to provide the dynamic force behind a European security identity, both France and the FRG will have to develop a more realistic appreciation of each other's security needs and interests. Furthermore, any bilateral arrangement would have to include consultations with the other NATO European allies (especially Britain) as well as with the United States. The French-German-British "eternal triangle" has a long history of political misunderstandings, strategic misconceptions, and outright missed opportunities.

As Dierckx notes, the smaller countries (like Belgium) tend to be "trend followers" in security and defense. Denmark, according to Faurby, is one NATO member state where a growing Europeanization of defense responsibilities would not be welcome; whether the external context and pressures by neighbors would oblige the Danes to conform is a moot point. These factors did succeed in convincing the Danes to support the EC reform package in the February 1986 referendum. For his part, Veremis characterizes official Greek response to the reactivation of the WEU as "patently cool." Both commentators express concern, however, over the future isolation of their countries if some plan of Europeanization is finally implemented. It is more than likely that these countries would revert to their traditional role of trend followers in any redistribution of NATO responsibilities.

In addition, the European allies react cautiously to any extension of Alliance commitments to out-of-area operations. While they admit the dangers of Third World upheavals, the Europeans remain reluctant to provide the United States with an interventionist carte blanche. But there exists no specifically European policy structure for dealing with relations outside of Europe. In moments of crisis, European leaders are mostly content to complain about "nonconsultation" by Washington.

What is most evident in this discussion is the imperative for NATO European policymakers and analysts to open up lines of communication and cooperation in order to overcome the conceptual and psychological frontiers existing between these countries. Brauch, for instance, provides an important examination of alternative, non-provocative conventional defense strategies proposed by West German experts. Unfortunately, the debate over these theories appears to be largely limited to the FRG, and its consequences for Alliance solidarity (and any Europeanization initiative) have not been fully explored. In his list of British political party options, Coker assesses both the Conservative project for a maritime strategy and Labour's schemes for unilateral denuclearization. These alternatives for Britain are not well understood in other

European NATO member states, even though their future implementation would have enormous repercussions on the collective defense. First and foremost, it is necessary to delineate the common security interests and perspectives of the European NATO countries before proceeding to formulate plans for Europeanization or "a European pillar" or "a revived WEU." The following chapters suggest that NATO Europe requires considerable "consciousness raising" in security and defense. These differences of opinion among allies have often been exploited by the United States to maintain its policy dominance over NATO. On the other hand, the United States has frequently expressed impatience at the lack of European cohesion on security issues (as was evident during the March-April 1986 crisis with Libya). In this sense, the elaboration of shared interests among Europeans has to precede any move toward a more equitable distribution of burdens and responsibilities in the Alliance.

The adaption of NATO military strategy is also essential to the success of any structural or institutional reform. Most contributors support the principle of a stronger conventional deterrent, thereby raising the nuclear threshold to a "not-so-early-but-still-credible" level. The problem, however, is financial and demographic. The escalating costs of advanced conventional weapons technology constrain any modernization plan on the order of the Rogers proposal (Follow-on Forces Attack, FOFA) or AirLand Battle. The need for greater industrial cooperation is acknowledged, but the organization and politics behind large-scale weapons collaboration are immensely complicated. Many of the southern countries seek national self-sufficiency in basic arms production as well as quick profits from overseas sales of "low-technology" equipment. But, as Ilari, for one, warns, Third World countries are demanding increasingly sophisticated weaponry and undercutting this potential market for Italian exports. The dependency of Europe on advanced U.S. arms technology is generally admitted, and the "two-way street" in arms sales is dismissed as a political fiction. The challenge of the Strategic Defense Initiative (SDI) and the bickering over the Eureka program are emblematic of European retardation in this industrial sector. Furthermore, as Makinsky observes, participation in SDI by European countries (especially the FRG and Britain) is attractive in terms of anticipated technology transfers and lucrative contracts. But such defections undermine efforts to build a truly rationalized European defense industry.

The financial crunch is regarded as the major obstacle to conventional modernization, but falling birthrates in nearly all these countries also present serious, long-term planning dilemmas. Brauch points to the agonizing West German decision to increase compulsory military service to 18 months as evidence of this official concern with depopulation. Western Europe is undergoing a demographic "implosion" that threatens to make the classic concept of a standing army obsolete, hence the West German interest in adapting theories of territorial defense to advances in high technology. In this perspective, any future European defense plan has to be "people-effective [sic]" as well as "cost-effective."

The response of the two European nuclear powers to these constraints is illuminating. The French have made considerable investments in an across-the-board modernization of their nuclear deterrent to the detriment of conventional forces. Makinsky is critical of the capabilities of the new Force d'Action Rapide which he labels a "tool for the management of budgetary scarcity," and Gnesotto sees financial constraints leading France inevitably to "the European option." Other French observers have described the excessive French reliance on nuclear weapons as evidence of a Maginot Line mentality divorced from strategic realities within Europe.[5] In their analyses of British defense policy, Booth and Coker emphasize the enormous financial burden represented by the Trident nuclear modernization project. To date, Britain has either avoided policy choices or imposed "equal misery" (Booth, chapter 1) on all defense sectors. Both contributors agree that this state of affairs cannot persist, but the proposed alternatives appear even more illusory; Coker cites economic critiques of Labour party conventional options and questions whether schemes for industrial conversion would not require a politically unacceptable degree of social engineering. Neither the French nor the British seem to be seriously considering any "pooling" or other cooperative venture in their nuclear weapons programs. Any effective future plan for Europeanization of defense responsibilities would require (at a minimum) closer consultation between the two nuclear powers, or better still, multilateral discussions including West Germany. This does not appear to be in the offing.

The Strategic Defense Initiative and its European variations evoke mostly skepticism among these observers. To Faurby, these proposals represent "imaginary technological fixes" that would exacerbate (rather than solve) U.S.-European differences. There is much suspicion about the feasibility of strategic defense, either on a global or continental scale. Brauch sees SDI and any European Defense Initiative as essentially destabilizing and contrary to the spirit of the Harmel consensus. Gnesotto and Makinsky worry mainly about the implications of Soviet strategic defense measures for the French deterrent and the high costs for France to engage in the new space race. The two French contributors perceive the space defense dimension as potentially uniting Europeans in a common effort to maintain their deterrent capacities; the logical vehicle for this undertaking, in Makinsky's view, would be the hitherto civilian Eureka program.

The four frontline neutral states base their security on an activist foreign policy, combined with a military strategy of "dissuasion," reminding a potential aggressor, in Frei's terms, "that a military invasion . . . would involve him in heavy losses in men and material, that he would have to count on much destruction and a lengthy campaign, thus being obliged to pay a 'high admission price' ." However, the two most exposed neutrals, Finland and Austria, stress the primacy of their foreign policy initiatives over security policy measures. Vesa perceives Finnish security in Europe to be best served by promotion of the CSCE process and the idea of a Nordic nuclear-weapon-free zone, while Gärtner sees Austria's role as a diplomatic middleman, whose political utility is the best guarantee of its continued independence. Both Austria and Switzerland have adopted doctrines of territorial defense, although the Austrian effort pales in comparison to the Swiss model. The Swedish concept of a "total security policy," as described by Huldt, also emphasizes the importance of a non aligned foreign policy. Huldt sees Swedish policy as being "challenged by the costs and technology explosion in the military sphere-and by a continuing transfer of resources from the external security sector and defense to the internal security sector-the welfare society." He also notes a growing "realism" in the Swedish debate, owing largely to the persistent Soviet submarine intrusions. The evolving dependency relations (largely economic and technological) have provoked a greater sense of the "dwarfing of Sweden" and have increased interest in Sweden as part of "a new Europe of the Europeans." Ireland, on the other hand, remains a captive of its parochialism; the first step escaping these narrow conceptual confines, according to Keatinge, "would mean establishing policy making procedures at the parliamentary and adminstrative levels that would make the appraisal of security policy a normal, periodic task of government." All the contributors, from both NATO and neutral countries, would agree with Keatinge's truism that "the future is bound to be 'surprising'."

It is the job of government to be prepared to cope with such surprises in the most effective manner possible.

The five neutral states also convey a long-standing commitment to the United Nations and to the collective security system it represents (although Switzerland, the host to numeral UN agencies and conferences, is not officially a member). The other four neutrals regularly provide peacekeeping forces for UN missions overseas. In Vesa's view, "associative peace strategies" - strengthening the UN, increasing international economic and social cooperation, pursuing general disarmament , and bridging the gulf between the rich and poor nations - represent the optimal means for ensuring Finland's position in the world. It is worth noting that contributors from NATO European states largely ignore the UN framework for collective security and mention economic development programs (or so-called North-South issues) only tangentially. Security, for Alliance members, is defined much more narrowly than for neutrals. Perceptual differences between the "separate" and "common" security paradigms manifest themselves quite markedly in this case. Still, Huldt, for one, gives the impression of the vulnerabilities of a European neutral state (Sweden) in the late 1980s, especially with respect to what he calls "peace crises" (cutoff of raw materials, economic boycotts, trade wars) which affect neutrals and Alliance members equally. Present policies, he writes, "generally signify a Swedish return to Europe, both in terms of security concerns and economic relations." To pretend that any of these five nations can function outside of a European context is to deny basic strategic realities. All five countries are too small, too poor in resources, and too economical dependent to live purely autonomous existences. Ireland is already an EC member and the other four have associative status. One measure of the realization of their common interests is their consultative process in the CSCE negotiations; another measure is their active participation in the French-proposed Eureka program. It must be admitted that all five neutrals are Western democratic societies by political structure and philosophy, sharing much more in common with NATO Europe than with the Warsaw Pact countries.

As stated earlier, political detente, the second pillar of the Harmel report, is a policy imperative for all European countries, both East and West, who have learned to coexist in a constricted geographic space saturated with military arsenals. For the coming years, Booth stresses "the desirability of adopting a less dogmatic and confrontational attitude toward the Soviet Union," while Faurby remarks that "a relaxation in superpower relations and a positive development in the arms control negotiations in Geneva in particular will contribute to a lessening of domestic problems over security policy and ease the way for a Danish policy more in line with the NATO mainstream than has been the case in the past few years." According to the prevailing European viewpoint, the future of detente depends overwhelmingly on the future of the U.S.-Soviet relationship. The NATO countries anticipate a greater willingness on the part of the United States to strive for a political and military accommodation with the Soviet Union, especially on European issues. Moreover, as Ilari cautions, "the West does not have any interest in an eventual internal destabilization of the East, because this would augment Soviet militarism, the arms race, and global instability . . . . The Soviet Union does not seem to be on the ropes or to have its ultima ratio in war machinery." The inference here is that continued confrontational policies on the part of Washington could well backfire and destroy the Alliance. This potential for conflict is more a matter of political intentions and outlook than specific proposals in diplomatic forums. Unlike the Reagan administration, the majority of Europeans still regard the detente process as a limited success and thus worth pursuing in all its manifestations. From this perspective, it is the United States that has diverged from the Harmel consensus. The neutrals also perceive their security futures as inextricably bound to the principle of sustained progress in superpower relations. In the end, the political and strategic composition of Europe for the year 2000 and afterward will be determined by the success or failure of the United States and the Soviet Union in learning to live together.

POSTSCRIPT

From this brief synthesis, it is evident that European security has become primarily a political rather than a military issue. A large-scale continental conflict, either nuclear or conventional, is inconceivable for Europeans because it would mean the effective destruction of Europe. The solution to Europe's security dilemmas will not be simple, but this awareness should not deter informed observers from making long-range prescriptions. Part of the psychological mindset of "Europessimism" is that the fundamental problems are insoluble, hence the fatalistic attachment to the Finlandization myth. These prophecies threaten to become self-fulfilling, as the ensuing policy paralysis engendered by this world view can only multiply political, economic, and military dependency. What Europe requires today and tomorrow is a renewed sense of collective initiative and dynamism, of the capacity to take risks. The Eureka program, for instance, grouping all the countries surveyed in this book, represents a potentially promising response to the technological challenges of the twenty-first century. The major difficulty for Western Europeans has been to translate the enormous potential of the continent into effective measures benefiting all the peoples involved. Inevitably, such efforts necessitate an intensified process of political integration. The stronger Western Europe grows, the more obsolete the artificial division of the Old World becomes. In security and defense, what is necessary, as stated earlier, is to stimulate a common European consciousness of strengths and weaknesses. Here we are talking principally about the NATO member states, even though the neutrals do share a number of security concerns. From all points of view, the twin pillars of the Harmel report (the essence of the present European elite and public consensus) embody the only acceptable future security policy for Europe. All Western European countries, both NATO and neutral, need to maintain a strong defense, while at the same time they make every effort to encourage East-West rapprochement and stability. This book will hopefully serve as an intra-European confidence-building and consciousness-raising measure. The European contribution to the world today is too great for Europeans to be satisfied with a subsidiary role in the twenty-first century.

NOTES

1. For reference, see Luc Reychler and Robert Rudney, eds., <u>Directory Guide of European Security and Defense Research</u> (Leuven : Leuven University Press/Pergamon-Brassey's, 1985); and Reychler and Rudney, <u>In Search of European Security : An Assessment of the European Security and Defense Research Sector</u> (Leuven : Leuven University Press, 1986).

2. Stanley R. Sloan has called for a similar, government-sponsored security assessment in his book, <u>NATO's Future : Toward a New Transatlantic Bargain</u> (Washington, D.C.:National Defense University Press, 1985) pp. 189-91.

3. The full text of the report is provided in <u>NATO Facts and Figures</u> (Brussels : NATO Information Service, 1971), pp. 365-67.

4. See Stephen F. Szabo, "European Opinion After the Missiles," <u>Survival</u>, November-December 1985, p. 265; see also Gregory Flynn and Hans Rattinger, eds., <u>The Public and Atlantic Defense</u> (Totowa, N.J. : Rowman and Allanheld, 1984).

5. See, for instance, Pierre Lellouche, <u>L'Avenir de la guerre</u> (Paris : Mazarine, 1985).

NATO Center

1 Britain: Forcing Choices

Ken Booth

The first half of the 1980s proved to be an unsettled period in European security affairs, and nowhere during this time was defense policy more a focus of attention than in Britain, the only Western European country to actually be involved in a shooting war. While there is a general assumption that European security affairs in general will be quieter in the late 1980s, it is unlikely that British defense policy will cease to be a focus of attention. As a result of internal rather than external considerations, changes may occur in the years ahead that could have a major impact on weapon procurement, strategy, and Alliance relationships.

Through the 1980s, the evaluation of the current security situation from the British perspective has been more contested than during almost any time since World War II. There has been something of a breakdown in what had hitherto been an impressive consensus of defense policy. Thus an evaluation of the present security situation depends very much on the standpoint of the commentator.

From the perspective of the British government, there is satisfaction at the state of European security and confidence that British defense policy is set on the right course. Since 1979 the Conservative government of Margaret Thatcher has devoted considerable effort to the country's defense policy, and it is proud of its achievements. Among these it would pick out for special attention a nearly 30 percent increase in the defense budget in real terms, the maintenance of a strong commitment to NATO, the rousing victory in the Falklands War of 1982, the defeat of the Labour party's defense platform in the general elections of 1983 and in 1987, the overcoming of the challenge of the antinuclear movement on the issue of the deployment of U.S. Cruise missiles in Britain, and the taking of a number of decisions (notably to develop Trident as the next generation of "independent deterrent") which it hopes will establish the basis for a sensible policy for years to come.

Despite the government's sense of achievement, there have been serious errors and disappointments. Of these, the most important were the collapse of British credibility in the south Atlantic, which made the Falklands War necessary, the considerable strains that developed in NATO in the early 1980s, and the growing strength of the critics of established defense policies. Despite the government's assertions to the contrary, the defense debate in Britain was not closed by the result of the general elections.

The late 1970s saw the start of a breakup in the impressive bipartisanship on defense matters that had characterized British political life for over 30 years. Through that period, which saw Britain's gradual retreat from empire and its increasing concentration on Europe, there had been broad agreement on the principles of defense policy, and often on matters of practice. In its major defense review of 1974, the Labour government of the day identified four priorities for British security : the maintenance of the strategic nuclear deterrent, the defense of the home base, the defense of the central front in Europe, and the defense of the eastern Atlantic. These priorities have remained basically stable under successive governments, although some adjustments were made by the Conservative government's defense review of 1981, and some shifts in resources were necessitated by the Falklands War in the year following.

Until the late 1970s, government policies to meet the country's security challenges had attracted widespread public approval. The security situation appeared satisfactory. Order had been maintained in Europe, it was believed, as a result of NATO's policy of stabilization through military balance. However, during the 1970s, establishment circles showed concern at the apparent expansion of Soviet military capabilities. This was of concern not only in Europe, but also, for the first time, in strategic areas beyond. Nevertheless, outside Europe the British defense community also looked back on its record with satisfaction : Britain had disentangled itself relatively painlessly from its distant obligations, while it had retained some capacity to show the flag for national or international purposes. The one running sore was closer to home, in Northern Ireland, where since 1969 the Irish Republican Army (a terrorist organization outlawed in the Irish Republic as well as in Britain) had conducted a campaign that successive British governments had not been able to eradicate, by either military or political means. It had proved possible to stabilize the situation, but not to ameliorate it.

At the end of the 1970s, the established consensus on defense in Britain began to crack. This was most visible in the revival of the antinuclear movement, which grew greatly in strength after a hibernation of nearly 20 years. The occasion for this was provided by the conjunction of two issues. The first was the government's need to make a decision about the future of the British "independent deterrent," and in particular whether to replace the aging Polaris system with Trident. Predictably, Thatcher's government remained committed to a nuclear strategy and in 1980 plumped for buying Trident from the United States. Second, following NATO's "twin-track" decision in 1979, there arose the vexing issue of the deployment of U.S. Cruise missiles on British soil, an issue made even more controversial by the government's refusal to acquire a "dual key" for the missiles, and hence a veto on their use.

The growing internal opposition to nuclear weapons spilled over into criticism of other aspects of defense policy, a trend which was greatly encouraged by what was seen as the unsophisticated and (on nuclear issues) dangerous "leadership" being offered by the Reagan White House. In Britain, criticism grew of U.S. bases, the U.S. presence in Europe generally, and the politics and strategy of NATO. As it happened, developments in NATO offered plenty of targets in the early 1980s : most prominent were the increasingly apparent weaknesses of flexible response, the crisis over INF, the perceived need for more conventional defense, and contested doctrinal innovations such as FOFA and the U.S. Army's AirLand Battle. Considerable strains developed within the Alliance during this period. However, apart from those sections of the peace movement that favored British withdrawal from NATO, the rest of the British community remained committed to the Alliance, although almost everybody tended to be rather more critical of particular developments than formerly.

The debate about Britain's commitment to European security was intensified by the failure in policy that tempted the Argentinian invasion of the Falkland Islands, and the subsequent success of the British forces in rescuing the islands and the Thatcher government's reputation. This experience resulted in a "Fortress Falklands" policy, a posture that attracted little public enthusiasm at a time when public expenditure at home was under considerable pressure. But in defense circles there was discussion over whether Britain's optimum effort should be "continental" or "maritime" -- should Britain make its effort on the central front or the open seas ? While this debate proceeded among the establishment, the peace movement attempted to translate its simple "Ban the Bomb" slogans of previous years into alternative and sophisticated nonnuclear strategies.

Politically, the growing crack in the consensus on defense became evident in Parliament as well as on the streets and in the media. The antinuclear cause found a home in a Labour party which at the time was unhappy and divided. And its divisions and underdeveloped ideas about defense did not help its electoral prospects with a public that generally supported an independent nuclear deterrent and was proud of the recent performance of its armed forces in the Falklands War. While not sharing Labour's "unilateralist" posture, the newly formed Alliance (the old Liberal party and the new Social Democratic party) was critical of important aspects of the Thatcher government's defense policy : it favored revoking the Trident decision, throwing Polaris into the arms control negotiations, and freezing or withdrawing U.S. Cruise missiles. Against the opposition, the Conservative party won the general elections of 1983 and 1987, but the impressive size of its victories was in Parliamentary seats rather than in popular votes : thus the apparently overwhelming endorsement of its defense policy was more a matter of the idiosyncracies of the British electoral system rather than popular support.

At the present time, the defense debate in Britain is not as rousing as it was, but that does not mean that all issues are settled. The Labour party is now more united and coherent, and its defense policy does not look so unpopular as to prevent future electoral success. Campaign for Nuclear Disarmament (CND), the leader of antinuclear criticism in the early 1980s, lost some momentum after the deployment of U.S. Cruise missiles at the end of 1983, but it remains a strong pressure group and has contributed to a general heightening of consciousness on defense questions. So, although Cruise missiles have been deployed and Trident has been decided upon, powerful political forces in Britain are committed to reversing or significantly changing major elements of existing policies.

Whatever party or combination of parties is in power in Britain, defense policy in the years ahead will be greatly affected by economic constraints. After six years of growth in the defense budget, the government announced that there was to be level funding after 1986. Because of the inflation in the costs of defense equipment, this will impose severe pressure on almost all decisions relating to Britain's security policy. It will force choices to be made, about missions (should Britain keep "the deterrent" or become the first ex-nuclear power?), between missions (should Britain concentrate on the central front or the eastern Atlantic?), and between weapons (should Britain acquire fighters or missiles for the RAF?). Alternatively, there might well be a decision not to decide; that is, a future government could agree to maintain exisitng priorities, but allow "equal misery" across the board in resource allocation. Britain would attempt to meet its existing obligations, but with a lower level of capability.

British defense policy therefore faces a crossroads, with a cracked consensus and declining resources. Whether this presages significant change or only less of the same, it is certain that its allies will have to pay more attention to British defense developments than hitherto. Major aspects of British defense policy cannot be taken in future as given as they have in the past.

As has just been indicated, there has been a breakdown in the established consensus regarding the future direction of British defense policy. There are therefore several potential answers to the question, "What policies will enhance Britain's security situation over the next 30 years?." The answers will depend on the way the problem is defined. Is Soviet aggression the major threat, or is it the nuclear arms race itself ? Is the most likely military challenge within Europe or "out of area"? Within Europe, is NATO the solution to the problem of security, or a big part of the problem ? Answers to these and other matters will be influenced in turn by the wide range of opinions that individuals have about such issues as the state of the East-West military balance, the nature of the Soviet threat, the reliability of the U.S. guarantee, and ideas about "how much is enough?" in defense. Given the range of opinions about such matters, it is hardly surprising that numerous contending schools of thought have developed in addition to the policy set down by the government. Some of these alternatives are reformist : others advocate more extreme positions, including neutralism or the adoption of a Gaullist stance.

Given the breakdown in the consensus, and the variety of ideas on offer in the British strategic marketplace, it is fruitful to reformulate the question "What policy changes would enhance the security situation of Britain over the next 30 years?" to "What policy can attract politically significant support?" Before identifying these, several prefatory remarks are necessary regarding public opinion and defense. First, it needs to be stressed that the British public usually tends to support the government of the day on defense matters, and that the British public is generally in favor of a sound defense posture. Second, even though public opinion polls have pronounced unfavorably on Trident, they have indicated majority support for an "independent deterrent" of some sort. Finally, British defense policy in the years ahead will be constrained by a mixture of domestic (primarily economic) and international (political and strategic) "necessities." These constraints mean that the scope for change may be less than some fear, but that the changes that do occur will probably command support. The latter might even be the case if a future Labour government terminates Britain's military nuclear capability; in this respect, British voters at the next general election will have an opportunity to make a decisive or perhaps irrevocable change in the country's defense policy. Whether particular reforms or new directions in policy would improve Britain's security remains to be seen : this will depend how any changes are carried out, and how they fit into the evolving international situation. Given the vagaries of political and military life, nobody can offer guarantees.

Because of the diversity of current British thinking about defense, it is no longer as easy to generalize about the priority of security concerns facing the country or whether some developments (such as the loosening of ties with the United States) would represent threats or promises. That noted, there is likely to be general agreement regarding the following concerns :

1. Nuclear war between the superpowers. The possible (interrelated) causes of such a catastrophe might be a decisive technological breakthrough, madness or miscalculation on the part of the decision-makers, the escalation of a conventional war in Europe or the Third World, or the spread of a regional nuclear war.

2. A war in Europe between NATO and the Warsaw Pact. The most likely cause of such an outcome is generally thought to be Soviet aggression following the spill-over of instability in Eastern Europe or U.S. isolationism. An alternative cause might be the spread to Europe of a regional (especially Middle Eastern) war.

3. Conflict outside Europe. Conflicts in various locations would affect British interests. They might result from superpower intervention or local ambition, nuclear proliferation, the collapse of particular states, competition over scarce resources, or attacks on Western assets (from oil supplies through diplomatic missions to individual nations).

4. Domestic security problems. The overriding problem in this regard will remain Northern Ireland; this is followed by the threat of terrorist activity in which Britain might be used as a battleground for distant quarrels. There is little expectation of trouble from indigenous nationalist movements (Northern Ireland apart); a more immediate concern is the prospect of violence arising out of local economic or racial problems.

The standard for judging whether or not particular defense policy changes will enhance the security situation of Britain will be judged in most minds by their effect on the threats just identified. Some of these inevitably overlap; so do some of the proposed policies for dealing with them. As ever, actual decisions will rest on a combination of risk assessment and what the government of the day believes the country should afford.

REDUCING THE RISK OF NUCLEAR WAR BETWEEN THE SUPERPOWERS

There is broad agreement here on some matters of principle (to pursue arms control and disarmament, and to support the nonproliferation of nuclear weapons for, example) but there is much disagreement about questions of practice. On arms control and disarmament, there is a fundamental split between the unilateralist and multilateralist approaches; on the particular question of proliferation, this split results in a gulf between those who say that Britain should lead by example, by renouncing Trident or nuclear weapons altogether, and those, like the government who stress the dangers of horizontal rather than vertical proliferation. The division of opinion on these matters is echoed in the issue of deterrence policy, by the division between those who stress that in order to maintain stability the priority is to maintain the strongest possible deterrent posture for the West, and those who advocate nuclear disarmament by Britain.

On other areas of strategy there is more agreement. In terms of relations with the Soviet Union, there is a growing recognition that it is necessary to move on from the confrontational attitude of the early Thatcher-Reagan years; a more sensible relationship should be cultivated with more emphasis on detente, and less on confrontation. While the Thatcher government was the most loyal of the major European countries toward the Reagan line in the early 1980s, nostalgia for detente remained powerful in major sections of British opinion, as it did on the continent; and Thatcher herself thawed somewhat in her attitudes toward the East. On the vexed and dominating question of Reagan's

Strategic Defense Initiative (SDI), Thatcher's government has also put some distance between itself and the White House, although not as much as most of the British defense community would like. SDI is generally regarded as an expensive and dangerous addition to the strategic equation, and one that Britain should not support.

In the proposed policy changes just discussed, the future of Britain's "independent deterrence" figures prominently. In this respect, despite the visibility of the antinuclear movement in recent years, general support remains for a British nuclear retaliatory capability. The familiar justifications remain persuasive for many people : the need for insurance against "blackmail," the value of a "second center of decision," the desirability of a force of last resort, and the necessity of a nuclear capability in view of long-term worries about the U.S. guarantee. Supporters of the British deterrent argue that all allied governments would be greatly concerned at the implications of unilateral British nuclear disarmament : they fear it would place the Alliance on a very slippery slope. Despite the general support for a nuclear deterrent force, the government's commitment to the Trident system has come under increasing pressure, even from within the pronuclear lobby. Rising costs have been a particular concern. Less extravagant options --in terms of capability as well as costs-- are favored by many : a sea-launched Cruise missile force has substantial support. As the next election approaches, the future of Britain's nuclear deterrent will again become a focus for debate. It remains to be seen whether Labour, for tactical reasons, will continue to play up the antinuclear issue, or whether it will seek to keep it in the background. Whatever the result of the election, it will have profound implications for British defense policy for decades to come.

REDUCING THE RISK OF WAR IN EUROPE BETWEEN NATO AND THE WARSAW PACT

There is plenty of controversy on this matter amongst interested British opinion, particularly on the question of future NATO strategy. There is disagreement over which reforms will both strengthen deterrence and provide the optimum capability should war break out. Criticism has grown, even from some NATO supporters, of the inflexibility of flexible response, and the inadequacies of forward defense. But there is also much disagreement about some of the proposed reforms (especially FOFA, AirLand Battle, and no first use) and the best focus for Britain's effort -- should it be on the central front or in the northeast Atlantic (or even in the open seas beyond) ? On some issues, however, there is growing agreement. Notable in this respect is agreement about the need to raise the nuclear threshold by improving the Alliance's conventional capability (through different tactics and exploiting new technology) and about the desirability of reducing and pulling back NATO's forward-based battlefield nuclear weapons.

There are disagreements not only about aspects of NATO strategy, but also about the very desirability of Britain's continued membership in the Alliance. A vociferous minority asserts that the Alliance exacerbates tensions and spreads danger rather than enhances European security; from this viewpoint, Britain gains nothing from membership. Those holding such opinions span left-wing elements of the peace movement and right-wing neutralists. The majority of British opinion, however, continues to see NATO as an essential part of the framework of British security. The way ahead is therefore seen through reform rather than withdrawal. Suggested improvements involve strategic reforms as discussed above, economies (by more standardization or a more sensible division of labor), and, finally, political changes (such as a greater British identification with its European partners rather than the United States). While British governments are likely to want to maintain as much as is possible of the Anglo-American "special relationship" in defense, it is increasingly accepted by all sectors of the defense community that the U.S. guarantee to Western Europe is not as credible as the Alliance approaches its fortieth anniversary as it was in the past, and that Europe is the key to British security. Consequently, more attention has been paid to the European dimension of defense, as seen in the government's involvement in the attempted revival of the Western European Union.

REDUCING CONFLICT OUTSIDE EUROPE

Although some conflicts in the Third World could have extremely serious consequences for Britain and Western Europe in general, these "out-of-area" problems are generally given a lower priority in British defense thinking than those discussed above. In most cases the issues are less immediate and Britain has limited power to do anything about them. In approaching these matters, there is a significant difference in emphasis between the Labour and Alliance parties on the one side, and the Conservative party on the other. In theory at least, the former appear to see security in wider terms than simply defense policy. Thus more emphasis is placed on supporting the United Nations, assisting Third World development, strengthening the nonproliferation regime and so on. In contrast, the Thatcher government has interpreted security more narrowly; this was evident in its non-signing (so far) of the 1982 UN Convention on the Law of the Sea. All sections of British opinion agree on the need to strengthen international law on such matters as international terrorism, but considerable differences exist on the question of the extent to which Britain should be able to "show the flag" in support of U.S. military actions ostensibly designed to support Western interests. In the past, such support as has been given has been appreciated by the United States, but the costs of maintaining even a modest capability are very high. But so might be the costs of apathy : in this event the Falklands War was a nasty reminder to British opinion of the instabilities that exist outside Europe. Naturally the experience has been used by the naval/high Tory lobby to support the case for more emphasis in defense policy on possible threats beyond NATO's formal limits. In contrast, the costs and dangers of the Falklands War, together with the subsequent heavy expenditure on "Fortress Falklands," have been used by a strong body of opinion to draw attention to the disadvantages of changing the emphasis in British defense policy. For political and economic reasons, Britain's out-of-area role is unlikely to grow.

CONTROLLING DOMESTIC SOURCES OF INSTABILITY

Ireland remains the dominating internal security concern, and a consensus remains on the need to hold the ring in a military sense, while a political solution is sought. Only a very small sector of British opinion favors the troops being withdrawn. Equally, there is an overwhelming support on the need to strengthen measures, nationally and internationally, to deal with international terrorism. A unanimous desire also exists to avoid those breakdowns that might result from economic and/or racial causes, such as occurred in the riots of 1981 and 1985 and in the miners' strike of 1984-85; however, different political parties have their own theories as to which policies are best calculated to produce a harmonious society. As in the other areas of national life, an era of "conviction politics" is antithetical to consensus.

On some issues in British defense policy, there are such fundamental differences of opinion that it is not possible to talk about a national consensus, future policy is in the hands of election winners. Having said that, there has been some movement of opinion in recent years that suggests a possible compromise between the more pragmatic members of the interested public. Among the issues around which a new consensus might emerge, the following are the most prominent : the desirability of strengthening Britain's conventional forces (and those of the Alliance in general); the possibility of adopting as a replacement for Polaris a system that falls somewhat short of the "best" independent nuclear deterrent; a continued commitment to NATO, but with a more European than Atlanticist orientation; the need to reform the strategy of flexible response away from the early use of nuclear weapons; and the desirability of adopting a less dogmatic and confrontational attitude toward the Soviet Union. In addition to movement along the lines indicated, there is also likely to be continuity of consensus in some areas. In particular, it is unlikely that the majority of British opinion will quickly be won over to supporting unilateral nuclear disarmament (although this will not necessarily stop large numbers from voting for a Labour government); there will be continued priority for maintaining the European commitment rather than taking on additional responsibilities elsewhere; and short of some unexpected international crisis, few are likely to advocate increased defense spending by Britain.

Although the package of policies just identified would command a good deal of support in Britain, different elements in the package will attract strong criticism : the peace movement will oppose a continued commitment to nuclear weapons; the defense establishment will oppose any run-down in defense effort (as is implied in the level funding that will occur after 1986); and many electors will oppose the strengthening of conventional forces if it means that increased amounts of public money would have to be allocated to defense.

As well as the interplay of domestic pressure groups, there are two other major factors that will affect the realization of changes in British defense policy in the years ahead. These are economic constraints at home and the "realities" of international strategic life (especially the relationship with the United States).

Except in moments of acute national emergency, defense policy in Britain has always been liable to be a matter of economics writ large. This is likely to be the case in the future, as it has been in the past. In this respect, the dominating fact is certain to be the slow and uncertain effort of British governments to lift the economy out of the depressed state of recent years. For defense policy, this means a continuation (at best) of the level funding referred to earlier. This is likely to be the case regardless of the political party in power. The problem of level funding will be more than usually acute because of the peculiar conjunction of the problem of continuous weapon innovation (Britain is at the threshold of emerging technology in the conventional field and the acquisition of Trident in the strategic) and the relatively higher inflation rates in defense equipment. Thus the same will buy less. As was discussed earlier, this means that either choices will have to be made between missions, services, and equipment, or alternatively, "equal misery" will have to be imposed across the board of British defense efforts. Different political parties will juggle the cuts, adjustments, and misery in rather different ways, reflecting their own ideology, multiple objectives, and assessment of the international situation.

In addition to making (or avoiding) difficult choices, future British governments will also be faced by the need to ensure that greater economy and efficiency is achieved with whatever resources are released for defense. This will involve waste cutting and reorganization. The reforms that have been discussed, tried, or proposed include international programs for procurement, more competition for equipment, more privatization (a Thatcherite favorite), or buying more major systems off the shelf from the United States.

Whatever the strategic consequences of the pressure on the defense budget, there will certainly be awkward political ramifications. There will be no decrease and there may possibly be some increase in such problems as Alliance burden-sharing, arguments about the "two-way street" in defense between Western Europe and the United States, and criticisms about the extent of Britain's commitment to Alliance strategy. If Britain comes to be seen to be doing less than in the past, this may well legitimize others in Western Europe to follow suit; such an outcome would be certain to provoke criticism (and possibly worse) from the United States. All in all, the political and military ramifications of defense economics will interact and dominate Alliance relationships in the years to come.

Of all Britain's Alliance relationships, that with the United States has been regarded as the most special; but no relationship in the future will be more sensitive or problematical. On the British side, there are concerns about the long-term reliability of the U.S. guarantee to Europe, anxiety about the implications of SDI, and worries about some of the directions and character of U.S. foreign policy. On the U.S. side, there is concern over whether Britain's commitment to Trident will lead to a failure to make improvements in conventional forces, anxiety about the implications for NATO of a future Labour government committed to a nonnuclear policy (not to mention the withdrawal of U.S. nuclear bases from Britain), and doubt about the seriousness with which future British governments will discharge their responsibilities both to NATO and those out-of-area problems that are bound to occur. As a result of diverging interests and perceptions between the old allies, there will be stresses and strains in the "special relationship." But it must be remembered, nostalgia apart, that this has always been the case. Since most British governments are likely to continue to see some advantages in the maintenance of at least a residual special relationship, its importance cannot be dismissed. Even so, it is likely that Britain will continue to look increasingly toward a European identity in defense. It is unlikely that the Anglo-American relationship in the future will be as warm as it has been in the Reagan-Thatcher period, when the mutual admiration of the leaders was made concrete by the Trident agreements, U.S. help to Britain in the Falklands War, British loyalty to U.S. positions on many issues, British support for Cruise, and Britain's steady commitment to NATO's 3 percent spending target. In the future, the way in which Anglo-American relations develop will significantly affect how and to what extent Britain will be able to discharge its various defense roles.

It is apparent from the discussion above that important changes are bound to occur in important aspects of British defense policy in the years ahead. Seen at its narrowest, Britain will seek to carry out existing policies with less money. At its broadest, the problem of British defense policy remains that of searching for the optimum strategy for a medium-sized power situated just off the continent of Europe. The reforms that different sectors of opinion believe to be necessary will not be easy to carry out, because of the lack of consensus and the range of internal and external constraints that have been identified. Logically, the situation points to the need for a major review of British defense; in practice, soldiering on, muddling through, and carrying on while sharing out the misery will be a great temptation to the most politicians. Unless the Labour party achieves power and turns Britain overnight into an ex-nuclear power, change in other areas of British defense policy will be slow and incremental. In the last part of the twentieth century, as in the first half, British defense policy will be prey to the national habit of willing the ends but not the means.

2 Britain: Psychology of Decline

Christopher Coker

Britain has been fortunate to enjoy 40 years of peace. It has also until recently enjoyed a favorable record of civil relations, and been comparatively untroubled by civil violence. Since the mid-1970s, however, civil threats have come to the fore of public thinking--reason enough, perhaps, to turn to them first.

INTERNAL THREAT

The 1980s have showed little respite from the seemingly intractable problem of Northern Ireland where political violence has required a British military presence since 1972. No other country in Western Europe has found it necessary to employ military force against terrorism--not even Spain, where the Basque conflict is closest to the condition of Ulster.

Terrorism has been a grim part of the province's life for more than 20 years. While the British mainland has also experienced the horror of bombs and wanton murder, the suffering of population on the mainland has been light. It may indeed be the hard-won success of the security forces in Northern Ireland that has pushed the terrorist high command to strike at targets in England, at army barracks, hotel resorts, and shopping centers where casualties may be high. Violence in the province is currently running at the 1984 level, the most "peaceful" year since 1970.

Indeed, with each year, the 9,000 soldiers in Ulster slip further from the public view. The virtual end of large-scale rioting and the narrowing of terrorist and counter-terrorist activity have lowered the military profile. The army (which now takes second place to the Royal Ulster Constabulary) has adapted, partly because the Provisional IRA has done so, to the idea that there will be no rapid end to the conflict. Victory or defeat in an insurgency is very much a matter of endurance.

What the future may hold, apart from an enduring pattern of violence, at lower levels than the 1970s, is still unclear, especially in the wake of the 1985 agreement with the Irish government. The army has always suffered from changes of mind on the part of the politicians about the precise nature of its role. Does it lead, protect or assist the police? Clearly, however much stress is laid on police primacy, nobody in the government, past or present, has ever suggested it should be withdrawn. Even a future Labour government, despite the links between the political wing of the IRA and left-wing activists, is unlikely to grasp that nettle either. It is certainly not official Labour party policy.

As for the IRA, the terror campaign now bears little relation to events in Northern Ireland, where even its own cause has made greater progress through the election of Sinn Féin candidates at local elections. Its campaign remains emotionally rooted in the late 1960s and early 1970s. The conclusion may have to be drawn that the movement has so divorced itself from the realities of Ireland that it has become a self-sustaining exercise, unrelated to anything that may happen in the wider political world. Some political observers are quite convinced that the campaign will trickle on until 2006, when there will be a Catholic voting majority in the North. Then the democratic process may take the North into the South, and Dublin will have to deal with the problem that will undoubtedly come from a discontented Protestant minority.

EXTERNAL THREAT

The problem with Britain is that it faces too many threats, all in theaters it considers vital to its security. Thus the defense estimates of 1984 described the defense of Britain as "the heart of our defense policy," claimed that the defense of the eastern Atlantic was "crucial to the conventional defense of central Europe," and went on to observe that the defense of the Rhine should be considered as "the forward defense of Great Britain itself,"before adding that the country must also be prepared to accept its "fair share of the burden" in the defense of areas outside the NATO area where it had historic ties, or where its security was involved.

Britain has to fulfill almost as many roles as it had 20 years ago, but with far fewer forces. Certainly, its armed forces are more professional than they were in the 1950s, the RAF and British Army of the Rhine (BAOR) much better armed. Defense budgets, in addition, far from shrinking, have actually increased, but they have merely bought less. That is the problem. The cuts of 1957-81 have been all but exhausted; there is much less fat, much less scope for waste. The scale of Britain's economic decline has, unfortunately, even now not clarified the priorities, but merely highlighted the extent of which successive governments have ducked the problem. If Britain has failed to clarify its priorities, it will not be the last country to discover the difficulty of reconciling ends to vanishing means.

Clearly, the government will soon find it difficult to sustain the variety of roles outlined in the 1984 Defense White Paper. On the basis of present trends, David Greenwood, Britain's foremost defense economist, estimates that the cost of the defense bill by 1989 may be as high as £24 billion, well above the projected level of defense spending (£20 billion). It is clear that military spending even under a Conservative government will not rise to close the gap, not even at the expense of social welfare which has already been cut beyond the point where it is politically viable.

If inflation rises above 3 percent (as it has for the last two years), the defense budget may have to be cut substantially. Equipment costs will continue to rise well beyond projected levels (witness the horrendous story of the Nimrod), and total defense costs may continue to rise faster than inflation. Whatever economies are secured, the future appears to hold out the promise of a further defense review, one far more savage than the last (1981).

At the same time, however, there is no evidence of any public pressure on the politicians to lower defense spending, or to contract out of any of the present defense commitments. For two decades, over half the respondents in Gallup's monthly political index thought that Britain was spending either too little on defense or what was justified by the international situation. Indeed, as the 1970s drew to a close, there was a significant fall of 10 percent in those who believed that too much was being spent on defense and not enough on social spending. Similarly, although the opinion polls clearly showed that in the same period people became even more concerned about the threat of nuclear war, their concern made them even more anxious to retain a national deterrent.

These trends are likely to continue. The most significant findings of all, however, apply to public attitudes about alliances and allies. It is here that the divergence between some of the Labour party's preoccupations and less self-regarding attitudes is most apparent. To begin with, the perception of a Soviet threat and the need for a concerted response are still strong. In a poll conducted in March 1982, 75 percent of those interviewed thought it would be better to fight regardless of the cost rather than succumb to Soviet domination.

Attitudes toward the United States are even more revealing. Although anti-U.S. sentiment is real, higher today than perhaps at any time, it is not manifested in declining support for NATO. Indeed, quite the reverse is true. Although many people trust the United States less than they used to, in part because of its bellicose attitude toward the Soviet Union, that same belligerence has inspired the man in the street with far more confidence that the United States will actually defend its allies. A substantial increase in distrust of U.S. intentions has not been reflected by any loss of confidence in the certainties in which the public has believed since NATO's inception. The preoccupation with survival to the exclusion of everything else that has possessed the Left since the late 1950s has not been communicated to the public at large.

ALTERNATIVE POLICIES FOR THE FUTURE

As the 1980s come to a close, Britain will be faced with four possible alternative strategies, each of which will be reviewed as they have been discussed in the two major political parties. It also seemw worth looking at the alternative defense policies proposed by the Alliance--the grouping of the Liberal and Social Democratic parties (SDP).

Conservative Option 1

The first option is to continue as usual. In defense as in so many other major areas of policy, the government has preferred the managerial to the radical approach. That is the philosophy that lies behind the cabinet's refusal to contemplate any further cut in government spending. It is based on a political fear of the consequences of radicalism. It is assumed (questionably) that radical reform in the structure of the armed forces would attract too much opposition.

But can the present policies be sustained for very much longer? At £17 billion (and rising), the defense budget is a fifth higher in real terms than when Thatcher came to power, and the largest in Western Europe as a percentage of GNP, in absolute terms and even per head of population. The statement on the 1984-85 defense estimates pointed out that even a government so sympathetic to the need of the military could not continue to commit limitless resources. This dilemma was posed strikingly at a meeting of the cabinet in September 1982, which concluded that the country could no longer continue to fulfill three roles simultaneously : to maintain an independent deterrent, a large blue-water navy, and a permanent force on the continent beyond 1986. One of the roles would have to be abandoned. If the commitment to Trident holds good (now budgeted at £12 billion, or 6 percent of the annual equipment budget in the peak years of the program), the choice may lie between the maritime and continental commitments.

Conservative Option 2

For several years, the maritime lobby in the Conservative party has argued for a more flexible approach to the use of British forces outside the NATO area, on the understanding that one of the consequences of the successful stabilization of the central front has been a Soviet attempt to undermine the West's position in the Middle East, Africa, and the Caribbean. As it happens, the present British government has agreed to set up a Rapid Deployment Force consisting of two brigades, one airborne and the other a commando, together making up a force of about 10,000 men.

The navy lobby also maintains that the case for sustaining substantial naval forces (70 percent of NATO's forces in the Eastern Atlantic) is far more convincing than the army's contribution on the mainland of Europe. It maintains, in fact, that the BAOR's permanent presence, with the garrison accompanied by all its dependents and their welfare, adds an unnecessary burden to the defense budget and helps to cloud NATO's tactical thinking, which for several years has cried out for revision. The peacetime establishment of the army and the RAF in Germany, it is alleged by some, has no tactical rationale. The line-up in central Europe makes military nonsense. It is born of old political formulae that have outlived their relevance.

Against this it can be argued that these "tactical rigidities" also happen to be important realities which are, like it or not, the price that Britain and its allies may have to pay for keeping Germany in NATO and persuading the German taxpayer to contribute four army corps and to keep 490,000 men in the field. The British contribution may be expensive in terms of money, but it is cheap in terms of men. The presence of 55,000 men, or only one army corps, is not regarded by its allies as an unwarranted expense from a country of 55 million people. Indeed, the fact that it has to rely on the rapid redeployment of one and one-third divisions out of four before it is even ready to defend its 40-mile front is regarded as less than satisfactory. Reducing the force still further (as some Conservative MPs propose to the equivalent of two divisions over five years) might look like the action of a country that no longer believed the defense of Germany to be "the forward defense of Britain itself".

Labour Option 1

Labour party options, by contrast, are much more radical and have the advantage of having been publicly debated, perhaps debated too much. The defense paper published by the Labour party in July 1984 commits the next Labour government to scrapping Britain's deterrent and expelling all nuclear bases from British soil. Within a year, Polaris would be decommissioned and negotiations opened to withdraw all Cruise missiles from the two bases at Molesworth and Greenham Common.

The party's ambitions do not stop here. Its leader, Neil Kinnock, has called for a complete freeze on nuclear testing. By the autumn of 1987 , thousands of millions may have been spent on the Trident program, but thousands more could still be saved by its cancellation. It is possible that a future Labour government in the mid-1990s might find that nuclear energy had been "disinvented" --that no more power stations need to be built, that work on the Heysham 2 and Torness advance gas-cooled reactors could be discontinued, the prototype at Dounereay dismantled, and work on all other fast breeder reactors phased out. If, in addition to all this, the design team at Aldermaston is disbanded, it would be extremely difficult ever to resume a British nuclear program.

Inevitably, a nonnuclear defense policy would put a high premium on conventional deterrence. Could Britain afford it? In a contribution to the 1983 debate, David Greenwood produced a preliminary model of what Michael Foot's government might have spent, had it ever been formed. On his own set of calculations, he surmised that keeping the budget down to £16 billion would have required a reduction in service strength by 200,000 men, three-fifths of the present total. It would also have meant the rundown of the fleet, and a substantial increase in home defense at the expense of the Rhine Army and the Second Tactical Air Force in Germany.

Today, such a program of cuts would mean more money for minehunters and fast patrol boats, but less for ocean-going warships. It would require the army to regard the defense of Britain, not the defense of the Rhine, as the most important of its roles, with all that this would mean for existing claims on equipment and resources. Any increase in defense spending would have to be at the expense of the service's direct contribution to NATO; it might lead the army to reduce its strength in Germany to 10,000 men in readiness for their complete evacuation at the expiry of the Paris Treaty (1994). As Greenwood has argued, having discarded the existing infrastructure of deterrence and defense, a Labour government, even of moderate credentials, would probably shy away from putting anything else in its place. It might particularly balk at the costs of "defensive deterrence," the expense of which might threaten its plans for Britain's economic and social rejuvenation.

Labour Option 2

On the far left of the Labour party, even more radical proposals are entertained. Those who advocate the conversion from weapons manufacture to the production of goods and services of more immediate social value have grown in number over the years, not so much in response to public anxiety about nuclear weapons, but in recognition of Britain's continued economic decline. A nation that helped to develop the bomb may wish to retain some responsibility for its use, but a country that pioneered the welfare state has no wish either to slip into the second league of welfare states.

A study commissioned by the Institute of Professional Civil Servants has estimated that 80 percent of capital equipment used in the production of nuclear weapons could be transferred directly to civil use. A detailed paper on the conversion of the conventional defense industry was discussed only once by the Labour party and the Trade Union Congress Liaison Committee before the 1983 election. Now, a plethora of such reports exist, including some by the Transport and General Workers Union, the Civil and Public Services Association, and the Society of Civil and Public Servants, all of which propose cost-effective ways of converting tanks into tractors, the modern equivalent of turning swords into ploughshares. At the highest union level, these reports have been complemented by studies undertaken by shop steward committees of some of Britain's leading defense contractors, notably at Vickers and Barrow and Lucas Aerospace.

The Labour party has already adopted a plan to establish a National Industrial Conversion Council (NICC) to oversee and assist the work of a number of regional conversion offices which will, in turn, be responsible for the emerging network of factory-based Alternative Use Committees.

The claim that reduced defense spending, however, would have an immediate social impact should be received with considerable skepticism. If the share of defense spending in GDP has remained at its pre-1979 level, only £2.3 billion would have been available for tax cuts, less than the cost of the 1984-85 miners strike. Expressed another way, it would have been equivalent to less than two pence off the basic rate of income tax, hardly enough to free the spirit of enterprise or put three million people back to work. Even if a future Labour government were to find the courage to sacrifice tanks and planes for more schools and hospitals, it is unlikely to resolve any of the structural problems of welfare spending that have prompted Ralph Dahrendorf to talk of "the end of the social democratic century."

The problems of conversion run even deeper. Where would the state find the money to retrain workers in the defense industry? Even if it succeeds, how would it stimulate market demand for the new products? Would the workers wish to be redeployed in urban development schemes, environmental protection programs, public utilities, or high school teaching? The program in its most stark and unqualified form would demand a degree of "peace planning" that would be politically acceptable only in time of war, even if its most coercive aspects were disguised by the phrase "community planning."

Alliance Option : The European Temptation

The SDP's misfortune is to have adopted policies which in the economic field offer radical ways of tackling the endemic decline of the British economy and yet in the field of defense promise to preserve the mold of NATO. This mixture of radicalism and conservatism would rest uneasily on any party's shoulders; it sits more uneasily still because the SDP is tied to Liberal allies who in defense offer a far more radical alternative, not entirely removed from the aspirations of many on the left of the Labour party. The solution the SDP has chosen is to think about how to obtain the objectives the Labour party has set by less radical means : nonnuclear defense, a minimal deterrent, arms control without abject surrender.

The Liberal party, by contrast, saddled with a hard-core leftist fringe from its

60 years or more in opposition, has found the task much more difficult and accommodation to political realities much harder. More recently still, the Social Democrats, as they have sensed that power was within their grasp, began to build up an image as a governing force rather than merely a vehicle of political protest, and have to this end tried not to formulate new policies but to capture popular moods and to give expression to popular fears --fear of the expense of the Trident program, of a future without arms control, of the alternative offered by the Labour party. This has meant that since 1983 the SDP has also become less imaginative, less challenging in the face of some of the old orthodoxies, but much more in tune with public opinion.

For this reason, it has become much harder for the two members of the Alliance to reach agreement, especially on nuclear questions. It is difficult to imagine what an Alliance policy will be with one party committed to Cruise, the other opposed to its deployment. How would an Alliance-supported government act when the Liberals support a nuclear freeze, and the SDP does not, when the Liberals would like to see a nuclear-free zone in Europe, an option their partners dismiss as a "cruel hoax"? As a leading Social Democrat acknowledged in the run-up to the 1983 general election, the two parties had reached their conclusions by "different routes"; indeed, the routes have led them to entirely different conclusions.

The SDP is committed to maintaining the Polaris fleet at least to the year 2000, or even 2005; prolonging its life to the end of the century would enable a future government to look at the whole prospect of the British deterrent in the light of the existing arms control regime and the state of the East-West relations. If this is not possible or even desirable, the party would prefer Britain to opt for a much cheaper system on the assumption that Britain needs only enough warheads to deter, not destroy, the Soviet Union, and the difference between an optimal figure and the number of warheads promised by Trident has been widened unacceptably by the switch from the C4 missile to the D5. The Liberal party, by contrast, has opposed an independent nuclear deterrent since 1957, a much longer time than the Labour party. The Liberal Assembly has also come out against the deployment of Cruise missiles and given unanimous support to a freeze on all further deployment of nuclear weapons. All this is difficult to square with SDP leader David Owen's insistence that an Alliance government would be prepared, if necessary, to use Polaris as a weapon of last resort.

In an attempt to gloss over their differences, the two parties have talked much more seriously than either the Conservative or Labour movements about a European option. For the Social Democrats, NATO's conventional deficiencies remain the most urgent and central question that merits no less than an authoritative declaration of intent similar to the Harmel Report of 1967, but a Harmel Report signed by the Europeans. A series of straw polls taken by the Liberal party chairman in 1984 also revealed that the great majority of Liberal MPs would prefer a larger European contribution and an emphasis on a conventional deterrent, nonprovocative in its intent. In the Gulbenkian Foundation Lecture, David Owen clarified this position by insisting that the answer was not a European defense community, or a European defense force, but the development of a European defense personality within NATO. The SDP's answer to reliance on the United States is neither to take it for granted like the Conservatives, nor deplore it like Labour's left-wing, but to reduce it as far as possible by forging a European alternative. For many Liberals, it is no longer a matter of choosing between a European and an Atlantic priority in defense but strengthening the European priority in order to maintain the Atlantic link. In the nuclear sphere, the Liberal party leadership claims that Europe has a vital role to play, one that warrants a third chair at the arms control talks, if for no other reason than that the new initiatives or perspectives that Europe might bring to bear might break the deadlock.

The problem with this European alternative is that it relies for the most part on a European nuclear force, along the lines proposed by Edward Heath in the early 1970s. Such a European defense system would have to include an Anglo-French deterrent held in trust for Europe as a whole. Unfortunately, there is no sign of any closer cooperation between the two countries on nuclear matters (on targeting, for example), let alone the joint design of nuclear weapons and procurement, an option that was actually discussed, only to be immediately rejected by the committee that looked into the successor for Polaris when Thatcher first came to power.

A problem with the Alliance alternative is that European defense is, in Nicole Gnesotto's words, "a French passion," and there is no sign at the moment that the French would even consider holding the force de frappe in trust for their friends in the European Community. That is one of the two main weaknesses of the SDP's case -- Britain itself cannot be central to the process if and when it happens. Any claim that it might once have had to leadership in Europe was forfeited years ago by its late entry into the EEC and its spoiling role until recently. Most Europeans would remain unconvinced by British enthusiasm and would see it as many see the Alliance formation itself, as marginal to the political debate.

The second weakness of the argument is that the Liberal party, for one, would have no interest in a European nuclear force. In a public address in April 1984, the party leader, David Steel insisted that, if Britain and France were invited to attend a nuclear summit, they would have to be prepared to negotiate a freeze on all future missile development, which would mean cancelling Trident and delaying the modernization of the force de frappe, that they would also have, first, to agree to merge the negotiations on strategic and intermediate range European forces, which would mean the inclusion of their own systems, and, second, to encourage NATO to abandon its damaging reliance on the strategy of flexible response. Even the SDP has argued that the British deterrent should be made negotiable if its European allies wished it to be, the clearest indication that they would be prepared to trade away Polaris if the Germans in particular were ever to feel that it failed to serve any useful purpose. All the indications are that a government dependent on SDP support would be forced to go along with any German desire for Polaris or Trident to be discussed at the next round of arms talks.

In short, the disparity between the SDP's views of European cooperation and those of the Liberal party and between the Alliance views in general and some views entertained in France would suggest that the Europeans may have traveled a long way from Messina, but that they are not all traveling the same road. Although even the present British government has expressed some interest in the Eureka program, it must be said that Britain remains a highly ambivalent supporter of European defense cooperation and in any event no longer has the power to lead any such move as it did in the creation of the first three European defense initiatives : the Brussels Pact, the Western European Union, and the Eurogroup, a reflection perhaps of the wasting of British military power, and Britain's diminishing influence in European counsels.

BRITAIN'S DEFENSE IN THE 1990s

The critical issue over the next ten years will be Britain's attitude toward nuclear weapons, which has only in part been brought into relief by the debate over the U.S. Strategic Defense Initiative. It is not only the Labour party which has expressed concern over the Atlantic Alliance's nuclear policies. Across the political spectrum, there has been support for confining NATO's nuclear arsenal to ballistic weapons, withdrawing battlefield nuclear weapons from service, and re-arming Cruise missiles with subsonic nonnuclear warheads, an option which, its supporters claim, would enhance Britain's security, while reducing the risk of a nuclear exchange.

Even if the country's nuclear deterrent remains, it could become a casualty of the next round of arms control talks. At any stage in the next few years, the Americans might rethink the wisdom of selling their closest ally one of the most lethal systems. Already U.S. strategic literature is replete with acknowledgment that tomorrow's generation of European nuclear weapons will be of a different order of importance from those of the past decade, and that their future will have to be reevaluated in the light of the progress or non-progress of SDI. Thus the intellectual framework has already been laid for the inclusion of these weapons in some form of arms control negotiations, whether or not that implies formal concessions.

Recently, Henry Kissinger has suggested that the British deterrent might be "folded into" arms control talks at a later stage, perhaps by substantially reducing the number of warheads the British plan to deploy. Influencing that decision will not only be the U.S. perception of its own national interest but German anxieties as well. For the last couple of years, the Germans have made it clear that they would like the British and French systems to be brought into the arms control discussions. Their representations have been polite, even oblique, yet their concern is real. Whether they would press the British and French to yield is another question.

In going forward with the Trident system, the government insisted that it would be prepared to concur with substantial reductions in the number of warheads or even to cancel the program entirely, if the international situation improved significantly, and arms control once again held out some promise of easing international tensions. That may well be a decision that a future administration will have to countenance.

On the nonnuclear front, the prospect of rational, or even sensible choices being made is no more compelling than it was 20 years ago. There is still little discussion of national security beyond partisan prescriptions, or calls to patriotism or international morality. There has been little real debate about the costs of Britain's membership in NATO, or the corresponding benefits. The public has supported defense spending at a level the politicians have cared to choose; cost accounting has been the guiding principle and passion. That has been the case even with Thatcher, who has broken so decisively with the past in so many other respects. Thatcher came to power with a clear vision of the Soviet threat, but no real vision of how to meet it. Indeed, the Conservative party's 1981 program implicitly accepted that defense would have to stand on the same footing as any other major government expenditure.

Writing of the 1962 Defense White Paper, The Economist opined that "the psychology of the declining power is not to choose but to wait upon events." Britain is no longer in the position of being able to do so. Unfortunately, as it begins to find in unilateralist or neo-gaullist solutions the reassurance many no longer seem to find in membership in NATO, the eventual choices made may well reflect the psychology of decline even more than the choices that have been avoided.

3 France: Principle and Pragmatism

Nicole Gnesotto

Against all expectations, the coming of a new millenium hardly appears to have brought about any apocalyptic visions. On the contrary, both Ronald Reagan and Mikhail Gorbachev (the former in his so-called Star Wars speech of March 23, 1983, the latter in his disarmament proposals of January 15, 1986) called for a world free of the nuclear menace by the year 2000, that is, in less than 15 years. The superpowers' rhetoric has recently become more pacifist and more antinuclear than the public opinion trends to which these speeches were directed, although for diametrically opposed reasons and toward altogether contradictory objectives. There is little doubt, however, that the East-West security equation will, over the next 15 years, still rely on a considerable number of atomic weapons, whatever the real or desired progress in the area of arms control. Nor is there any question that, in terms of European security, nuclear deterrence will remain as much a necessity as a problem, one which is even more complex and delicate to resolve. Since it is independent from the NATO military structure and yet united with its partners in the Atlantic Alliance, France must take into account the political-strategic changes that affect the security of the European continent. Defense is as much a matter of principle as of pragmatism.

Already, in the early 1980s, the intermediate nuclear force (INF) affair and notably the deep turmoil caused by the deployment of Pershing and Cruise missiles in the Federal Republic initiated the double orientation of French defense policy: first of all, more Atlanticist, thanks to President Mitterrand's personal support of NATO's double decision; but above all, more European with the inauguration and reinforcement of Franco-German cooperation in security measures, which in turn brought about an improved European cooperation within the Alliance. In effect, Ronald Reagan's unfortunate remarks about limited nuclear war, combined with doubts over the European-American strategic coupling and neutralist and antinuclear tendencies in the Federal Republic, created a real climate of anxiety in France concerning the two conditions essential to French security: a credible U.S. deterrent and a Federal Republic that is firmly anchored in the Alliance.

The reinforcement of Franco-German cooperation in security matters then progressed through several stages.

The reactivation of the military clauses of the Elysée Treaty in January 1983 remains the keystone of this cooperation, comprising consultations by the Foreign and Defense ministers before each summit and the creation of a Franco-German commission designed to deal with armament issues, military cooperation, and political-strategic affairs. The reanimation of the Western European Union in October 1984 was to carry this Franco-German dynamic onto the European level. Similarly, thanks to the Dutch initiative, the Independent European Program Group (IEPG) was bolstered as a technical organ in European armaments cooperation. In the autumn of 1984, the IEPG acquired a political orientation with the first meeting under its auspices of the member countries' Defense ministers; here the group was given the mission of encouraging a maximum of military and industrial cooperation.

The creation of the Rapid Action Force (FAR) was also to demonstrate the spirit of European solidarity in French defense efforts. Admittedly, by the force of circumstance, the French have the role of initiators, whether it be in the discussions with the Germans on the FAR's mission or on the pre-strategic (formerly tactical) nuclear forces. First, French Defense Minister Charles Hernu made a declaration in June 1985 concerning both countries' common security interests. That same August, Mitterrand and Helmut Kohl decided at their meeting in Brégançon to install a "hot line" between their two capitals. On January 8, 1986, it was announced that the French and German armed forces would participate during the same year in combined exercises at an unprecedented level (150,000 men). At Baden Baden on January 16, the two leaders reached an agreement in principle on a common study project concerning the conditions of an air defense that could be enlarged to include an antimissile mission. And, finally, the Paris summit of February 18 concluded with three decisions: the first on common training for the officers of both armies, and the second on "the continuation of studies relating to a better use of French forces in Germany and especially the FAR" with the confirmation of "common appropriate maneuvers" in 1986-87. The third decision reaffirmed the Baden Baden meeting a few weeks earlier on pre-strategic weapons: "Within the limits imposed by the extreme rapidity of such decisions, the President of the Republic commits himself to consult the Chancellor of the FRG concerning the possible use of French pre-strategic weapons on German territory. He reiterates that, in this matter, the decision cannot be shared."[1]

The actual deployment of the Pershing and cruise missiles in Western Europe and the weakening of the West German antinuclear protest movement still have not resolved the question of deterrence and of the Euro-American coupling, nor does it make the European orientation of French security policy superfluous. The INF affair had hardly been terminated before the U.S. administration itself seemed to reconsider the issue of deterrence. Didn't the Strategic Defense Initiative (SDI), launched by Reagan in 1983 with its expanded version of a missile-proof shield, undermine the concept of "extended deterrence," thus leaving the European continent open and vulnerable to any conventional attack? Was it really judicious to create the illusion of a world soon to be freed of the nuclear threat when the Atlantic consensus on deterrence was still badly shaken by the pacifist protest of large segments of European public opinion? In addition, Franco-German relations, it is true, went through new difficulties after 1984: the uncertainties over the Franco-German combat helicopter; the failure of the European combat aircraft project from which France was to withdraw in the summer of 1985; the reservations of the Federal Republic regarding the European space shuttle, Hermès; the German refusal to participate in the military communications satellite project proposed by France in November 1985; the budget cuts announced by Bonn, which limited German participation in the Eureka projects; and finally, the disagreement between Paris and Bonn over participation in the SDI research program which the Federal Republic officially accepted, but which Paris refused to support at the government level.

However, these temporary obstacles--doubtlessly exaggerated by the approach of elections in both countries--should not bring into question the necessity of Franco-German and European cooperation in matters of security.

Indeed, the evolution of the sociopolitical context presents a number of important trends, so that one can no longer afford to neglect European cooperation within the Alliance. These multifarious threats are military, political and economic.

Besides deploying an increasing number of SS-20s which directly threaten the European territory, the Soviets, for their part, have developed short- and middle-range ballistic missiles of such accuracy that they can be equipped with either conventional, nuclear or chemical warheads; the problems of an antimissile air defense have acquired a truly European dimension for all states concerned. On the U.S. side, the isolationist trend has persisted; whatever the present reality of the U.S. commitment in Europe, one should not totally exclude the possibility of a new definition of the commitment (reduction of U.S. troops in Europe, reorientation toward a more maritime strategy centered on the NATO Mediterranean bases, appeal for a greater European financial participation in the conventional area as a condition to maintaining U.S. troops on the European continent, etc.). On both the U.S. and Soviet sides, the prospect of antimissile defense systems, even partial ones, may undermine the nuclear deterrence system as it now functions in Europe. A mixed offensive-defensive system deployed by both superpowers might perhaps reduce the risks of a first strike and strengthen mutual deterrence. On the other hand, it could produce a new offensive and defensive arms race and entail even more alarming consequences for Europe, such as reconsideration of nuclear first use, the foundation of present NATO doctrine and of the U.S. guarantee to Europe, and possibly the decoupling between strategic nuclear forces and battlefield weapons (both nuclear and conventional) deployed in Europe. Finally, from the technological and industrial perspective, the immense military research and development effort in the United States presents Europeans with a challenge that threatens their very economic power and independence, if they do not unite to confront it.

It is in this evolving context that French security policy must be reassessed and readapted. The domestic consensus on defense constitutes, in this respect, an essential asset without equivalent in any other country of the Alliance. Since 1977, when both the French Communist and Socialist parties rallied to a national nuclear force, public opinion has appeared almost unanimous in its support of the main principles of national defense: independence, so-called nuclear deterrence "of the strong by the weak," and a global capacity for intervention and influence. Since 1983 this consensus has been reinforced within the political class (with exception of the Communists) by support for Franco-German coooperation, which has become as fundamental a principle as that of national independence. This continuous internal cohesion over defense policy thus categorically excludes two types of scenarios: on the one hand, return to NATO's integrated military structure, and on the other hand, neutrality and a nervous withdrawal inside the boundaries of the Hexagon.

The constant modernization of the French military forces remains nonetheless both a political and a military necessity, inasmuch as the credibility of French forces is indispensable to deterrence and national independence. The modernization of defense equipment, as defined in the 1984-88 military programming law, comprises the following :

1. For strategic nuclear forces, the introduction of the M4 missile on the nuclear missile-launching submarines; the first submarine equipped with M4s entered service in 1985 and two others are being readapted.

2. For pre-strategic nuclear forces, the first squadron of Mirage 2000s equipped with the new air-to-ground middle-range missile (ASMP) in 1986, and the development of the Hadès missile with the objective of replacing the aging Plutons by 1992. In total, nuclear forces have been allocated 33.4 percent of the credits (Title V) in the 1986 defense budget.

3. For conventional forces, the future tank, the combat support helicopter, a nuclear aircraft carrier, the new ACX Rafale combat aircraft are --among other programs-- part of the national defense modernization plan for the next decade.

If this modernization remains indispensable to the credibility of the French military apparatus, it is nonetheless necessary and inevitable to adapt to certain constraints, both of an internal and external nature. The debate over the potential antimissile defense capacity provides an example of this: the prospect of a Soviet antimissile system has already induced France to assign an extensive part of its military funds to silo hardening and to improving the penetration capacities of strategic missiles (all told, 842 million francs in the 1986 budget). The SX surface-to-surface missile, designed to give a new mobility to the strategic land forces, might also be reconsidered, and the final decision will take into account Soviet countermeasures and antimissile defense systems as well as the cost of this program (approximately 30 billion francs). The second type of constraint is indeed financial and just as fundamental as the evolution of East-West strategy. The defense budget presently represents 3.77 percent of the gross domestic product, that is, about 15 percent of the national budget. Given the existing international situation, however, economic difficulties may lead to severe cuts, especially as the cost of new weapon systems, particularly the most advanced technologies, increases all the time. Besides the SX program, the debate will also concern the future combat tank, the nuclear aircraft carrier, the future combat aircraft, and the communications and reconnaissance systems (satellites, AWACS, etc.). Most of these programs will have to be examined in light of the budget resources, but also in light of the objectives and coherence of national defense policy: national deterrence, European solidarity particularly in the conventional area, and intervention capacity overseas. The balancing act is extremely difficult in this field: the choice of an all-nuclear policy at the expense of conventional forces is incompatible not only with the very coherence of French deterrence doctrine but also with European cooperation, especially in a period when demographic decline will also raise serious problems for the Bundeswehr. On the other hand, giving up overseas intervention forces in favor of nuclear deterrence does not correspond either to the defense of French interests all over the world or to the need to meet any indirect threat to France and to the countries that have signed alliance agreement with her.

In light of all these constraints, the European option may prove, in many respects, more and more difficult to bypass. With respect to weaponry, space systems, and technological research, the national financial difficulties, added to U.S. pressures and the formidable technological advance of the United States, all point to European solutions: a space shuttle, communications and reconnaissance satellites, technological cooperation within Eureka, distribution of design leadership by system and by country (the helicopter to France, the future tank to the FRG, for instance). On the other hand, from a strictly military point of view, the adaption of air defense in Central Europe to the new Soviet capabilities (accuracy, double nuclear and/or conventional capacities of short- and middle-range missiles) should also induce common European solutions or, at the very least, joint research in the area of antimissile defense. In addition, at the strictly French level, the very development of the national deterrent leads France to be more selective in its use of forces. This concerns particularly the ASMP and Hadès programs, the first because of its increased flexibility and survival capacity, the second because its 350-kilometer range (that is, beyond West German territory) may result in more selective strike options at the French President's disposal. Finally, concerning negotiations over arms control, France, like all its European allies, remains vigilant and convinced of the necessity to maintain the 1972 ABM Treaty, the keystone of deterrence. Despite the disagreements over industrial participation in the SDI program, Europe unanimously agrees on the destabilizing strategic impact of antimissile systems. Future French security policy will thus continue to abide by the twin guidelines of principle and pragmatism.

NOTE

1. English translation printed in <u>Survival</u>, July-August 1986, p. 366.

4 France: What Vital Interests?

Michel Makinsky

Governments may change, but the French nuclear deterrent remains. As Ambassador François de Rose has stated, "Defense policy always demonstrates continuity regarding the essential options. This does not mean immobility."[1] From this principle, the two facets of French doctrine are apparent : the strategic nuclear option is definitive, but, on the other hand, its scope can evolve. At the request of General de Gaulle, the initial strategic model was constructed around a "constant," the autonomy of decision-making; today, it appears that this decision-making process has to respond at the same time to variable external contingencies. General Lucien Poirier, one of the most influential nuclear theorists, observed that, from its origins, "the fundamental problem of our military strategy has consisted of conciliating heterogeneous and complementary goals : the absolute will of autonomy and support for changeable external relations."[2]

We can understand from this why the permanence of strategic nuclear deterrence is periodically reaffirmed by the presidents of the Republic and the succeeding governments of the Fifth Republic. In the middle of the Greenpeace crisis in the summer of 1985, François Mitterrand , during a brief visit to the Muroroa atoll testing range, solemnly confirmed the importance of the French strategic deterrent and the government's determination to pursue the necessary testing for its modernization.[3] With the exception of the Communist party, all of the political parties have demonstrated their support of this major option, even though there are serious disagreements on defense policy between and inside the parties. This is a uniquely French phenomenon that is habitually designated by the slightly ambiguous term of "consensus." Yet, isn't it appropriate for a consensus to carry within it a sense of ambiguity? Whatever the case, all future presidents and prime ministers will have to assume this "heritage" and will not be able to question the principal pillar of French deterrence, its strategic nuclear force, even if the doctrine will have to undergo some alterations.

Today, we have to recognize that, while the principal component of French deterrence is to be at least preserved and possibly reinforced, the external environment as well as several internal factors have not only modified the tools of deterrence, but have also affected the conditioning strategic concept. These changes have manifested themselves as much in the geographic dimension as in the means of deterrence. The debate centers around the question of what deterrence covers at present; is the evolution that we observe derived from a simple adjustment to a changing external environment or from a more basic strategic restructuring?

It is not the purpose of this chapter to give a detailed response to this controversial question. Our objective here is to understand the defense policy of the present government and to evaluate the major trends of future defense policies. In this, we have to keep in mind the permanent contradiction that French strategy must resolve : autonomy of decision-making versus adaptation to external contingencies. As will be demonstrated, other factors have influenced and continue to weigh upon the security of France, and we will attempt to assess their importance. It goes without saying that we will refrain from formulating predictions for the next 30 years; we know by experience that the most sophisticated models can rarely resist confrontations with reality. In a more modest fashion, our prospective study will try to bring to light some lines of continuity -- and of rupture.

The right-wing government of Prime Minister Jacques Chirac, the first Fifth Republic government to represent a parliamentary majority politically opposed to the President, has had to confront the structural constraints of cohabitation. Both the President and the Prime Minister demonstrated a strong resolve to dominate the areas of foreign policy and defense. In the first months of the new government, however, France spoke with one voice, but "through two mouths." Mitterrand and Chirac undertook a close collaboration in these policy areas which are no longer the privileged reserve of the President. How long this "bicephalous" arrangement can last is questionable. Such a dyarchy is incompatible with the principle of nuclear deterrence. How can French foreign and security policies be split between two decision-making centers? This uncomfortable situation does have the merit of revealing a more fundamental problem : the absence of sufficient administrative coordination permitting the executive to undertake in-depth analysis and concerted action in the foreign and military domains. Various proposals have recently been made for the creation of a National Security Council and for the establishment of related task forces. But this organizational problem should not cloak the real issue at stake : what strategy for France? We are tempted to think that whoever the successor to Mitterrand may be, the orientations described here will remain the same. If major transformations do intervene, they will no doubt come from external circumstances.

The analysis of threat perceptions affecting French security has been the object of numerous declarations by public officials. These perceptions have been clearly defined and summarized by General Jeannou Lacaze, then Chief of Staff of the Armies, during a speech at the Institut des Hautes Etudes de Défense Nationale on May 19, 1984.[4] As Gen. Lacaze observed, Western Europe is confronted by the so-called direct menace throught the continuous deployment of SS-20 missiles, the increase in Warsaw Pact strategic and tactical nuclear capacities, as well as the increase in chemical and conventional capacities, all of which "make a formidable instrument for intimidation and possible invasion." To this, General Lacaze added a threat that he labeled indirect, consisting of "bringing together the conditions for a decoupling between the United States and Europe." In this indirect strategy, the Soviet Union has devoted itself to developing a number of propaganda efforts against the neutron bomb and against the deployment of the Pershing and Cruise missiles.[5] Added to this, one must note the omnipresence of the Soviet navy, especially in the Mediterrenean and the Baltic areas.

These intimidations aim to undermine the unity of the Alliance at a time when France is reaffirming both its independence and its solidarity with its allies (due to a much stronger threat perception). The main themes of French doctrine on potential threats deserve some clarification beyond the well-known generalizations.

To begin with, French political and military authorities today have a sharper perception of the Soviet threat in all its diverse forms than they had in the past. This means that, first, these threats themselves have become greater, and second, this growing danger has been perceived as such.

This evolution is very much due to the Soviets themselves who, by several acts, have undermined, according to Denis Delbourg, "the apparently reasonable model of East-West coexistence, of which Henry Kissinger was the most influential theoretician."[6] The SS-20 deployment, the military coup in Poland, and the invasion of Afghanistan all provoked a realization at the highest levels of state that the detente years had been "a decade of duplicity."

This was a brutal awakening for political figures who have now been made fully aware of the double trap that threatened the security of France and of Europe; the risk of nondeployment of U.S. Euromissiles, opening the door to blackmail by the SS-20s, and also the repeated Soviet efforts to integrate French strategic nuclear forces in a process of Soviet-American arms reduction, where France would be faced with the dissolution of its most important defensive asset. On October 3, 1985, during his official visit to Paris, Mikhail Gorbachev proposed that the strategic nuclear forces of France and Britain be detached from other Western forces and that separate negotiations be initiated for their reduction. To this subtle trap Mitterrand replied that two superpowers had first to come to an agreement among themselves and that the French force could not be amputated. The French President had forthrightly repeated on a number of occasions that this threat was unacceptable, notably through his approval of the "double decision" of 1979 and his celebrated remark that "the missiles are to the East, and the pacifists to the West." The speech by Mitterrand to the Bundestag in 1983 was a decisive step in the development of a political will to confront the Soviet threat. From this point on, the multidimensional character of this threat was recognized, including the technological thievery by Eastern intelligence services, resulting in the expulsion from France of Soviet agents operating under diverse covers.[7]

Admittedly, this perception, reflected since 1981 by a growing determination of policymakers in their negotiations with the Eastern bloc, reflects an important turning point. Michel Tatu rightly states that the heritage of General de Gaulle, breaking the monopoly of the two blocs through the establishment of a dialogue with Moscow in the so-called framework of détente, weighed heavily on his successors even when this dialogue lost some of its meaning and became an obligatory rite for reasons of internal politics (unity of the Gaullist majority, or efforts to mollify the Communist party with respect to French foreign policy).[8] In addition, this rite was essential for the notions of independence and national prestige.

Several factors pressured Mitterrand's predecessors to hold to this line. Tatu lists the following factors : the necessity not to appear to break with the past (in the eyes of the majority); the Ostpolitik of the Federal Republic of Germany associated with Willy Brandt; the Soviet-American dialogue reflected in the SALT agreements; the detente process culminating (according to Tatu) in the Helsinki accords. Ultimately, it was admitted that the concrete results did not match the hopes. In the second part of Valéry Giscard d'Estaing's term, a period of greater awareness dawned with the seizure of power by a pro-Communist government in Kabul in 1978, following the Cuban military interventions in Ethiopia and Angola.

The Shaba rescue operation was the first tangible reaction. In spite of this, Tatu stresses the need up until 1981 to maintain the detente dialogue at any price, a policy that became most apparent in the policy of accommodation during the Afghan crisis. This "soft-line" attitude toward Moscow is also evident in the absence of French guarantees for the Camp David agreements and the failure to apply economic sanctions to the Soviet Union. This position is also linked to internal preoccupations, that is reconciling the French Communist Party as the 1981 elections approached.

There has been no real revolution in the threat perceptions of the French political leadership since 1981, but rather the realization of a change in these perceptions, especially for the Socialist party leaders and their rank and file. This evolution is also reflected by polls on public defense consciousness, which we will discuss later. We will also have to modify our judgment of the real extent of Mitterrand's threat perceptions through two observations : one on the political context of this threat assessment, and the other on the non-correlation between the declared strategy and the material means at hand.

François Heisbourg observes correctly that "the Socialist Party has carried out a profound transformation on questions of defense during the 1970s."[9] It was only in 1978, he continues, that the party accepted the doctrine of nuclear deterrence. This was the product of a major effort of internal persuasion led by the party's Defense Commission under the direction of Charles Hernu, who was until September 1985 the "irreplaceable" Minister of Defense. This lengthy maturation process of the Socialist party has resulted in an internal "consensus," appropriately described by Jolyon Howorth as a "consensus of silence."[10] This consensus covers divisions within the Socialist party that the official line attempts to conceal.

The principal target of the Soviet threat in Europe is and will be the Federal Republic of Germany. This was already apparent under Giscard d'Estaing. The vital importance to France of its neighbor's security was considerably accentuated during the campaigns launched by the Soviets and the pacifists and Greens (not to mention certain SPD factions) to stop the Pershing deployment. France strongly supported the West German government in its commitment to this deployment. Having failed to block the Pershings, the Soviets proceeded to their second objective : the detachment of the FRG from NATO through blackmail and seduction. Such an eventuality is considered to be a threat to French vital interests. It confronts French strategy and related defense policy with an extremely complex question : the geographic extent of the deterrent. In other words, does the French deterrent cover the FRG? As a consequence, would the very nature of the French deterrent and strategy change, or would it simply be adapted to a new context? This challenge, this apparent contradiction already recognized at the time of Giscard d'Estaing presidency, appears in the 1980s to be a major question for the present government and its successors. The strategic upheavals generated by the new Soviet-American challenge (which far exceeds the Strategic Defense Intitiative) has pointed up the problematic nature of the balance between strategy and threat.

The defense of French interests is conceived according to the so-called theory of the "three circles," well-known to most specialists. The first circle is the national territory; the second, located in Europe, encompasses to a certain extent the approaches to the "sanctuary"; the third covers the rest of the world.

According to classic French doctrine, nuclear deterrence is reserved only for the national territory; the nonnuclear means are reserved for the two other circles and are subject to independent French decision-making processes. The appearance of the neutron bomb, a weapon long in search of a strategy, forced a reassessment of certain aspects of this doctrine. The contradiction that neutron weapons introduced was alleviated by putting ultimate control of nuclear employment at the highest political level. By insisting on a European orientation for French security, Giscard d'Estaing declared that a threat against France's neighbors was likely to affect national interests and possibly trigger the appropriate reactions. Subsequently, however, General Poirier has emphasized that there is no conceptual continuity between the first and second circles, thereby countering critics who contended that a "war-fighting" role for the nuclear deterrent would undermine its very meaning.[11] The introduction of the advanced Hadès "pre-strategic" missile has diminished the debate, even though the missile's deployment doctrine has never been fully defined.[12]

Indeed, the reports on defense and defense budget policy published in 1985 by the three major political parties demonstrate a rather large area of agreement (although with numerous nuances on the insertion of French vital interests in Europe). Thus, the authors of the Socialist party document on future defense policy declare explicitly that, although there is no automatic guarantee of French nuclear weapons use on behalf of its allies, France doubtlessly has an essential interest in the security of the FRG, "the most exposed and vulnerable territory in Europe, but also one bordering on France."[13] For their part, the Rassemblement pour la République (RPR) and the Union pour la Démocratie Française (UDF), the new majority coalition in 1986, also recognized Germany's central position in French interests.

In particular, the UDF proclaimed : "France has to display clearly its will to respond to a possible aggression from the very start with all its conventional means and, if necessary, with tactical nuclear weapons at the forward positions of Europe."[14] The RPR is not as categorical, owing perhaps to its Gaullist origins, but it certainly agrees with the UDF on the central nature of the stakes in Germany. Only the Communist party, for obvious reasons, remains definitely hostile to such a conception of French interests, along with certain isolated authors.[15]

The reason for this fading of an apparent contradiction in French strategy is quite simply that the Soviet threat directed against Germany has become more menacing in the eyes of the French at the same time as questions arose over the risks of the decoupling of Germany and Europe from the United States.

Last, two other dimensions of the threat have manifested themselves in a troubling way : first, there is the destabilization of those African states linked to France by international agreements and of other Third World countries where France has important interests. From this point of view, it seems that, paradoxically, the threat directed mainly by the Soviet Union has become more real and, at the same time, succeeding French governments (until March 1986) have tended to underestimate this threat and to minimize the strategic risks that it entails. The Chadian affair is typical. The delay in engaging French forces and the abrupt withdrawal of those forces after the meeting between Mitterrand and Khadaffi in Crete has had extremely grave consequences.[16] This failure led to a loss of French credibility in Francophone Africa.

Finally, it is necessary to ask why French political leaders had persisted so long in accommodating Libya, without any tangible results. The recent military success of the Chadian government has perhaps obscured this questioning.

Even more critical is the evident failure of these political leaders to understand the existence of a strategy aimed against France and the West via the Third World. The latest research, including the work done at the Fondation pour les Etudes de Défense Nationale, has thoroughly illuminated the existence of an "oblique strategy."[17]

The second dimension of the threat (which French governments have generally neglected) is internal destabilizations and terrorism. For years, independence movements have sought to detach French territories and overseas departments : New Caledonia, Guadeloupe and Martinique, Guyana and Réunion. In certain cases, the destabilization process is very much under way (New Caledonia). However, these territories and departments represent vital strategic interests, not only for France, but also for the West. Despite emphatic declarations to the contrary, succeeding governments (and especially under Mitterrand) let the situation deteriorate.

For New Caledonia, the left government, under Mitterrand's influence, had paradoxically encouraged the independence movements and hoped naively to "organize" independence while proclaiming loud and clear that this would not be a rupture. Socialist ministers understood (a little too late) the essential geostrategic location of this territory (resources in nickel, key maritime position) and clung to the illusion of maintaining French influence after independence, notably by reinforcing the military base there. Furthermore, the New Caledonian independence movements have received the support of Libya and other foreign powers.

In Guadeloupe during this time, movements openly supported by Cuba were fomenting a continuous agitation. The local authorities knew precisely how things stood, but up to March 1986, the political powers in Paris hesitated to regain control of the situation.[18] Guyana, where the Ariane rocket space center is located, has also had its external infiltrations, again organized by Cuba.

Terrorism offers the most appalling example of the lack of political will, since the strategic dimension of international terrorism is increasingly evident. Terrorist groups advocating an antimilitary, anti-NATO, anticapitalist, and pro-Soviet ideology have gone on a rampage in France and elsewhere in Western Europe. Despite the best efforts of police (often crowned with success), the political powers had until recently refused to take on international terrorism, either because the governments wanted to accommodate the Arab countries (petrole oblige), or because of an incapacity to recognize the existence of a strategy behind international terrorism.

This rather general picture of real threats affecting France thus assumes multiple aspects. We have shown the main orientations and policies adopted to confront these threats. Without abusing statistics, we would like briefly to describe the adequacy (or inadequacy) between the perceived threats and the means of response. To give an idea, we have to emphasize that the main priority, as with preceding governments, is the maintenance and modernization of the strategic nuclear arsenal and tactical nuclear weapons. The signs of this continuity are the introduction into service of the nuclear submarine Inflexible, the refitting of four submarines to carry M4 missiles, and the entry into service in 1992 of the Hadès missile designed to transport neutron warheads.[19]

Unfortunately, a more worrisome sign of continuity is operating in the other direction : the degradation of the French economy has provoked the delay in the program-laws determining the military budget. As the RPR report noted : "The growth rhythm of the defense effort has been broken : from 1982 to 1985 the military credits increased by only 0.5 percent per annum, as opposed to 5 percent per annum from 1977 to 1981. These credits represent less than 15 percent of the national budget and 3.71 percent of the gross domestic product, as opposed to 17 percent and 3.87 percent, respectively, in the previous period."[20] These figures speak for themselves. In addition to an economic situation that required budget cuts, the projections made since 1981 have been based on unreasonable monetary exchange rates, and many sectors of the army suffer from grave financial problems. Officially, the capital expenses are privileged, but in reality they have undergone reductions to avoid the complete asphyxiation of operating expenses. André Giraud, the Defense Minister in the Chirac government, has been critical of these financial manipulations in his new programming law covering the years 1987-91. In early 1986, Mitterrand published an anthology of his statements on foreign policy where he presented himself (in the preface) as the guardian of French orthodoxy in foreign and military affairs and expressed satisfaction over his achievements in office. In response, Giraud entitled his article in Le Monde, "Oui sur les grandes orientations, non sur leur mise en oeuvre" ("Yes to the major orientations, no to their implementation").[21]

The 1983 decision to create the Rapid Action Force (FAR) has been presented as a disposition capable of intervening on the side of France's European allies, a tangible proof of solidarity while conserving the autonomy of decision-making. General Poirier sees it as a means of filling the "hole" in our previously "all-or-nothing" defense, while, on the contrary, General Claude Le Borgne asks if the FAR deployment might not reveal that whatever justifies its dispatch is not a vital stake (i.e., one in which France does not intend to deter the adversary by nuclear means).[22]

In our view, it is not from a strategic standpoint that we must examine the FAR. The concept of an air-mobile force including a strong antitank helicopter unit was formalized at the end of 1983. Without a doubt, this concept is seductive, but we do not share Heisbourg's enthusiasm regarding its composition. According to Heisbourg, "the FAR is not so much characterized by the novelty of its means (for the men and their equipment necessarily come from other units) but rather by the new capabilities that this reorganization--with more than 200 helicopters--entails."[23] Drawn on the now weakened First Army, the FAR appears quite modest, especially if it does not have neutron weapons or aerial fire support. If the FAR had to be deployed in another theater, we do not see how its logistical lifeline can be ensured at a time when previous operations (Chad, Lebanon) have illustrated the difficulties in this area. Furthermore, we have to ask if the FAR is not in the end a tool for the management of budgetary scarcity, since there is nothing really in common between a powerfully armed force capable of consolidating a threatened front--or, even better, intimidating an enemy in time of crisis-- and this vulnerable tool which, moreover, diminishes existing units. There is a relative imbalance between the strategic objectives and the proposed means, especially if the FAR, which is hardly an intervention force on the U.S. or Soviet scale, is supposed to be a political gesture.

We have discussed the evolution of thinking in the Socialist party toward the acceptance of nuclear deterrence and the apparent maintenance of this option by the government since 1981. Public opinion has generally followed a parallel movement and, according to recent polls, young people approve (by 72.3 percent) of nuclear deterrence.[24] The causes of this evolution are easy to pinpoint : public opinion has reacted quite unfavorably to the Afghanistan invasion, the coup d'état in Poland and the South Korean Boeing affair. Even more significantly, for a majority of Frenchmen, the security of German has to be guaranteed.[25] In this manner, at a time when pacifist movements have had hardly any success, the tendency to accept nuclear deterrence is increasingly rooted in public opinion. During the Greenpeace affair, when the will to safeguard French nuclear potential was challenged, the public did not question this policy. This principle has now become a durable feature of the French political landscape.

How can we improve the security of France and Europe? That is the question that commands attention at a moment when the Soviet threat is growing and when the allies of the United States are increasingly uncertain about the effect of the Strategic Defense Initiative (SDI) on their own security. First of all, we will put forward those orientations that will certainly be adopted and then we will reflect on the changes in defense policy that may occur in the years to come.

France, with or without the cooperation of its allies, does not have the means to completely change its strategy. On the other hand, the French deterrent urgently needs to be adapted to new conditions. Indeed, it is vital for French defense to rapidly acquire a spatial dimension, taking into account the acceleration of the Soviet space threat. It is not the SDI that is capable of making the French deterrent obsolete : rather, it is the magnitude of the Soviet threat (engendering the SDI in the United States) which has to be confronted in future years. For this reason, a space studies group has been formed, and top priority is certainly being given to the improvement of observation systems, as well as to a substantial effort in the C3I area (command, control, communications, intelligence).[26] In the near future, there will be a realization of the need to incorporate "powerful and well-protected means of transmission from intelligence observation satellites, covering all of the planet and utilizing optical, infrared, radar, and electromagnetic sensors, in addition to navigation satellites to avoid being totally dependent on the American NAVSTAR system."[27] The VEC (voir - écouter - communiquer) program has had its objectives defined at the beginning of 1985. The multi-year (1985-92) plan already provides for a telecommunications satellite destined to replace the SYRACUSE I system in 1992. Other command and control systems will not enter into service until the ensuing period (1995-2005). Their realization will depend on European agreement, both on the acquired technologies and on the division of financing.

In the longer run, as General Lacaze implies, France will probably consider the study of an antisatellite system, which would rely on ballistic missiles, in case of a Soviet deployment of space weapons. In this context, such a capacity for antisatellite retaliation would reinforce French policy of independence and deterrence. In its space program, France only wishes to preserve its deterrent force, but, under present circumstances, this may mean nothing less than a perfect defense system--indeed, a strategic revolution.

These orientations are universally accepted by all of the political parties, with the exception of the Communists. The latter are, in general, hostile to reinforcement of the French nuclear capacities. Certain authors, like General Etienne Copel, draw attention to the risks of a massive Soviet chemical and bacteriological attack and call for adequate retaliatory measures for this type of threat.[28] If the chemical and bacteriological risk is real, given the Warsaw Pact capability for such an attack, the French response can only be nuclear. On the other hand, it is clear that the vulnerability of French territory and especially of the French population is very high. The question to be asked is whether the limited financial resources in a time of economic constraint would permit the contemplation of another strategy to meet this threat. In a book that caused a sensation and inspired other books, Guy Brossolet proposed a defense by internal "linkage," designed to ensnare an adversary who had invaded the territory.[29] To adopt such a strategy would be a complete, but not very realistic change, particularly when taking into account first, French geography and second, the strategy of the adversary. Moreover, this would signify that France accepts the idea of being invaded. France remains a power whose nuclear capacity is still taken seriously by its potential adversaries, and for this reason it cannot be compared to Switzerland, Yugoslavia, or Afghanistan. Other propositions, like those of Marc Geneste, have examined the U.S. strategic reorientation incarnated in the project "High Frontier" (space defense) and therein derived a response to the vulnerability of French land forces (in case of a blitzkrieg).[30] Contrary to what proponents of this thesis think, there is no efficient and financially acceptable alternative to the French strategic nuclear deterrent which ought not simply to be shelved in a damaged-goods shop. On the other hand, the operationalization in the near future of SDI space defense systems (in response to the Soviet threat) would obligate France to expand its present mode of deterrence.

There are good reasons to think that the United States will pursue its research linked to SDI, even if one cannot predict accurately which system will finally be chosen and, more important, if this system will ever be deployed. It is certain that the Soviet Union will pursue its studies in this area and undertake eventual deployment. This will be a race against the clock, unless the United States and the Soviet Union can finally conclude an agreement renouncing these systems. This eventuality would suppose that the Soviets accept verification of their activities in this field; such a system of controls would be difficult to obtain and to enforce. For France, this race poses a strategic challenge, but also, more immediately, a financial uncertainty. Only close European cooperation would make an effective response possible. Many obstacles to this have not yet been overcome. The participation of the Europeans in SDI research is only possible if there is a division of the technological spin offs between the United States and its allies. France has expressed certain reservations and initiated a project of European cooperation, Eureka, which received the political green light from sixteen countries at a Paris meeting in July 1985. Officially, this project is much more civilian than military; it signifies a commitment by France and other European states to remaining competitive in the technological race launched by the United States. Alone, France has no chance. The rationale for this program--in reality as much military as civilian--is to attempt through industrial and commercial advances to obtain the counterpart benefits in terms of military research stricto sensu.[31] This can be achieved only by the expansion of research. Such a program will include research projects parallel to those in SDI. In any case, there is no other way of avoiding a loss of competitiveness. The principal European firms have already shown an interest in Eureka.[32]

Looking more closely, one can foresee the French government not only encouraging French companies to cooperate among themselves in Eureka, but also in the contracts proposed by the Americans for SDI itself. On this point, Giscard d'Estaing has expressed the hope that French companies will sign contracts as part of the SDI program and that SDI will also be studied for its implications with respect to defense systems.[33] Giraud, the new Defense Minister, indicated, before taking office, that by launching the Eureka project, France had appeared to be rejecting SDI and carrying Europe in its wake. In fact this is more a question of nuance than of opposition to Mitterrand's policy. Eureka is compatible with SDI and, even if the two projects are formally distinct, there are bridges between them.[34] Moreover, several companies that cooperate in Eureka are candidates for SDI contracts.[35] Finally, France does not wish the FRG to become the unique or privileged beneficiary of SDI agreements (to the detriment of France).

This question became urgent when both the West Germans and the British announced their participation in SDI. These agreements largely undercut proposals for a

European Defense Initiative (EDI), designed to neutralize Soviet nonstrategic nuclear arms by conventional means. France thus found itself isolated in spite of the growing number of Eureka projects. The dilemma facing France is threefold : first, from a strategic viewpoint, the French (as well as other Europeans) have questioned the efficacy of a protective defense system covering Europe. Moreover, France has to take into account the consequences of Soviet antimissile systems on its own deterrent forces.

Second, from an economic and technological perspective, the temptation for Europeans to join the SDI program derives largely from the desire to benefit from technology transfers and U.S. contracts. Those NATO allies who do not participate in SDI risk technological retardation as well as a brain drain. Third, SDI complicates the bilateral relations between Paris and Bonn and thus strains European cohesion.[36] At the January 1986 Franco-German summit at Baden-Baden, Mitterrand underestimated the FRG's preference for the U.S. umbrella and attempted unsuccessfully to expand Bonn's support for the Eureka projects. In the future French leaders will be obliged (by budgetary constraints) to engage in increased international cooperation, while they put on a delicate balancing act aimed at maintaining a strong relation with the FRG without falling into the psychosis of a Paris-Bonn axis set "against" a Paris-London axis. This psychosis would only lead to political isolation from the two European partners. The present consensus on the shared destiny of France and Germany rests on certain unstated assumptions : the risks of the FRG being drawn away from the West; German economic superiority "compensated" by the fact that France exercises rights over German sovereignty and is a nuclear power. In our view, it should be added that the FRG does not appear to have an international "destiny" or "design," whereas France, in spite of its diminished means, has the potential for such a "calling," however vague it may be at present.

The principal obstacle that any French defense policy has to confront is of a financial nature. Thus, the last defense budget drawn up by the Socialist government defined several priorities: the Navy, the Rapid Action Force, the nuclear deterrent, space defense. But it was necessary to forgo temporarily the acquisition of Boeing AWACS planes which were ultimately ordered in 1987. Will the projected budget appropriations be sufficient for program implementation? Will Mitterrand's successors change the official line? It would be extremely imprudent to make any such prognostication.

France will face the accentuation of all these serious challenges, in addition to the destabilization of its territories and overseas departments as well as of traditionally friendly African states. In the same way, energy and strategic mineral supplies will be the object of multiple threats and will require an alert and flexible policy. Finally, certain imaginative authors foresee a lightning nuclear war launched by the Warsaw Pact before the deployment of U.S. SDI systems, or alternatively, a European capitulation (including France) before a massive blackmail by the Soviet Union. This somewhat audacious hypothesis seems to make very little of the existing systems of deterrence.

To put forth predictions on so vast a range of threats would exceed the limits of this chapter. France has, first of all, to undertake a precise analysis of enemy strategies and, subsequently, to define a global strategy of its own.

NOTES

1. François de Rose, "La Politique de défense du Président Giscard d'Estaing," in <u>La Politique extérieure de Valéry Giscard d'Estaing</u>, edited by Samy Cohen and Marie-Claude Smouts (Paris : Presses de la Fondation Nationale des Sciences Politiques, 1985) p. 177.

2. General Lucien Poirier, "Essais de stratégie théorique," <u>Cahiers de la Fondation pour les Etudes de Défense Nationale</u>, No. 22 (1982) : 293.

3. <u>Le Monde</u>, September 13, 1985.

4. General Jeannou Lacaze, "Concept de défense et sécurité de l'Europe," <u>Défense nationale</u>, July 1984, pp. 11ff.

5. On the function of propaganda in Soviet strategy, see Michel Makinsky, "La Fonction propagande et la stratégie global de l'URSS," <u>Défense nationale</u>, July 1985, pp. 75ff.

6. Denis Delbourg, "Est et Ouest : contrevents et marées," <u>Politique étrangère</u>, no. 2 (1985) : p. 322.

7. François Heisbourg, "Défense et sécurité extérieure : le changement dans la continuité," <u>Politique étrangère</u>, no. 2 (1985) : 391; see also Thierry Wolton, <u>Le KGB en France</u> (Paris : Grasset, 1986), pp. 107ff.

8. Michel Tatu, <u>Eux et nous</u> (Paris : Fayard, 1985) pp. 107ff.

9. Heisbourg, Défense et sécurité, p. 377.

10. Jolyon Howorth, "Consensus of Silence : the French Socialist Party and Defense Policy under François Mitterrand," <u>International Affairs</u>, 60, no. 4 (Autumn 1984) : 579; see also Jolyon Howorth and Patricia Chilton, eds., <u>Defence and Dissent in Contemporary France</u> (London : Croom Helm, 1984).

11. Poirier, "Essais de stratégie", pp. 287ff.

12. See especially Léo Hamon, "Le Sanctuaire désenclavé?" <u>Cahiers de la Fondation pour les Etudes de Défense Nationale</u>, no. 23 (1983).

13. Parti Socialiste, <u>La Sécurité de l'Europe</u> (Paris: 1985), p. 1.

14. Union pour la Démocratie Française, <u>Redresser la défense de la France : propositions de l'UDF</u> (Paris : 1985), p. 2.

15. For example, Paul-Marie de la Gorce, in a violent condemnation of these orientations, "Dissuasion française et défense européene," <u>Le Monde diplomatique</u>, September 1985, p. 1.

16. Elce et Hesse (pseud.), "La France et la crise du Tchad d'août 1983 : un rendez-vous manqué avec l'Afrique," Politique étrangère, no. 2 (1985) : 416.

17. Groupe d'Etudes et de Recherches sur la Stratégie Soviétique (GERSS), "L'USSR et le Tiers-Monde : une stratégie oblique," Cahiers de la Fondation pour les Etudes de Défense Nationale, no. 22 (1984).

18. The Greenpeace affair illustrates very well the difficulties of political power.

19. Le Monde, September 27, 1985.

20. Rassemblement pour la République, La Défense de la France : 4 ans de gestion socialiste. Propositions pour un renouveau (Paris : June 1985; under the direction of François Fillon), p. 2. This report presents a precise table on the decline in defense expenditure since 1981 and the gap between projections and reality.

21. André Giraud, "Oui sur les grandes orientations, non sur leur mise en oeuvre," Le Monde, February 12, 1986; François Mitterrand, Réflections sur la politique extérieure (Paris : Fayard, 1986).

22. Lucien Poirier, "La Greffe," Défense nationale, April 1983, pp. 5 ff., General C. Le Borgne, " Lettre à Lucien Poirier," Stratégique, no. 18 (July 1983), pp. 69ff.

23. Heisbourg, "Défense et sécurité", p. 385.

24. EPSI poll, published in Le Point-L'Etudiant, January 1985 and cited in Heisbourg, "Défense et sécurité", pp. 379-80.

25. Poll in Le Monde, June 28, 1985. The SIRPA (Service des Relations Publique de l'Armée) has greatly contributed to improving the public image of the Army and of deterrence.

26. Critias (pseud.), "Stratégie de l'espace ou l'espace d'une stratégie," Le Monde, June 7, 1985.

27. General Jeannou Lacaze, "L'Avenir de la défense française," unpublished speech before the Académie des Sciences Morales et Politiques (1985).

28. General Etienne Copel, Vaincre la guerre (Paris: Lieu Commun, 1984).

29. Guy Brossolet, Essai sur la non-bataille (Paris: Belin, 1975).

30. Marc Geneste and Arnold Kramish, "De la terreur à la défense : le changement de parapluie," Défense nationale, January 1984, pp. 35ff.

31. See Yves Stourdzé, "Vers une nouvelle coopération scientifique et industrielle," Le Monde diplomatique, August 1985.

32. Le Monde, June 27, 1985. In addition to the Matra-Norsk Data agreement, Siemens, Philips, General Electric, and Thomson are also cooperating.

33. Le Monde, September 17, 1985.

34. See "L'Europe face au project Eurêka," Le Monde, June 25, 1984, and André Giraud's article in Le Monde, February 12, 1986.

35. See the declarations of Jean-Luc Lagardère, President-Director General of Matra in Le Monde, June 9-10, 1985.

36. On this, see Alfred Grossner, "Franco-Allemagne: 1936-1986," Politique étrangère, no. 1 (1986): pp. 247ff.; see also Pascal Boniface and François Heisbourg, La Puce, les hommes et la bombe (Paris : Hachette, 1986).

5 Federal Republic of Germany: Defending the Status Quo?

Reimund Seidelmann

THE SECURITY POLICY TODAY

The present security policy of the Federal Republic, aimed at securing the integrity of its national territory and West Berlin, preventing direct or indirect military threats, and operating a foreign and domestic policy defined primarily by national interests, is shaped by three factors, which give the FRG a unique position within Europe. First, as a result of historical lessons, the FRG claims a special responsibility for peace in Europe.[1] As a consequence, the FRG's military forces are limited to sufficient and nonprovocative defense. Second, the FRG not only has a common border with two Warsaw Pact (WTO) countries, the German Democratic Republic (GDR) and Czechoslovakia (CSSR), but faces the highest concentration of the most advanced conventional and short-range nuclear forces within a range of 200 to 300 kilometers. Unable and unwilling to counter these forces by itself, the FRG has joined the NATO alliance not only for historical but military reasons as well.[2] Third, the FRG has twice experienced combined Soviet political-military pressure against West Berlin in the late 1940s and early 1960s. As a result, West Berlin's political status quo and its links with the FRG are regarded as a symbol of Western willingness and ability to withstand Soviet threats.[3]

External Threats

In contrast to prior historical periods, where Germany regarded France, Britain, and Russia as its economic, political, and military competitors, alliances and international integration since 1945 have left the Soviet Union as its only military threat. Successful military and economic integration into NATO and the EC, together with significant Western European and Atlantic political cooperation, exclude intra-bloc war as long as these structures exist. In addition, economic developments combined with progress in Western integration have limited the Soviet threat to a purely political-military one. In economic terms, the USSR and its bloc, WTO/COMECON, are not even small-scale competitors and nothing less than dependent markets.[4]

However, if a threat is defined as a combination of military capabilities and options on the one hand, and the political will to exploit opportunities on the other, then there has been and is a significant Soviet threat against the Federal Republic. It can be defined by types of weapons and strategic options which create a fundamental security dilemma for the FRG. There are four aspects of the Soviet conventional threat, posed by its forces stationed in Eastern Europe and the Soviet Union itself. First, the conventional threat to West Berlin cannot be matched by its allied forces, serving more political and "trip-wire" functions than as a military counterforce. Second, the conventional threat against the FRG in the first phase (roughly the first week of conventional warfare) is significant but of less concern. Although the main numerical force indicators show an indisputable Soviet numerical advantage and although the Soviet and GDR forces have improved their arms, command structure, and combat readiness in the past years, and continue to do so, they have no chance to surprise or to realize quick and deep attack operations against the FRG.[5] This results from the achievements in comprehensive antitank warfare that characterized the Bundeswehr and most of the NATO forces stationed in the FRG in the 1970s. The picture changes, however, when, third, the second phase of a conventional warfare is taken into account and reinforcements have reached the battlefield. Because of the Soviet geo-strategic advantage (i.e., the strength of its second and third echelon and its arms industries) NATO has to face a numerical superiority of between 30 and 60 divisions, which cannot be compensated by worn-out regular and insufficient reserve forces.[6] Although the Soviet Union might run considerable risks in intra-bloc cohesion and might face significant antiwar and anti-Soviet unrest, especially in the GDR and Poland, this numerical advantage would allow it to win the war, if the war remains conventional. Fourth, the Soviet naval build-up not only threatens the Atlantic reinforcements lines, but the global sea lanes as well, which are vital for a country whose economy depends both on unrestricted imports of raw materials and access to global export markets.[7]

Although chemical warfare is limited because of a significant lack of control of its effects on one's own troops, the Federal Republic nonetheless faces a Soviet chemical threat. Since roughly one-third of all WTO artillery ammunition in the GDR is chemical and WTO forces undergo systematic training to fight under chemical conditions, the Soviet no-first-use declarations might prove hollow. Chemical weapon use to attack military infrastructure (like air bases) in the FRG's hinterland or to enable the necessary conventional breakthrough are attractive as long as NATO seems unable and unwilling to retaliate adequately.

In contrast to most other Western countries, the Federal Republic is exposed to all Soviet nuclear options : tactical systems like SS-21 and SS-23 in the GDR and CSSR, short- and long-range intermediate nuclear forces (INF) like the SS-20 and SS-22, ICBMs and SLBMs, and finally all kinds of Cruise missiles. The nuclear threat to the FRG is not new. However, it attained a new quality in the second half of the 1970s when capabilities in tactical and intermediate forces grew with such a speed and to such an extent that long-existing hidden contradictions in NATO's flexible response doctrine became an obvious problem.[8] NATO's INF deployment and French and Britain nuclear modernization programs have reduced but have not overcome this problem (the loss of escalation dominance, the limitation of flexibility in flexible response, and the possibility of U.S. decoupling).

Altogether, these threats produce a security dilemma that cannot be solved by military means alone. West Berlin cannot be defended by military means. A conventional war would in its first phase lead to the destruction of roughly one-third of the FRG's infrastructure, production capability, and population. NATO's intention to compensate conventional inferiority with the use of tactical nuclear weapons, at least in the second phase of conventional war, means an additional destruction with a high risk of uncontrolled escalation into a continental and then an all-out nuclear war. In sum, if deterrence fails, the Federal Republic would be the first victim, whether the conflict is conventional or nuclear. And even if escalation control works and the war between NATO and the WTO could be limited, the FRG would nevertheless suffer vital losses. Finally, even an indirect, selective Soviet nuclear threat against the FRG would force the FRG to rely fully on the U.S. and/or French nuclear umbrella, with all its risks and costs.

In general, there is a consensus within the FRG political elite that the Soviet Union is saturated in Europe, pursues an overall defensive posture, and does not intend to use a direct military threat in the foreseeable future. However, Soviet conventional, chemical, and nuclear options are measured against the excessive increase of its military capacity, its unwillingness to evolve from "super security" to common security, and the use of military force to solve political problems even outside its own bloc.[9] Given the influence of a strong military-industrial complex within the Soviet Union, German experts have two major concerns : either misperceptions or mistakes in Soviet cost-risk evaluation, or perceived or real political opportunities might lead the Soviet leadership to a direct or indirect power projection in Europe.[10] Depending on U.S. nuclear guarantees and NATO's conventional solidarity, Federal governments therefore regard Alliance cohesion, U.S.-European coupling, and credibility of Western defense as essential preconditions for avoiding such risks. Consequently, West German governments tend to be hypersensitive to all intra-Alliance developments threatening these perceptions.

Internal Threats

The stability and legitimacy of the FRG's political and socioeconomic order rely on the economic growth, widespread private prosperity, public services including welfare, and a broad opportunity to participate in economic and political life. Together with a general search for consensus in its parliamentary party system as well as between trade unions and corporations, these factors have successfully discouraged the marginalized part of its society--the unemployed, poor, old, and disaffected--from political unrest and have been able to channel and partly reintegrate protest into extra-parliamentary, party, and other mass movements and organizations. The failure of extremist militants and terrorists to gain even limited support indicates the system's efficiency and flexibility in handling its internal problems. Although there is a limited potential for right-wing populism or neofascism, this cannot be regarded as a threat as long as these economic and political mechanisms are working. Anticommunist traditions and the deterring example of the GDR brand of socialism, together with the strength of Social Democracy, have reduced communist movements to insignificant levels, indicated by 0.2 percent vote for the German Communist party (DKP). In sum, there is no major threat to internal stability, and as long as economic strength prevails, the Federal Republic can proceed without major risks. However, it has to be underlined that social security, a necessary condition for domestic stability, is expensive, consuming roughly 30 percent of the GNP, compared with the 3 to 4 percent military share.[11]

Government's Security Policy

In response to the basic security dilemmas, generally unfavorable trends in cost-effectiveness of modern armament, longstanding arms race patterns in Europe, and recent problems in military manpower and public and elite acceptance, West German governments try to solve the security problem by political detente and military deterrence, as outlined in NATO's Harmel doctrine.[12] Its military component has followed three main principles since 1956. First, the Bundeswehr is as nonprovocative in defense as possible. It follows an operative forward defense strategy, thus accepting its own territory as a battlefield hostage. It is organized, armored, and trained in a way that simply does not allow deep attacks or counterattacks into Warsaw Pact and especially Soviet territory.[13] Finally, its political education and orientation rule out any aggressions or threats toward the East. Second, the West German armament policy follows the principle of restrained sufficiency. Nuclear, biological, and chemical weapons are neither produced nor possessed.[14] Necessary armament is regarded as only an adequate reaction to reestablish sufficient defense and is not aimed to fuel the arms race. Sufficiency means to accept numerous disparities in favor of the Soviet Union as long as overall deterrence seems ensured. Third, nearly all of the West German armed forces are fully integrated into NATO, thus ensuring allied control and linking its security, including that of West Berlin, both to Western European and U.S. NATO security. Although an adequate and credible NATO defense is regarded as a necessary insurance against Soviet military threats, opinion is widespread that real improvements in security can be reached only through political solutions.[15]

The detente component of the West German security policy consists of the interaction of three subcomponents. First, political detente using Ostpolitik to establish a network of bilateral treaties, under which FRG-Soviet relations played a special role, was a condition for initiating the multilateral reorganization of the European security order through the Conference on Security and Cooperation in Europe (CSCE) process. Although slowed down due to U.S.-Soviet "re-bilaterization," the CSCE concept of reducing the temptation to use military force by means of political solutions, economic interdependence, and sociocultural exchange has been regarded as a vehicle for reducing both the probability of military solutions and dependency on superpower security guarantees. Second, East-West economic cooperation, dominated by the FRG since the early 1970s, served limited economic but mainly political interests to establish long-term, mutually profitable relations with some leverage for the FRG. Third, military detente was expected to reduce gradually not only the will but the capability to implement military options in Europe through the development of these political and economic relations and the ensuing climate of cooperation. The FRG traditionally has supported not only the strategic arms control process, but is also engaged in Mutual and Balanced Force Reduction (MBFR) (i.e. reducing the conventional threat and the problem of unilateral withdrawal of U.S. troops) and confidence-building measures (CBM); i.e. reducing the chances for a Soviet surprise attack.[16] The Helmut Schmidt government has to be regarded as the architect of NATO's double-track decision, designed to give arms control a chance before INF deployment took place. However, the lack of progress in arms control affected the FRG's security concept in its crucial dynamic, the evolutionary change of priority from the defense to the detente component. As a consequence, the mixture of cooperating detente and conflicting deterrence policies prevailed, in which the continuation of detente depended to a great deal on U.S.-Soviet cooperation.

Within such a grand security strategy, the Federal Republic combines an Atlantic and European approach. The Atlantic approach aims to ensure close U.S.-FRG links, to overcome or at least reduce U.S. unilateralism and neo-isolationism, and to cement U.S. military guarantees. The European approach is to improve FRG-French military relations, because France is seen as a vital military partner and the Franco-German axis as a fundamental aspect of the FRG's European integration policies. Although West German governments have perceived Ostpolitik primarily as a policy of cooperation with the Soviet Union, inter-German relations are intensifying and now include general security and especially arms control policy. This development is not meant to create a new trans-bloc coalition, but rather to coordinate mutually beneficial "all-German" initiatives within each bloc.[17] Again, Ostpolitik aims first to harmonize FRG-U.S. positions within NATO and then to turn to the Soviet Union, using the GDR as a supplementary access to the Warsaw Pact countries.

Public Support and Acceptance

The past three decades of FRG security policy are characterized by periods of inter-party consensus and public protest and acceptance. After a period of public and opposition protest against rearmament and nuclear weapons in 1956-58, most aspects of security policy have been accepted by the public, which normally has not been aware of their implications and effects.[18] The Ostpolitik controversy between the Social Democratic-Liberal government and the opposition in the years 1969-75 nevertheless showed significant active public support for detente, whereas the defense counterpart remained largely undisputed. The peace movement of the years 1980-83 began, like the Kampf-dem-Atomtod-Bewegung in the 1950s, as a one-issue protest phenomenon. But in contrast to its predecessor, it developed into an anti-party, anti-parliamentarian movement mobilizing a broad social, political, and moral spectrum against the deployment element of NATO's double-track decision of 1979. When in 1982 the opposition Social Democrats changed their course and rejected deployment, they could neither control the movement's activities nor prevent its collapse after the start of the deployment process. Although the majority of the roughly 1 to 1.5 million peace activists retreated in disillusionment from political life and will not be easily mobilized again, the final spill over into the party system and the political elite is significant. Limited public acceptance of the deployment now coincides with a growing search for alternatives to mutual assured destruction and conventional defense. If today traditional defense policy is accepted, this is not because it is regarded as consistent and convincing, but because of a lack of alternatives that promote security at lesser costs and risks. However, skepticism toward the traditional defense formula is so widespread that, under the present domestic and international constellation, a major increase in real defense spending cannot be implemented.[19]

PERSPECTIVES FOR IMPROVING THE FRG'S SECURITY

Western integration and East-West relations have created such interdependencies for the Federal Republic that there is little freedom left to change national security policies unilaterally. The FRG is forced to develop and to exploit opportunities in responding to, stimulating, and transforming those structures and trends that are favorable for its security. Multilateral approaches and the search for integration are perceived as political strategies reflecting the concept of common security, an outcome of both the FRG's security dilemmas and its lessons from history. Options for increasing security can be found in three domains : defense, military detente, and changes within the Warsaw Pact.

Defense Options

There are three basic defense or military options. The first is to follow traditional reaction patterns and improve security by increasing defense capabilities. AirLand Battle, FOFA, the Rogers Plan, and reinforcements improvements are today's ideas that could be modified, extended, or supplemented in order to respond to potential improvements in Soviet conventional capabilities.[20] Concentrating on NATO capabilities to halt the Soviet first echelon and to counter successfully its second and third echelon would decrease Soviet chances of "winning" a conventional war either in its first or second phase, thus reducing the political effects of Soviet conventional options. Given the low cost-effectiveness trends in military hardware, the Bundeswehr's budgetary and manpower problems, national spending priorities, and public unwillingness combined with elite skepticism, this policy will receive only half-hearted and fragile support. Similarly, numerous proposals to establish an even more nonprovocative defense from experts and the opposition parties have increased doubts over continuing with traditional formulas.[21] Changing the general defensive formula or going beyond sufficiency could provoke political dissent and could trigger one-issue or broad protest movements as in the early 1980s.

The second military option is not to increase armaments but to improve existing military and defense cooperation. Joint armament research and development, improved military management and cooperation, and increased military integration within the NATO framework would not only improve NATO's military capability but its political effectiveness as well. Such improvements in NATO's unity and decision-making efficiency would overcome potential opportunities for the Soviet Union to single out weak member states or to launch a surprise attack. Reintegration of France into NATO's military organization and Europeanization, to establish a second credible and efficient European pillar within NATO, are political-military measures that would probably have a stronger effect on the Soviet grand strategy toward Western Europe than any Rogers Plan. Although there is considerable elite and expert support for such an option within the FRG, combined with a new wave of realistic Europeanism, the willingness to sacrifice national security "sovereignty" in order to improve security by Europeanization is limited, since both the FRG's parliament and its parties oppose any transfer of real power to European bodies. The attraction of a cheap and nonprovocative improvement of the FRG and Western European security competes not only with the comfort of the status quo (i.e. relying ultimately on U.S. guarantees), but also with the European nation-states' unwillingness to integrate fully their security policies.[22] This is less a question of public support and more one of the national orientation of the parties, the Bundestag and other political organizations.

The third military option to be mentioned is the nuclear one. Creating an independent nuclear force for the Federal Republic can be ruled out because such a force cannot be implemented.[23] The FRG's Basic Law does not allow it, the political elites are traditionally against it, public large-scale protest would prevent it, and both the neighboring countries and German interests to stabilize the military situation in Europe make such a policy infeasible, even if the present Soviet INF and tactical nuclear advantage is increased. There are more attractive nuclear options for the FRG that may reduce its decoupling trauma or the dangers of being a target of a nuclear war.

One of them is to reach bilateral agreement with France to include the Federal Republic in an enlarged French sanctuary, thus supplementing U.S. guarantees with French ones.[24] Such a model would not only follow the traditional dual Western policy of the FRG (cooperating with both the United States and France), but it would meet elite consensus and little public disagreement. Another option would be some kind of multilateral European nuclear force, made up of British and French forces, but including the FRG and other European countries in nuclear planning and targeting. Such a limited nuclear access comparable to NATO's Nuclear Planning Group would be acceptable in the Bundestag but might arouse public dissatisfaction. The final option would aim to modernize and/or increase U.S. nuclear forces in response to Soviet nuclear capabilities. This possibility seems politically unacceptable in the future for both the elite and the public, but could win elite acceptance if the Soviet rearmament and foreign expansionism continue.

In sum, both conventional and nuclear buildup options, even if limited and selective, will meet considerable skepticism and will be pursued only as a last resort. The reason for such restrictions in support lies less in the experience with the peace movement of the 1980s than in the awareness that such policies means increases in defense budgets and continued dependence on U.S. and other security guarantees, and do not solve the conventional and nuclear problems of a country that perceives itself as the first and main victim of any war in Europe. The political-military Europeanization option seems more promising because it does not have these financial and political implications. In addition, it seems more probable because of the long-term dynamics of the European integration process and the trend to supplement and stimulate EC integration with a gradual Europeanization of security policy.

Military Detente

Amid improving U.S.-Soviet relations and its "re-bilateralization" pattern and in view of a more flexible Soviet position on essential arms control principles, the return to military detente with new methods seems far more attractive for the Federal Republic than any other strategy to improve security. Military detente is regarded not only as reducing both the will and capacity to implement military options, but also as the cheapest way to increase security and reduce dependency on security guarantees.[25] Military detente includes the arms control and CSCE options, which complement each other.

Given the threat perceptions, FRG arms control interests concentrate on three issues. First, to reduce the conventional threat and to establish a balance of forces on a significantly lower level.[26] MBFR negotiations play an important role in avoiding unilateral withdrawal of U.S. and other troops, and in starting controlled mutual reduction on a collective basis. Associated confidence-building measures increase military security and encourage reductions of forces and weapon systems. The military relevance of MBFR contrasts with its limited public support, which is more a matter of limited information than dissent. However, MBFR finds significant and widespread support within the political elite and the military establishment.[27] Even limited and declaratory agreements would gain public support if popularized.

The second arms control option concentrates on INF and tactical nuclear systems. Unlike the MBFR talks, the FRG does not participate directly in negotiations on these issues, although it is one of the driving forces behind unilateral reductions. German interest, not only in control but in significant cuts, will continue, and the temptation to participate in such negotiations will increase. In the absence of antinuclear public protest, the Bonn government can and will exert pressure on its U.S. ally to respond to German security interests.[28] Even minor progress will attract active elite and public support which could be transformed into an electoral bonus incentive for the government in power. This is not a sign of pacifism, weakness, or Finlandization, but a result of the military situation and the experience with antinuclear protest which divide and strain German society. Despite the military problems of the nuclear-weapon-free-zone approach (NWFZ), this special option will continue to receive attention. Promoted both by the SPD and Greens, it reflects European Social Democratic thinking and a tradition in the FRG nuclear debate. Although this approach does not significantly increase the FRG's security, which is the argument of the present FRG government, it is supported mainly as a confidence-building measure, a starting point for control and reduction, and a testing ground for verification.[29] Although public support is sure, experts and parties will be divided as long as this approach is not accepted by NATO as a whole.

The third arms control and disarmament option concentrates on chemical weapons. Here at the moment the comprehensive global UN approach in Geneva competes with the recent proposal to establish a chemical-weapon-free-zone (CWFZ) in Central Europe, promoted by the opposition Social Democrats.[30] The present conflict between the global and regional approaches can be solved by a combination, seeking a CWFZ as an interim measure before reaching global agreements. Such combined efforts will receive not only elite but broad public support as well.

From a German view, the CSCE process plays a crucial role in transforming the present European security order into one with a significant higher stability and common security based on appreciably lower costs in terms of resources and dependencies. The CSCE grand strategy, originally linked to MBFR, is based on both the linkage between economic, sociocultural, and political foundations of security and a positive military security approach as well. The CSCE option not only consists of continued systematic efforts to create and enlarge interdependencies within the region but also of establishing those mechanisms and institutions that enable conflict prevention, provide nonmilitary conflict solution, and can be used for diplomatic crisis management. While the arms control option provides a negative strategy (to limit, restrict, and finally to abolish military capability), the CSCE option aims at the establishment of positive structures promoting the will and the interest to cooperate peacefully. Like arms control, this option is so attractive for the FRG that in principle there exists consensus and support among the elite and the public. This is not only because of the security aspect including the West Berlin problem, but also because of the long-term political and economic interests of the FRG in all-European cooperation and integration.[31]   A regionalized arms control approach reducing the conventional and nuclear threat and abolishing the chemical one, together with long-term CSCE perspectives, finds not only a general consensus within and between elites and public, but also a significant support from experts and politicians.

CONDITIONS FOR FUTURE SECURITY IMPROVEMENTS

Internal Conditions

Security policies reflect and influence domestic developments in the Federal Republic, although their impact is limited. Economic growth eases tensions about national spending priorities, thus enabling a small growth in defense expenditures or at least maintaining the present spending level. Economic decline, followed by the deindustrialization and marginalization of major parts of the population without adequate social security measures, might undermine the fundamental consensus within the FRG political system, which might eventually encourage neo-nationalistic militancy. Although such a scenario is highly improbable, the lessons of the Weimar Republic have to be kept in mind. The Falklands or the Grenada scenarios, (i.e. successfully mobilizing widespread chauvinistic support for a government in trouble by using military power in a situation without military risks), may work in the FRG as well. Again, this is improbable if NATO, which controls the Bundeswehr, is not supportive of such a policy.

Military detente is equally dependent on domestic developments. Inter-German relations and especially the situation of West Berlin depend very much on the general East-West climate. Both issues are important for voting patterns. Arms control success would not only overcome the legitimacy gap that confronts the traditional defense policy today, but it would attract the peace movement generation back into the Republic's political mainstream and the parliamentary party system. On the other hand, public protest and domestic dissent on arms control issues reduce the government's flexibility in negotiations. Anti-party and anti-parliamentary activities in favor of radical arms control or disarmament stands block or delay the ability and the will within the German political elite to support such ideas, whereas the combination of mass and intra-party activities can have significant effects on political change within the parliamentary party system. In general, internal conditions do not play a decisive role for the FRG security policies. Even in times of dissent between government and opposition, there will be a consensus on basic principles like Western integration, sufficiency in defense, and remaining nonnuclear. Although public protest will emerge from time to time, a skeptical and sometimes unwilling acceptance of basic defense necessities will persist. Pacifism exists only at the society's periphery, and sudden tensions or military threats might, in fact, encourage broad and intense measures for self-defense.

External Conditions

Whether and how the Federal Republic can improve its future security depends primarily on three external developments. First, Soviet military and foreign policies have to be taken into account. After a period of optimism during the detente era in the 1970s, Soviet willingness to respond to political and economic cooperation in terms of military restraints is questioned. German political experts underline the difference between arms control of strategic systems and nuclear and conventional arms control in Europe and seek reassurance that the Soviet Union will abolish its conventional, chemical, and nuclear advantages voluntarily and without radical pressure from the West. This is less a question of arms control offers and more one of concrete and significant actions. Thus, Soviet violation of Sweden's neutrality and its unwillingness to abide by Helsinki agreements after 1979 are seen as a significant lack of political restraint in sensitive security areas, signaling an important gap between peace rhetoric and military reality. In sum, the Soviet Union's willingness to change its security policy will be the essential determinant of FRG security policies. In addition, Soviet policies toward the WTO play an important role. Although the WTO is dominated by the Soviet Union, its internal cohesion, the stability of its economies, and its ability to allow the necessary liberalization in Eastern Europe are other factors in the future perspective of FRG defense and detente policies. Detente and especially the CSCE option depend primarily on the Soviet willingness to tolerate Europeanization and political-economic changes in Eastern Europe. Any Soviet military intervention would not only lead to a reevaluation of the military balance, but would force any West German government to abandon detente policies.

Second, developments within NATO or between the United States and the Federal Republic will also determine German security postures. This includes mainly decoupling and burden-sharing problem. Any major U.S. move to reduce military and political engagement in the FRG or in West Berlin will be interpreted as neo-isolationism, independent of the extent and nature of long-term U.S. economic and strategic interests in the FRG. This is primarily a political and not a military question, if adequate reinforcement could be secured, the Federal Republic could easily accept a reduction of up to one-third of U.S. troops on its territory. This political dependence puts the FRG on the defensive when it comes to burden-sharing. The threat to reduce U.S. military presence has always forced Bonn governments into compromises in burden-sharing and other questions. The growing political self-consciousness of the German successor generation will not change this as long as the Soviet threat exists. Given the ongoing relationship, the FRG's arms control and even military detente options will depend finally on U.S. support and acceptance.

Besides drastic changes in Soviet policies, the only chance for improving West German security policy against the desires of the United States is the third development, the Europeanization process. Successful Europeanization in terms of close cooperation or better integration of Western European security policies (from political aspects of security to integration of arms industries and then to military integration including nuclear planning) is the most promising perspective for securing FRG security. Europeanization (establishing an equal European partner for the United States within the Atlantic Alliance) is the only way, first, to overcome superpower "re-bilateralization" with all its drawbacks for arms control in Europe; second, to reduce and resolve the burden-sharing problem; and, third, to convince the Soviet Union that there will be no opportunity either to split or to dominate Western Europe. In spite of the difficulties for security policy, integration in Europe thus has to be regarded as the precondition for cost-effective defense, progress in European arms control, and implementing the final CSCE option.

In sum, the security problems of the Federal Republic are mainly external ones caused by the Soviet conventional, nuclear, and chemical threats, which are met by a political mix of defense and detente, Atlantic and European approaches, and attempts to reform intra-bloc and inter-bloc relations in Europe. An idealistic view of the developments that could take place in Europe would concentrate on progress in conventional and nuclear arms control; significant asymmetric reductions in conventional, tactical nuclear, INF, and chemical weapons; and implementation of confidence-building measures. Such arms control would be supplemented by progress in the CSCE process, establishing not only positive conflict prevention and management by peaceful means, but improving intra-European cooperation to reduce the impact of both superpowers' policies on Europe. Although such a perspective has to be regarded as the only solution of FRG and Central European security problems, a realistic view has to consider a number of factors, which might slow down, delay, or even disrupt such a process. Such factors would include, among others, the U.S. "re-bilateralization" and leadership interests or Soviet unwillingness to accept common security, arms control, and disarmament or to tolerate Europeanization trends within its bloc. Even more decisive would be the lack of political will between European states, elites, and peoples to develop joint or at least coordinated security policies, based on political instead of military solutions. In the end, it will be the Europeans' willingness and ability to Europeanize and to politicize security policies, which will decide whether the costly and unstable status quo will continue, or whether a new European security order with higher security for lower costs can be established.

NOTES

1. See Federal President Richard von Weizsäcker's speech to the Bundestag, Bulletin der Bundesregierung, No. 52, May 9, 1985, p. 446 : "Von deutschem Boden in beiden deutschen Staaten sollen Frieden und gute Nachbarschaft mit allen Ländern ausgehen." Similar remarks can be found in numerous statements and speeches of FRG politicians.

2. For details see Helga Haftendorn, Security and Detente : Conflicting Priorities in German Foreign Policy (New York : Praeger, 1985).

3. See the Federal Minister of Defense, White Paper 1979 (Bonn : GPO, 1979), p. 52 : "Berlin will continue to be a barometer of the political climate in Europe. The city is of vital importance to German politics and a touchstone as far as detente is concerned."

4. The exception is energy trade, which, however, does not exceed 5 to 6 percent of the FRG's prime energy consumption and where, due to the gas pipeline deal, numerous interdependencies have been created.

5. See the Federal Minister of Defense, White Paper 1985 (Bonn : GPO, 1985) passim : the WTO-to-NATO ratio in combat-ready divisions is 1.3:1; in main battle tanks, 2.0:1; in armed helicopters, 2.0:1. For a critical view, see Christian Krause, Kann die NATO auf den Erstgebrauch von Atomwaffen verzichten? (Bonn : Friedrich-Ebert-Foundation, 1985). FRG defense experts assume a minimum warning time of 2 to 3 days.

6. See U.S. Congress, Department of Defense report, Improving NATO's Conventional Capabilities (Washington, D.C. : GPO, 1984), p. xvi.

7. On average, 23 to 24 percent of the FRG's trade is foreign, of which roughly 50 percent is trade beyond EC boundaries.

8. For example, see Klaus-Peter Stratmann, NATO-Strategie in der Krise (Baden-Baden : Nomos, 1981).

9. An impressive example was the SS-20 buildup, going far beyond any legitimate modernization or compensation for combined NATO, British and French nuclear capacities.

10. Recent experience with Soviet intrusion into Swedish waters, Afghanistan, and Cambodia, and military threats before the "domestic" solution of the Polish crisis have reaffirmed memories of the West Berlin crises. For a general picture of mistrust in the longstanding goals of Soviet policies, see White Papers 1985, p. 64.

11. See White Paper 1985, passim. In NATO terms, the last figures are around 3.3 percent. If one adds expenditures for West Berlin, the figures are 4.2 percent. Another factor in future defense planning is the significant shortage of conscripts in coming years.

12. This is reaffirmed in numerous documents and statements; typical is one by Foreign Minister Hans-Dietrich Genscher, "Toward an Overall Western Strategy," Foreign Affairs (Fall 1982): pp. 42-66.

13. To underline this defensive character, the Bundeswehr's logistics were reorganized into depot logistics in the early 1970s. Soviet perceptions of FRG forces as "aggresive" do not correspond to realities. However, flexible response includes limited air attacks against military infrastructure targets in the enemy's hinterland. AirLand Battle and Follow-On Forces Attack (FOFA) will add offensive elements to NATO's defense, but are limited mainly to disrupt, delay, or reduce the second-echelon reinforcements, thus keeping the conflict conventional even for the second phase of war and putting the escalation blame on the Soviet Union. Again, FOFA cannot be regarded as a fundamental shift from a defensive to a rollback strategy.

14. The FRG's dual capacity systems can be equipped with nuclear warheads completely under U.S. control.

15. However, this does not exclude significant efforts to reduce existing threats through military measures. Here NATO and especially the FRG want to establish a nuclear "no-early-first-use" doctrine. Compare Karl Kaiser, Georg Leber, Alois Mertes, Franz-Josef Schulze, "Nuclear Weapons and the Preservation of Peace," Foreign Affairs (Summer 1982) : pp. 1157-70. Improving conventional defensive power by emerging technologies, improving reinforcement infrastructure, and early use of reserves, FOFA and other measures are mainly designed to avoid both a Soviet conventional breakthrough in the first and especially the second phase of conventional war and also first-use implications for NATO. Nevertheless, the ambitious NATO plan for a 3 or even 4 percent rise in defense budgets seems unrealistic under the present circumstances.

16. For details on MBFR, see Reinhard Mutz, Konventionelle Abrüstung in Europa, Die Bundesrepublic Deutschland und MBFR (Baden-Baden: Nomos, 1985).

17. In spite of reunification rhetoric and neoromantic sentiments, any type of reunification seems unrealistic when the economic, political, and military interests of both Germanies and their neighbors are taken into account.

18. In the mid-1950s, roughly three-quarters of the population opposed rearmament. However, the Adenauer government won the 1957 election for the first time with an absolute majority of 50.2 percent. This, together with the Christian Democratic Union (CDU) victory in the 1982 and 1987 elections, in which the Social Democratic Party (SPD) exploited the missile question, underlines the fact that security and military issues play only a limited role in the FRG's voting behavior.

19. The defense budget grew in the past ten years an average of roughly one percent per year in real terms; since 1983 there is nearly zero-growth in real terms. Nevertheless, the FRG has the highest per capita defense expenditure and the highest defense share of the overall budget in NATO-Europe.

20. On the Rogers Plan, see Bernard W. Rogers, "The Atlantic Alliance : Prescriptions for a Difficult Decade," Foreign Affairs (Summer 1982): p. 1145-56.

21. These alternatives range from a militia system to the establishment of an antitank cordon sanitaire behind the border, made up largely of light infantry. The lack of compatibility with other NATO forces, the inability to regain lost territory and to counter air attacks, and the political implications of these strategies, prevent these ideas from being implemented.

22. See Robert J. Jackson (Ed.), Continuity of Discord : Crises and Responses in the Atlantic Community (New York : Praeger, 1985).

23. See David Garnham, "Extending Deterrence with German Nuclear Weapons," International Security (1985) : pp. 96-110.

24. It is mostly overlooked that the ongoing French nuclear modernization program allows such an option. After having reached a "worst-case" second-strike capability far beyond what is necessary for defending the French sanctuary, France can afford to enlarge its nuclear defense perimeter without running the risk of having no more SLBM warheads left if France is attacked. If a total of 100 to 150 arriving warheads is considered enough to destroy vital parts of the Soviet Union and therefore provide deterrence, the French modernization program will establish a capability that is two or three times bigger, thus opening new options.

25. However, even if MBFR would lead to significant cuts in conventional ceilings, this would not automatically lead to proportional cuts in defense expenditures. In contrast to widespread opinion, the first stages of conventional and/or nuclear disarmament will not free large amounts of resources to be used for welfare or development aid.

26. See FRG Government, Report on the State of Efforts towards Arms Control and Disarmament and on the Changes in the Balance of Military Power 1984 (Bonn : GPO, 1984), p. 18 : "Decisions on the development of new weapon systems as well as the arms control negotiations should generally be oriented towards establishing a stable equilibrium with as few weapons as possible."

27. MBFR looks attractive not only because of issues under present negotiations but as an ongoing process, including even tactical nuclear weapons, other forces like those in the Baltic Sea, and other areas like Hungary and France.

28. For example, missile deployment at sea would reduce expected destruction of FRG territory in a counterforce attack.

29. See <u>White Paper 1985</u>, <u>passim</u>, and Ulrich Krafft, <u>Atomwaffenfreie Zonen in Europa</u> (Bonn : Konrad Adenauer Foundation, 1985).

30. A detailed discussion can be found in the journal <u>Deutschland-Archiv</u>, no. 9 (1985).

31. Any inter-bloc improvements would at the same time improve inter-German relations, a major priority in FRG <u>Ostpolitik</u> from its beginnings until today.

6 Federal Republic of Germany: Searching for Alternatives

Hans Günter Brauch

This chapter will focus on the most salient, politically relevant research that has had a political impact on the major parties; some 20 of the 37 authors who were invited to two public hearings on alternative strategies, organized by the Defense Committee of the Bundestag between November 1983 and February 1984, and to a second joint hearing, organized by the Defense and Foreign Affairs Committees of the Bundestag on SDI in December 1985, have been selected in a representative sample of the different schools.

This survey will include only the writings of German authors on the present and future security systems in Central Europe. Both collaborative efforts, such as the European Security Study (ESECS) publications, and publications by non-German authors writing on the future security system in Central Europe will not be included, nor will studies that deal specifically with arms control and disarmament planning.[1]

EXTERNAL THREATS AND DOMESTIC CHALLENGES

From an official point of view, both the external threat perception and the future domestic challenges have been put forward in the West German Defense White Paper on the Situation and Development of Armed Forces.[2] However, both the official threat analysis and interpretation of the future challenges have been contested by retired military officers, former defense officials, and independent social scientists.[3]

---

* Portions of this chapter are based on Hans Günter Brauch , "Official and Unofficial West German Alternatives for Reducing the Reliance of European Security on Nuclear Weapons--A Plea for a Pragmatic Approach," in Rethinking the Nuclear Dilemma in Europe, edited by Frank Barnaby and P. Terrence Hopmann (London: Macmillan, 1986). The author acknowledges the permission of both editors and publishers to use material in this chapter.

The Official Perception of the Soviet Threat

In the official view of the Defense White Paper, the Communist ideology remains a determining factor in Soviet policy whose major goals can be described as :

- to further develop socialism, to create desirable preconditions for its global expansion, and to extend Soviet influence in the Third World;
- to undermine NATO's cohesion and to drive a wedge between the United States and its European allies.

The Soviet Union is assumed to convey a fundamentally positive attitude as far as the use of force as a political means is concerned. If war should occur, the Soviet Union would pursue the offensive in order to achieve a military victory over NATO. In this case, Soviet offensive operations would be the predominant form of battle based on secrecy, surprise, initiative, and rapid, deep strokes into the opponent's territory. The military balance, the White Paper argues, is maintained roughly in the area of strategic nuclear forces but is challenged by Soviet superiority in medium- and short-range nuclear forces, in chemical warfare, and in conventional forces. In its overall comparison of NATO and Warsaw Pact forces, the German White Paper concludes: "In this respect, the armed forces of the Warsaw Pact must be interpreted as being offensive. The armed forces of NATO have to be interpreted according to the same criteria as being 'defensive.' The armed forces of NATO and the Warsaw Pact are a mirror image and the result of the opposite intentions and military strategic goals. "[4]

Insofar as Soviet space and ballistic missile defense systems are concerned, the White Paper argues that the United States has reacted to Soviet initiatives in these areas. The official threat analysis of the West German Defense Ministry reflects the joint threat analysis of NATO's intelligence services. However, the White Paper continues, the goal of Soviet policy can be described as "victory without war." The very fact "that no direct danger of war would exist in Europe should not lead to the wrong conclusion that no fundamental threat by the Warsaw Pact exists. Military strength will remain the political power instrument of the states of the Warsaw Pact toward the West and the Third World."[5]

Challenges to Official Threat Analysis

This official threat analysis, as well as the threat analysis of the previous Social Democratic-Liberal coalition government, has been challenged by social scientists, retired generals, a former Parliamentary Defense Secretary, and by the present opposition parties. In 1985, Andreas von Bülow, the chairman of the Social Democratic Defense Commission, observed in his dissenting threat assessment : "The Soviet Union will not have an opportunity to fight a successful war against Western Europe either by conventional or by nuclear means."[6] While Hans Rühle, the present director of the Defense Planning Staff and a critic of the alternative threat assessments, opted for a regional threat analysis, von Bülow preferred a global one --at least for the naval and air forces of both superpowers and alliances.[7] Von Bülow pointed to NATO's manpower and economic advantages, its naval superiority, and the supporting roles of China and

Japan in any major war, and concluded that "no reason exists for initiating a new conventional arms race by exaggerated means."[8]

The private consulting firm SALSS, in cooperation with the Study Group on Alternative Security Policy (SAS), in a qualitative analysis of the military balance in Central Europe for the Research Institute on Peace Policy in Starnberg, concluded "that a major superiority of the Warsaw Pact does not exist. More specifically, it is probable that the Warsaw Pact would have to launch a surprise attack with inferior forces in terms of fighting power and, even in case of a conflict launched after intensive preparations, the force relationship may only turn in NATO's disfavor if an extremely unfavorable mobilization period is assumed."[9]

DOMESTIC CHALLENGES FOR THE FUTURE

Confronted with the prospects of a severe manpower shortage in the late 1980s and the 1990s, then Defense Minister Hans Apel (in 1981) asked for an analysis of alternative options that would enable the Bundeswehr to fulfill its obligations within NATO. In its final report of June 1982, the official Commission on Long-Term Planning concluded that from 1987 onward the Bundeswehr would not be able to obtain its 207,000 conscripts and that by 1995, 104,000 conscripts would be missing. If no decisions were made soon, the manpower of the Bundeswehr would have to be reduced to 297,000 men by 1998.[10]

According to the Defense White Paper (1985), the Conservative-Liberal coalition government of Chancellor Kohl decided that the present strength of the Bundeswehr of 495,000 men in peacetime should be maintained in the future by the implementation of a combination of the following measures :

● a greater use of the age cohort of conscripts,
● an increase of the proportion of longer-serving soldiers,
● extension of the time for compulsory service,
● an increase in the exercises of reservists,
● changes in the degree of readiness of the armed forces.

At the same time the conventional fighting power of the Bundeswehr should be improved by :

● a further modernization of the equipment, procurement, and munitions;
● a creation of new possibilities for battle against follow-on-forces as well as for deep strike;
● an evolutionary development of the force structure of the armed forces.[11]

However, no detailed cost projections have appeared on how all these goals may be accomplished in the future. In the Bundeswehr Plan 1985 for the years 1985-88 (according to press reports), at least DM 10 billion appear to be lacking. If the West German government complies with the so-called Stoessel Plan of November 1981, it would have to spend at least DM 13 billion for such U.S. programs as Wartime Host Nation Support, Master Restationing Plan, construction of U.S. barracks and housing for soldiers, improvement of the social conditions of the U.S. soldiers and their dependents, and environmental protection. In May 1984 West Germany was expected by the United States to contribute DM 7.3 billion to NATO's infrastructure program for the years 1985 to 1990. Furthermore, Western European defense establishments have been confronted with new, extremely costly defense concepts, such as different versions of "deep strike" concepts (Follow-on-Forces-Attack, Rogers Plan, AirLand Battle, AirLand Battle 2000, Counterair 90, European Defense Initiative or extended air defense) requiring highly sophisticated emergent technologies. According to a proposal by the SACEUR, General Bernard Rogers, Western European governments were exspected to increase their defense spending in real terms by an additional 4 percent. Why have both Apel and Manfred Wörner, the present Defense Minister, not been more supportive of American expectations for a higher West German defense contribution? What would it cost to realize the long-term defense goals of the Kohl government? What impact would a real increase of West German defense expenditure of 3 percent, as NATO recommended in 1987, or of an additional 4 percent, as has been suggested by General Rogers, have on the Federal budget by 1990 and 1995?

The most original and detailed analyses on the manpower projections have been published by General Christian Krause and by Bernd Grass of the SAS, and a model of the future development of West Germany's social and defense spending from 1983 to 1998 has been published by Hartmut Bebermeyer (SAS), a former high-level official in the Chancellor's office and in the Economics Department.[12] Bebermeyer criticized the present long-term defense plan as unsound for the following reasons :

● While the official procurement of DM 13 billion in 1986 was to increase only slightly to DM 14 billion by 1998, Bebermeyer estimated that both the procurement and the military research and developments costs would have to be increased from DM 15.6 billion to DM 44 or 45 billion in 1998.

● While according to the official long-term defense plan, the manpower costs of DM 21 billion were to increase only slightly until 1998, Bebermeyer projected a drastic cost increase for manpower due to the shift from conscripts to regulars, up to DM 39 billion by 1998.

● According to Bebermeyer, the present long-term plan of the Bundeswehr could be realized only if the defense expenditure were increased from DM 52.6 billion in 1986 to approximately DM 110 billion.[13]

Based on the assumption of an average inflation rate of 3 percent for the time period from 1986 to 1998 and a real growth rate of 2.5 percent (as well as an otherwise constant federal budget), Bebermeyer projected an increase of the social expenditures from the present 32.6 percent to 39.4 percent of the federal budget in 1998 and an increase of military expenditures from 19.9 percent in 1986 to 28.2 percent in 1998. These projections do not include the additional cost increases that have been called for by SACEUR, and it does not reflect the potential additional costs of SDI or of a European Defense Initiative. Bebermeyer concludes that the present Bundeswehr long-term planning could not be financed in the early 1990s. It could only be implemented with drastic cuts in social expenditures, a measure that not even a Conservative government could countenance. The only alternative to this fiscal dilemma for the Federal Republic would be, in Bebermeyer's view, to shift to cheaper alternative concepts that could provide a more effective conventional deterrent.

Both manpower and financial constraints would have major repercussions on public support for official defense policy. The best military equipment, the most consistent doctrine, and the toughest rhetoric may not impress an opponent, if they lack the support of the people who are to be protected by the military establishment. The call for higher defense expenditures, the extension of the compulsory military service from 15 to 18 months (and probably even more in the early 1990s under the present manpower goals), and additional cuts in social expenditures in a period of economic crisis will not overcome the increasing skepticism about NATO's defense posture among the well-educated "successor generation," nor will it contribute to the thorough re-examination of the conditions for consensus advocated by many serious observers.[14]

The manpower problems will most likely cut into the procurement budget or lead to cuts in the social budget. The first step would undermine present long-term defense planning, while the latter step would undercut even further the support for the Bundeswehr among the younger generation and among other social groups comprising the political consensus. Manpower shortages, fiscal constraints, and consensual problems could very well precipitate a major crisis of legitimacy for West German defense policy within NATO in the 1990s. What policy changes would be needed to prevent this worst case from occurring?

ALTERNATIVE SECURITY OPTIONS

What alternatives have been formulated by the West German government and by the group of alternative thinkers to cope with both the perceived Soviet threat and the threefold domestic challenges of manpower, procurement, and consensus?

Categorization of Alternative Security Options

Alternative security concepts may be distinguished on four levels :

● By foreign policy framework (e.g., the overall orientation of West German foreign and defense policy : Atlanticism, trilateralism, Europeanization, nonaligned Europe, a neutral confederated Europe)
● By philosophy of security policy (e.g., policy of strength, balance of military forces, policy of common security, a deliberate policy of inferiority)
● By strategic concepts (e.g., the maintenance of NATO's deterrence strategy by upgrading either nuclear or conventional warfighting capabilities, or the replacement of deterrence by a gradual restructuring of the armed forces and by the gradual denuclearization of Europe or even unilateral disarmament)
● By force structure concepts (e.g., within the present force structure of the Bundeswehr and NATO, or by modification of the force structure with or without changes in the strategic concepts).[15]

This chapter will offer a brief survey of the alternative security options that have been provided by the West German government, NATO, and the group of autonomous alternative thinkers in the West German defense debate, especially on the question of force structure concepts.

Official Alternatives

Four official alternatives will be discussed briefly :

1. The official position of the West German government, as articulated in the German Defense White Paper 1985, that there is at present no viable substitute for NATO's strategy of flexible response including the nuclear first-use doctrine.
2. The announced NATO policy to reduce the number of battlefield nuclear weapons in Europe as an effort to raise the nuclear threshold.
3. The new operative doctrine of the U.S. Army (AirLand Battle, AirLand Battle 2000, Army 21) as well as the other deep-strike concepts (Counterair '90, Focus 21), and NATO's long-term defense guidance to deal with second- and third-echelon forces (Follow-on-Forces-Attack or FOFA).
4. The Strategic Defense Initiative of the Reagan Adminstration and the call for a European SDI or for a Tactical Defensive Initiative (TDI).

West German Position
The Defense White Paper 1985 states that at present there is no foreseeable alternative to nuclear deterrence and to NATO's flexible response doctrine. In the official German view, there will be no substitute to nuclear weapons so long as no better way of war prevention can be achieved. Both limited nuclear-weapons-free zones and a no-first-use posture are rejected. The official German view supports FOFA and SDI research and AirLand Battle as long as they are in agreement with the principles of NATO defense. The limitations of both financial and manpower resources are stressed, and the expectation for a greater balance in transatlantic armament cooperation is expressed.

The Defense White Paper 1985 rejects all unofficial proposals for an area defense and an inoffensive defense, as well as the renunciation of nuclear weapons. While admitting the domestic challenges for West Germany's defense policy in the 1990s, the White Paper does not present a persuasive argument as how those fundamental challenges could be met within the framework of the present doctrine, given the severe manpower and fiscal constraints. However, the official view avoids both a detailed analysis of the defensive conventional alternatives and a discussion of the implications of the three domestic challenges threatening a major crisis of legitimacy of West Germany's defense policy in the 1990s.

NATO Reduction and Modernization
NATO's Nuclear Planning Group (NPG) at its meeting in Montebello, Canada, announced on October 27, 1983 that 1,400 nuclear warheads were to be withdrawn from Europe in addition to the 1,000 warheads that had already been withdrawn since December 1979. In addition, NATO eventually agreed on several measures to modernize the remaining nuclear battlefield systems in Europe.[16] If the projected nuclear warhead production plans of the U.S. Department of Energy are realized, the following short-range theater nuclear forces (SRINF) could be added to the U.S. arsenals within the next decade and may also be projected for later deployment in Western Europe : a new Advanced Atomic Demolition Munition (ADM); up to 500 Enhanced Radiation Warheads (W-70-3) for the Lance missile; neutron warheads (W-

79-1) for the 203mm artillery shell; up to 1,000 W82 warheads, and (possibly) nuclear warheads for the Joint Tactical Missile System (JTACMs) and Patriot Anti-Tactical Missiles (ATMS).

Given Secretary Weinberger's posture statement and the nuclear warhead production schedule, it appears highly unlikely that the role of the nuclear weapons in the defense of Europe will be essentially downgraded. More likely will be a shift from short-range to medium rangenuclear systems. Some of these have already been mentioned in the context of concepts for maneuvers, such as AirLand Battle.

Deep Strike Concepts

With the adoption of Field Manual 100-5 Operations of the U.S. Army in August 20, 1982, a shift in the operative doctrine from frontal defense toward forward defense took place within the U.S. Armed Forces.[17] While FM 100-5 is, according to its preface, "consistent with NATO doctrine and strategy," the West German Defense Ministry initially denied its applicability for Europe and only relented in 1985, as long as the new doctrine was in line with NATO's defense principles. While supporting NATO's long-term defense guideline to fight against follow-on forces (FOFA), the Defense White Paper categorically excludes a forward defense.

But, with the increasing emphasis in the United States on deep strike concepts that stress offensive, Blitzkrieg scenarios to achieve victory in a future battle and emergent technologies, that call for near real-time intelligence and extreme accuracies, crisis stability is likely to decrease, as both sides may try to preempt an attack by this sophisticated weaponry. With the increasing possibility of surprise attacks by either side without strategic warning and without prior mobilization, political efforts to inhibit surprise attack options by confidence- and security-building measures (CSBMs) in the context of the Stockholm Conference become increasingly irrelevant. Deep-strike concepts and the complementary emergent technologies may undermine the second goal of NATO's Harmel Report, the pursuit of detente.

On November 9, 1984, the NATO Defense Planning Committee adopted FOFA or the so-called Rogers Plan as a long-term planning guideline.[18] However, it appears highly doubtful whether the Rogers Plan will be able to solve the structural problems of NATO and to raise the nuclear threshold as claimed. Given the dual capability of many of its launchers, it may increase the worst-case assumptions of an opponent and undermine the verifiability of ballistic and Cruise missiles in an arms control context. FOFA deep-strike systems may lower crisis stability and increase the probability of conflict escalation. Given the pressures for preemption, FOFA may also accelerate a process of delegation of authority from the political to the military level at an early stage in a conflict. The call for deep-strike standoff forces that will target the GDR, Czechoslovakia and Poland has already provoked countermeasures by the Warsaw Pact countries. Moreover, the call for an annual increase of an additional 4 percent over a ten-year period to finance the Rogers Plan is completely unrealistic. FOFA neither solves the manpower problem nor the problem of public acceptance, and may undercut both the Stockholm and Vienna negotiations as well as violating the spirit of the Harmel Report of 1967.

SDI and TDI

Both the High Frontier Group and President Reagan offered a space-based ballistic missile defense system as an alternative to the present nuclear doctrine of mutual assured destruction based on mutual vulnerability. Will a Strategic or a Tactical Defense Initiative for Europe be able to provide an absolute area protection against Soviet nuclear weapons? Or will SDI and TDI intensify the offensive nuclear and the defensive arms race?

Since President Reagan's so-called "Star Wars" speech, the expectations for a comprehensive and absolute area defense system that could protect the U.S. population and its allies have been toned down by spokesmen of the SDI organization. In the context of an even more ambitious plan, Strategic Defense Architecture for the year 2000 (SDA-2000), the U.S. Defense Department called for efforts not only against ballistic missiles, but against aircraft and Cruise missiles as well. Given the inability of SDI to protect Western Europe against Soviet SRINF (SS-21, SS-22 and SS-23), both American and European politicians have called for an extended SDI (TDI or EDI) for Europe.[19] However, neither antitactical missiles (ATMs) nor deep-strike weapons (like the U.S. Army version of JTACMs) that have been mentioned as potential systems for a Tactical or a European Defense Initiative provide an area protection for Western Europe.[20] A requirement of up to 1,000 Patriot-ATMs has been suggested to protect the Patriot air defense missiles, Pershing II missiles, air bases, and special ammunition sites against Soviet SS-21, SS-22 and SS-23 attacks. ATMs could provide only a limited point defense for the most vulnerable military targets. The second alternative favored by some Pentagon experts is the destruction of Soviet SRINF before they are launched. But the potential use of the army version of JTACMs for pre-boost phase destruction, an integral part of some deep-strike concepts, may increase preemptive pressures and may therefore decrease crisis stability. If the Soviet Union reacted to SDI, TDI, or EDI with a greater emphasis on forward-deployed short-range ballistic and Cruise missiles, it would increase the likelihood that Western Europe would become the first battlefield of a nuclear war. If both the United States and the Soviet Union deployed a space-based ballistic missile defense, escalation dominance would lose its credibility for both the Soviet Union and for the U.S. allies in Western Europe.

None of the four official alternatives includes a "no-first-use posture" for nuclear weapons, and none calls for an end to the modernization of new battlefield nuclear systems in Western Europe. It appears doubtful whether any of these alternatives can overcome the problem of public acceptance of nuclear weapons for the defense of Europe. No cost projections have been published for the implementation of FOFA, a Tactical Defense Initiative, or an improved air defense within the next 10 or 15 years. The costs of these programs have not been included in the long-term plans of the Bundeswehr before the end of the 1990s.

Any alternative to nuclear deterrence as a basis for European security should be in agreement with the double strategy of the Harmel Report : to maintain a credible conventional defense posture and to pursue a policy of relaxation of tensions in Europe. A twofold alternative strategy may be preferable to the official alternatives :

● a policy of restructuring of the conventional forces in such a way as to constrain them from offensive operations;
● a policy of confidence- and security-building measures that limit the most likely cause of war in Europe, that is an unintentional nuclear war as a consequence of increased crisis instability in Europe.

NON-PROVOCATIVE AND INOFFENSIVE DEFENSE POSTURES

Instead of efforts to counter the perceived Soviet and WTO forces through "mirror-imaging" by optimizing present force structures, increasing defense expenditures, and incorporating high technology components, many defense experts in both the United States and Europe have suggested putting more emphasis on force economy through structural change. Structural change should, according to Lutz Unterseher, lead to functional differentation with forces consisting of : a static area defense system which employs reactive tactics, mechanized troops forming the active element, and a "rearguard" or object-oriented system.[21]

The present German debate on structural changes of the armed forces was influenced by criticism of NATOs flexible response strategy by Carl Friedrich von Weizsäcker and Horst Afheldt, by the writings of the French officer Guy Brossolet, by the Austrian model, and to some extent by previous proposals by Col. Bogislaw von Bonin and Ferdinand Otto Miksche who were influenced by J. F. C. Fuller and Liddell Hart.[22]

There are three important structural designs for alternative defensive forces :

● the model of <u>area defense</u> (Raumverteidigung) proposed by Horst Afheldt;
● the <u>area covering defense</u> (raumdeckende Verteidigung) suggested by Jochen Löser, and
● the <u>fire barrier</u> (Grenznahe Feuersperre) advocated by Norbert Hannig.[23]

Profiles of Competing Structural Designs

The area defense model by Horst Afheldt would set up a network of techno-commandos all across the Federal Republic of Germany, excluding only the highly populated urban areas.[24] He calls for a static light infantry of several thousand autonomous units, each made up of 20 to 30 men who are familiar with a territory of 10 to 15 square kilometers that they are supposed to defend. In the forward area, these forces are active permanently in order to provide a protection against surprise. Further back, the reserve component is to be recruited locally. The equipment is based on means for blocking the aggressor (e.g., mines) and antitank guided weaponry (ATGW) for direct fire. The infantry component of the defensive network will neither be able to attack nor to mass forces. Any possible effort by the aggressor to concentrate his mechanized divisions will be countered by precise fire or artillery rockets directed at invading forces at the moment they try to cross the demarcation line. These rockets (ranging between 20 and 80 kilometers) are based deep in the defender's hinterland. Just like the camouflaged positions of the techno-commandos, their launchers are randomly distributed, in order to avoid easy detection.

In the context of his area covering defense model, Major General Jochen Löser (army, ret.) suggests, doubling the number of brigades of the Bundeswehr by relying more heavily on reservists (cadre-type organization)--the further away from FLOT (forward-line of troops), the higher the reserve proportion would be.[25] Löser proposes that during an early phase of adaption, "shield" forces consisting of light infantry should cooperate with traditional (allied and German) units functioning as "sword" forces. In this process of trans-armament, the covering elements should become preponderant, and even the remaining "sword" forces should approach the organizational pattern of light and small units. Löser maintains that the best troops would be those who could exploit the terrain by specializing in mine warfare, erecting field fortifications, fighting with light and easy-to-handle weapons like mortars, machine guns, and ATGW, and developing a high degree of fluidity (motorized with simple civilian vehicles).

The concept of a forward fire barrier has been developed by retired Air Force Lt. Col. Norbert Hannig, a former consultant with the German aircraft industry.[26] He suggests that a trip wire along the demarcation line, four kilometers deep, should be controlled permanently with electronic sensors, and, in case of conflict, it should become impossible to cross that barrier anywhere as a consequence of concentrated fire from the rear. The essential components of fire (ATGW, partly on elevated fighting platforms, mortars with terminally guided projectiles, artillery rockets of different calibres for projecting mines, and armor-piercing submunitions) are deployed in several echelons according to their range, primarily on lightly armored vehicles in a mobile mode. In addition, according to Hannig, anti tank helicopters would be needed. The firepower would be controlled by highly specialized units of about company size that receive their orders from a relatively centralized command structure.

In addition, several military experts, among them General Uhle-Wettler, the present director of the NATO Defense College in Rome, have argued that only the North German plains and probably parts of lower Bavaria may be defended in a cost-effective way with the present force structure. This would not be true for the wooded and mountainous terrain that is typical for wide areas west of the demarcation line.[27] More fundamental are the criticisms that the present doctrine (maintaining that the Federal Republic has to be defended with a phalanx-type deployment of mechanized units) is a contradiction in itself. NATO armored units need space to maneuver. In order to develop their true potential, they should be able to move freely across wide areas, both forward and backward.

Besides these commonsense considerations, operation research studies conducted at the University of the Armed Forces in Munich have indicated that multipurpose forces representing the current posture would be less able to stop or slow down a locally superior mechanized aggressor than several reactive defense options with light, motorized infantry.[28] Löser's proposal did relatively well in the early simulations but it has not yet been fully simulated, and it is doubtful whether motorized forces would be able to survive heavy fire.

Not only does the nuclear component of our defense offer risks of destabilizing political crises. The very structure of our conventional forces raises various problems :

● The concentration of heavy equipment and large bodies of troops on bases as well as on deployment in areas close to the frontier tend to be an invitation for enemy fire.
● If our mechanized forces, which could be used both for defense and counterattack have to be filled with reserves, the opponent may perceive a threatening increase in the offensive potential that should be countered as early as possible.

A static defense would avoid this problem : it cannot be overcome by area covering artillery fire.

Hannig's concept may demonstrate a high degree of stopping power, provided that the sensors are not fooled, the munitions supplies for the firing units are not interrupted, and the centralized coordination and command remain intact.

For all three alternatives, future technological problems have to be solved. While the armed forces of today do employ various principles of tank-breaking (e.g., kinetic energy and HEAT--high-explosive anti-tank warheads, innovations in the field of armor technology provide major challenges to those capabilities.

If a military exchange occurs on the battlefield, the warning of many experts will probably come true--armored and mobile units are not suited to holding a line. If our side opts instead for maneuver warfare, life in such an extended battle zone would be practically impossible for the inhabitants of Central Europe, even without the use of means of mass destruction. By adding the option of deep conventional strikes with precision-guided munitions (e.g., FOFA), the destabilizing tendency will be further enhanced. During a crisis, presupposing a sudden stroke by the other side, the rationale for enemy preemption becomes even more obvious. If one uses weapons that could carry chemical or nuclear warheads as well, the opponent has no way to determine what is going to hit him next : escalation will become a plausible reaction.

The alternative models are designed to provide as few targets as possible. To combine this concept with a structural inability to attack, thereby minimizing the perception of threat, would remove the reasons for a preemptive strike. The introduction of territorial reserves into a defensive organization increases the ability to defend ourselves but does not provoke the adversary.

Insofar as this common aproach is concerned, Afheldt's proposal seems to come closest to the ideal--namely "no targets" and absence of offensive potential. Regarding Löser's concept, there is the objection that "everything is moving," and only a verbal but no structural guarantee that those light infantry units will not infiltrate the opponent's territory. Hannig's concept, at least at present, resembles a fence, which may lead to the assumption that one could break through with concentrated fire (or go around it). For this reason (and not only as a measure against airborne assaults), both Afheldt and Löser provide an area protection. Finally, the concentration of fire in Hannig's model may be objectionable. Would not command posts (even if there were several of them) be rather inviting targets, for example, for electronic countermeasures?

As far as the protection of the civilian population is concerned, the reviewed alternatives seem to provide a better guarantee for a limitation of the battle zone and for a prevention of the use of nuclear weapons than does the existing NATO posture.

Hannig calculated that his proposal for trans-armament (vehicles, weapons, and munitions) would require 18 to 20 billion dollars. Over a ten-year time span, this could be financed if most of the resources planned for traditional weapon systems were to be reallocated. However, can the cost estimates of the defense industry (used by Hannig) be reliable for weaponry and equipment that at present are not yet ready for mass production?

He may also run into problems with the increasingly limited manpower resources. The "military work" inherent in his concept would be so demanding that a considerable proportion of functions could not be performed by reservists.

The somewhat simpler tasks in Afheldt's structural proposal may facilitate the integration of the reserve component. Moreover, his concept, in contrast with the other two alternatives and with the existing force structure, would be advantageous because it would not require maintenance costs for mobile and possibly armored carriers of defensive fire.

However, static defense, too, has its cost problems. One may be surprised at the prices that industry could demand for adequately precise and adequate artillery rockets (the trouble-shooters of the area defense network). As far as the resources needed for the alternative military concepts are concerned, more detailed studies will be required. Savings may be possible, not so much in technical trans-armament, but more in the area of maintenance costs and by the substitution of reservists for active soldiers.

Interactive Frontal Zone Model

The "mixed concept" of the Study Group on Alternative Security Policy (SAS) integrates suggestions by Guy Brossolet, Eckhart Afheldt, Richard Simpkin and Lutz Unterseher.[29] It tries to incorporate the following suggestions in as cost-effective a manner as possible :

● no manned aircraft or Cruise and balllistic missiles for deep-strike against second- and third-echelon forces that could be misunderstood as a provocation;
● lack of major targets for nuclear, chemical and conventional attacks;
● frontal defense by a combination of static and mobile elements;
● predominance of static forces that are incapable of taking the offensive in relation to the mobile components.

The alternative defense model of SAS consists of three major elements :

● a static area defense system (Fangnetz), which employs reactive tactics;
● mechanized troops (Feuerwehr or Kavallerie) consisting of relatively compact elements including armor, cavalry, and mechanized infantry forming the active element;
● and a rearguard (Rückendeckung) or object-oriented system.

According to Lutz Unterseher, the conceptual thinker of SAS :

> Close interaction between static and mobile elements could prove advantageous under many aspects : the area covering system would wear down the aggressor's strength, canalize his movements, and serve as a source of intelligence as well as cover for counteroffensives; as a result, quantity and unit size of our heavy counterattacking forces might be reduced. The mechanized force may not only be trouble shooters at the weak spots of the area defense system; there are also tasks like boosting morale of isolated outposts as well as evacuating them in case of imminent danger. There are indications that a combination of mobile and static elements could stop an invader east of the Weser-Lech line.[30]

The static area defense system of the SAS model calls for exploiting artificial obstacles while leaving cities undefended. In peacetime the static element would require about 150,000 soldiers, to be more than doubled by local reservists in times of crisis. Up to 80 percent of these reservists would be combat personnel. According to Unterseher,

"Mobilizing reserves for a <u>static</u> defense system could not be perceived as threatening by the adversary. The closer to the border, the higher the percentage of active personnel with the area defense: this is what safety from a surprise attack requires. Mechanized elements should consist entirely of active personnel (no build-up in times of crisis)."[31] This static infantry force, Unterseher argues, could be well protected from concentrated artillery fire if the following inexpensive measures are taken : small installations (two or three men per position only), hard cover (prefabricated concrete elements), three to five positions per crew, camouflage and decoys, dislocation in depth, and random distribution. Basic assets of static warfare are mines; other cheaply engineered obstacles; short-range, mass-produced ATGMs; and simple antipersonnel rocket launchers.

In order to reduce the costs of trans-armament, the mobile element could integrate about 70 modern fighting battalions of the Bundeswehr and 80 to 90 similar units of the allies. The German component would comprise between 75,000 and 80,000 soldiers, not all of them consisting of tank forces. According to Unterseher, "The mechanized part itself could undergo functional differentiation : besides a heavily armored force, it might consist of cavalry and mobile infantry mounted on light armored vehicles. In order to draw advantage from Western high technology, the mobile element of a future defense should include advanced antitank helicopters and rocket launchers for indirect fire."

The rearguard (<u>Rückendeckung</u>) would provide the protection of bases and of the rear area. The rearguard would be highly cadred and to varying degrees it could be manned with regional reserves. In times of crisis, it could comprise about 120,000 soldiers, 90 percent of them reservists.

As far as the costs of the SAS alternative defense structure are concerned, it is not assumed that precision-guided munitions and other required equipment would be cheaper. Most of the funds would be saved for active personnel (the requirements could be decreased from 495,000 to 330,000) and maintenance, because only one-third of the present mechanized vehicles would be required.

In the context of the domestic challenges confronting West German defense policy in the 1990s, the SAS model in comparison with the official alternatives would have the following advantages :

- it would reduce those components that might induce the adversary to preempt; therefore it would increase crisis stability and it would provide additional time for political crisis management.
- If deterrence fails, the pressure to escalate from a conventional to a nuclear war would be reduced.
- The social system could still be financed without major shifts from the social to the defense budget which could lead to social instability.
- The future soldiers of the Bundeswehr would not be confronted with a major increase of the period of their service from the present 15 months to 24 months or more.

In comparison to the pure alternative models, the combined SAS model could be more easily implemented in the present NATO context. Nevertheless, Unterseher assumes major obstacles against the implementation of the SAS model, especially bureaucratic sabotage against structural changes. As most components of the alternative model could be produced in Europe, a fundamental resistance by the German and European armament industry could be avoided. Given the severe economic problems of the Soviet Union and the Warsaw Pact countries, it could be expected that at some stage the East might have to reconsider its own military posture due to the immense costs in adapting to these changes.

EVALUATION OF ALTERNATIVE DEFENSE POSTURES

Given the domestic constraints of a decreasing manpower supply, increasing demands on the defense budget, and persistent criticism of nuclear weapons and NATO's first-use option, which of the official and unofficial alternative defense postures optimally offers an affordable defense, acceptable to the people concerned, and both credible but not intimidating for the assumed adversary?

In a synoptic comparison, Unterseher isolated basic elements for which military and technological characteristics may be offered. Assessing these elements, Unterseher argued that a combination of units both of the traditional force structure and the alternative defensive concepts could be developed.[32]

This approach broadens the public and the scientific debate which has focused nearly exclusively in the FRG on the proponents of pure alternatives : Afheldt and Löser. Most of the semi official critiques have concentrated on military efficiency and the Alliance context, and they were often based on best-case assumptions about the present defense and on worst-case assumptions about area defense and other alternative reactive defense options.

Military Evaluation Based on Operations Research Techniques

Hans W. Hoffman, Reiner K. Huber and Karl Steiger have undertaken a comparative systems analysis of alternatives for the initial defense against the first strategic echelon of the Warsaw Pact in Central Europe, consisting of reactive defense options. These included four active defense options consisting of structural variants within the present German army structure : four static area reactive defense options, including the Afheldt and SAS proposals and the Swiss Territorial Defense system and the Austrian Area Defense; three dynamic area reactive defenses, including Löser's area defense concept and the SAS battalion-size-cavalry regiment; two continuous fire barrier reactive defenses (CFB) including Hannig's fire barrier, and the Hoffmann team's own light infantry battalion.

The comparison of the relative investment cost requirements for these fourteen basic forward defense options by Hoffmann et al. indicates that most of the alternative ("reactive") defense options are obviously more cost-effective.

Systematic operations research tests and field exercises of the different defense options are extremely rare both in the United States and even more so in the Federal Republic of Germany.[33] The official rejection of alternative options by some arm chair strategists contrasts with the findings of a combat simulation of fourteen alternatives by Hoffmann et al. in 1984 :

> Overall, the results of our experiments suggest that the incorporation of properly designed reactive defense into NATO's existing force structure could indeed contribute to a

significant improvement of NATO's forward defense at acceptable cost and without having to rely on emerging technologies, whose operational performance tends to be overestimated, especially with regard to enemy adaptability and the demands of a battlefield environment.[34]

EVALUATION OF 25 ALTERNATIVE SECURITY CONCEPTS

In my own systematic armchair evaluation, I grouped 25 alternative security policy concepts in four broad categories : foreign policy outlook, philosophy of security policy, strategic concepts and force structure concepts. I then evaluated these alternatives in the framework on the following five criteria :

1. They have to be in conformity with both constitutional and the international law, especially with articles 24, 25, and 26 of the Basic Law and with the Charter of the United Nations and with the principles of the Final Act of Helsinki.
2. They have to be in conformity with both the NATO and the WEU Treaty and with the goals of the Harmel Report.
3. They have to be acceptable for the population concerned.
4. They must be achievable with the foreseeable manpower. Any suggestion that calls for an increase of the manpower of the Bundeswehr is unrealistic.
5. They must be in conjunction with available financial resources. Any alternative that calls for major increases, for example, of more than three percent per annum in real terms, is unrealistic.

In the next step, I distinguished among three overall political frameworks by which these theories are incorporated in the present debate : a conservative or traditionalist approach, a pacifist approach and a pragmatic reformist approach.

The conservative or traditionalist approach to security policy in the West German debate consists of close transatlantic ties, with the goal of German reunification in the NATO context. As far as the philosophy of security is concerned, it vacillates between a policy of strength and a policy emphasizing an overall balance of power. It calls for an improvement of both the nuclear and conventional war-fighting and deterrence forces. It supports the deployment of theater nuclear forces and the modernization of short-range nuclear systems; for tactical reasons (public acceptance), it prefers to be silent on the issue of binary weapons. While it stresses differences with the U.S. AirLand Battle concept, it supports without restrictions the Rogers Plan. This approach neglects to explain how the present manpower level can be maintained and how the future plans for a European Defense Initiative can be financed. Both the continued emphasis on NATO's first-use option to maintain the credibility of a deterrence posture and the support for SDI and EDI may intensify the problems of legitimacy of West German security policy in the 1980s and 1990s. The traditionalist approach is supported by the CDU/CSU and with certain reservations by the Liberal Party (FDP). In the words of Unterseher :

Nowadays, the Christian Democrats, perpetually ruling out the possibility of defensively oriented structural change, are trying to put together four elements of policy--the combination of which is inconsistent, beyond West Germany's resources, and dangerous : beefing up the mechanized forces, investing in a moderate form of conventional deep strike, but nevertheless insisting upon a first-use doctrine of nuclear deterrence based on adequate assets, while at the same time trying to get on Reagan's SDI ticket.[35]

The pacifist approach calls for a withdrawal of both German states from their military alliances with the aim of a non aligned Europe. This approach supports a policy of calculated inferiority beyond deterrence, based on steps toward unilateral disarmament. The proponents of this approach call for a policy of defense by non-military means (civil resistance) and are supported by a majority within the Greens and segments of the peace movement.[36] A minority within the Greens pleads for a non provocative defense during a transitional period.

The pragmatic or reformist approach calls for a realistic defense posture that takes into account the need to reduce the manpower of the Bundeswehr for demographic reasons, to reduce the reliance on tactical and theater nuclear land-based forces, and to move gradually to a policy of no first use in order to regain public support for future defense posture. Given the budgetary constraints for West German defense policy in the 1980s and 1990s, the pragmatic approach opposes both the perspective of SDI and EDI and the U.S. plans for deep strike. It calls instead for a restructuring of the conventional defense posture. The reformist approach sees the preservation of the welfare state as a necessary condition for maintaining domestic stability and strengthening the motivation to defend one's own territory without committing national suicide.[37]

The Social Democrats, once again in opposition, have gradually shifted away from their traditionalist approach to a pragmatic and reformist approach in the defense area. At the Party Congress in Essen in May 1984, the SPD adopted a formula that stresses a policy of Europeanization within NATO (the two-pillar concept), gradual denuclearization, a security partnership with the East, and a shift toward an unambigious "defensivity."[38] Unterseher correctly criticizes the lack of conceptual clarity both in the resolution adopted at Essen and in the work of the new security commission :

> The proposal of replacing nuclear rockets like Pershing I and Lance by conventional precision-guided missiles for deep strike purposes makes it obvious that neither the concept of security partnership nor the principle of defensivity has been understood properly. ... The subject of an alternative defense is currently treated in a somewhat dilatory manner --the perceived impact of the peace movement fading away and the lieutenants of Schmidt having regained their self-confidence.

Nevertheless, the SPD is still the only party that has been discussing the possibility of gradually moving towards a "defensive defense" posture since the early 1980s.

The pragmatic or reformist approach to the defense of Central Europe may provide an opportunity to initiate reforms in security if the Social Democrats return to power in the next election and if the Democrats form the next U.S. administration. A shift in the U.S.-Soviet relationship and a convergence in outlook between a new U.S. and a new German government could provide favorable conditions for an "agonizing reappraisal" of the present defense posture of NATO. In the foreign policy context, such a parallel conceptual innovation took place in the late 1960s and early 1970s, in the era of detente and Ostpolitik.

MAJOR IMPEDIMENTS TO ALTERNATIVE SECURITY OPTIONS

The pragmatist or reformist approach to security policy in the Federal Republic of Germany will be confronted with the following impediments :

Alliance considerations. It has been argued in the debate on the alternative strategies in the Bundestag on June 13, 1985, that the alternative force structure models could not be realized within NATO and with the Americans.[39] However, this negative assessment does not take into account that similar proposals have been made by U.S., British and French authors.

Lack of conceptual grand design and conceptual inconsistencies. The alternative strategies have been criticized for lacking any "big picture." But the official long-term plan of the Bundeswehr also lacks a conceptual grand design and a realistic assessment of the available scarce resources. The present policy may be described as an "adaptive security policy" that follows U.S. leadership, e.g. in the case of SDI, though often without enthusiasm. It lacks a clear formulation of specific German security interests as a divided country within NATO.

Lack of political will for implementation : against institutional stubbornness and inflexibility. The present military leadership has been openly critical of the concepts proposed by the alternative thinkers, even though many alternative thinkers are retired officers.

Against industrial interests. The West German defense industry, based on its close transatlantic and intra-European cooperation, may prefer established official plans. It can hardly be expected to propose alternative concepts to a government that has openly rejected these options beforehand. With the intensification of the inter- and intra-service rivalries in the Bundeswehr and with the likely reductions in the procurement portion of the federal budget, the West German defense industry may become more receptive to alternative defense options relying exclusively on European industrial components.

If SDI and a European Defense Initiative or an extended air defense should be realized, the dependency of European security, in either alliance, on the respective security schemes of the superpowers would increase. As a consequence, the political leverage of the European countries for alternative security options over the next 30 years would be drastically reduced.

CONCLUSION : "THE POLITICS OF MUDDLING THROUGH"

It appears unlikely that the present manpower and procurement goals formulated in the Bundeswehr Plan 1985, the long-term defense guidelines of NATO for follow-on-forces-attack, and the political preference of Mr. Wörner for an extended air defense can be implemented under the constraint of scarce resources. However, it also appears unlikely, at least until the late 1980s, that any of the alternative concepts will be initiated, given the present and future domestic power bases.

The most likely long-term security policy of the Federal Republic may be described as an "adaptive" policy of muddling through with the worst political alternative:

- of being unable to increase the domestic consensus for the Bundeswehr and for NATO's defensive posture;
- of being unable to provide a credible conventional deterrence against the Soviet Union;
- of being unable to provide an inducement for a policy of arms reduction, confidence-building, and detente in Europe.

NOTES

1. Among the latter are : Volker Rittberger, ed., Abrüstungsplanung in der Bundesrepublik, Aufgaben, Probleme, Perspektiven (Baden-Baden : Nomos, 1979); Volker Rittberger, ed., Neue Wege der Abrüstungsplanung (Baden-Baden : Nomos, 1981); Hans Günter Brauch and Duncan L. Clarke, eds., Decision-making for Arms Limitation--Assessment and Prospects (Cambridge : MA. : Ballinger, 1983); Hans Günter Brauch, Abrüstungsamt oder Ministerium? Ausländische Modelle der Abrüstungsplanung (Frankfurt: Haag und Herchen, 1981).

2. Der Bundesminister der Verteidigung, Weissbuch 1985--Zur Lage und Entwicklung der Bundeswehr (Bonn : Bundesregierung, June 1985).

3. Christian Krause, "Worst-Case Denken als Motiv westlicher Sicherheitspolitik," in Sicherheit durch Abrüstung. Orientierende Beiträge zum Imperativ unserer Zeit, edited by Wilhelm Bruns et al. (Bonn : Neue Gesellschaft, 1984); Wilhelm Bruns et. al., eds., Bedrohungsanalysen. Eine Sachverständigen Anhörung (Bonn : Neue Gesellschaft, 1985); Andreas von Bülow, ed., Die eingebildete Unterlegenheit. Das Kräfteverhältenis West-Ost, wie es wirklich ist (Munich : C.H. Beck, 1985); Forschungsgruppe SALSS in cooperation with SAS, Konventionelle Landstreitkräfte für Mitteleuropa--Eine militärische Bedrohungsanalyse (Starnberg : Forschungsinstitut für Friedenspolitik, 1984).

4. Weissbuch 1985, p. 49.

5. Weissbuch 1985, p. 65.

6. Von Bülow, Die eingebildete Unterlegenheit, p. 145.

7. See Hans Rühle, "Wunschträume statt Alpträume - Bedrohungsanalysen mit zweierlei Mass," in von Bülow, Die eingebildete Unterlegenheit, pp. 131-44.

8. Von Bülow, Die eingebildete Unterlegenheit, p. 115.

9. Forschungsgruppe SALLS in cooperation with SAS, Konventionelle Landstreitkräfte, summary. See also Erhard Forndran and Gert Krell, eds., Kernwaffen im Ost-West-Vergleich. Zur Beurteilung militärischer Potentiale und Fähigkeiten (Baden-Baden : Nomos, 1984); Erhard Forndran and Hans Joachim Schmidt, Konventionelle Rüstung im Ost-West Vergleich (Baden-Baden : Nomos, 1986).

10. Kommission für die Langzeitplanung der Bundeswehr. Bericht. (Bonn : Bundesministerium der Verteidigung, June 1982).

11. Weissbuch 1985, p. 398.

12. Christian Krause, Die Auswirkungen des Geburtenrückgangs in der Bundesrepublik Deutschland auf die Bundeswehr und Mögliche Folgemassnahmen, Working paper (Bonn : Friedrich-Ebert-Stiftung, 1979); Bernd Grass, "Manpower Shortage

of the Bundeswehr till the Year 2000," to appear in <u>Alternative Conventional Defense Postures in the European Theater - The Future of the Military Balance and Domestic Constraints</u>, edited by Hans Günter Brauch and Robert Kennedy (Boulder, CO : Westview, 1987); Bernd Grass, "Das Wehrpotential der 9Oer Jahre," in <u>Studiegruppe Alternative Verteidigung. Entwürfe für eine konsequente Defensive</u> (Opladen : Westdeutscher Verlag, 1984), pp. 35-47; Hartmut Bebermeyer and Bernd Grass, "Unsere Streitkräfte auf dem Wege in die Ressourcenkrise," in <u>Sicherheitspolitik am Ende? Eine Bestandsaufnahme, Perspektiven und neue Ansätze</u>, edited by Hans Günter Brauch (Gerlingen: Bleicher, 1984).

13. Hartmut Bebermeyer, "The Fiscal Crisis of the Bundeswehr," in Hans Günter Brauch and Robert Kennedy, <u>Alternative Conventional Defense Postures</u>; Hartmut Bebermeyer, "Verteidigungsökonomie am Scheidewege," in <u>Strukturwandel der Verteidigung</u>, edited by (Opladen : Westdeutscher Verlag, 1984), pp. 9-34.

14. Kurt Biedenkopf, "Domestic Consensus, Security and the Western Alliance" Address to the 24th IISS Conference in The Hague (London : IISS, 1982). See also Wolfgang R. Vogt, "Kopernikanische Wende in der Sicherheitspolitik," in <u>Streitfall Frieden. Positionen und Analysen zur Sicherheitspolitik und Friedensbewegung</u>, edited by Wolfgang R. Vogt (Heidelberg : C.F. Müller, 1984), pp. 3-34; Wolfgang R. Vogt, <u>Sicherheitspolitik und Streitkräfte in der Legitimationskrise</u> (Baden-Baden : Nomos, 1983).

15. See Hans Günter Brauch, "Sicherheitspolitik im Umbruch? Aussenpolitische Rahmenbedingungen unt Entwicklungschancen sicherheitspolitischer Alternativen," in Vogt, <u>Streitfall Frieden</u>, pp. 145-149; Hans Günter Brauch, "Official and Unofficial West German Alternatives for Reducing the Reliance of European Security on Nuclear Weapons--A Plea for a Pragmatic Approach," in <u>Rethinking the Nuclear Dilemma in Europe</u>, edited by Frank Barnaby and P. Terrence Hopmann (London: Macmillan, 1986).

16. See Caspar W. Weinberger, <u>Annual Report to Congress Fiscal Year 1986, February 4, 1985</u>, (Washington, D.C. : GPO, 1985), p. 221. See also William M. Arkin, Thomas B. Cochran and Milton Hoenig, "Resource Paper on the U.S. Nuclear Arsenal," <u>The Bulletin of the Atomic Scientists</u>, August-September 1984 : 12-14.

17. Huba Wass de Czege and L.D. Holder, "The New FM 100-5," <u>Military Review</u>, Vol. 62, No. 7 (July 1982) : 53-70.

18. Bernard W. Rogers, "Die langfristige Planungsricht-linie FOFA ; Behauptungen und Tatsachen," <u>NATO-Brief</u>, No.6 (1984) : 3-11. See also Institut für Friedenforschung und Sicherheitspolitik Hamburg (ISFH), "Angriff in die Tiefe : Ein Diskussionsbeitrag zum Rogers Plan," <u>S + F</u>, No. 1 (1985) : 53-58.

19. Konrad Seitz, "SDI--die technologische Herausforderung für Europa," <u>Europa Archiv</u> July 10, 1985, pp. 381-90; see my critical assessment in "Uberlegungen zur Militarisierung des Weltraums und zur Betroffenheit der Bundesrepublik

Deutschland," in <u>Die Friedenswarte</u> (Fall 1985).

20. Hans Günter Brauch, "Elements of a Tactical Defense Architecture," in <u>From Star Wars to the Strategic Defense Initiative-Implications for Europe--Perceptions and Assessments</u>, edited by Hans Günter Brauch (London : Macmillan, 1986); Fred S. Hoffmann, "The 'Star Wars' Debate : The Western Alliance and Strategic Defense: Part II," <u>Adelphi-Papers</u>, no. 199 (London : International Institute for Strategic Studies, 1985), pp. 25-33. Joseph Fitchett, "First Part of U.S. 'Star Wars' Defense Advocated by Mid-90s," <u>International Herald Tribune</u>, September 27, 1984.

21. Lutz Unterseher, "Konventionelle Verteidigung Mitteleuropas : Etablierte Struktur und Alternativen im Test," in Brauch, <u>Sicherhietspolitik am Ende?</u>, pp. 214-222. See also Lutz Unterseher, "Towards a Feasible Defense of Central Europe--A German Perspective--Empirical and Normative Theses," Unpublished paper presented at a German-American workshop conference, "Improving NATO Conventional Capabilities," Strategic Studies Institute, U.S. Army War College, Carlisle Barracks, PA, April 15-16, 1983.

22. See Carl Friedrich von Weizsäcker, ed., <u>Kriegsfolgen und Kriegsverhütung</u> (Munich : Hauser, 1970); Horst Afheldt, <u>Verteidigung und Frieden</u> (Munich : Hauser, 1976); Afheldt, <u>Defensive Verteidigung</u> (Reinbek : Rowohf, 1983); Afheldt, <u>Atomkrieg : Das Verhältnis einer Politik mit militärischen Mitteln</u> (Munich : Hauser, 1984); Guy Brossolet, <u>Essai sur la non-bataille</u> (Paris : Editions Belin, 1975); Alain Carton, <u>Dissuasion infranucleaire - l'école allemand de techno-guerilla</u> (Paris : CIRPES, 1984); Bogislaw von Bonin, <u>Opposition gegen Adenauers Sicherheitspolitik. Eine Dokumentation</u> (Hamburg : Neue Politik, 1976); F. O. Miksche, "Präzisionswaffen veränden das Kriegsbild," <u>Wehrtechnik</u>, 5 (1977) : 17-23.

23. Afheldt, <u>Defensive Verteidigung</u>; Jochen Löser, <u>Weder rot noch tot. Überleben ohne Atomkrieg--Eine sicherheitspolitische Alternative</u> (Munich : Olzog, 1981); Norbert Hannig, <u>Abschreckung durch konventionelle Waffen. Das David-Goliath Prinzip</u> (Berlin : Berlin Verlag Arno Spitz, 1984). Other variations are presented by : F. Uhle-Wettler, <u>Gefechtsfeld Mitteleuropa--Gefahr der Übertechnisierung von Streitkräften</u> (Munich : Bernard & Graefe, 1980); Steven Canby, <u>The Alliance and Europe : Part IV : Military Doctrine and Technology</u>, Adelphi Paper no. 109 (London : IISS, 1975); Steven Canby, "Light Infantry Perspective," unpublished Paper presented to Infantry Commanders' Conference, Ft. Benning, GA., March 6, 1984; J. J. Mearsheimer, "Why the Soviets Can't Win Quickly in Central Europe," <u>International Security</u> (Summer 1982) : 5-39; J. J. Mearsheimer, "Nuclear Weapons and Deterrence in Europe," <u>International Security</u> (Winter 1984-85) : 19-76; Dietrich Fischer, <u>Preventing War in the Nuclear Age</u> (London : Rowman & Allanheld, 1984); E. Afheldt, "Verteidigung ohne Selbstmord : Vorschlag für Einsatz einer leichten Infanterie," in <u>Defensive Verteidigung</u>, edited by Horst Afheldt (Reinbek : Rowohft, 1983); J. Gerber, <u>Bundeswehr im Atlantischen Bündnis, Sec. 10 : Analytischer Rückblick und prognotischer Ausblick</u> (Regensburg, 1984); Gerber, "Fordert die Wirtschaftlichkeit eine neue Struktur

des Heeres?" Heere International, vol. 3 (Herford : Mittler, 1984).

24. See also Horst Afheldt, "Tactical Nuclear Weapons and European Security," in SIPRI, Tactical Nuclear Weapons : European Perspectives (London : Taylor & Francis, 1978), pp. 262-95; Horst Afheldt, "The Necessity, Preconditions and Consequences of a No-First-Use Policy," in No-First-Use, edited by Frank Blackaby, Jozef Goldblat and Sverre Lodgaard (London and Philadelphia : Taylor & Francis, 1984), pp. 57-66; Horst Afheldt, "Flexible Response and the Consequences for the Defense of Central Europe," in Brauch and Kennedy, Alternative Conventional Defense Postures; Hans Günter Brauch and Lutz Unterseher, "Review Essay : Getting Rid of Nuclear Weapons : A Review of a Few Proposals for a Conventional Defense of Europe," Journal of Peace Research, 21, no. 2 (1984).

25. Löser, 1981, see Note 23.

26. Norbert Hannig, "Can Western Europe be Defended by Conventional Means ?" International Defense Review, no. 1 (1979) : 27-34.

27. Uhle-Wettler, 1980, see Note 23.

28. Hans W. Hoffmann, Reiner K. Huber and Karl Steiger, On Reactive Defense Options, (Hochschule der Bundeswehr, Fachbereich Informatik, Institut für Angewandte Systemforschung und Operations Research, Report No. S-8403, Neubiberg, November 1984); R. K. Huber, K. Steiger and B. Wobith, " Uber ein analytisches Modell zur Untersuchung der Gefechtswirksamkeit von Heeresstrukturen," Wehrwis-senschaftliche Rundschau no. 1 (1981), 1-10; R. K. Huber, "The Systems Approach to European Defense--A Challenge for Operational Research Gaming," Phalanx, 15, no. 3 (September 1982).

29. Lutz Unterseher, "Friedenssicherung durch Vermeidung von Provokation? Ein pragmatischer Vorschlag für eine alternative Landesverteidigung," in Vogt, "Kopernikanische Wende" (see Note 14), pp. 95-103; R.E. Simpkin, Mechanized Infantry (Oxford : 1980); Lutz Unterseher, "Für eine tragfähige Verteidigung der Bundesrepublik : Grundgedanken und Orientierungen," in Studiengruppe Alternative Verteidigung (see Note 12), pp. 108-30; "Arbeiten der Studiengruppe Alternative Sicherheits-politik (SAS) : Landstreitkräfte zur Verteidigung der Bundesrepublik Deutschland, Ammerkungen eines Logistikeers, Das Personal alternativer Landstreit-kräfte, über Luftstreitkräfte einer defensiven Verteidigung," in Strukturwandel der Verteidigung. Entwürfe für eine konsequente Defensive, edited by Studiengruppe Alternative Sicherheitspolitik, (Opladen : Westdeutscher Verlag, 1984).

30. Lutz Unterseher, "Towards a Feasible Defense" (see Note 21), p. 7.

31. Ibid, p. 9.

32. Ibid, p. 8.

33. See R. K. Huber, K. Steiger and B. Wobith, " On an Analytical Quick Game to Investigate the Battle Effectiveness of Forward Defense Concepts," Journal of the Korean Operations Research Society, 6, no. 1 (April 1981), 33-35.

34; Hoffmann, Huber and Steiger, On Reactive Defense Options, p. ii.

35. Lutz Unterseher, "Emphasizing Defense : An Ongoing Non-Debate in the Federal Republic of Germany," in Emerging Technologies and Militay Doctrines, edited by Frank Barnaby and Marlies ter Borg (London : Mac-millan, 1986).

36. Komitee Grundrechte und Demokratie, ed., Frieden mit anderen Waffen (Reinbeck : Rowohlt, 1981).

37. See Eckhart Afheldt, Verteidigung ohne Selbstmord. Vorschlag für den Einsatz einer leichten Infanterie, (Herbrechtingen/Starnberg : March 1982).

38. These policies wee reaffirmed at the SPD Party Congress of August 1986 in Nürnberg.

39. Deutscher Bundestag, 10. Wahlperiode, 143 Sitzung, June 13, 1985, pp. 10602-34.

7 The Netherlands: "Hollanditis" in Remission?

Jan Geert Siccama

There is little doubt that the image of consensus on Dutch security policy has been shattered by the nuclear issue. The process of crumbling consensus, which had started already with the planned deployment of neutron shells in 1977, often has been ascribed to the democratization of foreign policy. In this chapter, however, we will argue that the process of internalization of foreign policies has been overtaken by a process of externalization of internal policies. Questions of peace and external security have become prominent factors in the career prospects of party politicians, in differentiating between party platforms in elections, and--perhaps the most important effect in the multiparty system of the Netherlands--in influencing political parties to join coalition governments or to remain outside of government. Until now, attempts to acquire salient profiles in security policies focus almost exclusively on the nuclear issue, and even more specifically on the deployment of Cruise missiles in the country. Neither the peace movement nor the major political parties have attempted to present full-fledged alternative security policies. Precisely because the search for radical alternative security arrangements has remained confined to the extreme left, the underlying consensus may be greater than is realized within the present turmoil. Indeed, we will argue that some basic tenets of Dutch security policies are still present, and that the recommendations of "Europeanization" and "conventionalization," which are usually regarded as alternative approaches to the present security arrangement, may even strengthen consensus, although in a somewhat modified form.

PRESENT SECURITY SITUATION

The Perception of Internal and External Threats

As far as the Dutch population is concerned, unemployment ranks as their main problem.[1] In a 1976 poll, 81.1 percent of respondents mentioned unemployment as a very important individual problem. In comparison, international questions ranked low : defense of national interests against the superpowers was mentioned by 35.0 percent, and strengthening defense capabilities by an even lower 26.1 percent. In a poll on "enemy images," held in 1979 and 1980, 44.6 percent of the respondents considered health problems the most threatening to their individual well-being. Nuclear energy (31.6 percent), the threat of war (25.0 percent), and the arms race (17.7 percent) ranked lower. When asked which problems were considered the most threatening to Dutch society, 45.5 percent mentioned unemployment, 37.5 percent crime and 32.1 percent nuclear energy. Much lower scores were attained by the arms race (15.9 percent), immigrant laborers (11.4 percent) and communism (6.7 percent). In four polls held in 1981, the nuclear weapons issue scored fourth (together with "social security," "foreigners," "nuclear energy" and "environmental problems") with about 7 percent (unemployment rated about 85 percent, housing shortages about 20 percent, economic recession about 12 percent). Rather different results were acquired when the respondents were presented with a limited list of problems (Table 7.1).

Table 7.1 : Which of the following problems do you consider the greatest to your country?

Problems	I	II	III
Unemployment	70	74	70
Crime	45	53	47
Nuclear weapons	49	47	49
Threat of war	32	33	37
Too many government expenditures	20	25	17
Lack of political leadership	17	24	19
Social inequality	19	19	19
Inflation	9	12	10
Energy crisis	10	9	9
Insufficient defenses	5	7	5
Other/no answer/no opinion	3	3	6

Source : NIPO (International Herald Tribune/Atlantic Institute, and others).
I, September 1982; II, March 1983; III, October 1983. Figures are percentages; respondents were allowed more than one answer.

In comparison with the results for 1976, 1979, 1980 and 1981, the results for 1982-83 suggest that nuclear weapons have become a more important issue to voters. Moreover, while unemployment is a valence issue (everybody favors less crime and a lower unemployment rate, although ways of attaining that goal may differ completely and politicians may feel they are incapable of solving the problem), preferred armaments policies may vary from complete disarmament to superiority over the opponent, making the issue susceptible to political manipulations.[2]
Identifying nuclear weapons as an important problem, however, does not

necessarily imply dissatisfaction with nuclear deterrence. In various polls, some 70 percent of the population do not expect a third world war to break out in Europe, while the same percentage think they would not survive such a war if deterrence really failed (72 percent expect to die in a nuclear war, 59 percent in a chemical war, and only 21 percent in a conventional war).

Similarly, there is a clear understanding that the cutoff of oil supplies (as during the Arab oil embargo to the Netherlands in 1973-74) could really put the existence of the country at stake. In 1976, 16 percent considered the Arab countries a threat to the future peace in Western Europe, while 27 percent mentioned the Soviet Union. In 1978, 20 percent of the respondents considered the Arab oil countries an even greater threat to the Netherlands than the Soviet Union (15.5 percent). As a consequence of the invasion of Afghanistan, the Soviet military threat in 1980 was felt again by 69.6 percent of the population, albeit 64.4 percent of the respondents thought that the oil countries were responsible for the economic difficulties of the Netherlands.

Government Policies to Meet the Threats

In government policies, threats to economic security are usually sharply distinguished from threats to military security. An exception is the supply of energy, where economic measures (i.e., a distribution schedule of oil in times of crisis) and the possibility of maritime convoys have been planned. Additionally, security aspects of development aid are sometimes mentioned, although it may be doubted whether economic growth or a more equal income distribution within developing countries are indeed conducive to peace and stability.

The military policies of the Netherlands coincide almost completely with NATO policies. They aim at the protection of territorial integrity and discouraging external attempts to interfere with internal political decision-making (i.e., Finlandization). Within NATO, the Dutch have strived since World War II to attain four major goals, which are described by J. J. C. Voorhoeve as major themes of Dutch security policies :

1. Give priority to NATO interests, meaning that consolidation of the Alliance is considered the first and foremost aim.
2. Support U.S. leadership, thus retaining continued presence and military dominance of the United States in Western Europe.
3. Tie West Germany to NATO, thereby avoiding the need for an independent West German nuclear force or a rapprochement between Bonn and Moscow.
4. Concentrate on strategic deterrence. This goal seemed easier to obtain in times of U.S. nuclear preponderance. In the 1970s and 1980s, after U.S. territory had become vulnerable to Soviet nuclear retaliation, this aim has been changed into deemphasizing the role of nuclear weapons.[3]

Furthermore, in recent years additional requirements with respect to detente, arms control, and "conventionalization" have been introduced into the policies of the Netherlands.

Support of Public Opinion

NATO membership is supported by a solid three-quarters of the population. Similarly, some 50 percent of the respondents in polls conducted between 1963 and 1982 deemed the armed forces "necessary," while another 30 to 40 percent called them "a necessary evil." There is also a solid majority of two-thirds supporting the statement that Western Europe needs a military counterweight against the Soviet Union.

However, with respect to nuclear weapons, the picture is substantially complicated and some would call it inconsistent. Substantial majorities of some 60 percent opposed deployment of the neutron bomb in the Netherlands, a percentage that rose even further after the deployment decision had been cancelled. Support for deployment of Cruise missiles varies with the phrasing of the question. If one asks simply to choose between "in favor" or "against," majorities of 50 to 65 percent are opposed to modernization. But majorities in favor of deployment are sometimes observed if this decision is made part of an arms control agreement or if the Soviet Union is unwilling to diminish the number of SS-20 missiles. Furthermore, since 1983, some 80 percent of the population expects that Cruise missiles will ultimately be deployed in the Netherlands.

In some cases, the nuclear turmoil may even have had its main effect in mobilizing the proponents of nuclear weapons. In June 1975, before all the commotion about nuclear weapons, 59 percent wanted to remove all nuclear missions of the Dutch armed forces, while 22.7 percent wanted to retain these missions. In 1983 and 1984, however, percentages in favor of nuclear tasks of Dutch armed forces had increased to 33.0 and 35.1 percent, while 46.4 and 48.4 percent respectively wanted to do away with nuclear missions of the Netherlands. Similarly, in 1977, 71.5 percent of the respondents in the National Election Survey opposed every use of nuclear weapons. In October 1983, however, this percentage had dropped to 42 percent.

Apparently the nuclear issue has split the country into three parts : one-third favoring NATO nuclear policies, one-third opposed to all nuclear weapons, and one-third neither unconditionally in favor or against or simply indifferent or still ignorant. In a Netherlands Institute of International Relations poll (held in September 1983 by NIPO), 31 percent supported the activities of the Interchurch Peace Council (abbreviated in Dutch IKV), while 29 percent opposed IKV, and 40 percent did not speak out for or against. In all likelihood, future deployment of new nuclear weapons (e.g., a possible nuclear replacement of the Lance missile) will also meet strong criticism from large sectors of the public (although it is questionable whether they would represent a majority view). Moreover, NATO's first-use policy is supported by only a small minority of the population.

ALTERNATIVE PROPOSALS

Ideas about improving Dutch security vary a great deal. Of the small, left-wing political parties, only the Pacifist-Socialist party (PSP) rejects all armaments and NATO membership. Within the Radical party (PPR), the idea of nonviolent resistance was rather popular in the 1970s. Government-sponsored research showed, however, that this concept is theoretically unclear and that it lacks effectiveness against Soviet military power.[4]

The other alternative proposals tend to vary with respect to two dimensions :

Europeanization and conventionalization. A complete Europeanization of defense with emphasis on nuclear deterrence (i.e., a European nuclear force) always has been anathema in Dutch politics. In fact, this idea is now supported only by a few Europeanists, who want to substitute U.S. nuclear protection with the French force de frappe.[5] These authors think that coupling no longer exists, while others maintain that strategic nuclear weapons and the presence of U.S. troops in Europe will tie the United States adequately to Western Europe.[6]

The peace movement in the Netherlands has emphasized the antinuclear character of its struggle. Furthermore, since nuclear deterrence is ascribed to the superpower confrontation, the movement wants to dissolve the alliance blocs. In this view, the populations of Eastern and Western Europe have to support each other in their struggle against the occupying superpowers.[7] If the United States left Western Europe, the Soviet Union would no longer feel justified in retaining buffer states in Eastern Europe and would permit a "Europe for the Europeans."

Although the idea of a Western European nuclear force and the idea of a nuclear-free Europe only overlap with respect to the removal of the superpowers from the arena, the two ideas are sometimes coupled. The journalist W. L. Brugsma, for instance, has sketched a "journey of a thousand miles," which would start with French nuclear protection of Western Europe and end with a nuclear-free Europe, in which the Soviet Union would have withdrawn behind the Bug (the border river between the Soviet Union and Poland) and the United States beyond the Atlantic Ocean. Similarly, the former Socialist Minister of Defense, H. Vredeling, wants to use a potential Western European nuclear force as a bargaining chip with the Soviet Union.[8] If the Soviets were to withdraw from Eastern Europe, the Western Europeans would forgo both the nuclear option and the sustained presence of U.S. troops. The integrity of such a nuclear-free Europe would be guaranteed by the superpowers.

While the peace movement is lukewarm about conventional defense, others emphasize the desirability of a change to "defensive" or "nonprovocative" military postures.[9] In these proposals, nuclear weapons are only meant to deter a first use of this weapons category by the opponent.

Heavy reliance on conventional warfare has been criticized because conventional defenses have shown no significant deterrent effect in the past, and because a long war would lead to mass destruction in the vulnerable industrialized societies of Western Europe, even it were fought with non-nuclear weapons. In this view, Atlantic cooperation can be reconciled with the interests of the European nonnuclear nations only if the United States is willing to deter mass destruction by the first use of nuclear weapons against Soviet territory.[10]

The Dutch government, although quite reluctant about the Genscher-Colombo plan (because it looked so much like the Fouchet plan of the early 1960s) became much more positive as soon as discussions had started in the framework of European Political Cooperation (EPC). In a speech on October 2, 1984 in Brussels, the Netherlands' Minister of Foreign Affairs Van den Broek gave six reasons for closer security cooperation between the European allies : (a) the economic renaissance of Europe had made it as strong as the United States; (b) it should be made clear (for instance, to counter threats by Senator Sam Nunn) that Europe has not abdicated its security responsibilities; (c) geographical differences lead to conflicting security interests between the U.S. and Western Europe; (d) SDI, emerging technologies, and new military doctrines require European cooperation; (e) the European partners should develop a common viewpoint in "out-of-area" interventions; (f) there should be a closer armaments cooperation to attain a real "two-way street" with the United States. This security cooperation, according to the Dutch government, should take place within the framework of a "light-structured" Western European Union (WEU), thus tying France more strongly to NATO. In a comparable speech, Minister of Defense De Ruiter stressed the need for a "greater political unity" between the European nations.[11] In this way, European insights on strategy and arms control, and a more effective organization of Europe's contribution to military defense and weapons production would become more important. According to the Minister of Defense, European security cooperation within the EPC framework was the most natural way of proceeding, although other forums (e.g., the Independent European Program Group--IEPG-- then led by the Netherlands Defense State Secretary for Materiel Van Houwelingen) also had their roles. All these efforts to stimulate European security cooperation, one should note, were presented as attempts to strengthen the Atlantic Alliance.

Simultaneously, Dutch governments have been striving since 1971 to deemphasize the role of nuclear weapons or to become less dependent on them. At first, this goal was thought to be attainable through an Mutual and Balanced Force Reduction (MBFR) agreement, but in the late 1970s and early 1980s the instrument was sought in unilateral measures to strengthen NATO's conventional defenses.

Paradoxically, nuclear debate contributed in this way to a rapid modernization of the Dutch armed forces. While other departments had to implement severe budget cuts during a time of economic crisis, real defense expenditures rose substantially, albeit less than NATO's goal of 3 percent real growth. In its ten-year plan, the present government coalition put forward 2 percent increases of real defense expenditures for the period 1984-86, while for the period 1987-93, real military outlays should rise annually by 3 percent.[12] In a memorandum on emerging technologies, the Multiple Rocket Launcher (MLRS) is designated as the Dutch contribution to FOFA (follow-on forces attack) during the present planning period. The Dutch government also wants to improve defenses against short-range Soviet missiles (SS-21, SS-22, SS-23) by anti-tactical ballistic missile defense (ATBM) and feels rather favorable toward deployment of conventional missiles (T-16 or T-22, the so-called follow-on Lance) within the framework of Offensive Counter Air (OCA).

In contrast to the governing Christian-Democrat/Liberal (conservative) coalition, the Social Democratic opposition party (PvdA) has identified itself much more strongly with antinuclear and pro-European stances. An alternative Defense Plan, published in 1984 by the PvdA parliamentarians, is inspired very much by the notion of "common security" of the Palme committee.[13] Although the security relationship with the United States should be retained, conflicts of interest require that Western Europe should be "at least equal" within NATO to the United States. The party is said to have already made a fundamental choice against nuclear weapons ten years ago. The ultimate goal of the party is "a nuclear-free Europe." In the meantime, possession of nuclear weapons should be restrained to nuclear weapon states (France and Britain). In the short run, a nuclear-free zone of a width of 150 kilometers on both sides of the demarcation line in Germany is admissable, while in the still shorter run (partly to fulfill NATO obligations by retaining the nuclear mission of the Lance missile) this zone could be restricted to 50 kilometers on both sides of the dividing line. According to the Social Democrats, coupling between Western Europe and the United States can be sufficiently attained by conventional means.

SECURITY POLICIES IN THE FUTURE

At the time of this writing the Cruise missile is still of overwhelming importance for the Dutch debate. The Social Democratic party made participation in a coalition government after May 1986 dependent upon renunciation of the deployment decision of November 1, 1985. Apparently, the major opposition party tried to make itself indispensable in a new government by selecting the cruise missile issue (and not unemployment or income distribution) as the major vote-getting vehicle. But the deployment agreement with the United States was approved in early 1986 by the Second Chamber, and the May 1986 legislative elections retained the conservative coalition in power. One important factor in the debate is the fait accompli of a deployment decision : after seven years of deliberations, people were inclined to accept any reasonable decision. Nevertheless, it is probable that the nuclear issue will linger on to at least December 1988, when the Cruise deployment schedule has to be completed.

In the long run, the following factors are decisive for the Dutch security profile :

1. As in Germany, future security policies will to a large extent be determined by the attitude of the major Social Democratic party and the closeness of its relationship with the antinuclear movement. Currently, PvdA voters can be roughly divided into antimilitarists (one-third), true NATO believers (one-third), and others. While there is, on the one hand, a tendency for accepting compromises, there is also, on the other, the consideration that an attitude of nuclear pacifism may enhance the chances of individual politicians in campaigns for parliament or for the party leadership.

2. The peace movement which has become predominantly an anti-Cruise missile movement, will have to choose a new platform. Will the movement stick to its antinuclear stance, or will it succeed in uniting total pacifists, nuclear pacifists and opponents of the arms race with one full-fledged alternative security policy? Moreover, what will be the effect of not being able to attain once again the tremendous successes (400,000 demonstrators in 1981 and 550,000 in 1983; 3,750,000 petition signatures in 1985) that the movement has achieved in the past?

3. Until now, the commitment to Europeanization has been treated without much engagement. From an external point of view, revitalizing the WEU countered U.S. unilateralism and pressure by means of the Nunn Amendment. It seemed an additional instrument to tie the Federal Republic, where the peace movement showed tendencies toward arrangements with the East, to the Alliance, while at the same time, partially reintegrating France into the military structure of NATO and possibly even strengthening conventional defenses. The strength of these external pressures will be determined by continued U.S. threats if attempts to strengthen nonnuclear defenses fail and by continued regional military threats (conventional as well as nuclear) by the Soviet Union against Western Europe. From an internal point of view, the nonbinding character of European security cooperation may be explained by the lack of consensus on security arrangements other than within a NATO framework. In an elite questionnaire, published in 1978, the problem was raised about what would happen if U.S. nuclear protection of Western Europe were no longer considered credible. The answers were widely divergent: 22 percent expected a fragmentation of Europe, 20 percent a greater influence by, or

rapprochement with the Soviet Union, 33 percent expected increases in conventional and nuclear armaments, 3 percent a political unification of Europe, and 8 percent gave still other answers (13 percent don't know/no answer).[14] In surveys for the general public, opinions are also divided. In the National Election Survey of 1977, 38.6 percent rejected a Western European nuclear force completely, while 39.7 percent thought it acceptable under some conditions. A majority of 57.2 percent considered Dutch security to be possible only in a alliance with the United States (27.5 percent opposed). While only 36 percent wanted a United States of Europe, 63 percent wanted to confine European cooperation to economic affairs. In 1979, 61.3 percent preferred a security arrangement within NATO, although there were different perceptions of the role for a European pillar (Table 7.2).

Table 7.2 : Optimal security arrangements for the Netherlands

In NATO, as its exists	31
In a changed NATO, where Western Europe has a greater say because it assumes a larger part of the costs	15
Military withdrawal from NATO, but political membership	11
Establishing an independent Western European army unconnected with the United States	11
Rapprochement with the Soviet Union	6
Don't know/no answer	27
Total	100

Source : USICA poll 1981.
Figures are percentages.

Other results of public opinion research also lend support to the assumption of uncertainty about the future of Europe. While 50 percent want to maintain the right of veto in the EC, 56.3 percent give priority to Dutch independence over European integration and 66 percent want to keep European unity at its present level. There is a majority of 63.8 percent in favor of a European Defense Command, a majority of 70.1 percent in favor of a European approach to defense, and more than 60 percent giving priority to European interests over Dutch interests in the European Parliament. While 45 percent reject a united Western European government (37 percent in favor), 41.1 percent of the respondents would accept a single European foreign policy (34.6 percent opposed)).

A similar uncertainty surrounds the desired position of Europe with respect to the superpowers. In four polls (USICA 1981, Le Nouvel Observateur 1981, Gallup 1983, NSS 1983) the alternative "neutralist position" (of the Netherlands in Europe) is preferred above "choosing sides" in the conflict between East and West. This could indicate a flight from reality in which the Netherlands (whether one likes it or not) is partisan in the superpower conflict. Furthermore, those who want to choose sides choose the side of the United States. Various surveys about "anti-Americanism" and the image of the Soviet Union confirm that the population is certainly not indifferent to the superpowers. A reasonable degree of confidence in the United States, however, has replaced the unlimited confidence of the 1950s and the early 1960s. The image of the Soviet Union is still very negative. In 1979, 54.7 percent deemed that the Soviet Union wished to "dominate the world," and in 1980 this figure was 63 percent. Moreover, in 1981, 52.8 percent considered Soviet behavior the most aggressive.

4. With respect to the conventionalization of defense, one might expect that increased public awareness of the vulnerability of society to nonnuclear warfare would mitigate the desire to substitute deterrence by retaliation with deterrence in kind. It remains to be seen whether antinuclear feelings imply acceptance of substantially larger civil defense preparations, for example, protection against conventional and chemical warfare or against poisonous gases set loose as a consequence of conventional attacks on chemical factories or depositories. It is not likely that increased awareness of societal vulnerability coincides with pacifism. Although this percentage should be seen in perspective against other indicators and other countries, no less than 70.6 percent of the Dutch are willing to sacrifice their lives for their homeland.

Another important factor is, of course, the willingness to pay. Among other government tasks, defense spending is assigned the lowest priority, while various polls also reveal a clear willingness to accept cuts in defense spending in favor of social welfare. When people are asked whether they are willing to pay more for conventional defense in order to become less dependent on nuclear weapons, opinions differ, as is shown by Table 7.3.

Table 7.3 : If the West diminishes nuclear weaponry, conventional armament (artillery, tanks, aircraft) should become stronger

Fully agree	33
Fully disagree	32
Neither agree nor disagree	36

Source : Netherlands Institute of International Relations survey, 1983.
Figures are percentages.

CONCLUSION

We have tried to show that it is awkward to rely on public opinion as a guide for desirable security policies in the Netherlands. There are indications that people would accept attempts to strengthen Western defenses under U.S. leadership. Discontent with nuclear weapons may lead to a strengthening of conventional defenses. However, awareness of the vulnerabilities of industrialized societies and unwillingness to pay the cost of conventional weapons may also result in a desire for "inflexible response," as in France. Finally, there are signs of neutralism and anti-militarism, not only for the radical left (where the Pacifist-Socialists may benefit from the support for NATO by all major parties), but also among a substantial part of adherents to the Social Democratic party.

It is not necessarily true that this diffuse picture limits politicians in defining security policies. In recent years, they have used populist arguments to give their parties a specific profile in nuclear policy. Although the major request of the peace movement was a "renationalization" of security policy, Dutch security has in fact been incapacitated by the veto power of two influential groupings (the pro-NATO lobby and the anti-nuclear movement). Below the surface, however, the consensus may still be largely intact on the following elements :

- NATO membership
- A more influential European voice
- Deemphasizing the role of the battlefield nuclear weapons (even the PvdA is in favor of retaining one nuclear mission)
- Strengthening conventional forward defense
- Preserving detente with the East, but insisting on human rights
- Continuing arms control talks (even though substantial majorities think the Soviets will cheat on arms control agreements)

Summarizing, NATO's policies of deterrence and detente and NATO's strategy of flexible response are still accepted by all major parties. In the future, the question will be whether this consensus will hold together on NATO conventionalization and strategic defense--the issues of the post-Cruise missile era.

NOTES

1. References to results of public opinion polls not cited in the following footnotes can be found in C. J. Vaneker and P. P. Everts, Buitenlandse Politiek in de Nederlandse Publieke Opinie (The Hague : Netherlands Institute of International Relations, 1984).

2. Greater attention to nuclear weapons instead of crime in Dutch politics has been ascribed to the elite character of the missile issue. Cf. O. Schmidt, "Politieke Partijen en Internationale Veiligheid," in Wapens in de Peiling, edited by Jan G. Siccama (The Hague : Staatsuitgeverij, 1984).

3. J. J. C. Voorhoeve, Peace, Profits and Principles: A Study of Dutch Foreign Policy (The Hague : Martinus Nijhoff, 1979) Chapter 6.

4. K. Koch, Sociale Verdediging. Een kritische literatuurbeschouwing (The Hague : Staatsuitgeverij, 1982); A. P. Schmidt, Social Defence and Soviet Military Power : An Inquiry into the Relevance of an Alternative Concept (Leiden : COMT, 1985).

5. J. T. Degenkamp and J. J. A. van Rooyen, "Naar een zelfstandig West-Europees verdedigingssysteem," Nieuw Europa, no. 1 (1983): 9-21.

6. G. van Benthem van den Bergh and Bart Tromp, "De Partij van de arbeid en defensie uitgangspunten voor een Nederlands veiligheidsbeleid," Socialisme en Democratie, no. 9 (1983) : 3-15.

7. B. J. T. ter Veer, chairman of IKV at the time, has written "IKV and Western Europe," in Europese Integratie en Atlantisch Bondgenootschap (The Hague : Europese Beweging Nederland, 1982), pp. 81-89.

8. H. Vredeling, "Voor en tegen van een Europese kernmacht," in Europese Integratie, pp. 38-39.

9. The idea of "defensive deterrence" has been initiated by the late Groningen peace researcher, B. V. A. Röling. For the most elaborate exposé, see E. P. J. Myer, Militaire Veiligheid door Afschrikking; Verdediging en het Geweldverbod in het Handvest van de Verenigde Naties (Deventer : Kluwer, 1980); see also F. Barnaby and E. Boeker, Defensie zonder Kernwapens (Amsterdam : Meulenhoff, 1982).

10. S. Rozemond and J. G. Siccama, Evenwicht van de Kwetsbaarheid (The Hague : Netherlands Institute for Questions of Peace and Security, 1982).

11. Published in Atlantisch Perspektief, April 1984, pp. 6-13.

12. Defensienota 1984 (Defense White Paper) (The Hague : Staatsuitgeverij, 1983), p. 213.

13. <u>Vrede en Veiligheid : een nota van de Tweede Kamerfractie van de Partij van de Arbeid</u>, May 1984.

14. J.H. Leurdijk, "De buitenlands-politieke elite en het veiligheidsbeleid van Nederland," in <u>Elite en Buitenlandse Politiek in Nederland</u>, edited by P. R. Baehr et al. (The Hague : Staatsuitgeverij, 1978), p. 37.

8   Belgium: Security Through Intimacy

Steven Dierckx

In discussions on Belgian security policy, it is commonly observed that the country's security situation has to be placed in a European, and, to a lesser extent, a global international context. It thus makes little sense to speak of a specifically "Belgian" security position. This is not at all surprising if one takes into account, as Luc Reychler does , that "Belgium is one of the most interdependent and vulnerable countries of the world."[1]   Economically, this fact is reflected in the export-oriented character of Belgium's economy and its dependency on the supply of energy and raw materials. Militarily, Belgium's security position has to be considered within the framework of NATO and is clearly dependent on the U.S. (nuclear) guarantee. Moreover, a national defense conception, to a great extent, has lost its relevance in the nuclear age by reason of the increasing range and destructiveness of nuclear (and conventional) weaponry, especially for such a small and strategically located country as Belgium. Not only Belgian decision-makers, but the public opinion as well is clearly aware of this regional and global context of Belgium's security situation.

In analyzing elite debates on security issues, one can distinguish between four main lines of thought. A first distinction relates to "separate" versus "common" security approaches. The adherents of the former point of view conceive of security as a predominantly competitive good. Security is seen as a scarce resource of fixed quantity-- the more security "they" have, the less security "we" have. Nations with a different ideology, political regime, and socioeconomic system are considered to be opponents and potential aggressors; they have divergent interests that are mostly incompatible with one's own objectives. Military competition is to a certain degree a valuable means for defending one's own security position, eventually at a cost to other nations. The common security approach departs from different assumptions. Security, being a co-operative good, is seen as a resource of variable quantity; only cooperative measures will significantly enhance the security of both sides. In the nuclear age, all nations are

* This paper is partly based on elite interviews. I am most grateful to all my respondents for their openhearted answers to the questions submitted to them.

considered to be allies in the struggle against war and nuclear holocaust. They are doomed to strive for common advantages by means of arms control and disarmament. Excessive military competition, instead of enhancing one's security, increases the probability of war. The separate and the common security approaches, although both using multidimensional security concepts, tend to stress different dimensions. The former gives special notice to the East-West military balance, while the latter points to the problem of political distrust between East and West and the related arms race dynamic. Common security proponents also place emphasis on economic issues, especially in the North-South context.

Within both lines of thought, additional distinctions have to be made. The separate security approach can be further subdivided into the Atlanticists and the Federalists, as will be specified below. Within the common security school, the moderates, who have a large majority and the radicals, who are a marginal tendency, are represented. Before elaborating on these four viewpoints, it should be stressed that they constitute ideal types which in reality cover several variants. Moreover, some approaches may not fit into one of these types. Nevertheless, this paradigmatic aproach is in my opinion most relevant from an analytic point of view.

The Atlanticist school is mainly to be found among the Liberal parties and among most Christian Democrats. It should be noted that the youth organisations of these parties, while following in essence their parties' point of view, take a more reserved position and are inclined to describe themselves as "critical Atlanticists." The Federalist point of view is strongly represented in the Federalist parties, namely the Front Démocratique des Francophones and, to a lesser extent, the Volksunie, as the latter, being confronted with internal contradictions on security issues, seems to have opted for a low-profile policy on this matter. Although reflected in a more moderate and gradualist position and remaining a minority view, the Federalist standpoint is surprisingly well represented in Belgian military circles.[2] The moderate common security approach is strongly defended by the Flemish Socialists and, although much less pronounced, by their Walloon colleagues. The latter do not seem to consider security questions to be of vital importance. The moderate point of view is also adopted by a large majority of the Belgian peace movement and in particular by Pax Christi.[3] Finally, the radical approach is supported by the Communists and by some smaller peace organizations of the extreme left. It is also well represented in the environmentalist parties.

The remainder of this chapter can be outlined as follows. First, the threat perceptions of the main schools of thought in Belgium with respect to security will be analyzed, externally as well as internally. Second, and along the same lines of demarcation, different security alternatives will be discussed in European and international contexts. In conclusion, some tentative observations with respect to the future of Belgian security will be presented.

THREAT PERCEPTIONS AND GOVERNMENT POLICY

The Separate Security Approach

As far as threat perceptions are concerned, the Atlanticists and the Federalists take a similar point of view, except for their opinion of the United States' objectives and intentions with regard to Western Europe. They consider the most important external threat to originate from the Soviet Union, which is perceived as an expansionistic but opportunistic actor--while the Soviet leaders are ideologically motivated by imperialistic objectives, their foreign policy behavior is dominated by realistic political considerations. As the expected gains of military aggression do not at this moment outweigh the estimated costs for the Soviet Union, war is deemed very improbable by the separate security adherents. Nevertheless, there is a serious danger of Finlandization, as the Soviet leaders try to attain their objectives not through military aggression, but through political intimidation. It should be added that some "critical" Atlanticists consider the Soviet threat to be partly dependent on the extent of internal stability and economic reform.

The proponents of the separate security approach are strongly concerned with the increasing military imbalance in favor of the East, especially in the European theater, a concern that is closely related to their perception of the Soviet threat.

The Federalists and, to a lesser extent, some Atlanticists point to the danger of a politically divided Western Europe. Both agree that this dissension threatens Europe's power to resist the political influence of the Soviet Union, and may lead to a definite technological inferiority to the United States and Japan. However, the Federalists go much further in their analysis. They see the military dependency of Western Europe on the "unreliable" U.S. nuclear guarantee as threatening to European security. They consider the United States to be not a close friend (as do the Atlanticists) but rather an unreliable ally; while having some basic democratic values in common with Western Europe, the United States is a superpower with worldwide responsibilities and with divergent interests or at least different priorities. In the final analysis, it is unwise to remain dependent for one's security on the goodwill of other states that are primarily driven by their own interests. Western Europe is clearly unable to significantly influence U.S. foreign policy because he who pays the piper calls the tune, with all its consequences in case of a serious conflict with the Soviet Union.

In contrast with the Federalists, the Atlanticists consider the potential dissolution of Atlantic solidarity to be most threatening. They also point to the vulnerability of a democratic alliance such as NATO.

In addition to the actual external threats, both lines of thought refer to some potential long-term threats. In a North-South context, economic disequilibrium and, especially, the burden of debts of Third World countries could increase the political instability of these nations and potentially lead to violent outbursts. This is a threatening factor for Belgian security, as this country is highly dependent on the supply of energy and raw materials from the Third World. This potential threat is particularly stressed by the younger generation. Moreover, some Atlanticists and Federalists point to the recent evolution in international terrorism and to the danger of a spreading Islamic revival.

On a domestic level, the Atlanticists and the Federalists have similar threat perceptions. First, as far as actual threats are concerned, both lines of thought refer to the lack of internal consensus with respect to security policy, and to terrorist attacks and banditry to which Belgium increasingly fell victim during recent years (i.e., the "Combatting Communist Cells" and "the gang of Nijvel"). Some adherents of separate security regret the "growing indifference and lack of defensive preparedness" in public opinion, especially in the peace movement. Pacifist tendencies, defending "distorted analyses" on security questions, are considered to be dangerous, although they have the merit of "democratizing" public debate in this matter. According to proponents of separate security, there is an increasing trend of "banalization" in public discussions as a consequence of the gap between emotional concerns and objective information with respect to security issues. Further, spreading terrorist activities and the banditry are seen as a conscious attempt at destabilizing Belgian parliamentary democracy.

Among potential internal threats are mentioned, first of all, the high level of unemployment, especially among young people, which tends to decrease the legitimacy of the Belgian democratic system, and second, to a lesser extent, the problem of foreign workers.[4]

According to the Atlanticists, the government's policy, supporting the famous defense-detente tandem of the Harmel doctrine, is satisfactory, at least in a foreign policy context. While all of the Federalists critical of governmental policy, they differ in the degree to which they reject this policy. Some say hardly a good word for the government, while others plead extenuating circumstances, as they point to the government's endeavors to further European integration and invoke the limited margin for maneuvering of a small and dependent country in international politics. On a domestic level, most Atlanticists and the Federalists consider the government's position to be too defensive and deplore the lack of a serious and consistent information policy.

The Common Security Approach

The moderate and radical tendencies within the common security approach have mostly comparable threat perceptions, but, as the terms imply, the radicals are more "radical" than the moderates. The external threats are almost identically appreciated by both lines of thought. First of all, there are two crucial and interdependent threats to Belgian and European security, namely the arms race and the political distrust between East and West. The arms race is considered to be a threat in itself, first because it is politically destabilizing and thus makes war more possible, and second because the continuing weapons escalation enhances the probability of accidental war. Moreover, in the long run, the arms race will become too expensive and is thus economically destabilizing. Last, the common security adherents stress the inner dynamic of the arms race and the ungovernability of the process. Closely related to the arms race is the total lack of political understanding between East and West, as the proponents of common security argue. This problem of political distrust is, in turn, connected with the bipolar power structure in the international system, whereby Western Europe may end up completely at the mercy of the two superpowers. Western Europe is not only a nuclear hostage of the Soviet Union, but is also a military (and secondary) pawn on the U.S. chess-board. According to the defenders of common security, the greatest threat for Western Europe thus lies in the risk of becoming the theater for a global (nuclear) war between the superpowers, which Europe itself will not have willed.

In contrast with the proponents of separate security, the common security adherents hardly refer to the Soviet Union as a political threat, nor do they perceive a military threat emanating from the East. The alleged expansionist tendencies in the Soviet foreign policy are justified as a reaction to the Western threat, which is reflected in a supposed military build-up without precedent at the Soviets' Western border. There is a frequent reference to the "encirclement complex" of the Soviet Union, which has therefore taken precautions by forming a girdle of buffer states at its Western border. In fact, since 1945 the Soviet leaders have mainly been inspired by their own security needs, as has the United States. Most defenders of common security therefore see (almost) no moral difference in the foreign policy behavior of the two superpowers.

Insofar as one can speak of superpower "threats" to Belgian and European security, according to the radicals, the U.S. foreign policy is an even more real "threat" than the Soviet one, as the United States maintains troops in the Federal Republic of Germany, installs nuclear weapons on European territory and forms a dominant factor in the NATO decision-making process.

It is also remarkable that the common security adherents consider the East-West military balance to be of secondary importance in this context. Security is, in their opinion, first of all a political problem that has to be tackled by diplomatic means, while the military discussion only forms a technical aspect of minor importance. Moreover, according to the proponents of common security, there is no reason to be concerned with the present military balance in the European theater.

In the North-South context, common security adherents perceive above all potential long-term threats (i.e., Belgium's dependency on the supply of energy and raw materials) but simultaneously contend that, from a moral point of view, this dimension constitutes greater "challenges" than the East-West framework. In their opinion, one should not primarily reduce a European security analysis to the East-West relationship, because of the growing interdependence between the North-South and the East-West axes. Also mentioned are the increasing problems concerning ecological equilibrium in the world.

On a domestic level, the persistent unemployment problem, especially among the youth, is in the opinion of the defenders of common security the number one threat, insofar as the continuing lack of an adequate government response tends to decrease the legitimacy of the Belgian democratic system. The common security adherents mention as a second threat the terrorist activities, while simultaneously pointing to the danger of overly repressive reactions by the authorities. In contrast to the proponents of separate security, they evaluate the lack of internal consensus with respect to security policy not as a negative but as a positive evolution, because the public increasingly questions the policy assumptions, which have too long been considered as self-evident. Moreover, they warn the government against ignoring the demonstrated will of the "majority" of the population, as was the case, in their opinion, with the NATO double-track decision. The radicals think of the "undemocratic" government policy, not only with respect to security issues, but also in social-economic and other domains as one of the greatest threats to Belgian security. A potential long-term threat mentioned by proponents of common security is the foreign workers problem.

From the analysis above, it follows that Belgian security policy, especially in recent years, is not valued highly among common security adherents: in their opinion, political distrust between East and West has increased while the arms race remains uninhibited. More particularly, according to the common security school, the government only pays lip service to the Harmel doctrine by stressing the need of a stronger defense at the cost of the promotion of detente. Frequently, a straight comparison is drawn between the "autonomous, daring policy" of former Foreign Minister Pierre Harmel in the 1960s and the "excessive Atlantic amenability" of the present Foreign Minister Leo Tindemans. However, Harmel himself is not at all flattered with this kind of comparison and insists that the 1960s and the last decade (from 1974 to the present) cannot be compared. In a recent lecture he notes that "the present foreign policy of a country of our size is dependent on so many incertitudes and on such a vast sphere of influence that it cannot be compared to that of more open years. The governors have to take into account data which have become complex."[5] While pointing to the present lack of historical perspective, Harmel thinks that several factors may contribute to this "new critical phase," marked by a "universalization" of problems : the monetary instability since 1971, the economic crisis and the energy problems since 1973, the diminished ideological impact of the superpowers in the Third World and the related rise of the nonaligned movement, the rather unsuccessful interventions of the superpowers in regional conflicts, the ineffective attempts at significantly constraining the arms race, and finally, the continuing shift of the demographic focal point to the South.[6]

PRESCRIPTIONS : SECURITY ALTERNATIVES

The Separate Security Approach

Since they are opposed to any major changes in Belgian security policy, the Atlanticists strongly argue for preserving Atlantic solidarity as the cornerstone of Belgium's (and Europe's) security guarantee. They point to the fact that the small power was invaded at the beginning of both world wars, despite its explicit neutrality. From this experience, the Atlanticists have derived the lasting historical lesson that military independece and neutrality do not equal security. Therefore, as a result of a conscious choice made after the World War II, Belgium has sought durable security guarantees through its integration into larger alliances and, especially, through an intimate alignment with the United States in the context of NATO.[7]

The Atlanticists conceive of an autonomous European defense, decoupled from or only loosely associated with the United States, as undesirable for the following reasons. First, there remains a serious risk in decoupling Europe's security from the U.S. guarantee because of the Soviet geopolitical dominance on the Eurasian landmass; the price Europe would have to pay for its regained "independence" would probably be political blackmail by the Soviet Union, with the eventual risk of Finlandization. Second, after the withdrawal of the U.S. conventional and nuclear security guarantees, the European members of NATO would inevitably have to significantly upgrade their conventional and nuclear capabilities, thereby severely enhancing the financial defense burden on their reluctant citizens. Third, and very important from a Belgian point of view, one can wonder whether the small powers, trying to prevent the U.S. ally from monopolizing the NATO decision-making process, will not become confronted with extremely nationalistic behavior from their major partners within a purely European defense entity. By the same line of reasoning, taking into account the limited results of European integration, the Atlanticists refuse to barter the U.S. security guarantee for a fragile European security framework. Against a European nuclear force to which they are strongly opposed, the Atlanticists argue first that this would have a destabilizing impact on the world power structure and, in particular, on the East-West strategic relationship. Second, there is the problem of nuclear decision-making and especially of the German fingers on the nuclear button; the Soviets would not be at all pleased with the Federal Republic of Germany sharing a decision authority with other European countries on the use of nuclear weapons, not to mention the fact that Germany itself does not seem to desire such an authority.

While thus defending Atlantic solidarity, the Atlanticists are also in favor of strengthening the European voice within the Atlantic Alliance. The European and Atlantic security options are seen as totally compatible by a majority of the Atlanticists. Henri Simonet, former Minister of Foreign Affairs, conveys this standpoint when he states that the formation of a European pillar within NATO "would strengthen the Alliance, because it would provide more political equilibrium in West-West relations. One can easily see how naturally the Alliance could rest on these two main pillars."[8] One should add immediately that, on one hand, some "conservative" Atlanticists are skeptical about a two-pillar Alliance, as such a construction would in their view endanger the cohesion of NATO, which is currently led by one dominant power. On the other hand, some "critical" Atlanticists doubt the effectiveness of a European pillar as a means of articulating specifically European security interests.

As an alternative to Europe's current dependency on the U.S. security guarantee, the Federalists opt for the creation of a European defense community as a long-term objective. Some Federalists, especially the moderates, argue in favor of maintaining a close but redefined security relationship with the United States. In their conception, a limited nuclear force, under exclusively European control as the ultimate step in the shaping of a Defense Community, would have to remain predominantly tactical in nature and support primarily the air-ground maneuvers on the battlefield. Such a European nuclear force would operate in close conjunction with the U.S. strategic nuclear force, which is seen for the foreseeable future as a necessary security guarantee against the Soviet Union.[9] More radical Federalists tend to defend the creation of a neutral Europe, which would not take the part of one or the other side in the conflict between the superpowers. In their point of view, a limited European nuclear force can be credible enough on its own, if appropriate measures are taken to decrease its vulnerability. However, even the radical Federalists think that Europe will always remain closer to the United States than to the Soviet Union, because of common democratic core values.

While thus proposing the creation of a (more or less) autonomous European defense system as a security alternative, the Federalists are clearly aware of the enormous obstacles to such a system. These problems are most salient for the creation of a European nuclear force, especially in its radical conception. A first problem is how to control such a deterrent and how to decide on its possible use. It seems that a viable nuclear control structure can be set up only after the installation of an integrated European political decision authority. Related to the problem of nuclear decision-making are the role and intentions of the major European powers. To begin with, France should play a stimulating role in an autonomous European defense construction. However, it seems not at all prepared to give up its national force de frappe for the sake of a European deterrent. Second as Britain is an autonomous component with nuclear capabilities, it would also be one of the leading actors. This observation is not without difficulties as British public opinion is adverse to any kind of far-reaching European integration. Moreover, London would probably make its participation in a European deterrent subject to the condition that a close security relationship with the United States be maintained. Third, as for the already mentioned ticklish affair of the German finger on the nuclear button, the Federal Republic itself does not seem keen on acquiring nuclear decision power, fearing to destabilize the precarious balance between its NATO loyalty and its good neighbor policy with the East. In fact, the Soviet Union is strongly opposed to a European autonomous deterrent, especially a German nuclear decision authority. However, the Federalists raise the argument that the creation of a European nuclear force should not be interpreted by the Soviets as a militaristic position : a mainly self-reliant Europe means that it can only have defensive aspirations. A divided Europe, on the contrary, as a pawn on the U.S. chess-board, is a potential factor of war and could become involved in a superpower conflict through its security alliance with the United States. According to the Federalists, the U.S. political leaders themselves will probably not be flattered with a European defense community. Nevertheless, the security relationship between the Atlantic partners should be profoundly redefined in reciprocal, permanent and open-minded consultations. Also frequently mentioned is the danger of questioning the non-proliferation regime, as the European nonnuclear NATO members are parties to the NPT treaty of 1968. Further, while recognizing the financial repercussions of a European defense system, especially for the conventional arms, the Federalists at the same time point to the fact that the integration of national defense efforts would significantly enhance the rationalization of military output.

In the final analysis, advanced European political integration, which is currently not attainable because of prevailing nationalistic tendencies, is a necessary condition for the long-term objective of a European defense community. However, some first steps toward military integration in conventional arms, not requiring close political integration, can already be taken in the short term. For instance, such steps are suggested by General P. Cremer (Ret.) in his plan for a European Defense Union (linked in his conception to the U.S. strategic nuclear guarantee). Those measures respectively include : (1) the exchange among European NATO members, especially in Central Europe, of troops for time-limited exercises and maneuvers, and the related standardization of command procedures; (2) the respective and progressive standardization of weapons and logistics, of military organization and of tactics; (3) the gradual shaping of specifically European command structures.[10] Cremer notes that the dynamics of military integration could spill over to the political domain and vice versa.

As for the idea of a demilitarized, denuclearized, or chemical weapon-free zone in Central Europe, both the Atlanticists and the Federalists mention the following counterarguments : (1) East-West geographical asymmetry; (2) the increasing range of conventional and nuclear weapons; (3) the unsolvable problem of verification, which has two aspects : first, the issue of "pre-conflict verification" (how to control effectively the removal of certain weapon categories or systems from the "forbidden" zone without far-reaching verification procedures); second, the question of "in-conflict verification" (the Soviets' compliance during an eventual conflict can only be checked post factum, that is after a serious crisis has occurred). The separate security adherents do not consider nonviolent strategies to be a viable alternative for military defense.

The proponents of separate security consider the influence of small powers in international relations to be marginal. Small countries are heavily dependent on the state of superpower relationships. Nevertheless, one should not underestimate the potential role of small powers; precisely because of their limited international influence, these countries have sometimes more room for independent initiatives. "Critical" Atlanticists plead for a more active Belgian detente policy, even if opposed by the United States, while the Federalists strongly reject an "unconditional Atlanticism."

By intensifying bilateral contacts with Eastern European countries, small powers can contribute to a reduction of East-West political tensions. However, one must warn against encouraging excessive expectations. Small countries are not able to change Europe's political map. It is at the moment politically unwise to call into question the Yalta division. Illusions of transcending this division are based on a serious overestimation of the adaptation capacity of the rigid Soviet regime.

The Common Security Approach

Having a radically different security concept and threat perception, the common security adherents logically propose different security alternatives. As a key idea, they plead for the restoration of diplomacy's preeminence over defense policy. Security is first of all a political problem, therefore requiring political solutions, while defense is only the technical, second-order aspect of the matter. Thus the predominant goal of the Belgian security policy is East-West detente, whereby arms control and disarmament is a subordinate, but nevertheless important objective.

In the short and middle term, the proponents of common security advocate more daring arms control and disarmament initiatives in Europe in a bilateral and multilateral context. They repeatedly stress the importance of confidence-building measures as a means of reducing the risk of nuclear war. These proposed measures include : (1) a freeze on military spending, whereby more resources can be allocated to development programs; (2) a mutual East-West nonaggression pact or a pledge not to use nuclear weapons first; (3) a reorganization of both blocs' armed forces into "defensive" structures (e.g., by removing all "offensive" weapons in a 150-kilometer zone on both sides of the Iron Curtain; (4) the establishment of demilitarized, denuclearized, or chemical-weapon-free zones in Central Europe (e.g., the Belgian De Smaele project for a security zone in Europe).[11] The latter proposal seems to be a preoccupation of common security adherents in Belgium. It is said that such security zones will significantly enhance the consultation and decision time for the responsible governments, thereby promoting escalation control. This would especially be the case with respect to nuclear and chemical battlefield weapons, as these would be used first to escalate a war above the conventional level. The reintroduction of these weapons into the "forbidden" zone by one party in times of crisis would clearly constitute an important warning signal to the other side. In addition, defenders of security zones argue that the creation of such areas will contribute to confidence-building and detente between East and West, thereby making room for more far-reaching disarmament initiatives.[12] The plea for confidence-building measures by proponents of common security is consistent with the desire to continue the Helsinki process. In this connection, they also support the maintenance and extension of economic, social, and cultural contacts between East and West in order to build interdependencies between the two power blocs.

Referring to the INF issue, the common security adherents plead for unilateral steps to reciprocal disarmament. The radicals would even go further and promote complete, unilateral nuclear disarmament, if necessary, to stop the arms race.

At the moment, the moderate proponents of common security do not want

Belgium to withdraw from NATO. However, some moderates suggest reducing gradually the U.S. presence in Europe in order to loosen the assymmetrical security relationship between the Atlantic partners and to prepare the dissolution of the military alliances, both in East and West, as a long-term objective. On the other hand, some radicals demand that Belgium leave NATO or at least its military structure in the short run, thereby making an important symbolic act and striving for a neutral Europe.

This brings us to the conception of European security toward which most common security adherents aim in the long run. In the first instance, a European Union should be formed by the former European NATO members. This union should develop a common foreign policy, especially with respect to security matters, and dispose of closely integrated, but exclusively conventional forces, both goals implying an advanced stage of political integration. It is repeatedly stressed that Europe should not become a "third superpower" and should in any case renounce the possession of nuclear weapons, mainly for the following reasons. First, these weapons are morally reprehensible as a means of defense, by reason of their enormous destructiveness, while also maintaining the vicious circle of nuclear deterrence logic. Second, a European nuclear defense posture could be interpreted by the Soviets as a provocative stance and as a new threat to their security. Finally, there is the already mentioned risk of endangering the existing non-proliferation regime.

Instead of going nuclear, Europe should take its own line by developing an autonomous security policy, dependent neither on the United States nor on the Soviet Union. At the same time, however, Europe should seriously engage in a good neighbor policy with regard to both superpowers. Defenders of common security think (or hope) that initial intermediate changes within the Atlantic Community will spill over into Eastern Europe and will gradually produce similar effects. In the very long run, as a result of many progressive and pragmatic steps, a Pan-European Security Community should reciprocally be created "out of the facts." In the end, this new European construction would imply the dissolution of NATO and the Warsaw Pact, and the abolition of the longstanding Yalta division.

In this connection, proponents of common security point to "significant evolutions" in Eastern Europe as a result of Gorbachev's rise to power. Ideologically speaking, Eastern Europe is no longer a monolithic bloc, and a limited margin of maneuver has emerged for "change-minded" tendencies. According to common security adherents, Gorbachev's politique d'ouverture toward the West offers serious opportunities for a new era of detente, if Western Europe (and the United States) behave prudently.

Some moderate advocates of common security are rather skeptical about the feasibility of a Pan-European Security Community. They guard against prematurely designating Gorbachev's new style as "significant" and doubt the possibility of fundamental changes in Eastern Europe. Therefore, they also think of the dissolution of the military power blocs in East and West as being rather illusory. Finally, these moderates consider it necessary for the foreseeable future to maintain a preferential security relationship with the United States.

Common security adherents also stress the need to develop a close and symmetrical relationship between Europe and Third World countries, thereby giving special attention to the North-South context. Indeed, because of its colonial past, Europe has a historical responsibility in this respect. Moreover, it should be aware of the high expectations of developing countries vis-à-vis the former mother countries.

A most important difference between the moderates and the radicals within the common security approach concerns their respective views on the role of nonviolent alternatives in a future European defense posture. The moderates, on one hand, consider such strategies to be a valuable complement to conventional defense. The radicals, on the other hand, tend to see nonviolent alternatives as a viable substitute to traditional defense, at least in the long run. Both tendencies, at the same time, point to the lack of thorough research into the possibilities and constraints of nonviolent defense alternatives. Increased theoretical research efforts as well as practical applications on a limited scale (e.g., in internal conflicts) should therefore be encouraged.

The advocates of common security state that small countries can put a greater stamp on East-West relations. This is especially the case for Belgium; its strategic importance and its tradition of loyalty to NATO leave room for more daring bilateral initiatives toward its Eastern European counterparts, in the spirit of the Harmel doctrine. In this way, Belgium could fulfill the function of go-between in the East-West context, thereby making concrete contributions to the search for a new detente model. Admitting that the present lack of consensus with respect to security issues as well as the unfavorable superpower relationship (at least as of November 1985) created additional obstacles, Rik Coolsaet argues that "detente might (and should) adopt a more specifically European outlook, different from the earlier detente (of the Harmel period) which was actually a delegated policy, authorized by both Washington and Moscow" (emphasis in original) [13] In other words, autonomous detente initiatives by countries like Belgium need not and should no longer be made dependent on the state of the superpower relationship. In the short run, some proponents of common security also plead that Belgium would adopt the status of nonnuclear NATO members like Denmark and Norway by questioning its nuclear tasks within the Atlantic Alliance. A few of them make the transition to a nonnuclear status subject to the condition that, in the short term, no significant results are reached in East-West arms control negotiations.

SOME TENTATIVE CONCLUSIONS

Thinking about the future of different international policy domains is traditionally relevant because, as Dougherty and Pfaltzgraff indicate, "change must be anticipated if it is to be moderated for beneficial purposes."[14] It is perhaps even more important nowadays "as the lead-time for policy planning, the complexity of issues facing policymakers, and the urgency of problems have increased."[15] On the other hand, considering the present state of the social sciences, one has to make use largely of intuitive straight-line extrapolations based on a careful analysis of present trends. Such extrapolations are inherently inadequate as new trends that are now yet perceptible can become crucial in the future, and vice versa.[16] Therefore, one should always be cautious with speculations about future developments. This is not least the case for this study of future security trends in Belgium.

An important variable determining future developments is the interaction between public and elite consensus on security issues, and their respective impacts on defense policy. It is now a popular view in Belgian political and academic circles that the defense decision-making process has been democratized as a result of the INF experience. It is argued that the rise of the "new" peace movements in Europe and the related large-scale demonstrations against the Cruise missiles and the Pershing IIs have fundamentally changed the defense decision-making process. As the longstanding consensus in this field breaks down, according to the democratization theory, decisions will no longer be the exclusive privilege of a small and impenetrable elite pulling the strings. Public opinion will have become an important factor in the decision-making process.[17]

As far as Belgium (and, to an even greater extent, the Netherlands) is concerned, it is clear to this writer, that, to a certain degree, public opposition to the missiles has influenced the governments' policy. More particularly, both countries' governments postponed the decision as long as possible. Analyzing the INF case, one cannot escape the conclusion that a majority of Belgians were opposed in principle to the installation of Cruise missiles in their country. Evidence from different opinion polls reveals a relative or absolute majority of negative answers on unconditional questions such as "Do you favor or oppose new missiles on your soil?"[18] However, deducing from the INF case that security policy has been democratized seems to be a too far-reaching conclusion.

To begin with, the influence of the Belgian and Dutch peace movements on their countries' INF policies has remained limited, since the installation of Cruise missiles (at first limited to sixteen in Belgium) has finally been approved by the respective Parliaments. In a long-run perspective, more fundamental counterarguments emerge.

First, several pieces of evidence indicate that security issues remain a distinct minority concern in public opinion. For one thing, with the installation now a fait accompli, the peace movements seem unable to keep up a permanent mass movement challenging the basic premises of traditional defense policy.[19] In the Low Countries, this is partly the result of their fixation on nuclear weapons and, more particularly, on sheer numbers, since, simplistically stated, one of their fundamental assumptions is that more weapons equal more insecurity. In the public debate, the one-sided overemphasis on the INF issue has brought about a neglect of or a wrong approach to other, more important issues in security policy such as the political and military-strategic aspects of conventional defense and of the Strategic Defense Initiative, and more particularly their impact on the future of European security; the burden-sharing syndrome and the growing tensions in West-West relations; and threats to the political and military-strategic stability of the East-West relationship.[20]

Second, the peace movements failed to influence significantly the voting behavior of the general public in recent elections. In the Belgian case, a DIMARSO poll carried out by request of the Division of Political Sociology (Catholic University of Leuven) reveals that the intensity with which Belgians hold opinions on the INF issue is relatively low. On the question whether the Cruise missile installation would exert "much, little or no influence" on their voting behavior in the parliamentary elections of 1985 almost two out of three Belgians (63.8 percent) answered that this issue would have no or marginal influence. Only 22.5 percent considered the same impact to be high, while 13.6 percent didn't know. The INF issue thus comes far behind the top three economic issues, to with unemployment, level of taxes, and decrease of purchasing power. Its perceived impact is roughly comparable to that of hunger in the world or of linguistic community issues such as the federalization of education.[21]

These results clearly reflect the remaining low saliency of security issues in public opinion. There is another piece of evidence pointing in the same direction. Stephen Szabo notes that in 1984 "only 8 to 15 percent (of the Europeans) were interested in or followed international affairs 'very closely,' while "the figure for those with an interest in defense policy was an even lower 5 to 8 percent." These results are comparable to those of 1979.[22] Szabo as well as Flynn and Rattinger arrive at the conclusion that interest in security issues remains the "privilege" of a "small attentive public" which predominantly recruits among the younger, better educated part of the general public. They therefore argue that current defense policy is most intensely challenged by the so-called "successor genreration" and especially by younger citizens with a high-level education (a conclusion with potential long-term political implications). Moreover, the defense critics are situated from the center to the left in the political spectrum.[23]

Besides the argument that security issues remain a minority concern, a second main conclusion emerging from a cross-national comparison calls into question the popular democratization theory. In essence, it states that the amount of public opposition in different European countries is proportional to the degree to which the political parties of the left made an important issue of the nuclear problem, thereby fostering polarization. It can be argued that a "polarization gap" exists between Germany, the United Kingdom, the Netherlands, and (to a lesser extent) Belgium on one hand, and Italy and France on the other.[24] At the same time, the level of fear of war is not consistently different between these two country groups. Successive opinion polls carried out between 1977 and 1983 by the European Community even indicate that, in this respect, France took the lead in April 1980 and in October 1983. Moreover, Eurobarometer research reveals that fear of war and support for the peace movement are negatively correlated (R = -.422).[25]

If the hypothesis of a polarization gap is correct and considering the above-mentioned poll results, it can be argued, as Josef Joffe does, that "in the grand antinuclear drama of the 1980s, party was more important than populism, the 'top' more important than the 'bottom'.[26]

These arguments tend to support the politicization theory, the counterpart of the democratization approach. In contrast to the latter, the former argues that the INF issue has led to a breakdown of elite consensus on security, thereby fostering confusion among public opinion and weakening consensus. According to the politicization theory, "popular consensus is . . . to a great extent a function of political consensus."[27] Because of the continuing low saliency of security issues, the general public is highly sensitive to the influence of the government, the political parties and the media. When the intra-elite struggle is then given a public forum by opposition parties, the split within the elite makes public consensus more fragile.[28]

Considering the pros and cons of both theories, this writer is inclined to support to a large extent the politicization theory. Nevertheless, one should remain cautious with generalizations about the elite-mass influence relationship. A detailed study of Oldendick and Bardes concerning U.S. mass and elite foreign policy opinions reveals that "there is virtually no evidence that elites such as those interviewed for the [Chicago Council on Foreign Relations] studies have any influence over mass opinions." It questions "the conception of elites as agents for transmitting positions to the electorate."[29] The interaction between elite and mass opinions might well be highly specific and depend on a whole set of intervening variables (such as the nature of an issue, the political culture of a country, the amount of or lack of consensus within elite and public opinions concerning the issue involved, the amount of organization of public opinion in a specific policy domain, or the degree to which the elite effectively translates public concerns into decision-making).

A second variable shaping future security trends is the nature of elite and public consensus. As far as the general public is concerned, consensus has weakened, but not broken down. The focus of public opposition against traditional defense policy during recent years was the rejection of nuclear weapons and, to a certain extent, NATO's nuclear strategy. Besides natural fears about enormously destructive weapons, especially when confronted with the reality of deterrence on the occasion of the missiles' installation on one's own soil, the key factor in popular resentment against nuclear weapons seems to be a significant drop in confidence in U.S. leadership as a result of a changed perception of the United States by many Europeans. Both superpowers are increasingly seen as similar insofar as foreign policy behavior is concerned.[30] This crisis of confidence is clearly reflected in Belgian perceptions of the Atlantic partner. In 1982 only 44.7 percent of the Belgians were said to have "a great deal" or "fair amount" of confidence in the United States' ability "to deal wisely with world problems."[30] However, the core of Belgian defense policy, symbolized in the Atlantic Alliance, is not challenged by most Belgians. In a DIMARSO opinion poll, carried out between February 22 and March 18, 1985, at the request of the Center for Peace Research (Catholic University of Leuven), about 2,000 Belgians were asked if they "considered NATO to be necessary for Belgian security." Almost two out of three respondents (64 percent) answered positively, while 18 percent were negative and an equal amount had no opinion.[32] In a nutshell, one can say that, in spite of vociferous opposition against the INF missiles, the basis of Belgian defense policy remains widely supported in public opinion.

In contrast, elite consensus has clearly broken down into two fundamentally different approaches, reflected in contrasting security concepts ("separate" versus "common") and thus in diverging threat assessments and security alternatives. Despite this split in elite consensus, the Atlanticist school remains very well represented on the decision-making level , especially in the Foreign Affairs and Defense Ministry bureaucracies. One can expect the Atlanticists not to give up their approach as long as no "viable" and "equally cost-effective" alternatives are formulated. One can discuss the long-term desirability of a security policy dependent to a great measure on the U.S. (nuclear) guarantee of which the credibility can be doubted, but, according to this writer, one cannot deny that the present policy is a relatively cost-effective option in material terms. In 1980 the United States defense spending share in NATO amounted to 53 percent.[33] If the link between European and U.S. defense is significantly loosened or cut, this would have serious financial implications. The creation of a European (strategic or tactical) nuclear force and a serious upgrading of European conventional capabilities would then seem inevitable from a credibility standpoint. At present, there is an increasing military imbalance on the European front in favor of the East, especially in conventional forces. As for European theater nuclear capabilities, the Warsaw Pact is far ahead in the overall number of missile launchers and warheads, and of nuclear-capable aircraft, while NATO has a slight advantage in the number of nuclear-capable artillery.[34]

Trying to assess other proposed security alternatives, one should keep in mind the following general observations. The Federalist option, while theoretically attractive from a realistic conception of international relations (in which national interests are the driving force of state behavior), has to contend with formidable problems of political and financial feasibility, as most Federalists admit themselves. As for the common security approach, its adherents remain confronted with the problem of translating their idealistic points of view in operational policy concepts: in contrast to their assumptions, the present international system remains semi-anarchic in nature, whereby states are primarily driven by clashing national interests and the use of force is the ultimate resource for conflict settlement. Moreover, Western European countries seem unable to bring about fundamental changes in the rigid Eastern European political system, a necessary condition for the realization of a pan-European security community. However, as the successor generation, largely critical of present defense policy, gradually replaces the older generations and might increasingly support the premises of common security (e.g., by voting for political parties that defend these premises), Atlanticist influence on the decision-making level might weaken in the next decades.[35]

A third variable influencing Belgium's security future is the impact of the external context. To begin with the East-West context, "fragile structures have developed, consisting of power equilibria and of political, economic, military and cultural interdependencies, and setting bounds to the political freedom of maneuver of states."[36] As for the Atlantic framework, Belgium, confronted with a twofold failure of its historic neutrality policy, resolutely engaged in a policy of guaranteeing its security through intimacy with the United States by becoming a member of NATO. In a European context, Belgium became a founding member of the Brussels Pact and of the European Community, thereby actively contributing to "the outbreak of peace" within Western Europe. This integration policy has clearly enhanced Belgian influence on the international scene, in some respects beyond the small power's objective scope. At the same time, however, the Belgian margin of maneuver in foreign policy was severely reduced, as the influence of a small state seems to be closely related to a tradition of loyalty and reliability in the eyes of the international community or alliance of which it forms part. As Herman De Lange notes in the context of NATO, "the foreign policy of states which form part of alliances, is directly influenced, not only by the alliance as a whole, but also by the policies of individual members."[37] In this respect, some members, serving as external reference groups, are more important than others. As Belgium is traditionally a trend-follower rather than a trend-setter in the Atlantic Alliance, one can expect the small power to tune its policy to those of the United States, Germany, France, Britain, and the Netherlands.[38]

A fourth set of intervening variables the impact of which is at the moment unpredictable should be mentioned.[39] First, the composition of successive governments in the years to come may influence future security policy. As the breakdown of elite consensus has clearly limited the governments' room for maneuvering, the participation of political parties that support the common security approach (in particular the Flemish Socialists) might put current defense policy increasingly under pressure. Second, future developments will also be influenced by the nature of emerging issues with which successive governments will be confronted. As Reychler notes, "The key factor will be whether new issues arise that eventually will be perceived as requiring significant new commitments."[40] Third, the terms of public debate on new issues may be relevant. Much depends here on whether the government takes a rather defensive and reactive position, as in the INF case, or engages into a more assertive and leading role in public debate.

All in all, a high degree of continuity may be expected in Belgian security policy for the foreseeable future. In summary, this sense of continuity can be summarized in five lines of force: (1) to prevent a further deterioration of Atlantic solidarity; (2) to strengthen the European pillar within NATO; (3) to strive toward a more cost-effective security policy; (4) to avoid significant new commitments, increasing the material costs or perceived to raise the risks for Belgium; (5) to promote detente and arms control.[41]

A small power was once defined as "a state which recognizes that it cannot obtain security primarily by use of its own capabilities and that it must rely fundamentally on the aid of other states, processes or developments to do so."[42] This "small power consciousness" has been the basic inspiration of the Belgian security policy within the Atlantic framework and will probably remain so.

NOTES

1. Luc Reychler and Jorg Leenaards, "Belgian Defense Policy: A Preliminary Analysis," A.I.B.-Papers, no. 1, (1982) : 13.

2. A new European defense community has been proposed by H. Brugmans, "Geen vrede zonder federalisme," in : Hoe winnen we de vrede? edited by Leo Tindemans et.al. (Leuven : Davidsfonds, 1984), pp. 82-103.

3. See Pax Christi, Voor wereldvrede in veiligheid, vrijheid en rechtvaardigheid (Antwerp: Omega, 1984).

4. According to the Statistical Office of the European Communities, the Belgian unemployment rate amounted to 14.4 percent in 1984 (the European average, evidently not yet including Spain and Portugal, then came to 10.6 percent), while about one of three unemployed (36.9 percent) was younger than 25.

5. Quoted from an unpublished manuscript submitted to the author by Mr. Harmel.

6. Ibid.

7. The term "intimate" is borrowed from Josef Joffe, "The 'Scandilux' Connection : Belgium, Denmark, the Netherlands and Norway in Comparative Perspective," In: NATO's Northern Allies, The National Security Policies of Belgium, Denmark, The Netherlands and Norway, edited by Gregory Flynn (Totowa,NJ : Rowman and Allanheld, 1985), p. 231.

8. Henri Simonet, "La sécurité de la Belgique dans son contexte futur," Contact, no. 56 (1980) : 23.

9. A well-know proponent of such a European defense conception is Gen. P. Cremer (Ret.). See P. Cremer, "Pour une Union européene de défense. 4. L'objectif final : contenu et composantes--conclusions," La Libre Belgique, February 5, 1983, pp. 8-9.

10. See P. Cremer, "Pour une Union européene de défense. 3. L'approche et les jalons préconisés," La Libre Belgique, February 4, 1983, pp. 8-9.

11. See A. De Smaele, Veiligheidszone in Europa, unpublished manuscript (1981), 6 pp.

12. For an outline of these arguments in favor of (denuclearized and) chemical-weapon-free zones, see L. De Smet, Chemische wapens in Europa? (Antwerpen : IPIS, 1985), pp. 33-34. The author also mentions counterarguments.

13. Rik Coolsaet, Once upon a time... Belgian Ostpolitik, unpublished manuscript, 1985, p. 14.

14. James Dougherty and Robert Pfaltzgraff, Contending Theories of International Relations. (New York : Harper & Row, 1981), p. 564.

15. Ibid., p. 565.

16. Ibid., p. 565-566.

17. Stephen Szabo, "European Opinion After the Missiles," Survival, 27, no. 6 (1985) : 265.

18. For evidence from different opinion polls, see : "Euromissiles : les Belges disent oui à Reagan," L'Evénement, December 3, 1981, pp. 4-6; "Meeste Belgen tegen raketten," De Standaard, October 27, 1981, p. 1; "Panorama's grote raketten-enquête," Panorama, September 20, 1983, p. 31; "Raketten," De Standaard, September 20, 1984, p. 2; Luc Reychler, "Belgische Defensie in de peiling," Cahiers van het Centrum voor Vredesonderzoek 11 (1983) : 3.

19. Josef Joffe, "The Scandilux Connection", p. 246.

20. See Herman De Lange, "De buitenlandse en de defensiepolitiek van het kabinet-Lubbers," Civis Mundi, 25, no. 1 (1985) : 35.

21. I am grateful to Prof. W. Dewachter for allowing me to have access to unpublished DIMARSO poll results.

22. Stephen Szabo, "European Opinion", p. 266.

23. Gregory Flynn and Hans Rattinger, eds., The Public and Atlantic Defense (Totowa,NJ : Rowman and Allanheld, 1984) pp. 377-79.

24. Josef Joffe, "The Scandilux Connection", p. 246.

25. Eurobarometer 20, (1983) : 18-19.

26. Josef Joffe, "The Scandilux Connection", p. 247.

27. Gregory Flynn, "Public Opinion and Atlantic Defense," NATO Review 31, no.5 (1983): 7.

28. Stephen Szabo, "European Opinion," pp. 265-66; Josef Joffe, "The Scandilux Connection," p. 246.

29. R. Oldendick and B. Bardes, "Mass and Elite Foreign Policy Opinions," Public Opinion Quarterly 46, no. 3 (1982) : 379-80.

30. Stephen Szabo, "European Opinion," pp. 268-70; Flynn and Rattinger, The Public and Atlantic Defense, pp. 240-41.

31. "Belgen fluiten Amerikanen wel eens uit, maar willen/kunnen ze niet missen," De Standaard, March 8, 1982, p. 6.

32. Luc Reychler, <u>Belgische defensie in de peiling</u>, p. 7; A DIMARSO poll of 1982 seems to confirm these results. It reveals that 42.8 percent of the respondents consider NATO or a Western European defense organization within the Alliance as the best framework for Belgian security in the 1980s. Taking into account that 35.9 percent didn't know or gave no answer, one can argue that two out of three respondents making a choice between the proposed options preferred NATO or Western Europe within NATO as the most appropriate defense structure. (See <u>De Standaard</u>, March 8, 1982, p. 6.)

33. Flynn, <u>NATO's Northern Allies</u>, p. 266.

34. John Collins, <u>U.S.-Soviet Military Balance, 1980-1985</u> (Washington, D.C. : Pergamon-Brassey's, 1985), p. 270.

35. See Szabo, "European Opinion", p. 266.

36. Herman De Lange, "De buitenlandse", p. 32.

37. Ibid., p. 33.

38. Luc Reychler, "The Passive Constrained : Belgian Security Policy in the 1980s," In : Gregory Flynn, NATO's Northern Allies, p. 43.

39. Ibid., pp. 41-42.

40. Ibid., pp. 42.

41. For a description of these lines of force, see Ibid., pp. 43-51.

42. R. Rothstein, <u>Alliances and Small Powers</u> (New York : Columbia University Press, 1968), p. 29.

NATO North

9 Norway: Lingering Lagnaden

Baard Bredrup Knudsen

"Security" and "security policy" are comprehensive and multidimensional concepts. In brief, security policy includes all aspects linked to a nation's efforts to protect its integrity and existence against external threats.[1] Among these efforts are various "domestic" policies as well as policies explicitly directed toward the outside world, plus some areas that are not always considered "political" (e.g., psychological factors). In fact, in a world characterized by "complex interdependence,"[2] the traditional distinction between domestic versus foreign policies has become rather meaningless as most policies have both a domestic and a foreign component.[3] This means that most national policies, especially in a politically and economically integrated region like Europe, have impacts both at home and abroad, and that this mutual exchange of consequences creates uncertainty and aspects of powerlessness[4] for the national actors concerned, dependencies that may be symmetric or assymetric,[5] and, in the latter case, a structural basis for influence or "power" over others.[6]

In this brief evaluation of Norway's position in the context of European security, a comprehensive approach to security as such is not feasible. Therefore, security will be primarily treated as military security limited to an East-West perspective, although the broader political factors linked to foreign policy orientations will be given considerable emphasis as well. Central parameters behind this chapter's approach will be the need for a small nation to reduce uncertainty and to gain larger political control of the decisive factors that provide the general systemic framework within which a small nation's security policy operates. Central in that respect are attempts to modify asymmetric relationships or to obtain guarantees that asymmetries will not be used as a basis for asserting "power," thus forcing Norway to pursue policies or take actions that it considers to be against its own interests, values, or goals. Finally, Norway's particular situation will be treated as a problem of adaptation to transformed European and international realities.

FUNDAMENTAL CONSTRAINTS

In this section, a few major constraints or "realities" that represent salient background factors or parameters with regard to the future will be summarized. This brief review is necessary in order to better understand Norway's foreign and security policies and its position within the European and Atlantic framework of cooperation.[7]

Geography

In the European context, Norway is both a small and a large nation. Norway's mainland (excluding the Arctic islands that are part of Norway) covers a land area about equal in size to West Germany, the Netherlands, and Denmark combined. In fact, in terms of territory Norway is the fourth largest country in Western Europe, after France, Spain and Sweden. The name Norway (the "way to the north") is highly appropriate, considering that the distance from Oslo to Cape North is about the same as from Oslo to Rome in Italy. If one takes the map of Europe and turns it so that the Atlantic Ocean is at the top, and the observer places him/herself in Moscow and looks at the access to the Atlantic Ocean from that vantage point, one will notice that the Norwegian coastline represents almost half of Western Europe's coastline from the Arctic Ocean to the Mediterranean. In that sense, the Baltic divides Western Europe into two halves.

Land area is only one side of the story, though. In terms of nationally controlled ocean areas, Norway is by far number one in Europe, with an economic zone of approximately 2 million square kilometers, a figure nearly equal in size to the surface area of Greenland. Norway's continental shelf, with sedimentary layers that make exploration for petroleum an interesting task, comprises a total of 1.4 million square kilometers. In comparison, the Norwegian sector of the North Sea, which has already made Norway a significant exporter of oil and gas, represents only 142,000 square kilometers of the above figure. Norway, in these respects, is Western Europe's "maritime superpower."

Another geographical feature worth noticing concerns the nature of Norway as such : two-thirds of the land area consists of mountains and mountain plateaus and about 21 percent of forests. Only 3.1 percent of the nation's area is agricultural land. There are approximately 150,000 islands along the coast, with deep and steep fjords cutting into the interior mountain plateaus.

Finally, Norway has over 2,500 kilometers of borders with other countries, with 1,619 kilometers along Sweden, 716 kilometers shared with Finland, and 196 kilometers with the Soviet Union. Norway is the only one of the founding members of NATO with a common border with the Soviet Union.

Demography

From geography to demography, there is a considerable jump. Norway may be equal in size to West Germany, the Netherlands, and Denmark combined, but in terms of population, Norway has only 4.1 million inhabitants as compared with the combined figure for these three nations : of 81 million people. This gives Norway a population density of one-twentieth of the northern part of continental Western Europe--

about 13 inhabitants per square kilometer, the lowest population density in Europe apart from Iceland.

However, the population density within Norway varies considerably, with the main portion of Norwegians living on or close to the sea. The central Oslofjord area accounts for about one-quarter of the total population, while the northernmost county of Finmark (larger in size than countries like the Netherlands, Switzerland, or Denmark) has a total population of less than 80,000 people.

Geopolitical Implications

The simple conclusions drawn from this presentation of Norway's geographic and demographic realities are at least four : (1) close political links between Norway and her alliance partners, and a credible defense of Norway, is vital for the credibility of U.S. power projection across the Atlantic Ocean; (2) Norway, particularly the coastline, is of vital strategic importance for the defense of Western Europe; (3) the combination of a large and strategically vital area with a disproportional small population signifies vulnerability; and (4) since the country, topographically speaking, represents a series of natural barriers against the invasion, it may be effectively defended through contingency planning and reinforcement of sufficiently substantial military assistance from the outside.

NATO Membership

When Norway signed the North Atlantic Treaty in 1949, this represented a fundamental break with its historical policies. Geographically removed from continental Europe with its many turmoils, Norway had enjoyed the political consequences of its relative isolation since the Napoleonic wars. As a modern nation it had gained full national sovereignty only in 1905, when the union with Sweden was dissolved (although Norwegians will immediately point out that the kingdom of Norway was founded over 1,100 years ago, with approximately the same borders as today). After 1905, the lack of foreign policy experience, combined with domestic concerns linked to a rapid industrialization, contributed to a rather isolationist and neutralist foreign policy orientation. Thus, becoming a member of NATO, a political and military "bloc" in post-World War II Europe, represented radical change.

What had happened in the aftermath of World War II was that geographical remoteness was no longer perceived to be a sufficient defense. On the contrary, World War II had demonstrated the strategic significance of Norway's long coastline. Furthermore, Norway's implicit reliance on British sea power since the nineteenth century to prevent any foreign power (read : Russia) from gaining a foothold in Norway had failed in 1940 when Norway was occupied by Germany.[8] Consequently, when the concerns for national security increased with the emerging East-West conflict, the historical pattern presented no feasible alternative.

The answer to the conviction that Norway needed to be linked to a credible collective security system, to obtain security guarantees from the outside and a sufficient deterrent against potential threats to the nation's political sovereignty and territorial integrity, was found in the North Atlantic Treaty. The United Nations could not possibly fulfill that need. In some respects, the United States came to assume the historical British role as a benign naval protector. But now there was a perceived need for explicit guarantees--a commitment that would be considered to be binding, and thus credible, by all parties concerned. In fact, Norway rejected the notion of a separate Scandinavian Defense Union between Denmark, Sweden, and Norway, negotiated in 1948-49. Sweden wanted nonalliance--a Scandinavian version of the Swedish neutral model. The negotiations broke down because the Norwegian and Swedish bottom lines were mutually incompatible. Norway insisted on some kind of link to the West, particularly to Britain and the United States.

Cultural and Historical Roots

As for the most salient cultural and historical roots and determinants, two aspects are particularly important : (1) the generalized accumulation of past experiences, of which so-called historical lessons are the most important, and (2) what we may call "the merger of the people with the land" or the impact of geographic and climatic factors on the people and their general outlook and predispositions.

To evaluate the latter first, the notion of isolationism is quite central. This historical root was a result of geographical remoteness from European power politics. Furthermore, geographical remoteness and the smallness of the population, combined with a comparatively large territory, bred a Norwegian feeling of uniqueness. It all blends in with the impact of the land and its historical past--a hard life and battle for survival, in a country where nature and climate were harsh and food rare; a small and homogeneous population dispersed over a large territory full of natural barriers; a history of free farmers who owned their own land and never knew feudalism; modern industrialization and urbanization, which mainly took place in the twentieth century; the lack of a politically and socially dominant upper class; fairly recent struggle for national independence and sovereignty; strong democratic roots embedded in egalitarian values; and an evangelical Lutheran and pietist religion.

The combination of the two main factors--non-entanglement in power politics and feelings of uniqueness--merged into a feeling of moral superiority and promoted a moralistic approach to international politics, a feature that is in line with a pietist religion as well. In the words of the historian Olav Riste :

> Giving to their neutrality and non-entanglement the credit for a security which both nations owed largely to the shield of British sea power, Americans and Norwegians alike tended to approach the problems of international politics with a feeling of moral superiority. And in Norway's case, our membership in the League of Nations provided the perfect forum for the development of a philosophy which saw the small nation as a paragon of virtue, and European great power politics as the embodiment of evil.[9]

Historical lessons represent another culturally determined prism, as history is interpreted according to, inter alia, a cultural framework and perspective. Most important in this field is probably Norway's experience with unions with other nations.

During the mid-nineteenth century, the heyday of national romanticism (which forms the foundation of Norway's quite exuberant nationalism), the Norwegian counterpart to Lord Byron, Henrik Wergeland, in a well-known poem that most Norwegian children read in school, characterized the union with Denmark as "the four-hundred-year night." During the 91 years of union with Sweden (1814-1905), struggle for popular sovereignty and more democracy merged with the struggle against Sweden, which led to full national independence and sovereignty. There is no wonder that many Norwegians are still skeptical of "entangling alliances," particularly with more powerful partners. Historically, the Norwegians have experienced that "equal partnership" between unequal partners may serve as a means for the stronger to dominate and control the weaker. Note, however, that this same distrust has contributed to Norway's rejection of separate and bilateral arrangements with the Soviet Union.

The second historical lesson with explicit impact on foreign and security policies is what happened to Norway during World War II. A country that is a "natural fortress" (Festung Norwegen as the Germans called it before they surrendered in 1945) was occupied, quite clearly with much higher costs than originally envisaged in Berlin, but still fairly easily. Facing that shock, that humiliation, were a people and their political leaders who had been incredibly ill-prepared, mentally as well as materially. German forces had appeared in several places along the coast in the early hours of April 9, 1940; thus, the most frequent slogan in Norway's post-World War II defense debate has been "Never again a 9th of April!" This slogan, in fact, has been the cornerstone of Norway's politically broad defense consensus since rearmament as a NATO member took place in the early 1950s.

Finally, it should be pointed out that Norway's struggle against Nazism and German occupation during World War II did not imply the same things for the Norwegians as it did for many people in continental Europe. For the Norwegians, the goal was to restore the old status of national independence and integrity, while for significant political segments in continental Western Europe the old system of independent European nation states and a balance of power had become permanently compromised, and a vision of a new and more unified Europe dominated the thinking about the future. In the Norwegian exile government in London, as well as within the resistance movement in Norway, there were no visions of "supra-national" cooperation or a "United States of Europe."

Economics

A few notes should be made regarding economics. It should be pointed out that Norway's "natural" predisposition for pursuing a policy of relative isolationism never could, or did, imply economic isolation. For at least 200 years, Norway has been characterized by an "open" national economy, in the sense that economic transactions abroad represented a significant portion of the nation's economic life and realities. Despite the fact that there has been a steady increase in Norway's exports and imports (in percentage of GDP) during the twentieth century and since 1945 in particular, as early as 1870 the added value of Norway's exports and imports amounted to over half the value of its GDP. In 1984, this indicator was 87 percent.[10] Few nations in the world today have such an open economy.

Furthermore, Norway's historical position as a shipping nation of international importance is demonstrated by the fact that in 1880, Norway's merchant marine was the third largest in the world, after those of Britain and the United States. It peaked in 1968 with 10 percent of the world fleet. In 1984 Norway's fleet was the seventh largest in the world.[11]

The obvious discrepancy between active economic involvement and dependence on international markets and suppliers on the one hand, and the desire to avoid political involvement on the other, is thus a paradox with deep historical roots. When a majority of Norwegians (53 percent) voted against Norwegian membership in the European Community (EC) in 1972, 79.4 percent of Norway's total exports went to Europe, 47.4 percent to EFTA (the "outer Seven"), and 23.8 percent to the EC (the "inner Six"). In 1984, these figures were : 84.5 percent to Europe, 13.3 percent to EFTA, and 69.6 percent to the EC.[12] The tremendously increased figure for Norway's export to the EC reflects both the latter's enlargement to ten member states and Norway's steadily increasing integration with the EC. For all practical purposes (except agriculture), Norway has become an integrated member of a European "common market" or "economic space," without being a member of the EC in the political sense. This is an imbalance to which we will return, as it represents a fundamental source of insecurity, both politically and economically.

NORWAY'S PRESENT SECURITY SITUATION

In this section, the following three aspects of Norway's security situation in the mid-1980s will be discussed : threats (structural uncertainties as well as the perceptions), policy responses (including what happened in the 1970s), and domestic policies (consensus, cleavages, public opinion).

The Threat

Norway's exposed geographical location and its resulting inherent vulnerability make the notion of a specific military threat to Norway a political reality. This, of course, is according to the predominant perceptions of the nation's political establishment, as well as of public opinion which overwhelmingly feels the same way. In many respects, the general military threat to Western Europe that the Soviet Union presents through its extensive military capabilities is the same for Norway as for most other Western European countries. The Western European nations are in the same boat in that there is, and most likely will continue to be, a need to counter the military potential of the Soviet Union on the European continent. If some kind of acceptable balance is not kept, the political and psychological impact of Soviet power is likely to produce political consequences which are highly undesirable from a Western European point of view. At that level of analysis, to discuss the real intensions behind the Soviet military buildup --whether it is "defensive" or "offensive," whether it is purely a reflection of the desire to equal the United States as a superpower, or whether there are underlying or concrete plans for a continued expansion of the Soviet sphere of influence in Europe, if necessary through military means--is of a secondary importance. What the Soviet themselves refer to as the correlation of forces inherently produces its own logic with politically real consequences. Norway faces a problem similar to that of the other

Western European nations, whether NATO members or not. Furthermore, the Norwegian political response to that challenge, since the East-West confrontation emerged in the aftermath of World War II, has been to help secure a military balance in Europe through collective defense and a credible U.S. guarantee. In the final analysis, what has mattered until today is the U.S. nuclear guarantee for the defense of Western Europe, and that a substantial number of U.S. troops stationed in Europe have made this guarantee sufficiently credible. For political and largely moralistic reasons, however, the fact that the defense of Norway in the final analysis has depended on an U.S. willingness to use nuclear weapons has not been a popular topic in Norway's domestic debate.

With the Western European commonalities in mind, there are several elements that make the Norwegian situation somewhat exceptional. Norway is a flank nation that borders directly on the Soviet Union. Since the early 1970s, the Soviet Union has carried out a tremendous naval buildup, with an obvious emphasis on its Northern Fleet. Furthermore, there has been a relative stabilization and reduction of tensions in Central Europe during the same period. However, the continued superpower rivalry and (since the "demise" of the detente of the 1970s) aggravated strategic competition and political confrontation between the two superpowers have steadily moved the Arctic and adjacent waters and land areas into the strategic center. A polar map projection demonstrates the geopolitics behind this development, in which nuclear strategy plays a crucial role. In summary, while there has been a relative reduction of tensions on NATO's central front, the northern flank has experienced an increase in strategic importance and, thus, potential for more tense political relations. The Soviet military buildup in the North, as well as the adjusted U.S. military planning, reflect this reality and may have reinforced it as well.[13]

The response in Norway has been growing concern with regard to Norway's military capabilities and the political desire to preserve a status of low political tension in Nordic Europe. Obviously, Norway increasingly faced a potential conflict between the two main elements of its postwar policy toward the Soviet Union : a credible deterrent in the form of an efficient defense (NATO membership), and reassurance that Norway does not intend to become a "bridgehead" in an offensive strategy directed against the Soviet Union (Norway's base and nuclear policies and some additional confidence-building measures).

Evolution in the Threat

In early 1985, Norway's Headquarters Defense Command released a study of the military strength development in the Soviet Union during the past 20 years, with special emphasis on the areas bordering on the Nordic countries. The study enumerates a considerable quantitative increase, and qualitatively the Soviet equipment has almost reached Western standards.[14]

Although the increase of personnel from 1964 to 1984 in the Leningrad military district was lower than the general increase of Soviet ground forces, the report summarizes changes in Soviet force structure and weapons systems that gave reason for particular concern in Norway. The Norwegian authorities recognize that the main objectives behind the Soviet Union's military buildup in the Kola area are of a global nature (as opposed to regional), but it is quite clear that the area contains forces and weapons systems that realistically speaking have little, if any, utility against nations other than Norway. Of particular concern are, for example, the Soviet amphibious forces, as well as the Spetsnaz units. In addition to the Soviet forces permanently stationed on the Kola Peninsula, the increase in mobility makes it less relevant to focus on the Soviet deployment in peacetime. With 18 airports, the Kola area is capable of receiving major reinforcements on short notice.

It goes beyond the scope of this essay to review the details of the Soviet build up. But among the highlights of direct concern to Norway are increased range and capacity of both Soviet bombers and fighter aircraft; increased capacity in tactical and intermediate missiles (land-based as well as sea-launched); increased airlift capacity, including airborne mechanized troops; and build up to brigade strength of naval infantry. According to Norwegian estimations, however, the Soviet forces in the Kola area would need substantial reinforcements from the southern parts of the Leningrad military district to launch a viable large-scale attack against northern Norway.

The Soviet naval build up deserves separate attention, since the consequences of the significantly increased Soviet naval capacities in the north are particularly important to Norway's general position within the Atlantic framework. First of all, with the introduction of the most modern Delta and Typhoon class submarines, the Soviet union is no longer dependent on the long and vulnerable transit toward the western north Atlantic to be able to reach strategic targets in the United States. Since about two-thirds of the Soviet sea-based strategic deterrent are found in the submarines deployed out of the Murmansk area (about 75 kilometers from the Norwegian-Soviet border), the protection of this area and its adjacent waters are of vital importance to the Soviet Union, if a viable and credible nuclear second-strike capability is to be ensured. The obvious priority given to the Soviet northern fleet's build up of ocean-going and highly modern surface ships probably reflects this vital importance. Thus, the Soviet Union is now capable of carrying out large naval operations in the northeast Atlantic and the Norwegian and Barents seas, as last demonstrated during the summer of 1985 (Summerex-85). The general pattern of these exercises indicates a desire to block out NATO's maritime forces from these ocean areas, which leaves most of Norway behind a forward Soviet defense line which has now been pushed far south.

Norwegian Responses

Norway has responded to this challenge in various ways. Most important is the increased emphasis on prestocking of heavy allied equipment in Norway, as part of a more sophisticated contingency plan. The main objective here is to make it possible for allied reinforcements to be airlifted to Norway on short notice, without having to rely on passage by ship or transporting by ship equipment that could not be airlifted.

During the late 1960s and 1970s, Norway signed a series of agreements with several of its allies (the United States, Britain, West Germany, Canada, the Netherlands) about prestocking of fuel, ammunition, and spare parts at Norwegian airports, naval bases, and other places, to be able to receive and support aircraft and naval units from these allied countries. Most important among these agreements is probably the one for the Canadian Air/Sea Transportable Brigade (which has just been terminated by Ottowa) and the agreement of 1981 between Norway and the United States concerning prestocking of heavy equipment in central Norway (Trondelag) for a U.S. Marine Amphibious Brigade.[15] Norway has also signed a Memorandum of Understanding with the U.S. Air Force (in 1974) on the use of certain Norwegian airports, frequently referred to as the COB Agreement (Collocated Operating Bases). In 1977 this agreement was extended to include aircraft from the U.S. Marine Corps as well.[16]

Behind these agreements is a desire in Norway to preserve the deterrent effect of a credible defense through allied reinforcements (in addition to Norway's own ability to mobilize 300,000 trained men), without having to reevaluate its base policy since 1949. When Norway had decided to become a member of NATO, the then Labor government declared that no foreign (i.e., NATO) troops would be stationed in Norway as long as Norway was not under attack or did not feel exposed to the threat of a military attack. In 1951, this policy had been outlined more explicitly, and it was pointed out that the base policy did not prevent Norway from making bases available in the event of an armed attack on Norway or any other NATO member, or if Norwegian authorities considered themselves under threat of an attack. Furthermore, Norway would prepare for such military reinforcements in peacetime, allowing NATO exercises on its territory.[17] However, in the 1970s, the ability to receive such military reinforcements at the time of crisis or war was seen as severely weakened due to the Soviet military build up. The choice was seen as one between reduced credibility of an early allied defense of Norway, or to open for permanent allied presence, or to make it possible for reinforcements to be airlifted into Norway, with the necessary heavy equipment already in place. Although the Norwegian response to this challenge (emphasis in allied prestocking) aroused some opposition in Norway, the general postwar defense consensus between the Labor party and the nonsocialist parties was capable of ensuring fairly swift political decisions.

In summary, developments since the early 1970s have made Norway more exposed, and the Norwegian response has been attempts to tie the United States more directly to an early defense of Norwegian territory. This is in line with the idea frequently heard in Norwegian politics that Norway is foremost and above all an Atlantic nation which depends primarily upon the U.S. security guarantee, and only secondarily a European nation linked to the other European NATO members through collective self-defense. This notion is well-expressed in the following observation : "that Norway is a country with its back to Europe and facing the Atlantic describes a state of mind as well as a geographical position."[18] In a major parliamentary debate on foreign policy in 1984, this perspective was expressed even more directly : "for Norway NATO is but a multinational framework around an American guarantee."[19] In the early 1980s, however, such "traditional" Atlanticist views have come increasingly under fire from a growing "Europeanist" school of thought, which stresses that politically, culturally, and economically Norway is above all an integrated part of Western Europe, and that a process of Europeanization in the field of security and defense policies--including a trend towards an Atlantic "two-pillar system"--is in Norway's interest as well. This is an aspect to which we will return.

"Europe versus America"?

Increased cooperation between Norway and the United States has been politically justified primarily on purely military grounds, although other factors like memories from the aftermath of World War II and feelings of kinship have played a role as well. A supplementary cause behind this development toward more explicit bilateral cooperation between Norway and the United States, however, was Norway's relative isolation from the mainstream of European politics since 1972. Norway had decided not to join the EC, and the general feeling, once the initial shock in major parts of Norway's political establishments had been overcome, was that the free-trade agreement accommodated Norway's commercial interests in a sufficient way and that there were no major negative political consequences lurking in the immediate future. But without a "European leg" as a support in foreign and, increasingly, security policies (i.e. the evolving pattern of European Political Cooperation (EPC) in the 1970s and early 1980s),[20] Norway had in reality only an "Atlantic leg" on which to lean. Thus, a more explicit dependence on bilateral relations with the United States turned out to have become an implicit and largely unexpected consequence of Norway's 1972 decision. The inherent irony, of course, is that for the anti-EC membership proponents on Norway's political left, Norway's membership in NATO was in 1972 a highly undesirable fact of life that many among them tacitly hoped might be changed once Norway was kept outside of the EC.

A rather brutal awakening in Norway to new political realities in Europe (EPC), as well as to transformed circumstances in U.S.-European relations, occurred when sharp disagreements over policy, and what the media soon called a "crisis" in transatlantic relations, followed the events of 1979-80 (Iran and Afghanistan). As it turned out, the political consequences of the inauguration of Reagan as president of the United States were later to aggravate the situation. In these transatlantic disputes, Norway's political reaction and views were "European" on virtually all issues, a fact that immediately caused problems in the country's relations with Washington. Suddenly there was a growing realization in Norway of an emerging separate European "identity" in the field of foreign policy, demonstrated by common or concerted attitudes and views among the ten EC member states. In this political setting, EPC was "discovered" politically in Norway. The implication for Norway of the close consultation and cooperation among the EC member states on foreign policy as well as on most political aspects of security policy (under circumstances of significant disagreement across the Atlantic Ocean, harsh rhetoric and a hardline turn to the right in Washington, and increasing tensions between East and West in general and Moscow and Washington in particular) made Norway feel exposed, isolated, and alone. Thus, at a time when Norway's geographical location had moved it toward the center of the East-West conflict in strategic terms, and the oil and gas production in the North Sea had significantly raised most Norwegians' notions about Norway's international role and importance, the country suddenly found itself not only exposed and vulnerable but in a (self-inflicted) situation of political marginalization within the European and Atlantic frameworks of cooperation. Most important, however, was that Norway felt exposed politically and military, as a result of the perceived increase in political distance between Western Europe and the United States, and because of Norway's strategic location in between two superpowers that were waging a verbal war in a increasingly tense political confrontation. And not taking part in EPC, Norway lacked the collective shield of protection that EPC provided for the participating nations.

The result was that Norway in the fall of 1980 asked for a consultation arrangement with EPC. This was obtained, but could not solve Norway's basic problem. At an early point it became clear that Norway could not participate in EPC without becoming a full member of the EPC at the same time. That, however, was not feasible, given the vivid memories of the bitter domestic Norwegian strife in the early 1970s and the potential negative consequences of reviving the issue for the internal cohesion of the

Labor party as well as for the non-socialist coalition opting for power. Norway's dilemma was put in harsh terms when the prime minister of the soon-to-be-defeated Labor government in May 1981 gave a speech at a conference with the theme : "Europe and America in the 1980s : Must Norway Choose?"[21]

"Europeanization"?

The answer, obviously, was that Norway needed both the United States and Europe. U.S. power constituted the only credible deterrent for Norway in the north, in the face of the Soviet military build up and the uncertainties created by the Soviet invasion of Afghanistan. As far as Western Europe was concerned, Norway was, despite her refusal to join the EC, an integrated part of Europe in all respects, geographically, historically, economically, and culturally. But the problem was that Norway, in a way, was no longer politically an integrated part of Western Europe. At the same time, many Norwegians felt uncomfortable with the political shifts in the United States and the policies of the Reagan administration. The latter made too close ties to U.S. problematic or even undesirable for important political segments in Norway and created in itself a source for increased domestic conflict over foreign, defense, and security policies.

After 1982 and the disastrous "pipeline dispute," the general disarray in transatlantic relations was smoothed out, and in 1983 the INF issue dominated the political agenda, with a focus on the Geneva negotiations and the NATO deployment. Early in 1984, however, the news about the French initiative to "reactivate" the dormant Western European Union (WEU), to provide a more suitable European forum for discussions on international security issues, made headlines in Norway and revived Norway's dilemma. In March 1984, a major foreign policy debate took place in Oslo, with particular focus on the development in U.S.-European relations, the U.S. role for the defense of Norway, the potential development toward an two-pillar Atlantic system, and how it all might affect Norway's position as a European NATO country not part of the EC. The newest concern in this debate was how a "Europeanization" in the field of defense and security policies would affect Norway, if a reactivated WEU turned out to become a building block in the EC's attempt toward the goal of a European union. When the defense and foreign ministers of the seven WEU member states met in Rome in October 1984, the Norwegian government and Norway's political elites were watching with keen attention. And when it became clear that no major changes could be expected in the near future, there was a considerable degree of relief in Norway. Nevertheless, there was a realization that a process had been started and that the conceivable consequences for Norway had merely been postponed.

By the end of 1984, three different schools of thought had emerged on the Norwegian response to the dilemma : (1) that Norway should take part fully in what is referred to as a Europeanization process in the fields of foreign and security policies, and actively work to help create a two-pillar Atlantic system; (2) demands that Norway should stay out of any such Europeanization in continental Europe and, if necessary, increase her bilateral cooperation with the United States; and (3) demands that Norway should opt out and act unilaterally or in concert with its Nordic neighbors, in defiance of the international framework and what its allied partners decide to do.

NORWAY'S DOMESTIC POLITICS

In summing up the most salient domestic conflicts and views with regard to Norway's foreign, defense, and security policies, including the consequences of the main events of the 1970s, the following observations seem relevant. First of all, Norway's "9th of April" syndrome still produces overwhelming support in favor of a strong national defense. In a survey published in April 1981 (the year the Europeans supposedly were "going neutralist" and accommodating the best they could to the Soviet Union, if a major part of the U.S. media was to be believed), 81 percent of all Norwegians felt that a strong national defense was important, and 70 percent said they would want to take an active part in an armed resistance to defend their country.[22] And the support for Norway's membership in NATO has been higher in the early 1980s than ever before. In 1984, 67 percent of all Norwegians felt that Norway's NATO membership promoted its security, as opposed to 10 percent who felt that it increased the danger of an attack.[23]

The challenge that the Soviet Union's military build up represents for the defense of Norway has been reflected through major procurement programs and increased defense budgets. The increase in defense spending has been particularly noticeable since 1982. According to Norwegian national figures (based on the year the appropriations were granted, as opposed to when the money actually was spent), the average annual real increase in the Norwegian defense budget for the period 1974-79 was 1.4 percent, compared with 3.1 percent for the period 1980-86 (corresponding NATO figures, based on NATO's definition for defense spending are 2.2 percent and 3.3 percent).[24] During the past few years, the only political disagreement over defense spending has been between the previous nonsocialist coalition government's goal of a steady 3.5 percent real increase for the rest of the decade versus the Labor party's goal of a 3.0 percent real increase (disregarding the traditional antidefense spending proposals from the Socialist Left party).

According to NATO figures, Norway currently spends about 3.1 percent of GDP on defense, which is slightly below the European NATO average. According to defense expenditures per head, however, Norway is behind only three other NATO members (the United States, Britain and France).[25] If Norway's defense efforts were to be calculated the same way the United States (the CIA) calculates the Soviet Union's defense spending, Norway's defense efforts, in terms of proportion of GDP, would approximate the U.S. level, at about 5 to 6 percent of GDP.[26]

During the past decade, the slogan "Norway Out of NATO" has virtually vanished from the domestic political debate. This does not mean that the nation's defense and security policies have not been contested, however. In Norway's post-World War II defense and security policy debates, the main cleavage has not been between the socialist and nonsocialist blocs of political parties, but between a broad consensus among the nonsocialist parties and the politically dominant social-democrat wing of the Labor party at the one hand, and the Labor party's left wing and various political groupings to the left of Labor on the other. The opposition to the official policies (Norway Out of NATO) and antidefense spending on the left and abolishing Norway's historical base and nuclear policy on the right) has been left in the cold with virtually no influence on national decision-making. As a result, Norway's readjustments and responses to the perceived increase in the Soviet threat and challenge in the 1970s and early 1980s were fairly easily accomplished, with the traditional opposition on the political left as a highly vocal but politically impotent critic. On a few occasions, the Labor party adjusted its policies to avoid an internal polarization or deepened conflict between its social-democratic and socialist wings or political tendencies (for example, with regard to the geographic location of prestocking for the U.S. Marine brigade which the Labor government suddenly decided to locate in central instead of northern Norway) but until the INF issue became a contentious issue for the Labor party in 1982 and 1983, the traditional broad domestic consensus was kept intact.

The INF Controversy

As the negotiations, that were part of NATO's dual-track position stalled completely, the Labor party in the fall of 1982 proposed that Norway should not appropriate money for the part of NATO's infrastructure program that paved the way for deployment in Europe in 1983 of U.S. intermediate missiles.[27] As it turned out, several MPs who belonged to the Conservative government's two parties in the Storting (parliament) joined ranks with the Labor party and the government came extremely close to a major parliamentary defeat when its motion , which was to carry out NATO's agreed policy, obtained a majority by a single vote.

The appropriation issue itself referred to a minor sum of money. The political aspects which came to the forefront, however, were linked to issues like arms control, nuclear rearmament, and accelerated arms race, alliance solidarity, and Norway's political credibility with its the NATO partners. The conservative government claimed that its policy simply was to carry out, in a loyal fashion, the policy that the previous Labor government had taken part in designing a few years before and that the Labor party, once in opposition, had reversed its former position. The Labor party, on the other hand, denounced the claims that it had become unreliable on national security issues and pointed out that the original conditions for implementing the dual-track decision no longer existed. Consequently, it was the situation that had changed and not the Labor party's position with regard to the original 1979 decision. For example, spokesmen for the Labor party claimed that the United States had not ratified the SALT II treaty, and realistic arms reduction had not been attempted through serious negotiations.

In January 1983 the Labor party presented a report on arms control and disarmament issues. In brief, this report proposed that the INF negotiations ought to continue beyond December 1983 and that, meanwhile, NATO ought not to prepare any deployment of Pershing IIs and Tomahawk Cruise missiles. The aim should be to obtain sufficient Soviet reductions of SS-20s at the negotiation table to make the planned NATO deployment unnecessary. Furthermore, the Labor party argued for British and French nuclear weapons to be accounted for in the negotiations in Geneva, so that a negotiated solution without new Western deployments could be reached.

The Norwegian government, on the other hand, insisted that Norway should stick to the original NATO deal and stand firm on the policy to deploy U.S. INF systems in Europe unless a negotiated agreement in Geneva made such deployment unnecessary. The strong disagreement about the dual-track decision dominated Norwegian politics throughout 1983 until NATO's ministerial meeting in Brussels in December. The nonsocialist coalition government that had replaced the Conservative minority government in the early summer of 1983 had managed to keep a parliamentary majority for its policy, partly through explicit demands for loyalty to the government from the three parties' parliamentary groups. It seemed quite clear that the government would have resigned if its policy on the crucial issue had been voted down, which in turn would have paved the way for the Labor party to resume executive power. Especially as seen by the Conservatives, there was no way they would take part in making Norway another "footnote nation" in NATO, like Denmark and Greece.

As for public opinion and the INF issue, a considerable number of polls created an overall picture that is somewhat difficult to interpret. There was a clear-cut difference between the surveys that only asked about deployment and those that also included negotiations and arms control. The negative attitude toward NATO deployment was more pronounced when only deployment was mentioned, in contrast to when NATO's deployment was linked directly to the outcome of the Geneva negotiations. Over time, those who supported NATO's dual-track decision gained support, but a large number of people remained in doubt and had no explicit view. Nevertheless, it is clear that a deep-rooted skepticism regarding nuclear weapons was and probably still is widely shared in the Norwegian population and is found, by and large, within all the political parties. However, conservative voters seem less skeptical than those of the other parties.

In summary, two-thirds of Norway's population said that they would positively consider protesting against nuclear weapons. This indicates a substantial potential for opposition in Norway on issues linked to nuclear weapons. In international comparison, Norway, together with the Netherlands, stands out as a country in which the population was particularly concerned about the dangers of nuclear weapons at the time of the INF controversy.[28]

Despite this fact, the result was that Norway completely supported NATO's dual track decision. But the price was high--an unravelling of the defense and security consensus that had guaranteed continuity and nonpartisanship for three decades. In the spring of 1984, there were major attempts to repair the damage and to reach a common understanding and a general agreement with regard to the proper mix of military defense, arms control, alliance solidarity, and leeway for national initiatives. The latter was of relevance in particular with regard to the notion of a Nordic nuclear-free zone, which had been brought up by the left wing of the Labor party in 1980 and, subsequently, was coopted by the party officially, in close contact with its Nordic sister parties. The attempt to build bridges to restore the previous consensus in 1984 included an apparent modification of the Conservative party's rather negative position with regard to investigating the feasibility of formalizing a Nordic nuclear-free zone; this issue was included as part of a broad but vague package deal. By the end of 1984 and the early part of 1985, however, it became clear that significant disagreement between the Labor party and the government, particularly the Conservatives, remained unsettled. Thus, security issues came to play a major role in the election campaign during the early fall of 1985, with "reliability" and "alliance solidarity" as the main topics. And by the end of 1985, the disagreements between the government and the Labor party regarding the prerequisites for any attempt to create a Nordic nuclear-free zone came to the forefront once more.[29]

A New Conflict : "Europeanists" versus "Atlanticists"?

Another issue, which has been briefly discussed above, concerns the question of Europeanization of defense and security policies and Norway's relations with the United States. The conflicting views about policy options (summarized as

Europeanization, bilateral cooperation with the United States, or "opting out,") make a simple restoration of Norway's previous domestic consensus on security issues rather improbable. The new situation simply does not fit the old mold, and new political cleavages and the potential for some peculiar alliances have already emerged. Thus, while some people on Norway's political left (including the Labor party's left wing) would prefer Europeanization over close bilateral cooperation with the United States (the so-called neo-Europeanists), others despise the idea of European integration so much that they (opportunism or not) warn about the potential negative consequences for Norway's U.S. security guarantee (the neo-Atlanticists). The political mainstreams within the Conservative party's two past coalition partners (the Center party and the Christian People's party) are "traditional Atlanticists," but these parties contain a small group of rebels from that line, with views that frequently seem to approach those of Norway's socialist left. Except for a small group within the Christian People's party, the two are unanimously in rejecting any notion of Norway reevaluating its present situation with regard to participation in European integration. To them, Norway's position in Europe was settled once and for all in 1972. Among the Conservatives and the social-democratic mainstream of the Labor party, there are both traditional Atlanticists who consider Norway's relationship with the United States as the lifeline in Norway's foreign policy, as well as proponents of Norway actively taking part in a process of Europeanization and engaging herself in the creation of an two-pillar Atlantic system between two more equal partners. This internal division in both parties seems to be somewhat linked to age, with the postwar successor generation largely in favor of Europeanization. However, there has been a general trend in both parties toward acceptance of the idea during the past two years. Finally, the Progressive party (to the right of the Conservatives) strongly rejects the notion of Europeanization and argues strongly in favor of bilateral security arrangements between Norway and the United States, if NATO were to change.

Before the parliamentary elections in September 1985, the Conservative party's program for 1986-89 specifically stated that Norway should consider becoming a member of the WEU, if the developments in Europe made that a relevant option. A working group on the Labor party's European policy made the same proposal in 1984, but that recommendation was not included in the Labor Party's final and official program presented before the elections. Norway's Conservative prime minister in 1985 made some strong statements in favor of Europeanization and the need for "more balance between European and American input in the policy-making process of NATO,"[30] and the leader of the Labor Party (now Prime Minister) has argued in a similar vein (although with a stronger accentuation of the need to counter certain U.S. policies). And late in 1985, one of the Labor party's staunchest traditional Atlanticists came down in favor of Europeanization, as did the leader of the party's youth branch (the traditional organizational center for the Labor party's internal opposition on foreign, defense, and security issues) in 1982.[31] Finally, it is politically significant that there has been no overt opposition in the Storting to obtaining a "consultative status" for Norway at the WEU in 1985, as the only non-member with a consultation agreement at a political level.[32] By the end of 1985, there were a number of official statements that stressed that the Norwegian government considers the European nations to have an independent responsibility to guard Europe's security interests. These statements can only be interpreted as overt support for WEU and Europeanization in security, despite the Reagan administration's warning early in 1985 against the WEU putting the Strategic Defense Initiative on the agenda for its ministerial meeting on April that year. Behind Washington's letter to the seven WEU governments was an obvious lack of enthusiasm at seeing SDI discussed among America's main European allies, in a forum in which the United States did not take part.[33] It should be stressed, however, that the Norwegian government has repeatedly pointed out that Europeanization in the security field is a way of strengthening the Atlantic Alliance and not a separate alternative to European security.

NORWAY'S DEBATE ABOUT FUTURE SECURITY

"Status quo" versus Change

No one would argue that international circumstances, opportunities, and constraints do not change. But when it comes to the East-West division of Europe, NATO, and U.S.-European relations, there seem to be a considerable number of people who would agree with the French maxim : "Plus ça change, plus ça restera la même chose." Such a view, at least, seems to characterize the most common Norwegian outlook with regard to European security, and the need for the United States to maintain the same role that it has played in European politics since 1945. Norwegians, of course, are not the only ones to argue for (or just tacitly assume) such a predominantly status quo perspective. The outlook and general world views of the 1960s seem to be alive and well in various political quarters in many countries, sometimes almost living their own secluded lives. Furthermore, a status quo perspective of Europe after 1945 has been given some intellectual underpinning as well (in books like Anton W. DePorte's Europe Between the Superpowers : The Enduring Balance).[34]

In sharp contrast to the status quo perspective, we find a different school of thought, the notion of a future Europe in which the East-West conflict has disappeared or, at least, lost most of its importance, a Europe characterized by superpower disengagement and a dissolution of the military blocs. The latter perspective is frequently set up as a long-term desirable future, as an ideal suited for speeches with a "vision." In that way the future ideal may, in fact, be combined with the need to ensure a continuity of most of the present policies, since wishful thinking about a distant future should not interfere with realpolitik and the need to credibly counter Soviet power today and tomorrow. Nevertheless, critics of what (by them) is perceived as a continuation of the cold war mentality and an arms race at an even higher level, will tend to put the ideal forward as a vision that may be created here and now, if "alternative" policies (normally those of the political left could be implemented. It follows from this somewhat simplified presentation that traditional Atlanticists and anti-NATO groups of the political left may agree on the vision of a desirable European future in the abstract. When it comes to the political means, however, they differ drastically. The former say, "Don't rock the boat, it may sink," while the latter are of the opposite opinion : "Do rock the boat to change its course."

As a brief and schematic summary, the above situation seems quite an appropriate characterization of Norway's foreign policy and security debate. On one hand, the opposition to Norway's policies in the security field has wanted change now, opting out of a realpolitik conceptual framework that was alien to its ideological predispositions and which, in any case, led to political consequences its proponents did not like. Within Norway's postwar and politically dominant foreign and security policy consensus, on the other hand, the predominant way of thinking has been that Norway adapted pretty well to international realities upon becoming a member of NATO in 1949 and that what was needed afterwards was simply to "stay the course." To Norway's political establishment, thinking and writing about alternatives to Norway's already established policies easily became suspect, unless it was obvious that the future vision of a better world, as presented, did not seriously jeopardize or demand any major alteration of current Norwegian policies.

The United States, Europe and Structural Uncertainty

As a consequence of the implicit status quo approach discussed above, the politically dominant circles in Norway's foreign policy debate have largely avoided discussing the (potential) consequences, for the relations between Eastern and Western Europe and for NATO and transatlantic relations, of a slowly evolving trend toward a European Community with ambitions and growing ability to play an international role separate from that of the United States--politically, economically and in nonmilitary security. This attitude might be summarized : "If you don't like its potential implications, don't talk about it and it may go away." Behind it we may detect worry about the domestic political consequences of explicitly discussing new international issues that fundamentally break with the world views of the 1960s, on which Norway's defense and security consensus of the 1970s was founded. Quite clearly, the potential centrifugal consequences for the nonsocialist coalition that currently constitutes the only viable alternative to the Labor party minority government obviously have persuaded the Conservatives to avoid discussing the kind of European security issues named above, at least openly. In the same vein, the Labor party is still struggling with its vulnerable internal cohesion on many foreign policy issues. Nevertheless, the then Labor party foreign minister Knut Frydenlund, made a rather unique statement when, during the parliamentary debate on foreign policy in March 1984, he observed : "the logical solution ought to be that a potential American withdrawal takes place simultaneously with a larger Western European role for the defense of Western Europe. The American forces have been in Europe for 40 years. One cannot take for granted that they will stay for another 40 years."[35]

Again, Frydenlund's observation was unique in the sense that Norway's foreign policy establishment constantly seems to be afraid of creating doubt about the U.S. security guarantee. Thus, major developments within the United States during the past two decades are largely disregarded in Norwegian politics. To point out that many Americans seem to be fed up with Europe and think that the ungrateful Europeans ought to manage on their own, without having U.S. soldiers to protect them, if they refuse to follow U.S. "leadership," tends to be perceived as "covert anti-Americanism" and slander of Norway's most important ally.[36] Consequently, the most sturdy Atlanticists in Norway experienced severe discomfort in 1984, the year in which Henry A. Kissinger presented his plan for a "reshaping" of NATO, former Under Secretary of State Lawrence Eagleburger warned that the United States might turn its back on Europe and concentrate on the Pacific rim, and the Nunn-Roth amendment in the Senate implied use of U.S. troops in Europe as a crude leverage against the European allies.[37] It is hard to evaluate to what extent these three events solely reflected certain U.S. frustrations with Europe in 1984 or whether they were a sign of things to come. In Norwegian politics, however, the former interpretation apparently has been taken for granted, and memory is short when it serves political purposes.

The Debate about the Future : A Political Void

It follows from the above that the debate in Norway about future security regimes or systems in Europe has been rather scant , except for a handful of intellectuals with little, if any, political impact. Between the vision or ideal of a better future, and the immediate tasks and problems for Norway, NATO, or East-West diplomacy, there has been a vacuum, an intellectual and political void. Analytic thinking (for example, in terms of scenarios) about alternative future possibilities or developments until the turn of the century or beyond, simply is not Norwegian. There is a substantial element of Norway's cultural heritage underlying this situation, of which Norway's lack of foreign policy experience and tradition is a major factor. But beyond that are the historical roots of isolationism and the small nation that reacts to the developments that affect it and avoids taking part in any conflict-provoking shaping of the future international system. And lurking even deeper, at the roots of Norway's cultural heritage, is a belief in lagnaden (fate). What happens happens, and you try to make the best out of the situation. In political language, this approach is called pragmatism--an honorary term in Norway. Norwegian politics, including foreign policy, is geared to solving practical problems, without fussing about abstractions. So, Norway became a member of NATO because practical problems demanded that solution. Far-fetched notions about an "Atlantic Community," however, never inspired the Norwegian imagination.[38] Likewise, dreams about the future "unified Europe" had no practical meaning to the Norwegians when they were facing a period of reconstruction after World War II, so why should they become interested?

Pragmatism implies that you don't always know in advance where exactly you will end up, as in, for example, the field of international relations. Nevertheless, it suits most Norwegians better to tackle practical and "real" problems than to develop the kind of hypothetical and politically "unrealistic" schemes and political plans for which the French are famous (and which they themselves subsequently abandon). So, when the Norwegian politics and the country's political debate almost exploded over the EC membership issue in 1972, no one really asked how it might affect Norway in the next decade or two, in terms of possible or probable international developments and Norway's national security interests, if Norway did not become a member of the EC or if it decided to join. In fact, there was a tacit agreement among the predominant leaders on both sides of the membership issue not to discuss national security issues or NATO. As to the subsequent results of this immense shortsightedness, we have already discussed how Norway, in 1981, suddenly woke up to transformed international realities and was forced by external events to discuss the future in terms of a drastically put dilemma : "Europe and America in the 1980s : Must Norway Choose?"

Once the transatlantic disputes had calmed down, however, Norway's foreign policy debate could concentrate on current events once more : INF, Norway's practical problems, and the moral obligations of being a wealthy nation in an imperfect world. As already mentioned, the prospects of a "revitalized" WEU early in 1984 provoked a major parliamentary debate in Norway, in which the country's long-term priorities and interests were discussed in terms of possible, probable, and desirable trends and developments in

Europe and in transatlantic relations. The years 1985-86, however, were marked by the old preference for discussing the events the media happened to put on the political agenda that week, as well as more parochial issues like whether a separate Nordic nuclear-free zone ought to be established and whether Norway should vote for a nuclear freeze resolution in the UN, to demonstrate good will with regard to the need for nuclear disarmament. And, of course, moral issues in connection with North-South relations remained central.

This rather critical evaluation of the Norwegian debate with regard to future security issues is hardly complete, but it illustrates what this author considers to be major weakness in Norway's domestic debate about national security and the international context. In short, the general Norwegian outlook has been too confined to the status quo and the willingness to concentrate on (potential) international trends or changing conditions with major implications for Norway or vital Norwegian interests is lacking. This critical view does not imply that there are obvious international trends that could not be argued or disputed, simply that they ought to be argued and disputed. Neither the long-term prospects and possible trends in Soviet policies, the conceivable consequences for Norway and available Norwegian responses, nor the implications for Norway of a possible trend toward a gradual or major change within NATO or in U.S.-European relations are sufficiently discussed. What is disturbing is that the very same status quo approach characterized Norway in the 1960s, after Norway had followed Britain in a European controversy that ended up in a temporary division in Western Europe between the Common Market and EFTA. When Britain applied for membership in the EC in 1961 ("if you can't beat them, join them"), and renewed its application in 1967, Norway was mentally and politically unprepared and was taken by complete surprise. The same thing happened in 1969 when European politics suddenly went into high gear (the Hague summit of the EC in December, which set the stage for the Community's first enlargement in 1973 and the development of EPC). A major question, therefore, is what kind of surprises Norway may be in for in the late 1980s or eaely 1980s, particularly with regard to European security and U.S.-relations, that is, changes in the international framework to which Norway adapted early in the post-World War II period. But that question is not seriously asked in Norway.

NORWAY'S POLICY RESPONSES AND THE PROBLEM OF ADAPTATION

Despite the general lack of public debate and political analysis in Norway about alternative future security regimes or systems in Europe (except for the long-term vision of a peaceful Europe without the present military blocs) Norwegian authorities have a clear view of which immediate political changes might improve Norway's their country's security. At the broader European level, that view looks favorably toward a renewed dialogue between the two superpowers, arms control and disarmament, and a continuation of the CSCE process. Futhermore, trade and other forms of commercial interaction between East and West in Europe are beneficial as "stabilizers,"[39] and should not be used to serve short-term political purposes. This Norwegian view on East-West relations in general, and detente in particular, unambiguously defines Norway as a European nation with a European outlook.

The Immediate Future

As to the more specific security issues that are likely to remain on the political agenda for the years to come and which affect or directly involve Norway's national security interests, Norwegian authorities have kept a keen eye on how broader NATO or Western proposals and negotiation platforms may affect Norway and NATO's northern flank. The following points illustrate this and demonstrate the Norwegian emphasis on concrete issues as relevant security concerns :

1. At the European Disarmament Conference (CDE) meeting in Stockholm, there were Western proposals to reduce the threshold for advance notification of military maneuvers from the current 25,000 men to the division level (it would imply that the Soviet Union had to notify Norway each time one of the two Soviet infantry divisions on the Kola Peninsula were to move).
2. At the CDE meeting in Stockholm, Norway had pushed for advance notification of amphibious activities involving more than 3,000 men (i.e., the Soviet naval infantry brigade stationed close to the Norwegian border).
3. At the Mutual and Balanced Force Reduction (MBFR) negotiations in Vienna, Norway has worked hard to establish the principle that reductions of arms or troops in Central Europe must be linked to guarantees against adverse effects for the security of the flank nations.
4. As for the U.S.-Soviet negotiations in Geneva, Norway has supported the principle of 50 percent reductions in the strategic arsenals on both sides, partly on the basis that such drastic cuts might reduce the number of Soviet strategic submarines operating out of the Murmansk area. Norway has also stressed that such an agreement must not lead to an increase in the relative importance of the sea-based strategic systems.
5. As for the INF negotiations in Geneva, Norway has stressed in allied consultations the need for a balance at the lowest level possible, and that an agreement should include a reduction of the number of Soviet SS-20s deployed in the Asiatic parts of the Soviet Union (these are capable of reaching Norway). Furthermore, Norway has pointed out that an INF agreement should prevent an increase in Soviet SS-23s and reduce the number of SS-12s and other nuclear weapon systems that may reach the Nordic area from bases in the Leningrad military district. In addition, Norway has emphasized that Soviet sea-based Cruise missiles with a range of less than 600 kilometers must be included as well, and not only those with a range over 600 kilometers (the latter Soviet proposal would exclude from an agreement some of the most important weapons systems in the Soviet northern fleet).[40]

The Medium- and Long-Term Future

As for the more medium- or long-term issues and problems in the field of European security, particularly with regard to the developments in Western Europe and transatlantic relations, there are no clearly defined Norwegian policies. As shown in the presentation of Norway's domestic politics by the mid- 1980s, a certain process of political maturation seems to be under way, and this process has resulted in an increasingly positive Norwegian understanding of the principle of Europeanization. In operational terms, however, nothing more substantial than a passive "wait and see" policy has developed. When it comes to the need for a larger European role for the defense of Western Europe, which assumes an increase in European tasks and responsibilities and a relative reduction of those of the United States, the Norwegian government pays lip service to the principle as such but possesses no clear policy according to which Norway has an active role to play in bringing about such a change. Furthermore, Norway pays lip service to the principle of achieving predominantly conventional defense of Western Europe in the future, although such a strategy, if it were implemented, would become a predominantly European responsibility. Including the available reserves, total U.S. military manpower is only half that of its Western European allies (3 million as opposed to 6 million men). A conventional defense of Western Europe, which is seen desirable because it would raise the nuclear threshold, might turn into a complete reversal of both leadership roles and political influence within the Atlantic Alliance in the future. Such a change, however, would most likely imply a reorganization and upgrading of the WEU, including extending WEU membership to most European NATO members. In addition, it seems reasonable to assume that such a WEU would be closely linked to the goal and process toward a European union, as one organizational building block among others (the EC as regulated by the Treaties of Rome and Paris, EPC, EMS). As a result, Norway's predominantly status quo policy with regard to its current position in Europe and European politics would face the end of the road. Little seems to be done to prepare the Norwegian public for that possibility, however.

Scenarios like the one above belong to the sphere of speculation about the future. But although the scenario of Europeanization of security is not at all certain, it is not entirely improbable or unrealistic either. What seems unrealistic, by the late 1987, is that Norway would play an active role in making such a development happen. The domestic political constraints, as well as Norway's historical roots, seem to make unlikely a Norwegian initiative to join in and help develop such a Europeanization process. Instead, Norway is likely to continue to watch such a development from the sideline, until it faces a situation that demands action in terms of concrete adaptation to new international realities. Then Norway will adapt (whether it will be reluctantly or not is hard to tell) and Norway's pragmatic approach to practical problem-solving will start operating within the new framework.

To believe that there would be feasible alternative solutions available (withdrawal and opting out of the larger European framework, or trying to reach a separate and bilateral arrangement with the United States) seems highly unrealistic. That does not mean, however, that the temptation to pursue both alternatives does not exist. On the contrary, such temptations are likely to remain an inherent part of Norwegian politics. In addition, the conflict or dilemma between Norway's perceived military needs (a credible deterrent and the U.S. security guarantee) versus domestic and external political needs (low tensions with the Soviet Union and closer links to the rest of Western Europe) will remain and is likely to become aggravated. An illustrative example is that early in 1986 there was an emerging debate about the desirability of requesting the United States to deploy U.S. naval units on a more permanent basis off the Norwegian coast. The issue of how to counter the military and political impact of the Soviet Union's new naval capabilities and forward defense strategy is likely to remain and to become linked to the broader political questions discussed above.

Despite such disagreement about Norway's future orientation in the field of foreign and security policies, one objective and fundamental fact remains : in terms of geography, history, culture, economics, and vital security interests, Norway is an integrated part of Western Europe. One crucial aspect that has not been discussed in this chapter, for example, is that the economic costs of Norway's current position outside the EC may turn out to be considerably higher in the next decade, compared with the 1970s. Furthermore, Norway has become increasingly dependent on oil and gas revenues for its economic well-being. This represents a major vulnerability in the face of an unstable international oil market. A solution that reduces this unacceptable uncertainty can only be found within the framework of a long-term European energy policy. Thus, many factors seem to pull in the same direction. For Norway to face the logical consequences of this trend, however, there is a need either for considerably more time or external events that make the decision inescapable.

NOTES

1. For a discussion of security policy in a very comprehensive manner, see Nils Andrén, Den totala Säkerhetspolitiken (Stockholm : Utrikespolitiska Institutet, 1972).

2. Cf. Robert O. Keohane and Joseph S. Nye, Jr., Power and Interdependence : World Politics in Transition (Boston, MA : Little, Brown, 1977).

3. A discussion of how issue areas may be defined, inter alia in terms of distribution of consequences, is found in Arild Underdal, "Issue Variables in the Study of Foreign Policy Decision-Making," unpublished paper, Institute of Political Science, University of Oslo, December 1981; earlier version published in Cooperation and Conflict 14, no.1 (1979).

4. For the notion of "powerlessness," see Knut Midgaard, "Co-operative Negotiations and Bargaining : Some Notes on Power and Powerlessness," in Power and Political Theory : Some European perspectives, edited by Brian Barry (London : John Wiley, 1976).

5. CF. Keohane and Nye, Power and Interdependence.

6. For a classical definition of "power" in political science, see Robert A. Dahl, Modern Political Analysis (Englewood Cliffs, NJ : Prentice-Hall, 1963).

7. For a more comprehensive discussion, see Baard Bredrup Knudsen, "Norway's Defense and Security Policies : Domestic Roots, current Issues and Dilemmas," in Evolving European Defense Policies, edited by Catherine M. Kelleher and Gale A. Mattox (Lexington, MA : Lexington Books, 1986).

8. Cf. Olav Riste, "The Historical Determinants of Norwegian Foreign Policy," in Norwegian Foreign Policy in the 1980s, edited by Johan J. Holst (Oslo : Norwegian University Press, 1985).

9. Ibid., p. 14.

10. The "open" nature of Norway's economy, as a historical pattern, is demonstrated by the following figures :

Added value of exports and imports as a percentage of GDP

1870	1900	1930	1960	1970	1980	1984
54.9	64.5	59.6	77.9	84.9	88.5	86.7

Source : Historical Statistics 1978, Table 51; Statistical Yearbook 1974, Table 82; Statistical Yearbook 1985, Table 106 (Oslo : Central Bureau of Statistics).

11. Store Norske Leksikon : "Norway, Shipping"; vol. 8, p. 695 (Oslo : Kunnskapforlaget, 1982); Statistical Yearbook 1985, Table 545 (Oslo : Central Bureau of Statistics).

12. Statistical Yearbook 1974, Table 208; Statistical Yearbook 1985, Table 226 (Oslo : Central Bureau of Statistics).

13. Cf. Barry R. Posen, "The U.S. Military Response to Soviet Naval Developments in the High North," unpublished paper presented at the Harvard Nordic Conference, Harvard University, April 19-20, 1985, as well as Deterrence and Defense in the North, edited by Johan J. Holst, Kenneth Hunt, and Anders C. Sjaastad (Oslo : Norwegian University Press, 1985).

14. A summary of the report was published by Norway's Ministry of Defense in April 1985, as Current Defense Issues no. 0185; cf. as well former Minister of Defense Anders C. Sjaastad's speech on "Threat Development and Defense," January 7, 1985.

15. Cf. "Lagring av utstyr i Norge for en amerikansk brigade," FAKTA no. 0684, August 1984 (Oslo : Ministry of Defense).

16. Cf. "Memorandum mellom Norge og USA om felles bruk av visse norske flystasjoner," FAKTA no. 1783, December 1983 (Oslo : Ministry of Defense).

17. The declarations are quoted in Chris Prebensen, Norway in NATO (Oslo : Ministry of Foreign Affairs, 1974).

18. Johan J. Holst, " The Military Build-up in the High North : Potential Implications for Regional Stability. A Norwegian Perspective"; unpublished paper presented at the Harvard Nordic Conference, Harvard University, April 19-20, 1985, p. 2.

19. Guttorm Hansen (Labor) in the foreign policy debate in the Storting, March 15, 1984; Stortingsforhandlinger, Sesjon 1983-84, no. 29, p. 2903.

20. A detailed discussion of European Political Cooperation (EPC) and its development and organization is found in Baard Bredrup Knudsen, "Europe Versus America : Foreign Policy in the 1980s," The Atlantic Papers, no. 56 (June 1984).

21. Cf. the Conference Report "Europe and America in the 1980s : Must Norway Choose?" NUPI-Rapport no. 54 (Oslo : Norwegian Institute of International Affairs, 1981).

22. Polls listed in Norsk Utenrikspolitisk Årbok 1981 (Oslo : Norwegian Institute of International Affairs, 1982), p. 519.

23. Poll listed in Norsk Utenrikspolitisk Årbok 1984 (Oslo : Norwegian Institute of International Affairs, 1985), p. 417-18.

24. According to data received from the Ministry of Defense, the annual figures are (real growth in Norway's defense spending in percent per year) :

Year	National Definition	NATO Definition
1974	-3.6	-3.6
1975	+0.1	+5.2
1976	+2.5	+0.4
1977	+3.2	+1.8
1978	+3.6	+7.7
1979	+2.8	+1.9
1980	+1.5	+1.8
1981	+2.8	+2.7
1982	+4.0	+4.1
1983	+2.8	+4.0
1984	+3.5	-4.6
1985*	+3.5	+15.7*
1986*	+3.5	-0.8*

* Forecast

Norway's national definition is based on the figures in the defense budget plus extra appropriations directly related to that budget. The NATO definition is based on accounts. The Coast Guard is excluded from both definitions. The NATO definition includes certain expenses not listed as part of the defense budget according to the national Norwegian system.

25. See "Defense Expenditures of NATO countries 1949-1983," NATO Press Release M-DCP-2 (83)28 December 2, 1983.

26. Norway has universal conscription for men, and according to the CIA method the value of this manpower (for reasons of equitable comparison) should be calculated according to U.S. personnel costs. The claim that this method gives Norway close to same as the U.S. figure for defense spending in proportion to GDP is based on information presented in Report on Allied Commitments to Defense Spending, a report to the United States Congress by Caspar W. Weinberger, Secreatry of Defense (Washington, D.C. : GPO, March 1981), p. 8.

27. Cf. Arne Olav Brundtland, "Gjenopprettet enighet om sikkerhetspolitikken" (Restored Consensus on Security Policy), in Norsk Utenrikspolitisk Årbok 1984, pp. 11-31. (Brundtland's conclusion about a restored consensus was premature, though.)

28. Cf. Bernt Aardal, "Meningsmalinger om forsvars- og sikkerhetspolitikk med hovedvekt pa NATO's dobbeltvedtak : En oversikt og evaluering"; Aktuelle Forsvarssporsmal No. 0384, February 1984 (Oslo : Ministry of Defense). The international comparison is based on a series of surveys sponsored by the Atlantic Institute for International Affairs, reported in the International Herald Tribune, October 25, 1982.

29. The Norwegian government's policy at that time was that (a) a Nordic nuclear-free zone arrangement must be linked to Soviet reductions of nuclear and conventional weapons to ensure a better balance between East and West; (b) such an arrangement must be subject to efficient safeguards and means of verification, which can only be obtained within a larger East-West agreement; (c) efforts to create a Nordic nuclear-free zone should not be made in advance of or simultaneously with negotiations to reach a broader European solution, but should be postponed until there is a general agreement between East and West on the main European security issues. Cf. State Secretary of Foreign Affairs, Torbjorn Froysnes' speech of January 7, 1986, published in UD-Informasjon No. 1, January 9, 1986 (Oslo : Ministry of Foreign Affairs).

30. Cf. former Prime Minister Kaare Willoch's speech at the International Democratic Union meeting in Washington, D.C., July 25, 1985.

31. Cf. former President of the Storting, Guttorm Hansen's speech in Oslo Arbeidersamfund November 13, 1985, and Egil Knudsen and Jens Stoltenberg, "Sikkerhetspolitiske utfordringer i 80-Åra. Momenter til et program" (Challenges for Security Policy in the 80s. Elemnts for a Program), in Europe eller USA : Ma Norge velge i 80-Årene?, edited by Bernt Bull and Sverre Jervell (Oslo : Universitetsforlaget, 1982).

32. Cf. a press release by the Foreign Ministry in Oslo dated November 19, 1985, and published in UD-Informasjon no. 25, November 21, 1985 (Oslo : Ministry of Foreign Affairs).

33. See Aftenposten, April 4, 1985.

34. Anton W. DePorte, Europe Between the Superpowers. The Enduring Balance (New Haven, CT. : Yale University Press, 1979). For a critical evaluation of DePorte's status quo perspective, see Baard Bredrup Knudsen, "Europe Between the Superpowers : an All-European Model for the End of the 20th Century", Cooperation and Conflict, 20, no. 2 (1985) : 91-112; cf. as well Knudsen, "Europe versus America."

35. Stortingsforhandlinger, (see Note 19) p. 2921.

36. For a U.S. evaluation of NATO's future that points to the existence of anti-European feelings in the United States and the need for structural change, see Stanley R. Sloan, NATO's Future : Toward a New Transatlantic Bargain (Washington, D.C. : National Defense University Press, 1985).

37. Henry A. Kissinger, "A Plan to Reshape NATO," Time, March 5, 1984; Lawrence Eagleburger, "The Transatlantic Relationship : A Long-Term Perspective," U.S. Department of State Bulletin 84, no. 2085 (April 1984) : 39-42. The Nunn-Roth Amendment was presented as an amendment to the Fiscal Year 1985 Department of Defense authorization bill in June 1984. It was defeated in the U.S. Senate by a vote of 55 to 41.

38. Cf. the notion of an "Atlantic Union" as reflected by the Atlantic Convention in Paris, January 8-20, 1962; see Christian A. Herter, Toward an Atlantic Community (New York : Harper & Row, 1963) as well as Harold van B. Cleveland, The Atlantic Idea and Its European Rivals (New York : McGraw-Hill, 1966).

39. Cf. Kjell Goldmann, "Change and Stability in Foreign Policy : Detente as a Problem of Stabilization," World Politics 34, no. 2 (January 1982).

40. Cf. State Secretary Torbjorn Froysnes' speech "Norway in NATO--Current Issues," published in UD-Informasjon, no. 1, January 9, 1986 (Oslo : Ministry of Foreign Affairs).

10 Denmark: Increasing Isolation?

Ib Faurby

"It is difficult to predict--particularly about the future," goes the almost proverbial saying by the Danish humorist Robert Storm Petersen. It will be recalled by any Dane trying to make predictions. Danish security policy was remarkably stable during the long period of fundamental shift from neutrality to Alliance membership completed in 1949 and until the very end of the 1970s. Since then, and particularly since the autumn of 1982, Danish security policy has been in a state of flux and has not yet found a stable pattern. That makes it all the more difficult to attempt predictions beyond the immediate future. Furthermore, even if particular Danish circumstances are important for understanding the complexities of the present situation, there can be no doubt that Danish security policy first and foremost is determined by external factors and not by domestic ones. Thus any attempt to predict the long-term future of Danish security is faced with the even more difficult if not impossible task of predicting the development of these external factors; a task that in any case is well beyond the scope of this short chapter.

Consequently the predictions, or rather speculations, in the following analysis will tend to have a perspective much shorter than the next 30 years. The speculations will take as their point of departure the past pattern and recent developments in Danish security policy and emphasize domestic factors, even if these may not be the most important factors shaping the future of Danish security policy. The chapter will contain more details on the present and the immediate future and be rather hazy as it peers into the distance.

STRATEGIC IMPORTANCE AND THREAT PERCEPTIONS

Geography and Strategy

The Kingdom of Denmark consists of Denmark proper, Greenland, and the Faroe Islands. The strategic importance of Denmark proper is derived from its geographical position at the gate of the Baltic Sea as an appendix to Central Europe. Traditionally, the function of the Baltic Straits as a maritime passage has attracted the greatest strategic interest. The question of the Soviet Union's need for passage into and out of the Baltic in case of war is of paramount importance for any evaluation of Denmark's strategic situation. Contending answers, very dependent upon the scenarios on which they have been based, have been formulated over the years. There can be no doubt, however, that the ability to sail in and out of the Baltic is a major Soviet interest, particularly if a war with a long conventional phase is expected.

Added to this age-old question, military evaluations have in recent years stressed the strategic importance of Danish air space. As it is less heavily defended than the air space on both sides of the divide in Central Europe, both NATO and the Warsaw Pact could use Danish air space to circumvent the central front with airplanes of all types and possibly with Cruise missiles as well. Furthermore, Danish territory could be used as a basing and transit area for NATO reinforcements to the central front. Likewise, Denmark could be a stepping stone in a Warsaw Pact thrust toward Britain and southern Norway and in an attempt to control the North Sea and the southern Norwegian Sea. Finally, the island of Bornholm in the Baltic is an important location for peacetime surveillance of Warsaw Pact activities.

Of the two North Atlantic parts of the kingdom, Greenland is strategically the most important. Geographically speaking, it is a part of the North American continent and its strategic importance is first of all derived from its location on the shortest route between the Soviet Union and North America and thus on the most likely path of ICBMs and of SLBMs from the Soviet northern fleet. Second, the naval buildup north of the Greenland-Iceland-Britain (GIUK) gap has increased superpower presence in waters adjacent to Greenland, although it is difficult to point to specific strategic implications of this development for Greenland. The Faroe Islands, although centrally placed in an area of increasing naval importance, are probably of marginal strategic importance due to the limited possibilities for their large-scale military use.

In sum, quite different strategic problems pertain to the different parts of the kingdom. Increasingly, the strategic importance of Denmark proper has been seen to be tied to the situation on the central front, whereas the strategic nuclear balance between the United States and the Soviet Union and naval deployments in northern waters are particularly relevant to Greenland.

The Threat

The official definition of the military threat has not been constant but has changed in emphasis over the years. Immediately prior to joining the Atlantic Alliance (and an important element in the decision to join) was the fear of a surprise attack like the one in April 1940. In the 1950s, NATO membership led to a decrease in the fear of an isolated attack on the country. However, the debate in the 1960s within the Alliance over the credibility of the U.S. guarantee, the concept of limited war, and the strategy of flexible response meant that the possibility of an isolated attack on Denmark again gained in currency. Yet by the second half of the 1970s the threat perception changed again and gave way to the belief that the main threat against Denmark was the threat of an attack that was part of a larger Warsaw Pact attack on NATO in Europe. This last change could at least partially be seen as a consequence of the close integration of Danish and West German forces and the important role of the Federal Republic in the defense of the Danish area.

Today the official threat perception treats the following scenarios :

● an attack on Denmark as part of a general attack on NATO in Western Europe and adjacent waters,
● an isolated attack on Denmark or a limited part of the country,
● political intimidation brought about by the limited use of military means or the threat thereof.

It should be added that the official threat perception is not one of an immediate, premeditated and large-scale bolt from the blue, but of an attack resulting from a major international crisis.

Popular threat perceptions are more difficult to describe than official ones. The popular threat perception during the cold war of overt Soviet aggression has faded and almost disappeared during the years of detente. And it did not reemerge in its original form and scope with the breakdown of superpower detente in the second half of the 1970s. Even if a clear majority of the population views the Soviet Union with profound skepticism, there is only limited fear of overt Soviet aggression. The Soviet military buildup is seen as a major cause of international tension--just like the Western military buildup in many circles--but not as an acute military threat. It is not the threat, but rather the immediacy of the threat that is denied. The threat, as perceived by articulate groups in the public debate, is not one of deliberate Soviet aggression, but of war brought about by uncontrollable escalation.

The Soviet Union is seen, as in other Northern European countries, increasingly as a normal great power pursuing its interests in the way great powers do and in ways that often conflict with Western interests. This, however, cannot be changed by Western armaments, and the West will have to learn to live with the Soviet Union. There is, one could say, a strong wish to return to the policies of the detente period.

YESTERDAY AND TODAY

Like most other countries, Denmark in its security policy attempts to combine elements of deterrence with elements of reassurance. Deterrence is sought through membership in the Alliance and through the country's own military efforts. Reassurance is sought through certain self-imposed restrictions and through bilateral and particularly multilateral attempts at promoting stability and detente in general, and arms control and other tension-reducing arrangements in particular. Stated in general terms, it could be said that the main theme of the country's security policy debate is what the two elements (deterrence and reassurance) should consist of and how they should be balanced.

Alliance Membership and Defense Policy

Joining the Atlantic Alliance in 1949 was not a foregone conclusion. The government's preferrence had been for a Scandinavian defense arrangement which, however, did not work out. Although opposition to NATO membership was far from negligible, the three large parties--the Social Democrats, the Liberals, and the Conservatives, and thus an overwhelming majority in Parliament--brought Denmark into the Alliance. Since then, there has been not much public debate over the fundamentals of membership, although there have always been smaller parties and groups opposed to it.

Until recently the strategy of the Alliance, including the role of nuclear weapons in the strategy, had not been a contentious issue in the Danish security debate. Part of the explanation for that is undoubtedly to be found in the fact that nuclear weapons have never been stationed in the country. In 1957 the government declared that Denmark did not want nuclear weapons stationed "under the present circumstances," a formula that was later interpreted to mean that Denmark did not want nuclear weapons stationed in peacetime. This policy contributed to the depoliticization of nuclear issues in Danish politics for many years.

Neither has there been much public debate or many government pronouncements on Alliance strategy. Implicitly the dominant role of the United States in the formulation of Alliance strategy was accepted and the worries over the credibility of the U.S. guarantee, which from time to time have beset other Western European governments, were never pronounced in Denmark. Moreover, there were no demands for a stronger European role in the formulation of Alliance strategy.

Although the enhanced radiation weapon in 1977-78 did cause some debate, it was not before the autumn of 1979 that the nuclear policies of the Alliance began to generate more widespread debate in Denmark. Shortly before the NATO Council meeting, the Social Democratic government proposed a six-month postponement of the deployment part of the dual-track decision in order to test the willingness of the Soviet Union to negotiate reductions in intermediate-range nuclear weapons. When the Danish proposals did not win any support from the other NATO members, Denmark joined in the dual-track decision on December 12, 1979.

By endorsing the future nuclear force structure of the Alliance through a collective Alliance decision, Denmark became more directly involved in the nuclear policies of the Alliance than the country had been hitherto; its "nuclear profile" was raised, so to speak. In the following years, the public debate and the attitudes of the Social Democratic party on the dual-track decision became more critical. And from the autumn of 1982, when the Social Democrats went into opposition, they became increasingly skeptical toward the nuclear policies of the Alliance in general, a fact that had immediate effects on the country's security policy, as the new Conservative -led government did not command a majority in Parliament.

Another important aspect of Danish NATO membership has to do with allied reinforcements. In 1953 Denmark had declined to have allied troops stationed "under the present circumstances"--again later interpreted as meaning during peacetime. However, following NATO's adoption of the strategy of flexible response in 1967, the planning of reinforcements has become an important aspect of NATO planning. In 1976 Denmark entered into a COB (Collocated Bases) Agreement regarding U.S. Air Force reinforcements, and in 1982 SACEUR's Rapid Reinforcement Plan (RRP) was approved by the Danish government and Parliament. The reinforcement plans will bring five U.S. and two British squadrons of combat planes and a British infantry brigade to Denmark. Besides these forces, a U.S. Marine Amphibious Force of approximately 40,000 and a British-Dutch unit of Marines are assigned to NATO's Northern Region in general. Of SACEUR's strategic reserve, a British squadron and a U.S. infantry division have the northern region as their first priority. The reinforcements to Denmark do not require prestocking of heavy equipment, but prestocking of fuel, ammunition and spare parts has taken place.

The defense of Denmark is closely integrated with the defense of the Federal Republic north of the Elbe River, that is, in Schleswig-Holstein and Hamburg. In 1962 a common command (BALTRAP) was established for this area. Integrated at the corps level, it is the most closely integrated NATO command, and Denmark's national defense forces are to a large extent tailored to the needs of BALTRAP.

The budget and force structures of Danish military forces are normally decided through defense agreements among the major political parties and last three to four years at a time. The present agreement lasts until the end of 1987. According to this agreement, the standing army consists of approximately 10,000 men. The full peacetime strength, including conscripts undergoing training, is about 20,000. Fully mobilized, the army will consist of 72,000 men.

The navy will in the future have 35 combat units, 23 surveillance units, plus ships for fishery inspection. The peacetime force consists of approximately 8,000 men and the wartime force of 13,000. The air force has some 90 combat planes; by 1988, 57 of these will be F-16s. Peacetime strength is approximately 9,000 and wartime strength 19,000 men. Besides these forces, there is an almost completely volunteer home guard of about 80,000 for local defense, surveillance, and guard duties.

Reassurance

In addition, the reassurance aspect of Danish security policy consists of different elements. One of them is the self-imposed restraint on nuclear weapons and the stationing of foreign troops in time of peace, which has already been mentioned.

The reservation about the permanent stationing of foreign troops (also called "the base reservation" is, like the reservation on nuclear weapons, a unilaterally declared policy that is defined and can be modified by Danish authorities as they see fit. It does not, however, include Greenland. A Danish-U.S. treaty from 1951 makes the defense of Greenland a joint task, and the United States has two bases in Greenland at Thule and Sonder Stromfjord, plus a few other facilities. The reservation on nuclear weapons, however, also applies to Greenland.

Finally, Denmark exercises some self-imposed restraints related to the island of Bornholm in the Baltic. Allied forces are not allowed there even for exercises, and Danish forces do not participate in exercises east of Bornholm.

That these reservations should be seen as a deliberate policy of reassurance or nonprovocation can be illustrated by the reason given by the government in 1958 for the reservation on the stationing of nuclear weapons : "It must . . . be of importance that we in our area refrain from arrangements which--even unjustly--could be perceived as provocation and thus hamper detente."

Besides such restraints, Denmark has always given high priority to the pursuit of detente in East-West relations. The Harmel studies and the ensuing Harmel Report were supported wholeheartedly. Likewise, Denmark was the first NATO member to welcome the idea of a European security conference. Since becoming a member of the European Community, European Political Cooperation (EPC) has become an important forum for the country's support of the CSCE process.

Finally, disarmament or arms control policies can be seen as an element of the reassurance aspect of the country's security policy. However, Denmark is not an important participant in the international arms control and disarmament process. It is not a member of the UN Committee on Disarmament in Geneva and, as a flank country, it is only an observer at the Mutual and Balanced Force Reduction (MBFR) negotiations in Vienna.

However, through the 1980s, there has been an increased interest among the public and the Parliament in arms control and disarmament policies. This interest has mainly led to resolutions in Parliament, votes in the UN, and footnotes to NATO documents. The main theme for these manifestations has been nuclear policies of the Alliance, that is opposition to the deployment part of the dual-track decision and support for no first use of nuclear weapons, for the freeze of nuclear arsenals, and for the creation of a nuclear-weapons-free zone in the Nordic region.

The Domestic Politics of Danish Security

Three historical situations have been of particular importance in forming general attitudes on foreign and defense policy in Denmark. A hazardous foreign policy based on unrealistic assumptions about the country's military strength led to the War of 1864 and the subsequent loss of two-fifths of the kingdom. This experience laid the foundation for the image of Denmark as a small and powerless state dependent on Germany. In some political circles it led to the belief that any Danish defense effort was inherently futile. In the 1880s and until the turn of the century, defense policy furthermore became the major issue in domestic politics. The political left used it in its struggle with the government over the principle of parliamentarianism and Parliament's sole right to appropriate money. Thus defense policy became a field for partisan infighting.

The policy of the interwar years was one of almost unarmed neutrality. The immediate surrender and the following German occupation during World War II made the Social Democrats abandon unilateral disarmament. It also set in motion the development which, following the advent of the cold war, made the Social Democrats, the Liberals, and the Conservatives give up neutrality. The small but influential Radical party, however, could not accept membership in NATO. And when it finally did, partly for reasons of coalition-building in Parliament, the Socialist People's party, founded in 1958, took over the role as the defender of the antimilitarist tradition.

The three "old" and large political parties are the traditional artisans of Danish security policy. They are the supporters of NATO membership and they were the main participants in the aforementioned defense agreements.

The traditional consensus between the Social Democrats, the Liberals, and the Conservatives was not based on complete identity of views. To put it simply, the Social Democrats traditionally have emphasized the reassurance aspect of the security policy somewhat more strongly than the two large bourgeois parties who have, for their part, given a very high priority to a clearly demonstrated Alliance solidarity. In spite of these differences, all three found it in their best interest not to politicize issues of security policy and to arrive at a consensus either by splitting the differences (as in the defense agreements) or by the two bourgeois parties reluctantly accepting decisions made by the Social Democratic governments (as in the case of the self-imposed restraints on nuclear weapons and foreign bases).

The recent politicization of security policy can hardly be said to be stronger in Denmark than in most other Western European countries. In certain respects it has been weaker, and the peace movement in Denmark is unquestionably weaker and has less support than the peace movement in, for example, the Federal Republic and the Netherlands. Thus when searching for an explanation why the upheavals over security policy that have characterized all of Northern Europe have had greater consequences for official security policy in Denmark than anywhere else, one has to look at the particular parliamentary situation in Denmark.

Majority formation in the Danish Parliament today is more complicated than it has ever been. The government is a four-party coalition, yet it does not command an automatic majority but needs the support of at least one other party. Its normal parliamentary basis is provided by the Radical party, which protects the government against votes of no confidence and supports the government's economic policy.

When it comes to the general question of Danish membership in the Alliance, the government is supported by the Social-Democrats, the right-wing, so-called Progress party, and, in fact, by the Radicals. On defense policy, the traditional majority consists of the present governing parties and the Social Democrats--and in recent years the Progress party as well.

However, on almost all questions pertaining to nuclear weapons (INF, no first use, nuclear freeze, SDI, and a nuclear-weapons-free zone in the Nordic area) and a few lesser issues, the government is faced with an "alternative majority" made up of the Social Democrats, the Radicals, the Socialist People's, and the Left Socialists. Time and again, the government has been in a minority on these issues, but has chosen not to make them into cabinet issues and instead reluctantly accepted resolutions with which it did not agree.

This complicated situation probably could not be solved through an election. Even if an election were to be called on an issue of security policy, it would quickly turn into a "normal" election where economic policy would become the paramount issue. Furthermore, in spite of all the instability of the Danish party system throughout the 1970s and the 1980s, there has been remarkably stability in the overall distribution of votes and seats between the left and right. Thus, no election by itself seems to be able to change the relative strength of supporters and opponents of particular security policies. The election in January 1984 took place after more than a year of bitter disagreement over security policy. Yet even if there were considerable changes in the relative strength of individual parties, the overall balance between left and right was almost unchanged, and the "alternative majority" on security lost only two seats to the government, a loss so small that it did not change the basic situation.

TOMORROW

International Developments

The breakdown of domestic consensus in the early 1980s was not a particular Danish phenomenon; it happened throughout Northern Europe. Without analyzing that complex process in any detail, it does seem as if the following developments were important:

- The advent of nuclear parity between the United States and the Soviet Union gave rise to doubts about the credibility of the Alliance's strategy of flexible response by undermining the escalation dominance that was a precondition for its credibility.
- The breakdown of superpower detente meant that progress toward solving some of the major problems resulting from security policies based on the balance of terror was halted.
- The U.S. and Western Europe have diverging economic interests and explicitly stated differences over policies toward the Soviet Union as well as in relation to the economic and political problems of the Third World.
- The economic crisis following the 1973-74 oil supply crisis and particularly the 1979 oil price hike put pressure on public expenditure and, more important, demonstrated the increasing difficulties of public institutions in managing societal developments, and may--together with a greater awareness of environmental problems in the industrialized world--have contributed to a more pessimistic view of the future.

If these were the relevant factors behind the development in general of Western European attitudes, it is understandable that the breakdown of detente raised the specter of military confrontation in Europe and led to politicization and polarization over issues of security policy. And if these factors were crucial for the breakdown of traditional consensus, it does seem plausible that similar factors will determine the future development not only of Danish security policy but of the security policies of several Northern European countries.

Considering the importance traditionally attributed to reassurance and detente in Danish security policy, there can be little doubt that the general development of East-West relations in the years to come will be the most important factor shaping Danish security policy. Continued tension between East and West will keep domestic disagreements alive, while a relaxation in superpower relations and a positive development in the arms control negotiations in Geneva in particular will contribute to a lessening of domestic problems over security policy and ease the way for a Danish policy more in line with the NATO mainstream than has been the case in the past few years.

This general evaluation also holds when it comes to the specifics of NATO strategy and the role of nuclear weapons in that strategy. No marginal changes in that strategy or grand propaganda campaigns in favor of existing strategy will make it more acceptable to its present critics in Denmark or in other Northern European countries. Nor do imaginary technological fixes of the SDI variety or tactical ABM systems in Western Europe solve the inherently political problem. On the contrary, they could lead to an even greater disagreements than hitherto experienced. It is, on the other hand, quite plausible that a period of genuine detente between East and West will push issues related to nuclear weapons down on the political agenda, even if it is inconceivable that they would disappear completely.

Tension in the Nordic Area

A country with strong political and cultural affinities to other Nordic states, Denmark's popular and political perspective on security problems is often a Nordic one. Danish security seems more often to be discussed in a Nordic than in a broader European perspective.

In many writings about the security policies of the Nordic countries, the concept of a "Nordic balance" takes on a central role. Often the Nordic area is also characterized as an area of low tension, that is, an area where East-West tension is not as high as in Central Europe. This idea rests on at least three premises. First, relations between the Nordic countries are such that it is inconceivable for any of them to resort to arms in order to solve conflicts with other Nordic countries. Second, due to the neutrality of two Nordic countries and the self-imposed restrictions in the security policies of the Nordic members of NATO, the two military blocs are not as directly confronted with each other in the Nordic area as they are in Central Europe. Third, it is assumed that the two superpowers have a common interest in preserving the Nordic area as an area of low tension and consequently hold back on their military activities in the area.

It is this last assumption that is the most dubious of the three. It is somewhat parochial in its perspective. It implies that local considerations, and not the global perspective, determine the behavior of the United States and the Soviet Union in the area. Military developments over the past ten to twenty years do not confirm that view.

The growth of the Soviet northern fleet from a small coastal fleet to a major oceanic fleet, the importance of Soviet SLBMs in the northern fleet for the strategic balance, and the expansion of the Kola Base in general took place for reasons unrelated to the security policies of the Nordic countries, but nevertheless changed the strategic equation in the area and had far-reaching consequences for the security of the Nordic countries.

This development has in turn increased U.S. and NATO strategic interests and military activities in northern waters. In addition, the U.S. debate over naval strategy, the forward deployment of carrier battle groups, and the hazy concept of horizontal escalation contributed to moving the confrontation into the Nordic area. Finally, Soviet submarine activities in the territorial waters of Nordic states belie the idea of special considerations for the stability of the region.

The strategic developments in northern waters over the past years have drawn the Nordic countries closer to the cockpit of East-West tension. This has been reflected in several ways in the foreign and defense policies of Norway and Sweden, and to some extent of Finland. It is difficult, however, to detect any direct influence on Danish security policy.

It is improbable that northern waters should decrease in strategic importance in the years to come, and it thus seems likely, particularly if there is no fundamental change in East-West relations, that the implications for Danish security (not least for the security of Greenland) will become a more important and a domestically difficult issue in the future.

Europeanization of Security

The development of East-West relations over the past decade and the divergence in U.S. and Western European interests on economic matters and (not least) on how to deal with the Soviet Union have been at the foundation of a growing Western European perspective on questions of security and a wish to increase Western European cooperation in this field--not as an alternative to the Alliance but in order to give Western Europe a stronger voice within the Alliance.

The most important institutional elements in this process have been the EPC and the so-called revitalization of the Western European Union (WEU). Bilateral security cooperation has also increased, as most prominently illustrated in relations between France and the Federal Republic.

How would Denmark react to increased security cooperation between the Western European countries? As a member of the European Community, Denmark has, of course, participated in EPC for several years and considers this cooperation as a most important element in the country's foreign policy. There are, however, narrow limitations on how far Denmark could go in such cooperation. The issue of the country's role in the process of European integration is still a highly politicized and controversial one in domestic politics. Anti-marketeers are vocal and skepticism toward Danish membership continues to be strong. According to public opinion polls, about half the population shares this skepticism, and the Popular Movement Against the EEC has managed to poll one-third of the votes in the two direct elections to the European Parliament. Furthermore, at least half of those who support Danish membership are against further steps toward political integration. Such attitudes heavily influence the positions taken by the Social Democrats and the Radicals, without whom no majority can be found in Parliament.

The domestic limitations on Danish participation are particularly strong in two respects : there is a broad-based opposition to any ideas about increasing the supernational character of the Community and giving more power to Community institutions. This skepticism has been transformed into official policy as illustrated, for example, by the numerous Danish reservations to the Stuttgart Declaration of 1983. It has been revealed most prominently in the reaction to the reform package of December 1985. The Social Democrats and the Radicals (for different reasons) opposed the package, and it was decided to settle the issue through a referendum. The February 1986 referendum was won by the supporters of Community reform, but with only 53 percent of the vote. Even though a majority was in favor of reform, the uncertainty about the country's role in the EPC adds to the difficulty of making predictions, even about the immediate future.

The second limitation on Danish European policy is directly related to security. Any integration in the field of military affairs is rejected by an overwhelming majority, in the public at large and in Parliament. It is almost an article of faith that the European Community should have nothing to do with military affairs, which are the sole preserve of NATO. Thus any attempt in EPC to go beyond the "political aspects of security" would meet outright opposition from Denmark.

Denmark is not a member of the WEU and it is unlikely that Denmark should ever apply for membership. Thus, if the WEU becomes an important forum for security cooperation, possibly because such cooperation cannot be taken very far in EPC, Denmark runs risk of becoming increasingly isolated from increasing West European cooperation in security. But that seems in any case to be the logical implication of the policy preferred by a majority in Denmark, although it may not be perceived in those terms today.

The Nordic perspective preferred by many Danes has been manifested in recent Danish security policy in the proposal of a Nordic nuclear-weapons-free zone. However, there is no Nordic alternative to Danish membership in NATO and the European Community, and it is inconceivable that the Nordic nuclear-weapons-free zone will ever be established (except under international circumstances fundamentally different from those existing today). Present Danish policies thus seem to hold no alternatives to increasing isolation within Atlantic as well as European cooperation.

Toward a New Consensus ?

Traditionally, Danish security policy, as already described, has been conducted by a broad-based majority in Parliament. That consensus partially broke down during the first half of the 1980s. However, in June 1984, a leading member of the Social Democratic party proposed that an attempt be made as had been done in Norway to study the possibility of a new security policy consensus. The government quickly seized this opportunity and within a week appointed a high-level committee of civil servants to produce a study on Danish security in the 1980s. By the end of the year, the committee presented its report (generally known after its chairman as the Dyvig Report). The governments submitted the report to Parliament which in turn established an ad hoc committee to study the report and discuss all matters pertaining to the country's security policy.

By the end of 1985 the committee had not yet reached a consensus and the work had not progressed as quickly as had been expected by many people inside as well as outside the committee. Actually, in the spring of 1985, the work had been interrupted for some months due to disagreement between the government and the Social Democratic party on how to react to the U.S. Strategic Defense Initiative.

Reaching a consensus is, of course, not the purpose for everyone. The parties to the left of the Social Democrats fear a new consensus between the Social Democrats and the government that would bring to an end the unique influence the left wing has enjoyed on the formulation of policy since the Social Democrats went into opposition in the autumn of 1982. The Social Democrats themselves are split on the question on the desirability of a new consensus, and even among the four governing parties there are nuances as to the political price to be paid for a new consensus.

At the time of this writing, it is thus difficult to foresee whether or not the work of the ad hoc committee will result in some kind of a new consensus. Working in favor of a consensus is the untenable position--contrary to conventional principles of parliamentary government--which the government is in and which undermines its credibility at home and abroad. Nor is the situation completely comfortable for the Social Democrats. The party's new security policy has not measurably increased its electoral support, and when some day it returns to power, it will not be able to conduct its security policy with its present partners in the "alternative majority." It will need the cooperation of the parties of the present government.

Looking slightly beyond the present situation, it does appear, as already mentioned, that the main precondition for future Danish security will not be domestic but international. In this respect one can also point to the strong influence of other social democratic parties on their Danish sister party. Much of the inspiration for the party's security policies in recent years has come from Scandilux, the forum for discussions on security policy between the social democratic parties in Norway, Denmark, and the three Benelux countries and where the British Labour party, the French Socialist party and (not least) the West German Social Democrats participate as observers.

Economics of Defense

Among the foreseeable problems in Danish security policy in the years to come is the economic problem. In particular, the renewal of heavy equipment is going to be a growing quandary. Immediately after World War II, defense equipment was extremely scarce. The problem at the time was solved primarily due to the U.S. Mutual Defense Assistance Program. Although some of this heavy equipment is still in service after several rounds of modernization, most of it has been phased out. Consequently, there is a need for considerable investment in modern heavy equipment in the years to come. Yet it is difficult to see how such major investments could be made within politically realistic budgets.

A more general problem facing all NATO members, but especially the smaller ones, has to do with the economic-technological squeeze. The steeply rising costs of the modern weapons systems (ships, airplanes, and tanks) make it increasingly difficult for the smaller states to maintain a diversified and modern defense force. The number of systems a country can afford decreases with each new generation of weapons, and the small countries will be the first to reach the lower limit of what is necessary if basic defense tasks are to be fulfilled.

This development will soon raise difficult and quite fundamental questions about the future structure of the Danish defense forces. Some of these difficulties are in fact already being felt. The two full-size frigates have been mothballed in 1987, and it is inconceivable that Denmark will ever again acquire frigates, although the navy does have three completely modern mini-frigates (so-called korvets). As for submarines, it took long and complicated political negotiations to arrive in 1985 at a decision to procure three used submarines to add to the two old ones, which can continue in service. The idea of phasing out the entire, quite antiquated submarine force had strong political support.

In the air force, the F-16 is becoming the main combat aircraft, but the introduction of this modern system has necessitated a further reduction in the total number of combat planes. In 1984 it was 96 and in 1988 it will be 89. There is also a considerable need for modern low-level air defense systems, particularly for the defense of airfields.

Parts of the armored units are still equipped with Centurion tanks although these have been refitted several times. Among the items on the army's shopping list are also helicopters for antitank operations and other tasks.

In the present economic circumstances, with serious balance-of-payments problems and strict limitations on govenment spending, it will not be politically possible to expand the defense budget in order to meet the needs for new heavy equipment. In a more favorable economic climate, internationally and domestically, defense appropriations could be increased somewhat and thereby at least postpone the problem.

However, even such increases would not solve the problem. If not before, then by the turn of the century, fundamental readjustments in the structure of the Danish defense forces seem inevitable.

Ideas about the so-called non-offensive defense or territorial defense without large and technologically advanced weapons systems have recently become popular on the political left, and they could, to the extent that they are accepted by the Social Democrats, come to influence future defense agreements and serve as arguments for a defense structure without the traditional emphasis on large weapons systems. Such a restructuring would, however, create problems in relation to NATO planning and would hardly be compatible with the present integration of Danish and West German forces in BALTRAP.

Cohesion of the Kingdom

Although the question of the cohesion of the Kingdom of Denmark is not a normal topic for articles on Danish security policy, it seems, nevertheless, pertinent to include it, when asked to speculate about the very long term. Since 1948 the Faroe Islands have had home rule and have been self-governing on most domestic issues. Greenland was a colony until 1953, when it was fully integrated into the country as a county. In 1979, Greenland gained home rule under statutes similar although not identical with those of the Faroeese.

Foreign and defense policy is conducted by Copenhagen on behalf of the realm. The two self-governing communities in the North Atlantic thus, through the common Danish membership, belong to NATO. As far as the European Community is concerned, the situation is more complicated. Greenland, as an integral part of Denmark, joined the EC in 1973, although in the preceding referendum there had been a majority against joining in Greenland. The Faroe Islands did not join but received a free trade agreement with the Community. After gaining home rule, Greenland, based upon a referendum in 1982, chose to leave the Community and in 1985 received OCT (Overseas Countries and Territories) status in relation to the Community.

Greenland's departure from the EC has in some circles led to speculations about the possibility of Greenland also leaving NATO and, in the end, the Kingdom of Denmark. There are at present, however, no signs of such a development. Although Greenland has (as almost everyone else) experienced increased public interest in questions of security in recent years, the issues have mostly been related to specific problems and not to the fundamental question of Alliance membership.

The most important forces working against the official line on security policy are a small political party on the left wing holding two of the local parliament's 21 seats and the transnational Inuit Circumpolar Conference (ICC) of indigenous peoples of the Arctic area. The ICC has called for an Arctic nuclear-weapons-free zone and for the demilitarization of the Arctic.

Leading politicians in Greenland, aware of the strategic importance of Northern waters and of Greenland for the early warning on the North American continent, know that such ideas are utopian and that Greenland cannot withdraw from the strategic realities nor provide for its own defense. Even the peacetime assertion of sovereignty is a demanding task on this huge and forbidden island. However, the governing party and the local parliament have several times declared that Greenland must not under any circumstances be used for offensive purposes and have stated that Greenland should remain nuclear-free, even if it is acknowledged that this issue rests with the government in Copenhagen. Thus even if one can speculate about whether Greenland someday may become a fully independent country, there is nothing in present developments indicating radical changes with implications for security in the foreseeable future.

As far as the Faroe Islands are concerned, opposition to Danish rule is stronger and more articulated in certain political quarters, and the islands' status within the kingdom is a political issue of some importance. But this is nothing new, and there are no signs that these attitudes are gaining in political strength. However, neutralist and antimilitarist attitudes are quite widespread and stronger than anywhere else in the kingdom. The very small military (mainly communication) facilities on the islands from time to time give rise to heated political controversy, and the use of the island in connection with NATO exercises is a contentious issue. Furthermore, in 1984 the local parliament declared the islands nuclear-free, even if this was not in accordance with the provisions of home rule.

There is little reason to believe that the Faroe Islands will leave the realm, given the time perspective within which it is meaningful to speculate. However, small, insensitive moves on the part of Copenhagen, Washington, or NATO in the Faroe Islands could be interpreted as constituting an increased "militarization" of the islands and could easily provoke a conflict leading to the estrangement of the Faroeese from the Alliance.

CONCLUSION

The traditional consensus in Denmark has broken down and the country's security policy is at the moment in a flux, giving even short-term predictions of limited credibility. Future Danish security policy will, however, first and foremost be determined by external factors outside the control of Danish decision-makers.

This essay has pointed toward some of the dangers of Denmark becoming increasingly isolated from its partners in NATO, particularly in the case of no break-through in East-West relations, and in the European Community, where Denmark is extremely reluctant to move in the direction of closer cooperation, particularly on issues of security policy.

None of these gloomy speculations may necessarily come true. Political developments often, even in the short run, overtake and repudiate purely theoretical speculations.

11 Iceland: Guarding the Gap

Gunnar Gunnarsson

Located in an area of increased military competition of the superpowers, Iceland is generally regarded to have a high strategic value. At the same time, Iceland is one of the few nations in the international community that keeps no armed forces. The basic framework of Icelandic security policy, membership in NATO and a defense agreement with the United States concluded in 1951, should be viewed in this context.

Iceland has at times been described as a "minimalist member of NATO," which reflects its standing as an unarmed nation but also the fact that it has been an inactive member of NATO. Security policy has almost exclusively been a matter of bilateral relations with the United States. Iceland will probably remain an unarmed nation. However, it is gradually moving in the direction of becoming more involved in the Alliance.

In the first part of this paper, developments in the strategic environment as they relate to Iceland are reviewed, as well as the role of the Keflavik base. The second part describes the basic framework of Icelandic security policy and recent developments in policymaking. The domestic political context is the subject of the concluding section.

THE STRATEGIC CONTEXT

Since the beginning of the 1960s, the North Atlantic area has increasingly become the focus of the central strategic interests of the superpowers. This is mainly a result of two major developments : the advent of the ballistic missile-carrying submarine and the expanded Soviet general purpose naval capabilities deployed to the Northern Fleet at the Kola peninsula.

Strategically, the North Atlantic area may be seen as split into two main regions, the area north of the Greenland-Iceland-Britain gap (GIUK gap) and the area south of the gap. The northern region, the Norwegian Sea and the Barents Sea, have become a focal point of the strategic interests at stake. This reflects its position as the main operating area of the strategic offensive and defensive forces of both superpowers, while also being the principal domain of Soviet naval power in the Atlantic.

The main sea lines of communications across the Atlantic are in the southern region. Depending on the duration of war in Europe, the sea lines could serve a function similar to the role they played in the world wars. Their defense is thus of major concern to NATO to secure reinforcements and resupply operations from the United States to Europe. As assessed by NATO, the northern fleet is the principal threat to the sea lines, in particular its attack submarines and bomber force. It is primarily in that connection that the strategic position of Iceland should be seen. The GIUK gap constitutes a choke point through which the Soviet Navy would have to transit for operations in the Atlantic. Based on the traditional naval concept of gaining sea control by access denial rather than attempting control throughout an area, NATO strategy would aim at preventing Soviet transit by erecting an air, surface, and subsurface barrier in the GIUK gap. It can be argued that the central position of Iceland in the gap places the country in a unique position as a basing area for the conduct of sea control operations in the Atlantic. In fact, Iceland is conceded to have such importance that it is widely seen as the linchpin in the defense of the north Atlantic.[1]

The protection of the sea lines has been throughout the postwar period the main rationale for the U.S. naval posture in the north Atlantic. In view of the principal threat, ASW (anti-submarine warfare) forces have been emphasized. Since the first Soviet ballistic missile submarines were deployed, the ASW posture has not only been developed to protect the sea lines but also to create the option of destroying Soviet ballistic missile submarines in the event of war, in order to limit damage to U.S. territory from nuclear strikes.[2] Developments in the Soviet missile submarine program have influenced the way that damage limitation could be approached. Barrier operations, intended for sea line defense at choke points such as the GIUK gap could also be utilized to prevent submarines equipped with short-range missiles (Yankees) from reaching their operating areas off the U.S. east coast. Since 1974, the Soviets have equipped new submarines (Deltas) with longer range missiles which have gradually provided for a strategic force securing a second-strike capability from the Barents Sea. As a consequence the need to break through barriers has clearly diminished.[3]

From the point of view of Icelandic security interests, the diminished importance of the GIUK gap in Soviet nuclear strategy is an important development. For NATO, the importance of the gap for the protection of the sea lines of communications and in a more general sense for the control of the Atlantic remains undiminished.

THE KEFLAVIK BASE

With the exception of a small base with personnel of approximately 100 located at Höfn on the southeastern coast, the U.S. military presence in Iceland is concentrated at Keflavik. Both bases are under the operational command of the U.S. Navy. Navy and air force personnel number around 3000.

The undiminished importance of the GIUK gap in NATO planning is reflected in an ongoing project to upgrade its air barrier by increasing the air defense capabilities of the Keflavik base. Instead of twelve F-4E fighter interceptors, eighteen F-15 fighter bombers have been deployed to Iceland since 1985. They are directed by ground-based radars, an extension of the DEW line, located at Keflavik and Höfn, and two AWACS aircraft. An update of the radars is planned, and two new radars are being built in the western and northeastern parts of Iceland. The project also includes hardened aircraft shelters, new command and control facilities, and a new system for the reception, storage and distribution of aviation fuel. An examination of the military background to the project shows that it has its origin in a decision to expand the role of land-based forces in maritime operations, in particular to defend against long-range Soviet bombers armed with Cruise missiles. The aim seems to be the simultaneous enhancement of the air defenses of Iceland, the sea lines of comunications, and carrier battle groups.[4] The Icelandic government had authorized the whole project by 1985, primarily on the basis of developments in the Soviet bomber force and Cruise missiles.[5]

Submarine and surface surveillance is carried out by a squadron of nine Orion P-3C maritime patrol aircraft which, in coordination with an ASW command and control center, are aided by localization data on submerged submarines from a SOSUS (sound surveillance system) in the GIUK gap. Since 1985, Iceland has permitted the stationing of one Orion with a Dutch crew for training purposes. Also located at the Keflavik base are tactical and strategic communication facilities providing coverage for U.S. naval units in the north Atlantic and Norwegian Sea.

Apart from providing for the defense of Iceland, the main wartime contingency roles for the Keflavik base would include ASW operations, air support of naval operations in the north Atlantic, and support of reinforcement operations from the United States to Europe.

THE POLICY CONTEXT

The decision by Iceland to enter NATO in 1949 was intimately bound up with the question of whether this would entail an obligation to permit the stationing of foreign troops and military facilities on Icelandic soil. Alliance membership was thus considered an adequate guarantee against external aggression.

The Defense Agreement of 1951 between Iceland and the United States was entered into during a period when the first steps were being taken toward the military integration and political organization of the Alliance. The agreement may be seen to reflect changing perceptions of the need to provide defenses for the country, and as a recognition that Iceland could not refrain from contributing to the overall defense effort of NATO.

Although security policy has enjoyed majority support in the Althing (Parliament) during most of the postwar period, it should be noted that the presence of the U.S. base has been considered neither a desirable nor a permanent solution. Yet, the only alternative security arrangement considered to be open to Iceland, unarmed nonalignment, has not been regarded as a policy that could secure the independence of the country. Iceland itself has remained unarmed for centuries, and a change in that state of affairs has never been seriously considered. It is also extremely doubtful whether the necessary resources for any meaningful defense could be made available. This becomes apparent, if for no other reason than the size of the population, which now stands at around 240,000.

At the same time that the security policy has enjoyed a political majority, it has caused one of the most fundamental conflicts in Icelandic postwar politics. It has been and still is a consistent subject of debate, and it may be contended that there is no issue that is as sensitive in the Icelandic political arena. The focus of the controversy has essentially been on the Keflavik base rather than NATO membership. It has twice found expression in the declared policies of Icelandic governments to terminate the Defense Agreement, in 1956-58 and in 1971-74. In both cases, the policy was not carried out, apparently due to lack of consensus within the coalition governments once they had taken office.

Partly as a consequence of the security arrangement for which Iceland has opted, the development and conduct of security policy (especially regarding the military and defense) has had a very limited scope. Iceland has been inactive on these issues. This may also be explained to a large extent by the unarmed status of the country, the general attitude of Icelanders, who tend to regard military affairs as something strange and alien, and the political controversy on security policy.

The security arrangement has thus only recently found a rationale in threat scenarios provided by official authorities. In order to provide a framework for civil defense planning, the previous government (a coalition of the Independence Party and the Progressive Party) issued a statement declaring that it does not under the present circumstances regard an attack on Iceland as likely, except in the case of general war. In that case, it might come to bombing attacks, and attempts might also be made to gain a foothold in the country with airborne forces. Chemical weapons might be used and nuclear missile attacks could not be disregarded.[6]

Iceland does not participate in the NATO Infrastructure Fund, nor has it at any time been a member of the Nuclear Planning Group. Since 1984, however, it is represented on the Military Committee by a civilian, which is one indication of new developments in security policy. Before discussing these, a note should be made of Icelandic policy towards the Keflavik base.

BASE POLICY

According to the Defense Agreement, the number of personnel as well as the general development and use of the Keflavik base are dependent on the consent of Icelandic authorities. The main restriction in this regard has been to ban the stationing of nuclear weapons on Icelandic soil. This restraint has not been as well known outside Iceland as the nuclear weapons policies of Denmark and Norway. Statements on this issue, however, have repeatedly been made by all Icelandic foreign ministers since 1964.

The question of nuclear weapons in Iceland has been central to the debate on security policy in recent years, in view of allegations that there were or might be nuclear weapons stationed on Icelandic soil. The main debate on the issue took place in the summer of 1980, mainly on the basis that the Marines who are responsible for security at the Keflavik base operated according to a manual with the title "The Navy Nuclear Weapon Security Manual." The basic problem was the U.S. refusal to confirm or deny the presence of nuclear weapons anywhere. This was pointed out in a statement by the U.S. ambassador to Iceland, which further referred to the Defense Agreement, stating that the conditions under which U.S. forces "may enter upon and make use of facilities in Iceland" is dependent on the consent of Icelandic authorities. The implication was obviously that the U.S. government respected Icelandic policy on nuclear weapons.

The fact that there are no nuclear weapons stationed at the Keflavik base was further confirmed in December 1984, when classified U.S. documents from 1975 were made available to the Icelandic government. At the same time they showed that Icelandic policy was being respected, the documents revealed contingency plans to move nuclear depth charges for the Orion P-3C into Iceland in time of war.[7]

Nuclear weapons became once more a subject of debate in 1985. This centered around whether the policy of excluding nuclear weapons also included warships that came into port or passing through Icelandic territorial waters. Foreign Minister Geir Hallgrimsson (1983-85) stated that the policy on nuclear weapons also included warships in Icelandic territorial waters. This was subsequently interpreted by many in Iceland and abroad as similar to the policy of New Zealand. The minister explained, however, that Icelandic policy was similar to that of Norway, in that the policy was respected by the NATO allies. Icelandic policy in this respect is therefore not comparable to that of New Zealand.

Efforts have also been directed toward reducing the perceived cultural impact of the U.S. presence in Iceland. This has been a direct result of the controversy on security policy which has in the past been heavily focused on this issue. Thus U.S. personnel have largely been confined to the base area with strict rules governing their movements outside it. Furthermore, on the basis of a bilateral agreement with the United States in 1974, restrictions have been put on manpower levels, limiting the number of base personnel to around 3,000. This measure has apparently been considered by the U.S. Navy as a major restraint with regard to increasing the sea control capabilities of the base, which is now limited to upgrading the types of equipment deployed and to improvements in their support systems.[8]

DEVELOPMENTS IN SECURITY POLICYMAKING

In the past, Icelandic governments have from time to time had to call on foreign experts for advice, as expertise on security affairs has been virtually nonexistent in the country until recent years. The first steps toward amending this situation and providing the necessary basis for a more independent evaluation of national security affairs were taken with the establishment of the Icelandic Commission on Security and International Affairs in 1979. The commission, which is composed on two representatives from each parliamentary party, has as its main task to supervise research and distribute information and analysis on security policy. It does not make policy proposals to the government. However, its work has clearly had an impact on the debate in the country, and according to one observer it has been "instrumental in diminishing political disputes on security policy."[9]

As for policymaking, the main new development is that security policy has been institutionalized. For some years debates in the Althing have demonstrated a consensus between the political parties that experts should be engaged at the Ministry for Foreign Affairs. The largest political party in Iceland, the Independence party, has furthermore propagated a more active participation in NATO and a more independent assessment of the defense of the country. This process was started early in 1985 when Hallgrimsson announced the establishment of a defense office within the ministry. The office is responsible for the conduct of security policy, and experts have been engaged for that purpose. Iceland's participation in the NATO Infrastructure Fund is being considered and, as was noted above, it is now being represented on the Military

Committee. A further development is that the two new radars being built in the country will be manned with Icelandic personnel. In addition, the possibility is being considered of equipping the Icelandic Coast Guard for mine-sweeping.[10]

THE DOMESTIC CONSENSUS

The controversy on security policy and, in particular, the declared policies of Icelandic governments in the 1950s and 1970s to terminate the Defense Agreement are probably the main reason behind the relatively strong image that seems to have been created outside of Iceland that security policy has an unstable background in the internal political system. The fact is that, although security policy remains a controversial issue, it may be argued that it is no longer an issue in Icelandic politics that is likely to become a subject of sudden change in the near future. As a result of the policy on the Keflavik base, the cultural aspect of the U.S. presence has not been very noticeable in the debate during recent years, and it can no longer be regarded as a major issue in Icelandic politics. Instead, military aspects of the base have become prevalent in the debate. However, this has not had any comparable effects on policy, which may be partly explained by the fact that the cultural issue has resonance far beyond those circles that are opposed to the security arrangement. An outline follows of the political support for security policy in Iceland.

The Political Spectrum

The general election of April 1987 produced a political stalemate and jockeying among parties to form a coalition. The Independence party, usually ranked on the right of the political spectrum, is the largest, but lost much support in the last election. The party played a decisive role in the formulation of Icelandic security policy and has been its most consistent supporter throughout the postwar period. As mentioned previously, the Independence party has in recent years propagated a more active participation of Iceland within NATO and stressed the necessity for an independent Icelandic evaluation in matters of defense.

The Progressive party is the second largest in Iceland. It is in favor of NATO membership and supported the Defense Agreement with the United States in 1951. However, since 1956 it has been the declared policy of the party to terminate the agreement as soon as "conditions" permit. This policy formulation may probably be understood in the context that a substantial proportion of party supporters are opposed to the agreement. This cannot be regarded as an active policy, in spite of the fact that the Progressive party headed the coalitions in 1956-58 and 1971-74 which had the termination of the Defense Agreement on their agendas.

The Social Democratic party, the third largest in the Althing, has always supported Icelandic security policy with the exception of the period 1956-58. There has always been some opposition within the party to NATO membership and especially to the Keflavik base. This has not been reflected in its policy, however, except for the period mentioned.

The People's Alliance,the fourth largest party, lies furthest to the left in the party system. The party is opposed to NATO membership and the Defense Agreement with the United States and favors a policy of non-alignment. It used to make it a prerequisite for participation in coalition governments that Iceland terminate the Defense Agreement. This policy has changed, and, in 1978-79 and 1980-83 the party participated in coalition governments on the basis of status quo security policy. It has also taken a somewhat different approach in its opposition to security policy in recent years. Rather than generally emphasizing that Iceland terminate the Defense Agreement and leave NATO, it has focused its attention more on specific military aspects of the Keflavik issue.

The Women's Alliance is a new party which has its origins in the feminist movement in the country. The party doubled its popular vote and Althing representation 1987 election. It has avoided taking a specific stand on Icelandic security policy. Generally, its attitudes toward international affairs might be termed as pacifist. The fact that the Women's Alliance has the abolition of military alliances on its agenda would indicate that official security policy is not favored.

Public Opinion

An opinion poll on Icelandic attitudes toward security affairs was taken in 1983 shortly after the general election.[11] As shown in Table 11.1, NATO membership has the support of a clear majority of 80 percent of those stating an opinion whereas 20 percent are opposed to it.

Table 11.1 Attitudes Toward Iceland's Continued Membership in NATO

Approve	53%
Disapprove	13%
No opinion	34%
Total	100%
(N = 979)	
Of those stating an opinion	
Approve	80%
Disapprove	20%

Source : Icelandic Commission on Security and International Affairs poll (1985)

When it comes to the question of the Keflavik base, the results are different. As shown in Table 11.2 approval (64 percent) is considerably less than for NATO and disapproval is considerably greater (36 percent).

Table 11.2 Attitudes Toward the Keflavik Base

Strongly approve	23%
Tend to approve	31%
Makes no difference	15%
Tend to disapprove	15%
Strongly disapprove	15%
Total	99%
(N = 970)	
Of those who either approve or disapprove	
Approve	64%
Disapprove	36%

Source : Icelandic Commission on Security and International Affairs poll (1985)

A further examination shows that 76 percent of those supporting NATO membership approve of the base whereas 14 percent disapprove it. Note should also be made of the fact that 41 percent of those expressing no opinion on NATO approve of the Keflavik base.

The differences the poll shows between support for NATO and the Defense Agreement with the U.S. were to be expected but may, however, seem somewhat puzzling, as many would see these issues as two sides of the same coin. Some explanations for this may possibly be found in history. On entering NATO, Iceland made the reservation that membership would not entail an obligation to have a foreign military presence in the country during peacetime. As a consequence, the Keflavik issue has not necessarily been represented in Icelandic politics as closely related NATO membership and has been treated frequently as a separate issue.

More men (64 percent) approved of NATO membership than did women (41 percent) whereas the difference by sex is marginal among those who disapprove. No opinion was given on the question by 47 percent of the female respondents, as opposed to 22 percent of the male. Support for NATO is strongest in the age bracket 40 to 69 (65 percent) with no opinion given by 25 percent of the respondents, and weakest in the age of bracket 20 to 29 (39 percent), with 46 percent of the respondents stating no opinion. On the Keflavik issue, the same analysis shows only expected and insignificant differences, except in the case of the age bracket 20 to 29 where 45 percent approve and 37 percent disapprove. Although this may simply show a pattern comparable with the past, it inevitably leads to speculation on whether there is a trend toward declining support for the base and increasing opposition to it. As this is the first reliable opinion poll in Iceland on security affairs, no comparable data from the past exists and therefore no extrapolations can be drawn.

CONCLUSION

Although recent developments in the strategic environment have had considerable impact on the position of Iceland, the country remains of key strategic importance to NATO in the protection of the sea lines of communications across the Atlantic. In view of developments in the Soviet bomber force and Cruise missiles, the Icelandic government has authorized a project to upgrade the air barrier in the GIUK gap by increasing the air defense capabilities of the Keflavik base.

The main new development in Icelandic security policy is that the past inactive stand of the country is changing. By institutionalizing security policy in the Ministry of Foreign Affairs in early 1985 and engaging experts, a process was started that aims at a more active participation of Iceland within NATO and a more independent evaluation with regard to national security affairs. It is too early to be very specific about what impact this development may have on security policy in the long run. Substantial changes in security policy are not to be expected for the time being. However, it would seem likely that this will result in a gradual move from an almost exclusively bilateral relationship with the United States in security affairs toward closer cooperation with the European members of NATO.

Security policy has broad support among the Icelandic population, although it remains a controversial issue in the political arena. It will continue to be so, with a greater focus on the military aspects of the Keflavik issue than in the past. It remains to be seen what impact this will have on policymaking, but it seems unlikely to have an impact comparable to the cultural issue.

NOTES

1. See Bert H. Cooper, Maritime Roles for Land-Based Aviation, Congressional Research Service, report no. 83-151 F (Washington, D.C. : GPO, 1983), p. 20.

2. Congressional Research Service, Evaluation of Fiscal Year 1979 Arms Control Impact Statements (Washington, D.C. : GPO, 1979), p. 115.

3. For a more detailed exposition of this development, see Gunnar Gunnarsson, "Icelandic Security Policy: Context and Trends," Cooperation and Conflict 17, (1982) : 257-72.

4. See Gunnar Gunnarsson, The Keflavik Base : Plans and Projects, Icelandic Commission on Security and International Affairs, Occasional Paper no. 3, 1985.

5. Report of Foreign Minister Geir Hallgrimsson to the Althing (Reykjavik, March 1985), p. 28.

6. The text is printed in a report on the strengthening of civil defense published in April 1984 by a parliamentary committee.

7. On the contingency plans, see Leslie H. Gelb, "U.S. Contingency Plan Would Put A-Arms in Four Atlantic Nations," New York Times, February 13, 1985.

8. Congressional Research Service, United States Foreign Policy Objectives and Overseas Military Installations (Washington, D.C. : GPO, 1979), p. 26.

9. Björn Bjarnason, "Iceland's Security Policy : Vulnerability and Responsibility," in Deterrence and Defense in the North, edited by J. J. Holst, K. Hunt, and A. Sjaastad (Oslo : Norwegian University Press, 1985), p. 144.

10. Report of Foreign Minister Geir Hallgrimsson, pp. 26-31.

11. Olafur Th. Hardarson, Icelandic Attitudes Towards Security and Foreign Affairs, Icelandic Commission on Security and International Affairs, Occasional Paper no. 2, 1985; Olafur Th. Hardarson, "Icelandic Security and Foreign Policy : The Public Attitude," Cooperation and Conflict, 20 (1985) : 297-316.

NATO South

12   Spain: Problems of Integration

Antonió Sánchez-Gijón

EVALUATION OF THE PRESENT SECURITY SITUATION

From the perspective of the general public and social and institutional groups (political parties, Parliament, the armed forces), Spain's security is not at great risk and is unlikely to be within the foreseeable future. However, there are external and internal causes for concern.

External Factors

As an ally and economic associate of most of the Western European countries, Spain shares their concerns about peace and stability in Europe, but has a somewhat higher threshold level of threat perception than most of them. Spain is relatively immune from the anxieties that the enormous Soviet military presence in Central Europe creates in West Germany, for example; it has not experienced the worst fears of the cold war, nor has it taken up any major responsibility in checking Soviet power, as have Britain, Norway, the FRG, or Italy. This was due in part to its isolation from European affairs in the peak years of the cold war, to the nature of the Franco regime, but also to its introspective political culture and self-absorption over the moral and political consequences of the civil war.

Nonetheless, Spanish public opinion, as represented by its well-informed, educated segments, was always interested in the maintenance of good security conditions in Europe, and was concerned about such actions as the Berlin blockade, the Soviet invasions of Hungary and Czechoslovakia, and the tensions stemming from ideological confrontation, bloc politics, and the armament race.

A sharper perception of threat was apparent in the decolonization process, especially insofar as it affected the last remnants of the subject territories. This referred only to the Maghreb context, especially Morocco, the sole country against which Spain has resorted to the use of major armed force in the course of the twentieth century, first to impose its protectorate in northern Morocco, and then to fend off military pressure (in Ifni, in 1956). Spain also suffered extreme political pressure from the Moroccans when Rabat launched its "green march" into the Spanish colony of Western Sahara in 1975; Morocco is again the only country that has a claim over Spanish territory (the cities of Ceuta and Melilla, and a few islets along the Mediterranean coast). Compounding this potential for tension is the unresolved competition for hegemony in the Maghreb region between Morocco and Algeria, revolving around the issue of who is going to control in the end the Western Sahara : Morocco, which occupies most of it, or the Algerian-backed Polisario front, which is fighting for independence. The tension between the two Magreb countries spilled over to Spain, when Algeria, distrustful of a Spain (which failed to concede independence to the territory and, moreover, transferred its administrative powers over the Western Sahara to Morocco and Mauritania by the Madrid agreement of February 1976), gave diplomatic and material support to a miniscule Canary Islands independence group, the MPAIAC, active until the early 1980s.

Soviet military power and political designs are looked upon with caution, if not suspicion, by practically all political forces, except the Communist parties (Partido Comunista de España, the historical Communist party, and the Partido Comunista, a splinter group of Soviet obedience), but there is not a clear vision of how Soviet actions could affect Spain, short of a general European conflict. Soviet naval presence (transit through the Strait of Gibraltar, monitoring of Spanish naval bases and U.S. facilities) is constant but not heavy along the Spanish coast, and is also frequent around the Canaries.

Internal Factors

Modern Spain perceives only two internal threats, one of them potential, the other actual. The potential one is separatism by any one of the historical nationalities that form the Spanish state and nation. The actual one is terrorism.

Suspicions of separatism attributed to Cataluña and the Basque country were one of the factors that moved the armed forces to rebel against the Spanish republic in 1936. Franco sternly suppressed Catalan and Basque aspirations for larger autonomy, thus stimulating even more nationalistic feelings among the population of the two regions. In the Basque country, those feelings were inflamed by the confrontationist tactics adopted by the Basque nationalist groups, leading to the appearance of an extremely violent terrorist organization, the ETA, which has been much more active in democratic Spain than in Franco's times, while in Cataluña a more compromising approach, under the democratic monarchy reinstated in 1975, allowed for a generally peaceful process of political, economic and administrative devolution.

Democratic Spain has instituted itself as a state of autonomous regions, each with its own government. While the main Catalan nationalist party (Convergencia i Unió) backed the approval of the 1978 constitution, the Partido Nacionalista Vasco refused to support it by abstaining in the referendum; this undermined the legitimacy of the constitution in the eyes of important sectors of Basque society. Nevertheless, the Basque nationalist government abides by the constitution, although it engages in a constant tug of war with Madrid for larger home-rule powers. The ETA seems to be unmoved by the increasing devolution process; its final aim is independence and socialism for the Basque country; its strategy is that of forcing Spanish authorities to grant the right of self-determination to the Basque people, which is excluded by the constitution. This they expect to obtain by the systematic use of terrorism against police forces, military officers, individuals suspected of being police informants, and those resisting their financial exactions. The ETA had killed only 20 people while Franco ruled Spain, but more than 500 since then. Bombs planted by the ETA can be counted by the thousands; the economic decline of the Basque country is attributed by the present autonomous government to terrorism, through a process of de-industrialization and investment flight. The ETA has assassination groups within Spain but has its command and financial infrastructure in the French Basque country. What was perceived as French tolerance toward Spanish Basque terrorism under the presidency of Giscard d'Estaing was interpreted by Spanish analysts as a tactic to keep nationalist pressure off the French Basque country and further debilitate a Spain that wanted to join the EC, to the discomfort of French farmers. The attitude adopted by the Mitterrand government has been much more cooperative, and has eventually led to a relative decline in the frequency of acts of terrorism within Spain.

ETA killings were one of the excuses taken up by the armed forces groups that inspired or joined the failed coup attempt of February 23, 1981. Determined action by the king, obedience of the large majority of the armed forces, and calm civil response to the provocation did away, no doubt definitively, with the threats of military intervention that had festered since the consolidation of democracy. Although the ETA did not reduce its rate of assassinations after the attempted coup, there is no prospect in modern Spain for an armed forces clampdown on terrorism that would imperil democratic rule. The ETA has offered to negotiate a truce in direct talks with the army that would lead to the withdrawal of the armed and police forces from the Basque country, the legalization of separatist parties, and the right of self-determination. There is not the least likelihood that a Spanish government would ever accept such terms, as admitted by the president of the Basque government in a public plea to the ETA to halt terrorism on September 20, 1985.

In summary, separatism is not a risk in the present political context; terrorist groups have very little chance of forcing a political solution on their terms, although there is not much hope, either, that terrorism will fade away in the foreseeable future. Rather, it is going to be maintained as a way of prolonging the mystique of Basque national independence.

Aspects of Modernization

Internal and external factors have nurtured the pervading fear, among both government and industrial elites, of Spain being left behind in the new industrial revolution. Priority attention given to the political aspects of modernization by democratic Spain has caused neglect of economic reform and industrial renovation. Only very recently has democratic Spain awakened to the reality that it had missed the first waves of the third industrial revolution. This consideration bears heavily on the conscience of Felipe González's government, which has moved to adopt a more pragmatic approach to matters of international security. One of the excuses given by the Socialists to explain their change of heart toward the Atlantic Alliance (from opposition to Spanish membership to lukewarm adhesion) is that NATO allows access to advanced technology through joint weapons procurement and development projects in cooperation with other allied countries. Access to new technologies has also been the factor behind the Spanish decision to accept the rulings of the COCOM group for monitoring exports of dual-purpose technologies, taken in September 1985, and to join the Eureka program.

POLICY CHANGES FOR ENHANCING FUTURE SECURITY

Internal Factors

Not only obedience, but loyal adherence to the constitution from the main Basque political party, would be the single factor that would most reinforce political stability in Spain and debilitate terrorism. For that, the constitution would have to be amended in order to allow for self-determination. It appears unthinkable that such a right would be admitted by the Spanish parliament when terrorism is in full swing and when there exists a very high degree of political coercion against non-nationalists in the Basque country. It should be noted that only a fraction of the nationalist vote (60 percent of the total) is separatist.

The centrist and Socialist governments have followed a policy of encouraging the abandonment of arms on the part of Basque terrorists, which has been successful in the case of one faction of the ETA, called politico-militar, whose members have entered normal life and legal political activity. The more radical branch, called militar, has rejected any such pardon and demobilization, due in part to the fact that there would be much less leniency for their bloodier crimes. A new Basque nationalist leadership, which took over government in early 1985, and the Basque Socialist party entered into a parliamentary agreement to vote together in the Basque parliament, where the nationalist governing party does not enjoy a full majority, in order to make the country governable. This pact has greatly contributed to the political and social rejection of the ETA's methods.

Accepting the ETA conditions for peace would be perceived as a debasement of the Spanish government by the Basque population. Thus, the very act that would end armed conflict would endanger the unity of the country. That would not be acceptable to very large sectors of Spanish society, and would be seen as highly suspect by the armed forces. Thus, there is no way of ever considering the possibility of self-determination while the ETA is up in arms. Even if it were not, the consent to self-determination would be something very difficult to achieve from the point of view of Spanish Parliament and public opinion, unless the continuation of the basic tenets of the present unity are ensured : one market, no frontiers, and one crown, with all that this implies (one single armed service to the king, one foreign policy, one common flag). But in order to reach even a reasonable level of free debate around those alternatives, a long period of peace and accommodation would be needed. In the meantime, Spanish membership in the European Community (EC) will make its effects felt in Spanish society in a fashion that is not easy to foresee.

Spanish EC membership can either alleviate tensions between conflicting national loyalties within Spain, by a transfer of nationalist fervor to European ideals, or exacerbate these loyalties as certain regions seek a national profile differentiated from the rest of Spain within the Community. The result will greatly depend on how the economic opportunities offered by a large, more advanced market are shared among the different regions of Spain; Cataluña is probably the one region best placed to take advantage of EC membership given its social and economic fabric and its greater proximity to the European core, while large sections of the rest of Spain are likely to be harmed by integration. The Basque country, which in terms of industrial base, infrastructure, and proximity to the rest of Europe, can be compared to Cataluña, will probably fail to profit from EC membership while political violence, social strife, and industrial decline persist.

What effect EC membership will have on the Spanish internal balance among different regions will greatly depend on the ability of the government to mobilize human and capital resources to confront the European challenge. In this regard, one differential factor must be pointed out: while in Cataluña and in a few other regions local government and business share a common economic outlook, thereby facilitating concerted efforts to confront Community challenges, the Spanish business community at large resents the economic policies of the national and regional Socialist-controlled governments, thus weakening the chances of a healthy response to European competition. So it can be predicted that the nature and quality of leadership exerted by the national and regional governments will have, in the long-term perspective, a specific bearing on matters of internal security. A Spain in which resentments would explode because of perceived discrimination in the process of integration within the Community, would only compound what is already a delicate balance within conflicting nationalist tendencies.

External Factors

The Socialist government recommended a positive vote in the referendum they promised on the continuation of Spanish NATO membership, and the March 1986 plebiscite resulted in a 53 percent majority in favor of the Alliance (39 percent opposed). NATO membership will constitute the main security factor affecting Spanish military and international policies, at least while the Alliance lasts.

The Socialist government still embraces the option presented by Prime Minister Felipe González in October 1984, when he outlined a ten-point security policy, whose main tenet was maintenance of Alliance membership and no military integration, together with a reduction of the U.S. presence on Spanish territory (including base closures). He also announced that Spain would consider joining the Western European Union and signing the Non-Proliferation Treaty.

Opinion polls published from 1982 (the year when Spain joined the Alliance) up to the end of 1984 tended to show a declining support of Spanish membership in the Alliance. Polls published later, at the same time that the government was changing its attitude toward NATO, and negotiations with the EEC were ending, show a slow growth of those opinions in favor of remaining within the Alliance, with a majority of the people unable to state an answer. In any case, it can now be taken for certain that Spain will remain within the Alliance, without initially seeking full participation in its integrated military commands.

Spain is likely to increase its participation in different NATO bodies, which already is quite substantial at the civilian level, especially in those sectors that have to do with common development of weapon systems and joint procurement programs.

The question of full military integration will have to be tackled at some time when the government decides how it intends to discharge its duty to assist the allies in collective defense. An allied policy that would enhance NATO prestige in Spanish public opinion would be that to entrust Spain with the coordination of defense in the area of the western Mediterranean and the eastern Atlantic, which hinges on the Strait of Gibraltar, where a British, U.S., and Spanish (not to speak of a Soviet) presence, is constantly maintained. The ideal axis running from the Balearics to the Canaries along the strait constitutes the main geostrategic feature that inspires Spanish military efforts, as reportedly expressed by the Strategic Joint Plan, the secret master document that sets out military guidelines for defense. The plan has been in constant revision for many years and has not yet been officially approved by the government, for the avowed reason that it needs to take into account the revision of the Armed Forces Investment Allocations Law which regulates the resources designated for weapon systems acquisition. This law was intended to ensure a steady annual 4.432 percent increase in real purchase terms from 1982 to 1990. In 1985 the law was the object of strong criticism for creating defense investment growth while many social investment programs were being reduced in size.

The maintenance of the 4.432 percent increase commitment would be the single factor that would contribute most to enhance the security situation of Spain until the end of the century. It would make the process of military reforms (including deep cuts in personnel) more palatable to the armed forces, thus buttressing their morale. The present Investment Law only guarantees the armed forces of the acquisition of a much smaller number of weapon systems than had been contemplated by previous governments. For instance, the air force had been promised 144 advanced combat aircraft and received only 72 F-18As; the navy expected five FFG missile frigates and received only four for its carrier combat group; the army expected to develop a new tank to replace its very old armor, and had to be content for moment with the overhaul of 146 AMX-30 tanks. There was widespread fear among the armed forces that not even the reduced plans could be realized if the Investment Law was reviewed.

One policy that could help to legitimize heavy investment in weapons procurement is that of military exports. The Socialist government is making a great effort in expanding weapon sales and in substituting Spanish-built equipment for imports.

The planned major changes in the development of the Spanish armed forces will contribute greatly to strengthen defense; the changes mean a shift of units from central and northern Spain toward the south and southeast, to reinforce the axis laid out in the joint strategic plan. Andalucia will be the army's stronghold, while Rota, where the United States enjoys the use of vast facilities, will be the headquarters of the carrier combat group. The air force deploys most of its power in Valencia and Albacete, close to the Mediterranean shores. A third phase of the air control system, together with an area and point air defense, will complete the picture of the Spanish armed forces deployment.

As can be imagined, the characteristics of the described deployment have a certain ambivalence; on one side it confronts the areas interfacing with the Maghreb countries and on the other it gravitates around a critically important choke point that connects the Mediterranean and the Atlantic, serving as a communication lane between Northern and Southern Europe, and between the United States and the Middle East and NATO southern flank countries. It seems only natural that any potential contribution to NATO would develop from a defense configuration that is properly Spanish.

As has already been observed, Spanish security perceptions reflect concern for the consequences of political tension coming out of the Maghreb. The current theoretical discussion revolves around the idea of applying a balance-of-power or global approach to Maghreb policies. The experience seems to validate the balance-of-power policy. Thus, when Algeria was pressing Spain for rapid decolonization of the Western Sahara while at the same time intimating a threat against the Canaries, Spain chose Morocco for a political settlement of differences, in spite of the fact that the "green march" had involved quite a lot of pressure. When Libya and Morocco signed their spectacular act of union in 1984, it did not take much time for Spain to open a rapprochement with Algeria by ending the long dispute over Algerian claims on a big natural gas contract that Spain had not fulfilled. The solution of the problem involved large industrial and building contracts to compensate for the high prices Spain had to pay for Algerian gas. A long-term Spanish policy should be to open many avenues of cooperation with the two main Maghreb countries, in order to be able to play the balancing game without undue, definite losses.

One very specific policy that Spain could adopt with respect to the Moroccan territorial claim on Ceuta and Melilla would be to assure this country that the economic viability of the two cities would not be attained to the detriment of Moroccan economic interests, namely, among other things, by smuggling. Another would be that if the population composition of the cities shifted toward a majority of Moroccan citizens, a special interest would be granted to Morocco over the consequences of Spanish administrative powers. No doubt these policies would assuage to a certain extent Moroccan feelings, short of outright takeover of the enclaves; however, these policies would be very difficult to implement given the Spanish public's present mood.

Much diplomatic attention will be given by Morocco and other countries to the way Spain approaches the negotiations with Britain for settling differences on Gibraltar. Although there are substantial historical, political, and demographic differences between Ceuta-Melilla and Gibraltar, at least they are similar in that they concern populations who feel loyal to countries alien to the geographical situation where those cities are located, and in the irrendentist attitude adopted by the two claimants. One substantial difference is that Spain and Britain are allies and associates in the EC and NATO, while Spain and Morocco have as much mutual distrust as reason to be on good terms. A settlement on Gibraltar that would reconcile the wishes of the native population with the interests of Spain would have an exemplary effect on the case of Ceuta and Melilla and would indicate clearly to Morocco the baseline of a permanent solution for Spain.

Policy Opponents

Full Spanish assumption of NATO responsibilities would be strongly opposed by the extreme left, namely the Communists of every obedience. A rather tepid opposition is presented by large segments of the intellectual elites, which identify themselves with progressive causes, but only to the point where they become bored by the subject.

A policy of accommodation with Morocco on the terms suggested above would be looked upon suspiciously by the present diplomatic and military establishments and rightist parties. The same could be said about a policy that tried to reconcile Spanish interests with the wishes of the population on Gibraltar, with the added opposition of the moderate left.

FACTORS ENHANCING/INHIBITING SECURITY POLICIES

Internal Factors

Slow or zero economic growth would produce a negative impact on the basic fabric of the Spanish policy; there would be regions that would claim a right to disengage themselves from the political and economic lot of the more retarded areas; the logic of market forces, as enshrined in the EC basic philosophy, would be used as an argument for disparaging economic and hence political evolutionary processes.

Another negative factor of an internal nature is the reduction of the Spanish demographic growth rate, which in 1981 was 1.9 percent and today is perhaps less than 1.7 percent, compared with higher rates in Portugal and, above all, Morocco. Although there are no official statistics, the Spanish press reports increasing numbers of poor Portuguese and Moroccan immigrants entering a country with no jobs to offer.

External Factors

In the long term, it is the Moroccan population growth that shows greater potential for risk in the region, due to the refusal of the ineffective elites of that country to provide the social and economic changes that would accommodate the new generations in a stable manner. The frustration of the younger generations of Moroccans has triggered social explosions from time to time; they invariably have been suppressed very sternly. How long the ruling Alaouite monarchy can avert open social conflict is anybody's guess in Spain. A revolutionary situation, combined with a surge of religious fundamentalism and/or nationalism, can mean real trouble for Spain.

The effectiveness of the balance-of-power game that Spain plays in the Maghreb is dimisnished by the narrower parallel game the Polisario front plays with Spain. Its political leadership courts Spain so that it will not recognize full Moroccan sovereignty over the Western Sahara (the Spanish position is that the process of decolonization must be consummated through an act of self-determination), while its military leaders seize Spanish citizens and fishing boats along the waters of the Sahara; seventeen acts of aggression against Spanish trawlers have been registered since 1977, with several deaths. Consequently, so long as peace is not attained in the Western Sahara, Spain will not be able to see its relations with the Maghreb as stable and risk-free.

The relationship with Community and allied countries has become, and will remain, the central concern of Spanish foreign policies. This tendency will enhance internal as well as external stability, although some potential for tension should not be overlooked in relations with the United States. Although the centrist and rightist forces are in general pro-U.S., and the Socialists have shown a great talent for accommodation with the great "imperialistic, capitalist hegemonic power," there are some points where they would be put in an impossible situation due to certain U.S. policies; the main cause of tension between a Socialist government and the United States is Washington's policy toward Central America, where this implies the use of armed force. A U.S. intervention in a Spanish-speaking country would put good relations in jeopardy, at least for a few years; and this would be so in spite of the fact that the governing Socialists are more and more outspokenly disillusioned with the turn of the Nicaraguan revolution and the

Salvadoran guerrilla movement. Action by the U.S. Goliath against the revolutionary David is too much a symbolic image to be resisted by those who like to think of themselves, at the bottom of their pragmatic souls, as true progressive idealists. Moreover, the Socialist government tries hard not to hide criticism of the Strategic Defense Initiative, though they seem to see in it another trick of the old "military-industrial" complex designed to build up East-West tension. A U.S. foreign policy that is less assertive and militant than the one pursued by President Reagan would help the Socialist government to encourage a smoother integration into NATO structures, and would make Spain feel more comfortable within the Alliance.

13 Portugal: The Strategic Triangle

Alvaro Vasconcelos

Geographically close to Africa and on the route to the Americas, Portugal, with its Atlantic archipelagos of Madeira and the Azores, is part of a zone of transition and an area of great importance in the strategy of the Western Alliance.

A historian at the beginning of the twenty-first century will perhaps be able to contend that, for Portugal, the third millenium began when, after two years of turmoil following the uprising of April 25, 1974, the democratic parties successfully opted for European integration and the Atlantic Alliance as the major priorities of Portuguese foreign and defense policy. The European option was consolidated with membership in the European Community as of January 1, 1986.

Portuguese security priorities had been dominated in the twentieth century by the perceived need to maintain a large colonial empire--from Macau, Goa, Damão and Diu, and Timor in Asia, to Mozambique, Angola, Guinea, Sao Tomé e Príncipe, and Cape Verde in Africa. Following the collapse of the last European empire, Portuguese foreign and security policies have been reshaped along Euro-Atlantic guidelines, thus becoming more similar to those of most members of the Western Alliance. These policies are likely to remain the dominant Portuguese security concerns over the last decade of the twentieth century.

THE SHAPING OF A DEMOCRATIC CONSENSUS

In predicting Portuguese security concerns and defense policy for the turn of the century, one must bear in mind what factors have until now shaped the international posture of Portugal and how they may develop in the future.

Prior to 1974, Portuguese defense policy was determined by the geostrategic position of the country, the preservation of the empire, and the dominant anti-communist ideology.

Portugal is geographically situated on the southwestern periphery of Europe and linked to two Atlantic archipelagos : Madeira, closer to the African continent than to

Europe, and the Azores, on the Atlantic Ridge, lying approximately 2300 miles from the United States and almost 1000 miles from the Portuguese mainland. The Portuguese position was clearly significant to the strategists who shaped the configuration of a U.S.-European alliance system designed to contain the Soviet challenge in Central Europe. This was all the more evident in that Spain could not be invited to join NATO, due to Franco's involvement with the Axis. At the end of the 1940s, it was the conventional dimension of Western deterrence that was stressed, making the military reinforcement of Europe from the United States even more vital. The Azores were seen as part of the Atlantic strategic border of the United States, in a position symmetrical to that of Hawaii in the Pacific. The islands provided an important refueling stop for the reinforcement of Europe (already demonstrated by the Berlin supply operation of 1948-49), as well as an ideal base for anti-submarine warfare.

The Salazar regime understood the importance to its own political survival of being a member of an alliance of democratic countries and viewed NATO as a way of gaining international and domestic support. This idea was enhanced by the fact that the Alliance was created to face what was perceived as a Soviet military threat to Western Europe, a purpose well in accordance with the dictator's anticommunist crusade.

From 1961 (when the war in Angola began) until 1974, the main and almost exclusive foreign and security policy concern of the Portuguese regime lay in Africa. In 1974, more than 150,000 soldiers were fighting in Angola, Mozambique, and Guinea. The participation in the Alliance and, in particular, the bilateral agreements with the United States, dating back to 1951, were also perceived as a bargaining chip to try to reduce allied opposition to the African policy. That was clearly the case during the Kennedy administration and afterward, in 1973, in the wake of the Yom Kippur war, when Premier Marcelo Caetano (who was Salazar's successor following his illness and subsequent death in 1968) tried with a certain degree of success to convince the Nixon-Kissinger administration to find a way around the obstacle raised by the U.S. Congress in the form of an arms sale embargo.

On April 25, 1974, the military, seeking a negotiated solution for the African wars, overthrew the regime and began the democratic transition. Part of the former political and security concerns disappeared or would disappear with the forthcoming independence of the African colonies.

The Communist party, clandeste for more than 40 years, was for a short while regarded as an ally of the democratic parties. The Socialist party (PS) was founded in 1973 and, in the year after the coup, the two other major parties appeared--the Popular Democratic party (PPD), later renamed the Social Democratic party (PSD), and the party of the Democratic and Social Center (CDS), the Portuguese Christian Democrats. In 1985, a new political party, the party of Democratic Renewal (PRD) was founded by General Ramalho Eanes, the former president of the republic : this party tried to pass as successor to the democratic military left wing within the Movement of the Armed Forces.

In the post-revolutionary period, the notion emerged among the military leaders and in the political elite and public opinion that Portugal had no enemies and could afford a more neutral position in East-West relations. The question was never whether Portugal should opt out of the Atlantic Alliance--not even the Communist party has ever suggested that possibility. Rather, in that period, the Portuguese constitution expressed the idea that Portugal should seek the elimination of both military alliances--NATO and the Warsaw Pact. It is evident what such a situation would mean : in the East, it would bring no change in the grip of the Soviet Union over Eastern Europe, while in the West, Europe and the United States would drift apart. The Portuguese posture subsequent to the 1974 coup reflected the sentiment that there was no longer any need for a strong commitment to the Alliance, since NATO's "supportive neutrality" in relation to Portuguese African involvement was no longer required. Moreover, there was no clear perception of an external military threat to Portugal, a country far from the European front, although it is in a region of submarine and antisubmarine warfare (but submarines are by definition invisible to the eye).

It was the evolution of the democratic political struggle in Portugal that has shaped the present strong ideological commitment to the Atlantic Alliance. In the years 1974-75, during the battle for freedom and democracy, the democratic parties were compelled to overcome their differences and unite, to align with those sectors of the armed forces that opposed a Communist takeover, and to seek support from the member countries of the Atlantic Alliance. Portugal was divided between, on the one hand, the pro-Western and pro-European forces and on the other, the Communist party and its allies within the armed forces, supported by the Soviet Union. It is still a matter of debate whether the Communist party and the Soviet Union actually did want to seize power in Portugal or if they were destabilizing the country in order to gain greater influence over the independence process of the African colonies. But the fact remains that they were gaining control of the economy, state bureaucracy, and the media. As a result of the 1974-75 experience, the Portuguese have clearly taken sides. Still, the determining factors of geography and threat perceptions were responsible for a prevalent neutralist influence on the general approach to defense issues.

A EURO-ATLANTIC DEFENSE POLICY

The role that Portugal is likely to play in the Western security system will be shaped not only by security concerns, but especially by domestic factors, including the success of European integration. It will also depend, of course, upon the development of East-West relations. In any case, the current evolution of both NATO and U.S. strategy, the crisis in nuclear deterrence, the emphasis on the conventional deterrent, and the arguments about the present level of U.S. forces in Europe all convey a greater need for reinforcement from the United States. Consequently, those factors contribute to the U.S. request for more access to air and naval facilities in Portugal, in particular in the Atlantic-Mediterranean direction, all the more so since a decline of U.S. military presence in Spain is to be expected, as indicated by current bilateral negotiations. The Portuguese attitude is likely to depend as much on the evolution of Portuguese party politics and the results of U.S. "best efforts" in support of the re-equipment of Portuguese armed forces as on the degree to which Portugal will insist on relegating those facilities mainly to the European theater. A major problem for Portuguese-U.S. relations in the years to come may arise from misunderstandings regarding the use of Portuguese bases for possible U.S. involvement in the Middle East.

The U.S. interest in facilities for out-of-area conflicts, especially in the Middle East and the Persian Gulf, was at the center of the Portuguese-U.S. negotiations for the renewal of the defense agreement signed on December 13, 1983. Portugal then made it clear that "under no circumstances can clearance for the use of the Lajes base in the Azores be considered as automatic outside the NATO area."[1]

In the present situation, the disparity between the importance of facilities granted to NATO allies and the means of the Portuguese armed forces is considerable and unanimously recognized by civilian and military experts. This situation is not commensurate with the needs of the country's national defense or with those of the Alliance; the void of military power creates the perception in Portugal that, in a situation of crisis, forces other than Portuguese would be called on to act. And here again one finds another source of difficulty in the relations with the allies. It is thought that "in spite of the country's small physical dimensions, Portugal cannot, due to its past, due to its historical wealth, due to its self-consciousness as a nation, accomodate itself in a situation that could be defined as similar to that of Iceland."[2]

It is not foreseeable that, in the near future, Portugal will be in a position to increase military expenditure significantly. On the contrary, the military budget has decreased in real terms over the last ten years, and in 1984 it represented 2.45 percent of the country's gross domestic product. Although some degree of rationalization may be introduced, it will not be possible to modernize and re-equip the Portuguese armed forces without significant allied aid.

The willingness to contribute forces to the allied security system is clearly shown by the fact that Portugal's First Mixed Brigade is earmarked for deployment in northern Italy and that the modernization program is clearly designed to meet NATO as well as national requirements. This is the reason for the priority given to frigates and aircraft for anti-submarine warfare and for the implementation of air defense systems and other naval and air equipment for the protection of sea lanes and Portuguese harbors and airfields.

The present air-naval orientation of Portuguese strategy is stressed in the existing defense concept documents, which point to "the fundamental strategic importance of the maritime and air border and of the inter-territorial space," that is, the Atlantic waters between the different components of the territory of Portugal, the so-called strategic triangle (the mainland, Madeira, and the Azores).[3] The definition of the role of the army is limited by the fears of politicians about possible lingering political temptations of the officer corps. The thorough "normalization" of politico-military relations in the future will result in a reinforcement of the role of government and Parliament in the defense decision-making process.

Over the next decade, at the regional level, it will be necessary to manage the sensitive process of Spanish integration into NATO. Portugal will oppose any solution that would entrust Spain with a role of military coordination in the area and would certainly veto a unified military command for both countries. The Portuguese will undoubtedly favor a two-command solution, which would reinforce the Portuguese contribution under SACLANT. One of the subordinate commands to SACLANT, IBERLANT, under the direction of a Portuguese admiral, has always been located in Oeiras, near Lisbon.

If it is more or less clear what the Portuguese contribution to Western security in an East-West scenario would be, it is less clear what role Portugal will be called upon to play in North-South military cooperation. As already stressed, there is a close geographic proximity to Africa; the Algarve in southern Portugal is only 220 kilometers from the Moroccan coast, and Madeira is the southernmost position of the NATO command structure. The political, economic, and demographic developments in North Africa, tensions within the Maghreb, and the struggle for hegemony among Algeria, Morocco, and Libya, of which the conflict in the Western Sahara is the most spectacular manifestation, are all factors that must be taken into consideration by

Portuguese security policy. Portugal sooner or later will need to improve naval and air cooperation with Morocco.

Further to the south are situated the former Portuguese colonies in Africa. Military cooperation with them will be a task that Portugal will have to envisage and to perform if it wants to play any significant part in the European-African dialogue. That would depend, especially with respect to Angola and Mozambique, on the internal situation in those countries, torn apart by civil wars that also divide Portuguese public opinion and make it difficult to respond to the former colonies' military demands.

ECONOMIC DEVELOPMENT AND SECURITY CONCERNS

In the years to come, the main concern of Portuguese foreign policy will be the management of European economic integration. At the same time, Portugal will seek a greater participation in the ongoing process of reinforcing European political and military cooperation, as its application for membership to the Western European Union would seem to indicate. But the primary concern would appear to be how to succeed in economic integration within Europe, and how to turn Portugal into a modern country where living standards can compare with those of other European partners. The first indication of this new mood was the accession to the leadership of two major parties, the PS and the PSD, of two well-known economists, Vítor Constâncio and Anibal Cavaco Silva. This new trend, together with the fact that the memories of the 1974-75 crisis are fading away (even if the Communists still represent 15 percent of the vote), should shape a more pragmatic and less ideological approach to foreign policy. The 1987 legislative elections--a major success for the PSD--confirmed this public preoccupation with economic modernization.

At the turn of the next century, more than 200 million Portuguese-speaking people, in Brazil, Angola, Mozambique, Guinea Bissau, Sao Tomé, Cape Verde, and Portugal, will see the relationships among these countries as a major priority of their foreign and security policies. That will, in turn, reinforce Portuguese autonomy within the European-Atlantic relationship.

Economic development can have a positive effect on the understanding among the political leaderships of the need for a more dynamic external role in the East-West but also in the North-South direction, and, in that regard, the importance of having modern armed forces.

The success of European integration would create favorable conditions for this approach. If it does not succeed, however, Portugal could enter into a difficult process that might threaten the existing pro-European-Atlantic consensus. All the domestic and external conditions do exist to prevent that from happening.

NOTES

1. José Calvet de Magalhaes, Chief of the Portuguese delegation to the Portuguese-U.S. negotiations, in interview with Diáro de Notícias, January 1984.

2. General José Lemos Ferreira, chief of staff of the armed forces, "Alguns Apontamentos sobre Defesa Militar Portuguesa no Contexto OTAN," unpublished speech to the Lisbon American Club, March 1985.

3. Ministry of Defense, "Strategic Concept of National Defense, Major Options of the Strategic Concept of National Defense, and Strategic Military Concept," Lisbon, December 1985.

14 Italy: Mediterranean or European?

Virgilio Ilari

The chief problem of Italian security is to balance between the Mediterranean and European connections.

The Atlantic Alliance will remain in future years the best means for maintaining Italy within a Western geopolitical and socioeconomic framework. For this reason, a substantial Atlanticist consensus will prevail and even include the Communists in some ways.

But the Alliance cannot ensure an overall strategy for Mediterranean security or the defense of the totality of Italian national interests. Since the 1970s, Italy has enhanced its "Mediterranean option," that is to say, a more autonomous policy of economic and military cooperation with non-Western Mediterranean partners.

Opponents of this option within the political majority have sought to balance it with a "European option," focusing on European cooperation in defense industry. In the 1980s, both the Mediterranean and European connections have expanded into two potentially conflicting global security policies. This opposition between the two schools of thought will dominate in future years, but the Italian system's trend toward political stability should permit a more realistic and less ideological attitude and should re-establish a consensus in Italian foreign policy between its two historical contexts.

THE PRESENT SECURITY SITUATION

The threat analysis may be summarized by three main assumptions:

The political and military apparatus of the Soviet Union is the only source of an external threat against Italy.

There is no actual Soviet threat, only a potential one. Its purpose is not military aggression, but rather to put political pressure and limits on Italian foreign policy and to weaken the cohesion and strength of the Alliance.

Among NATO European partners, Italy seems to be or to have been the most vulnerable to indirect strategy and destabilization techniques, due to the presence of the biggest communist party (PCI) in the Western world. However, the Soviet Union does not seem to be interested in a proletarian revolution in Italy. In fact, the Soviet interest in the hopeless adventure of the Red Brigades may have been designed to weaken the Italian political system and to discredit Eurocommunism.

Thus the only external threat against Italy is a Soviet one, even if it comes from the territory of, or is apparently led by, a Mediterranean country. This view implies that Italian security can be ensured at all levels by a collective Atlantic defense.

But such a theory does not enjoy universal acceptance. In particular, the Foreign Office seems more sensitive to the Italian navy's warning concerning the possibility of a non-Soviet threat against Italian "national" or "vital" (i.e., economic) interests in the Mediterranean and the Persian Gulf. Such a theory apparently entails autonomous defensive tasks for the Italian armed forces, in particular the navy, beyond the NATO mission. But this concern really calls for some sort of international military cooperation outside the Atlantic Alliance, rather than an autonomous defense. Indeed, Italy must face the general problem of the Atlantic Alliance's southern boundary, that is to say, the weakness (if not the failure) of the Alliance to deal with indirect threats against Western interests and economic resources in the Mediterranean and the Persian Gulf. This weakness is due to economic competition and differing policies of the Western powers in the Mediterranean and the Persian Gulf; Italy has often supported the positions of the United States and Arab moderate countries rather than those of the French, British or Israelis.

At present, Italian security in the Mediterranean region is based on a mixture of political, economic, and military cooperation based on multilateral or bilateral agreements and memoranda of understanding with other NATO partners (e.g., the United States, France, Spain, and Greece) and with other countries like Malta, Tunisia, Algeria, Egypt, Sudan, and the Somali Democratic Republic.

Since the 1970s, Italy has had to face another threat coming from Colonel Khadaffi's Libya. Although direct disputes between Italy and Libya have been relatively limited, Italy may again be involved in the frequently occurring disputes between Libya and other Western or Mediterranean countries.

Soviet naval forces in the Mediterranean lack substantial sea and air bases and are in themselves unable to open a true southern front in case of war. Their main purpose is a political one, of "showing the flag" in what was, until 1965, a Western lake. At the most, in purely military terms, the Soviet fleet would be able to keep open the Dardanelles Straits in case of war.

To the northeast, Italian security was enhanced by the 1975 Osimo Treaty normalizing relations with Yugoslavia. A secret agreement on common defense planning was also unofficially reported. It is logical, at any rate, that Italian "forward defense" has been strengthened by the pro-Western attitude of the other Adriatic power.

In 1980-82, however, some Italian strategists argued that a forward defense oriented to the northeast on the Gorizia gap was out-of-date. They suggested that the most likely starting point for a supposed Soviet attack against Italy would not be Hungary, but Libya. Both the Italian general staff and the Ministry of Defense thought this view to be excessive. According to the official view, the Soviet threat coming from the south would consist of limited air strikes, or landings as diverting maneuvers supporting the chief attack over the Gorizia gap. To face this possibility, the Italian general staff holds that it is sufficient to complete the early warning system and to redeploy some interceptor and fighter-bomber squadrons in southern Italy, as well as improving the army's operational mobility from one end of the national territory to the other.

The Italian general staff, however, has expressed some concern over the military weakness of Austria and Yugoslavia, due to the belief that these two neutral countries could be easily overcome as part of a hypothetical Soviet attack against Italy. Lacking in modern mechanized forces for an effective forward defense, both Austria and Yugoslavia base their strategies on territorial defense and guerrilla warfare, without any capability of stopping or seriously damaging Soviet forces coming from Hungary, at least during the first days of a war. In this respect, a few years ago, some military analysts suggested that Italy abandon forward defense for territorial "deep" defense, with the aim of avoiding tactical nuclear weapons employment and sparing financial resources to develop naval, air, and long-range intervention forces. But such a claim was rejected by both the defense staff and government.

The internal threat of revolutionary terrorism has been finally terminated by the Red Brigades' political and military defeat. Unlike the German RAF, the Red Brigades had a potential socio-political base of support and a truly ideological/historical raison d'être, based on the revolutionary culture of the Communist party and on the historical legacy of the postwar political crisis that nearly erupted into civil war. But the failure of the Red Brigades has effectively destroyed both the revolutionary culture and "hero" guerrilla myths. In the future, the only internal threat would be "Euroterrorist" or other marginal groups; but this should be classified as an indirect external threat.

THE ATLANTICIST CONSENSUS

The Atlanticist consensus asserted itself definitively in the early 1970s and will maintain itself over the next three decades. Indeed for Italy, the Atlantic Alliance is much more than a way to ensure its security; one could even contend that the North Atlantic Treaty is the third pillar of the Italian political system together with the Republican Constitution and the Concordat with the Holy See.

Italy has several political (as well as military) reasons to participate in NATO. Relating to external policy, NATO is, together with the EC, a way to avoid supposed French, British, or even German hegemonies or directorates over Europe, counterbalancing their influences with the U.S. presence.

In the immediate postwar period, NATO solidarity deterred both proletarian revolution and socioeconomic changes incompatible with the capitalist model. Moreover, full Atlanticist loyalty is today one of the chief conditions for being admitted into government by the other coalition partners, and the absence of this loyalty is at present the chief argument, if not the only reason, for the general conventio ad excludendum against the Communist party. The latter passed the examination concerning its democratic commitment by virtue of its cooperation against the Red Brigades, but thus far it has not gained the other parties' consent because of its lukewarm commitment toward NATO. However, in the future, the Communist party will no doubt try to give new evidence of its compatibility with the Alliance.

Since 1973 the PCI has in substance accepted Italian participation in the Atlantic Alliance as well as the 1975-85 Italian rearmament programs; the Communists even began participating in the North Atlantic Assembly in 1975. Moreover, the sixteenth

PCI Congress in 1983 rejected a "Stalinist" motion denouncing the North Atlantic Treaty by a 95 percent majority. The PCI's decision to take the leadership of the Italian peace movement against the Cruise missiles was due to electoral motivations rather than to an anti-Atlanticist move, but its political isolation and subsequent electoral setbacks proved this to be a miscalculation. The PCI Congress of April 1986 formalized the acceptance of NATO, but added that this move would not imply automatic approval of all Alliance political and military decisions. This new Communist policy should strengthen a more "national" attitude in future years toward Italian participation in the Alliance.

In contrast to the German and French cases, any nationalist appeal against the Alliance is absent in Italy. Italian "Gaullist" elements were active in the late 1960s within the Christian Democratic Party's right wing. They had the aim of creating a national nuclear deterrent, but after their failed attempt to impede the Non-Proliferation Treaty ratification, Italian "Gaullists" limited themselves to voicing support for a European (British-French or French-German) deterrent.

It was the Communist party, however, that raised the question of national and popular sovereignty with regard to the Cruise missile deployment at Comiso air base, demanding that the final decision be submitted to the electorate. But this was legally impossible under the Italian Constitution, which excludes a referendum in defense and foreign policy matters. Moreover, the question of sovereignty was unpopular within the peace movement, whose militants were more sensitive to ideological rather than political questions. Thus, the two really important political questions (i.e., dual-key control for the Cruise missiles and the advantages of conventional rather than nuclear deterrence in Central Europe) were ignored during the ineffective campaigns for a nuclear freeze, denuclearization, and demilitarization.

The Italian political system may be easily understood if we realize that competition is not between different programs of foreign policy, but between different political-economic groups. The ideologies of the latter are not a recapitulation of their programs, but only their own particular languages and internal procedures for decision-making as well as for obtaining consensus--like ecclesiastical rites. The effective content of these languages and procedures is ideologically irrelevant in itself, and it is not surprising that different ideologies may have the same effective contents. The accordance between ideologies and effective decisions is only a problem of propaganda.

Thus Radical and Catholic-moderate pacifists did not join the Catholic-leftist and Communist-led peace movement, to which they opposed their own ideological aims (i.e., conscientious objection and antimilitarism). The government parties and press exploited the "true" pacifism of the Catholic-moderates (i.e., the politically ineffective kind), and supported more or less openly the Radical party in its struggle against the Communist party for the peace movement leadership. Indeed, both Catholic and Radical pacifisms, as utopian visions, are not only politically harmless, but even useful as a outlet to moral, ideological or psychological pressures against the real decisions about rearmament and defense policy. It is probable that in the future Catholic movements will enhance their pacifist and anti-militarist self-commitment. Their final aim is, however, not to influence effective political decisions or to impede rearmament, but only to assert a separate Catholic status within the Italian Republic. Far from hampering the Christian Democratic party's involvement in rearmament decisions, the Catholic movement's pacifism may even enhance it. Peace is not of "this" world, and Catholic pacifism reflects this outlook. The Radical party plays a very similar role for the Socialist and other lay parties.

The 1949 Italian admission to NATO was the major historical victory of pro-Western forces and marked their permanent political hegemony over the Christian Democratic party, at least in the field of foreign and security policy. Such a hegemony will persist and grow stronger over the next three decades, overcoming the more nationalist forces in foreign policy. The Foreign Minister in 1949, Count Carlo Sforza, the chief architect of Italy's admission into NATO, stated that admission and participation could not be negotiated. According to this permanent principle of Italian foreign policy, Italy did not negotiate its assent to 1959 and 1979-83 decisions concerning the deployment of U.S. intermediate nuclear forces (INF) on its territory, despite the contrary advice expressed in 1959 by the chiefs of the Defense and Army staffs.

There is no reason for Italy to change its policy in the future. From an Italian perspective, the NATO decisions about collective security are generally irrelevant, since the true historical reason for Italy's participation in the Alliance is not so much to enhance its national security, but to ensure the place of Italy within the Western world.

"MEDITERRANEAN" VERSUS "EUROPEAN" OPTIONS

In the postwar period, Italian soldiers and diplomats regarded U.S. support of Italy as the quickest and surest way to regain the position lost in the Mediterranean and Europe because of military defeat. Italy's admission to NATO was, in fact, a further development of the military and political guarantees previously granted by the United States to Italy under the 1947 agreements. Furthermore, some members of the Christian Democratic leadership (and the Vatican) saw the United States as "God's country," counterbalancing the Communist party and secular interests.

In 1945, the Mediterranean was a Franco-British lake, but Italy did not cooperate to keep it so. Eleven years later, Italy refused to join Britain and France in the Suez intervention, and subsequently supported Tunisian and Algerian independence. Since the mid-1960s, Italy has been the second Alliance military power in the Mediterranean after the United States, since France left the NATO command in 1966 and Britain withdrew its forces westward to Gibraltar. Moreover, unlike West Germany, Italy ensures its own defense with national forces, which are supported only by small U.S. and Portuguese air/land reinforcements as well as by U.S. tactical nuclear weapons according to the flexible response strategy.

Apart from some limited polemics and disagreements with Colonel Khadaffi's Libya, Italy has no reason for quarrel with the Arab and OPEC countries. Ultimately, Italy may be limited in its friendly relations with the Arab world by loyalty to and solidarity with its Western allies as well as by the growing disputes within the Arab world itself.

Therefore it is not surprising that Italy has no interest in an eventual extension of NATO southern boundaries that would compromise its role as a "bridge" over the Mediterranean. This does not imply that Italy would intend to drop out of Atlantic collective defense in case of war, or to betray Western solidarity in a Mediterranean crisis; the Italian navy, on the contrary, is now enhancing its cooperation with other NATO navies (particularly with the French and Spanish), and is planning a forward-strike capability in the Eastern Mediterranean. Moreover, in 1984 Italy formed a small division-sized combined Rapid Intervention Force (FIR), even though at present its potential missions and capabilities are a matter of controversy. But military cooperation in dealing with the Soviet threat or managing external crises in the Mediterranean should not imply a reduced national independence in foreign and economic cooperation policy.

Limiting Atlantic commitments to merely military aspects and expanding national autonomy and initiative in all other fields of foreign and security policy are in substance the "Mediterranean option," that is to say the Italian equivalent of German Ostpolitik. Enrico Mattei, Amintore Fanfani, and Giulio Andreotti followed one another as the Mediterranean option's mentors. Avoiding any ideological implications, Andreotti tried to obtain U.S. support for the military dimension of this policy when, as Premier in 1972, he granted additional naval/air bases and facilities to the U.S. Sixth Fleet, bases that were used by the U.S. Air Force during the 1973 Yom Kippur war for supplying the Israeli army. But at the same time, Italy demonstrated its independence by setting free PLO terrorists and supplying M-113 armored personnel carriers to the Libyan Army. The last development of such a policy was the November 1978 Ruffini-Brown Memorandum of Understanding, as part of the "two-way street" policy in U.S.-Italian military cooperation. According to this agreement, Italian military industry was to enhance exports to the Third World and coordinate with the United States instead of with the European military-industrial complex. The "Mediterranean option" in foreign policy was fully congruent with the "historical compromise" in internal policy, that is to say, with the general alliance between the Christian Democratic and Communist parties, reducing the Socialist and lay parties' influence both in internal and foreign policies.

The "Mediterranean option" opponents were more or less the same as those against the "opening to the Left": Antonio Segni, Arnaldo Forlani and Giovanni Spadolini followed one upon the other in the leading role against the "Mediterranean option." Even though Andreotti was the Minister of Foreign Affairs in the Bettino Craxi Cabinet, the "Mediterranean option" was counterbalanced by the opposing "European option" advocated by Defense Minister Spadolini who stressed European cooperation, support for Israel, and strong Atlanticism. Differences between the pro-Israel and pro-Arab factions within the Italian government became evident during the Italian participation in the 1982-84 multinational peacekeeping force in Lebanon, the first postwar Italian military operation that was officially justified for "national security" as well as humanitarian reasons. Using his powers as Minister of Defense, Spadolini tried to build up a Mediterranean policy more congruent with a general "European option" and to counterbalance Andreotti's attempts to give the PLO some sort of political recognition. Recently, Spadolini offered Italian military observers to survey the Lebanese southern boundary after the withdrawal of the Israeli army, and he also visited Spain, Portugal, Israel, Somalia, and Tunisia with the purpose of enhancing Italian military exports in the Mediterranean.

For his part, Andreotti used his Minister of Foreign Affairs' office to run a security policy in line with the more independent "Mediterranean option." Thus he modified Italian positions about INF and SDI (as in the February 1985 Andreotti-Gromyko joint communiqué condemning the militarization of outer space), explaining at the time that such an Italian Ostpolitik was not the same as the German policy and should not imply any interest in Germany's unification. In spite of Premier Craxi's cautious support, Andreotti has not had much success in this reorientation, and even the Communist party refused its assent. Indeed, the Reagan administration seems to have disavowed (at least openly) any Italian initiative for an opening to Libya and the PLO. For their part, Libya and the Soviet Union did not agree with Andreotti's attempt to involve them in the Italian initiatives for including all Mediterranean states in the CSCE process and for founding a nonsecret, scientific "World Laboratory" concerned with defense and peace research.

In October 1985 the Israeli and U.S. retaliatory operations against the PLO brought these political disputes into the open. The overt violation of international law and the national sovereignty of friendly allied countries such as Tunisia, Egypt, and Italy was the worst political and strategic error of the Israeli and U.S. "hawks" since the "Peace in Galilee" operation, which only enhanced Syrian influence over Lebanon.

For the first time since 1915, foreign policy was a matter for an Italian cabinet crisis which implied a change of majority. The political forces supporting the U.S. and Israeli actions, namely the Republican, Radical, Liberal, and Neo-Fascist parties, would have been isolated in the Parliament by an 85 percent majority including the Communists, if the Christian Democratic party had not impeded a parliamentary debate before the formal cabinet resignation.

Italian public opinion (75 percent in most polls) has not been sympathetic with the Reagan administration's crusade against "international terrorism" and condemned the Sixth Fleet's provocative exhibition in the Gulf of Sirtis and the brutal bombing of Tripoli in March-April 1986. The desperate retaliation by Libya against an insignificant NATO installation on the island of Lampedusa did shock the Italian public, but the general consensus laid political and moral responsibility on the U.S. government and regarded Khadaffi's threats against Italy as mere boasting. Nevertheless, Italy needs to maintain good relations with the United States, and Craxi ultimately took a softer line on U.S. Mediterranean policy, publically disavowing his Foreign Minister at the Tokyo summit. Relations with Libya were reduced, and Libyan diplomats and workers were expelled. The Lampedusa incident also impressed upon the government the need for a tightened national chain of command and a more effective air defense system.

Because of these heightened tensions and instabilities, it is extremely risky to forecast what could be the Italian Mediterranean policy over the next three decades. In the future, the internal incentives for more autonomy in Mediterranean policy could disappear, owing to the Italian political system's tendency toward stabilization. Such a political stabilization could enhance a more realistic, less partisan attitude toward true national interests in Mediterranean security and economic development. Once competition between the parties is reduced, rigid opposition between the "Mediterranean" and "European" options may be overcome. In the end, all the NATO partners--and not merely the United States--could be convinced that more independence for Italian Mediterranean policy, far from weakening collective security, would enhance it in both political and military terms. The pluralistic nature of the Atlantic Alliance allows for political flexibility, but ensures cohesion in the long term.

ITALY AND THE EMERGING TECHNOLOGIES

The so-called emerging technologies will dominate both economic development and security issues over the next three decades. Italy runs the risk of becoming marginalized within this process if it does not rationalize its political and economic decision-making system, thus promoting the capabilities of Italian industry.

The emerging technologies may realize revolutionary changes in the realm of conventional deterrence and strategic defense. Concerned by the threats to the U.S.-European coupling, Italy has an interest in raising the nuclear threshold. Therefore it welcomed and supported the Rogers Plan, as well as the NATO decisions about the new Follow-on Forces Attack (FOFA) operational doctrine for defending Central Europe. FOFA, however, does not have direct influence on the Italian operational doctrine, because of the political-strategic particularities of its forward defense system as well as its poorer military equipment. Futhermore, Italy does not allow the deployment of chemical weapons on its territory.

During the last decade Italy has made a great financial effort to rearm and modernize its armed forces. This effort will progress over the next decade, but it will imply international cooperation in arms procurement. Italy has a limited interest in the eleven programs forming Secretary of Defense Weinberger's "conventional defense initiative" (CDI); moreover, the only program in which Italy was particularly involved is the Multi-Launch-Rocket System (MLRS). Italy would be interested in a European Defense Initiative (EDI), that is, German proposals for air and tactical ballistic missile defense, on condition that EDI would not simply be a new name for an old program.

The postwar Italian defense industry policy has traditionally been balanced between U.S. and European cooperation. U.S.-Italian cooperation in defense industry and arms trade was settled by the 1978 Ruffini-Brown Memorandum of Understanding. But the results up to now have been extremely unsatisfactory. The imbalance in U.S.-Italian military trade is about 5:1, and the military represents only 4 percent of the entire U.S.-Italian trade. However, the military imports from the United States are essential, for providing the technological "know-how" and software components of Italian weapon systems. Even though the "Mediterranean option" enhanced Italian military exports to the Third World in the past decade, this "low-technology" military production excluded Italy from the European market, and compromised Italian long-term competitiveness in the Third World market as well, since the Third World armies are becoming increasingly modern and sophisticated. Moreover, Italian "low-technology" production does not assure the Italian armed forces' own needs, and contracts granted to the Italian military industry run the risk of becoming mere public assistance projects.

This deficiency increased the Italian tendency toward joint ventures in Europe. But there are also basic difficulties in agreements relating to the size and structure of the Italian defense industry within a European context.

Defense Minister Spadolini tried to enhance European cooperation promoting both a defense industry reassessment and the Western European Union (WEU) reform at the Rome meeting of October 1984. Such a reform does not imply an Italian initiative for a new European Defense Community. Indeed, Italy has never supported the idea of an autonomous European defense, which would consist ultimately of a European sharing of the French deterrent modernization costs. Instead, according to the Italian view, the WEU should become the primary forum of a European cooperation in conventional weapons production, a role very similar to the Eurogroup. Furthermore, with the exception of the Communist and Radical parties, all the Italian representatives in the European Parliament agreed with the 1979 decision to include defense industry policy within the European Parliament's authority. But the recent European Fighter Aircraft (EFA) affair proves that European cooperation in defense production will remain very difficult over the next decade.

A field of potential cooperation between the U.S. and Italy could exist in the SDI research program. Italian industries and scientific-technological research centers have long-term experience in cooperating with the U.S. space programs. The same sectors are involved in the SDI. Up to now, only industrial cooperation on an individual basis has been envisaged. A more systematic collaboration in the future was ensured by the signing of a formal U.S.-Italian agreement in September 1986. Such an attitude, however, could have deep negative implications both on Italian policies toward the Soviet Union and Eastern Europe and on the trade issues between Italy and the Soviets.

At the same time as Italian firms established the Italian Consortium for Strategic Technologies (CITES) in April 1985, the government set up an ad hoc Interministerial Committee to evaluate Italian participation in SDI. Its concern was to ensure participation on an equitable basis, particularly by securing technological and economic spinoffs for Italian industry. But the United States seems unable to guarantee substantial parity in know-how exchange, at least, in cases where Italian firms would be commissioned by U.S. primary contractors instead of dealing directly with the Pentagon. While the Italian government pondered its final decision, the Pentagon and the U.S. space industry have signed several contracts with Italian firms, who fear being excluded from this business. On the other hand, the Italian National Council of Research (CNR) estimates that the entire Italian share in SDI will be only 300 billion lire ($165 million).

Under the influence of Minister Andreotti, Italy has agreed to participate in the Eureka project. The official Italian view seems to be that Eureka will balance, rather than substitute for, SDI. But there are some concerns about the possibility that Eureka would become a French-German condominium, and there are some reservations about the viability of this project as well.

FUTURE SECURITY TRENDS IN EUROPE

For a long time, both Italian public opinion and politicians disregarded security and defense policies. The trend changed in the 1980s due to growing fears about nuclear war as well as growing economic implications of security and defense decisions. This trend will maintain itself in the future and will produce a new political culture. In general, Italian decisions in the field will be less improvised than they were in the past. Although at present there are no precise mechanisms to deal with national security as a whole, it seems that in the coming years, a greater coordination between defense, economic, and foreign policies will take place.

Italian security was in the past a sum of separate decisions, made in response to external (namely U.S. and NATO) initiatives, if not directives. The only national features and logical coherence of such decisions were to limit risks and costs as well to translate them into the Italian political language. Since the 1970s, however, this kind of decision was increasingly limited only to the field of defense policy. Foreign and economic policies (including defense industry and arms trade policy), although relevant for collective security, were fashioned more and more according to national points of view. Finally, in the 1980s, national initiative entered the field of defense policy too, although it was limited to decisions concerning the Mediterranean.

This seems to be the extreme boundary of national initiative in security policy over the next decades. Italy does not have the means or interest to extend its national initiative in the field of European defense policy; therefore it will continue to enforce rather than influence the Atlantic decisions concerning collective defense in Europe. But this does not imply that Italy will give up its autonomous initiative on defense industry policy as well as economic and foreign policies relevant for European and international security.

The chief Italian policy problem over the next decades will be to reconcile Western -Atlantic-European solidarity with Mediterranean solidarity, as well as to enhance detente and economic cooperation in East-West and North-South relations. One possible avenue may be to include Italy and Hungary in the Mutual and Balanced Force Reduction negotiations, and all the Mediterranean countries in the Conference on Security and Cooperation in Europe. As shown by the recent Soviet initiative of passing messages to the West through the Italian Premier, Italy could carry on an important role in East-West detente. One matter for contention in future years may be U.S. insistence on imposing restrictions on high technology transfers to the East. Italians (and other Europeans) regard industrial trade as a means of ensuring increased international security and even a certain liberalization within the Communist countries. In this sense, Italy rejects the idea of an "economic NATO."

As long as the Yalta settlement maintains itself in both Western and Eastern Europe, peace and detente will not be seriously compromised. This implies very high costs, namely Germany's continued division and military occupation, as well as limitation on human rights and freedom in Eastern Europe and the Soviet Union. But there are no other means for ensuring an effective balance of power in Europe. The West does not have any interest in an eventual internal destabilization of the East, because this would augment Soviet militarism, the arms race, and global instability. Moreover, it seems terribly wrong and even dangerous to depict the Soviet internal system as a mere police state without social consent, as is more and more frequently done by some Western analysts. In the same way, it seems an exaggeration to forecast Islamic revolution within the Soviet Union by contagion from Iran and Afghanistan. The Soviet Union does not seem to be on the ropes or to have its <u>ultima ratio</u> in war machinery.

Factors of continuity should prevail. The SDI and its Soviet counterpart will not make offensive arms obsolete. The United States will not be tempted by a "no-first-use" option. It is even possible that the new FOFA doctrine may enhance preemptive use of intermediate nuclear, neutron, and chemical weapons, thus keeping Europe under the threat of a limited nuclear war. Any conceivable Central European denuclearization would compromise the U.S.-European strategic "coupling" and undermine both the Atlantic Alliance and ultimately the Warsaw Treaty, that is to say, the Yalta settlement. Therefore it is highly unlikely that decisive changes in strategic confrontation will take place in Europe as long as the U.S. and Soviet forces do not withdraw.

On the other hand, the balance of power will be more unstable in the Mediterranean, Persian Gulf, and sub-Saharan Africa. Owing to a very great delay in developing its nuclear power stations, Italy depends more than other Western countries on oil supplies as well as on other raw materials; 95 percent of Italian imports and 65 percent of exports pass through the Mediterranean, but Italy lacks any means of controlling maritime traffic lanes and terminals outside the Mediterranean. The Italian navy failed in its historical aim to take off the British corks that bottled up in the Mediterranean, yet today Italy enjoys the presence of the U.S. Sixth Fleet. But these advantages are counterbalanced by the limitations of the dependency relationship with the U.S. Italian Mediterranean policy traditionally tried to overcome these limitations according to national interests, but this will be possible in the future only if the Soviet threat coming from the south and the Mediterranean countries' own instability do not exceed present, very worrying levels. To confront sudden crises in the Mediterranean, Italy formed its Rapid Intervention Force, as both the Italian contingent in UN or multinational peacekeeping operations and a national "fire brigade" to react to limited hostile actions against Italian sovereignty and national interests abroad.

In 1982 the United States gave up the idea to base RDJTF (Rapid Deployment Joint Task Force) in Europe; thus Egypt took the place of Italy as the Mediterranean logistical and training base of U.S. CENTCOM (Central Command), which succeeded RDJTF. But Italy may again be involved in possible U.S. military operations in the Mediterranean, as in August-September 1981, when the Sixth Fleet shot down two Libyan fighters in the Gulf of Sirtis, as well as in the March-April 1986 confrontations. Colonel Khadaffi threatened retaliatory air bombing against U.S. nuclear depots and bases in Sicily, thus provoking Italian defensive countermeasures. For the first time since 1945, the armed forces were ordered to plan preemptive strikes in the event of military menaces against the national territory. Any future involvement in U.S. operations would not receive general Italian support, even if Colonel Khadaffi does not enjoy high popularity in Italy. In spite of its limited commitment and the high emphasis on national pride, the Italian contingent in Lebanon had to be withdrawn for fear of provoking popular and political dissatisfaction in the long run, as it became evident that its main task was to free Israel from the Lebanese trap.

Italian security policy over the next three decades does not require substantial changes but rather a basic determination to coordinate both Mediterranean and European orientations within wider and more far-sighted policies. This implies less ideology and more realism, as well as a national solidarity concerning defense and security policy similar to the national solidarity that defeated the Red Brigades. Such a national solidarity should not be a mere moral attitude, but the widest contribution of all political forces, including the Communist party, to common decisions. In this connection, a determining factor will be the eventual development of a national-minded political culture in the field of defense and security, whose viewpoint would replace the present strategic thinking, which is overwhelmingly influenced by the United States.

15 Greece: Between Turks and Slavs

Thanos Veremis

THREAT PERCEPTIONS AND POLICIES

The strategic significance of Greece's territory has been confirmed repeatedly in our century, since the country became a theater of operations in both world wars and in regional conflagrations as well. As the proverbial crossroads of the Mediterranean, Greece is simultaneously a link between Western Europe and Turkey and an obstacle to a southward drive of Warsaw Pact forces from the north. The two NATO members of the southern flank have been linked in the defense of Thrace and the Dardanelles. If, in the event of a war, this line were to collapse, it is expected that a second line of defense would develop in the Aegean Sea based on the archipelago of Greek islands.

The United States and NATO rely on bases in Greek territory for the support of the Sixth Fleet. The Souda Bay complex houses fuel and ammunition and provides port services, an anchorage that can accommodate practically the entire Sixth Fleet, and an airfield used for military reconnaissance operations by U.S. units. Furthermore, Greece provides intelligence and communication links between Turkey and Western Europe, nuclear weapons storage, and facilities for exercises and training.

Historically, the two most persistent Greek security concerns have been the Ottoman Turks and the Balkan Slavs (especially Bulgaria). The two sources of threat, however, rarely appeared simultaneously. It became a doctrine of Greek diplomacy to improve relations with one side when there was tension with the other. The end of World War II transformed the regime of flexible alliances in the Balkans into ideological camps permanently attached to the superpowers. Greece's relations with Turkey were recast on premises dictated by the role that both countries had undertaken within the Western alliance.

Greece's foreign policy orientation and security priorities were to a large

---

* I would like to acknowledge the assistance of George Tsitsopoulos in formulating certain parts of this chapter.

extent determined by the outcome of the civil war that devastated the country between 1946 and 1949. The armed struggle between the nationalist forces of the government and the Democratic Army, dominated by the Communist party, ended with the defeat of the latter and had serious repercussions for the political life in Greece for years to come. U.S. support and the substantial role of U.S. missions throughout the period of the fratricidal war not only determined Greece's subsequent loyalty to the West, but also the total integration of Greek defense priorities into the Western collective security system. Until the 1960s, the country's defense orientation was therefore based on the U.S. assumption that Greece's main security concern was of an internal rather than external nature. In case of a Soviet attack in the Balkans, however, the Greek forces were expected to delay the aggressor in spite of their limited capabilities in arms and equipment. The threat of internal subversion by the outlawed Communist party became the security preoccupation of the conservative governments of the 1950s and an unlikely excuse for the colonels who installed themselves in power in 1967.

With the collapse of the military dictatorship following the Cyprus crisis of 1974, the entire Greek defense posture was revised to fit the new challenges. These challenges can be summarized as follows : since the invasion of Cyprus, Greece has been faced with what was perceived as a barrage of Turkish demands on various fronts. The continental shelf issue preceded the Cyprus crisis but acquired special significance after 1974. Turkey considers its continental shelf to be an extension of the Asia Minor hinterland into the sea, west of Greek islands to which it altogether denies possession of a continental shelf. Greece, while referring to the Geneva convention, which recognizes the right of islands to a continental shelf (although Turkey has not signed this convention) reserves the right to extend its territorial sea limit to 12 miles. Such an act would automatically solve the controversy in Greece's favor, but would, according to Turkish statements, constitute a <u>casus belli</u>, because it would limit Turkey's access to international waters. Greece's invocation of the right to extend its territorial waters was also provoked by Turkey's refusal to recognize the former's ten-mile-limit airspace after 44 years of compliance verified by official Turkish messages conveyed to the appropriate Greek authorities. Since 1975 Turkish military aircraft have violated Greece's territorial integrity in the air, propounding by force the argument of asymmetry between a ten-mile airspace and six-mile territorial waters. Turkey deplores the consequences of an extension of Greek territorial waters to cover the "asymmetry" between air and water and reverts to the threat of war.

A pending matter within the framework of NATO assignments in the Aegean is the allocation of operational responsibilities over the sea. After Greece's withdrawal from the military arm of the Alliance, Turkey sought to redraft the entire scheme of command and control arrangements in a manner that would in fact place the airspace of Greek islands under Turkish operational control. If all the above-mentioned claims of Turkey were to be satisfied, a third of Greek islands would be alienated from the Greek mainland and would be enclosed within a Turkish zone of influence.

Although the declaratory politics of the Greek Socialist Party (PASOK in power since 1981) have created the wide impression that Greece's "New Defense Doctrine" was put into effect in 1984, in fact the so-called doctrine has been evolving since 1974. This new posture consists of a shift in the emphasis of Greece's defense from the north to the east. According to official statements, this new codification of defense priorities primarily concerns units that have not been assigned to NATO's Naples headquarters.

The reinforcement of Greece's eastern defenses, however, including the militarization of the islands of Lemnos, Lesvos, Chios, and Rhodes, may also serve in wartime as a formidable obstacle to a Soviet naval incursion in the Aegean. The first three islands are located in the outlet of the Dardanelles and would greatly contribute to the defense of the Straits. The militarization of the Dodecanese in the southern Aegean provides the defense of the sea with depth and could impede the movement of the Soviet Fifth Eskadra in that region. Demilitarized and therefore defenseless islands would become the easy prey of any aggressor in times of conflict. Lesvos and Chios have been militarized over and above the limit allowed by the Lausanne Treaty of 1923 in response to what was perceived as a threat to their safety not emanating from the Soviet Union. The same is true for Rhodes, whose status is defined by the Paris Treaty of 1947 between Italy and the Allies.

THE MILITARY ESTABLISHMENT

Greece's military expenditure in terms of GNP percentage has been the highest among European NATO members for the last eight years. Since the military budget steadily exceeds the sum allocated for public investment, the long-run effect of such spending on the economy is potentially disastrous. Greece established its own arms industries to secure partial independence of armament and a source of income from the export of weapons. The national arms industry includes a rifle assembly plant, ammunition factories, facilities to upgrade older tanks, and the production of communication systems. The Hellenic Aerospace Industry can overhaul, repair, and modify military and commercial aircraft, engines and electronics. The Hellenic Shipyard has been building patrol boats and the Steyer-Hellas Company assembling heavy-duty military trucks.

The total regular strength of the Greek armed forces is 206,500 men which represents 2.2 percent of the total Greek population, a ratio among the highest in the world. Of these, 152,000 are conscripts serving for a period of 22 months (24 months in the air force, 26 in the navy). The strength of the army is 163,000, the navy 19,500 and the air force 24,000. There are also 25,000 gendarmerie and 100,000 national guardsmen.

The army is mainly an infantry force made up of eleven infantry divisions, one armored division and three independent armored brigades, one mechanized division, one para-commando division and fourteen field artillery battalions. There is also a marine brigade, three anti-aircraft artillery battalions, three surface-to-surface missile (SSM) battalions (with twelve Honest John missiles each), two surface-to-air missile (SAM) battalions, and fourteen army aviation companies and one independent aviation company. The tank division has six tank battalions of 55 tanks each, four motorized infantry battalions and reconnaissance battalions, three self-propelled artillery battalions and one mixed artillery battalion plus a combat engineer battalion, communication battalion, army air corps company, and logistical support subunit. The total strength is 13,000 men and 360 tanks. The independent armored brigade consists of two tank battalions, one motorized infantry battalion, one self-propelled artillery battalion (total, 36,000 men and 119 tanks). The para-commando division consists of one parachute and one marine brigade, plus one commando and one marine battalion.

The air force is divided into tactical, training and material commands. The tactical air force has seven combat wings containing eleven ground-attack fighter (FGA) squadrons, five interceptor squadrons and one FGA/reconnaissance squadron, one independent wing of three squadrons, and one maritime reconnaissance squadron, three transport and three helicopter squadrons. The air force's FGA squadrons are equipped as follows : three squadrons with 54 A-711s and six TA-711s Corsair IIs; two with 36 F-4s and RF-4s; two with 40 F/TF-104 Gs; two with 42 F-5A/Bs and RF-5s; and two in reserve with 54 F-84Fs. There are five interceptor squadrons, one with eighteen F-4Es, one with 21 F-5A/Bs, two with 36 Mirage F-ICGs and one with 24 F-104. The air force has one SAM wing consisting of one battalion with 36 Nike Hercules and one with 36 Nike Ajaxes.

The navy is made up of ten submarines, sixteen destroyers (five with ASROC), six frigates (one with Harpoon SSMs and Sea Sparrow SAMs), 25 fast attack aircraft (eight with Exocets, six with Penguin SSMs), nine coastal patrol craft, two coastal minelayers and thirteen coastal minesweepers, plus 84 landing craft. The navy also maintains two ASW helicopter squadrons.

The armed forces are divided into three military regions, two of which are located in northern (Thessaloniki) and northeastern Greece. The third army headquarters, in Athens, controls forces in the rest of Greece (continent and islands).

FUTURE SECURITY PROSPECTS

Greece's policy toward Turkey since 1923 has been one of maintaining the status quo as defined by the Treaty of Lausanne. Faced with what was perceived as a concerted challenge from the other side of the Aegean Sea, the two Greek political parties that have been in power since 1974 practiced a policy of defending past arrangements in the region. This policy has varied in form rather than substance. Indeed, basic foreign policy prescriptions, which have been considered vital for Greece's present security since 1974, have secured a consensus among the Greek public. Although the Conservative New Democracy and the Socialist PASOK, now in power, differ in the tone of their leaders' security parlance, both acknowledge the priority of Turkey in Greece's considerations. The position of the present Greek government on issues that touch upon its triangular relationship with Turkey and the United States could be summarized as follows :

a. Withdrawal of the Turkish occupation forces in Cyprus is seen as the prerequisite for a rapprochement with Ankara. Although this will not solve the other pending issues in the Aegean, it will serve as a confidence-building measure, which is sorely needed in the relations between the two countries.

b. Certain issues of legal nature merit a settlement by international legal arbitration. International aritration would not entail the loss of face by either side, thereby facilitating the acceptance of any court ruling by the leadership of both countries.

c. Settlement of the operational control question within the NATO framework must precede the establishment of a NATO headquarters in Greece.

d. Participation of Greece in NATO exercises that take place in the area near Lemnos presupposes that the island in question is not excluded from exercises.

e. Maintenance of the seven-to-ten ratio in U.S. aid to Greece and Turkey, respectively, will secure the regional balance and will make a local conflagration less likely.

An effective peace process between Greece and Turkey requires the services of a long-term educational program aimed at altering diverse images that each nation harbors about the other. The introduction of Turkish and Greek history in school and university curricula would help to familiarize the younger populations of Greece and Turkey with the character and culture of its neighbor. An encouragement of tourism and commercial and scholarly exchanges would also facilitate the bridge-building process between the two states.

Currently the most dangerous point of potential clash in the Aegean is Turkey's violation of the ten-mile limit of Greek airspace. These violations imply interceptions and aerial maneuvers that could easily escalate into a conflict. The consequences of armed collision would not only prove disastrous for both countries, but would also mean a dramatic widening of Soviet influence in the area. There is a difference in the prescription of crisis management that each side chooses to put forth. Greece appeals to foreign meditation as well as to the jurisdiction of the International Court of Justice, while Turkey believes that all bilateral questions should be solved between Greece and Turkey alone. Both major Greek parties in Parliament tend to agree that the United States was responsible for supporting the Greek military regime which through its Cyprus blunder disrupted the regional balance, and the United States must therefore make an extra effort to mediate between the two NATO allies.

The interdependence of Greece and Turkey in facing a threat from the north can be viewed both in a regional Balkan context and in a larger NATO context whereby the two states and Italy form a continuum that bridges the eastern Mediterranean. The deployment of Soviet forces in the region could be somewhat hindered by unfriendly Communist states, but their capabilities in the Balkan front of NATO's southern flank appear to be considerable. The Warsaw Pact has deployed 33 divisions on the Greco-Turkish borders against a total of 25 divisions of the two NATO allies. The Pact possesses an advantage of three to one in terms of mechanized and armored capability. The Soviet Union has also deployed intermediate-range ballistic missiles (IRBM), including the SS-20 with three multiple independently targetable re-entry vehicles (MIRV), in the Crimea and the northern Transcaucasus. Although the Soviet naval presence has expanded significantly during the last decade, its capabilities are impeded by the lack of important sea-based and land-based air power. The appearance of the Backfire bomber, which is based in the Crimea and can cover most of the Mediterranean basin, has partly offset the impediment. The introduction of this modern aircraft has made the role of Greek and Turkish air defense vital in this region.

The evolution of the eastern Mediterranean into a separate theater of particular interest to the West has been marked by the development of the Iran-Iraq War and the effort to establish alternative routes for the flow of Gulf oil into Western Europe. Besides global factors that affect the security environment of the region, the interdependence that emerged between the Persian Gulf, the Red Sea, and the eastern Mediterranean during the past years promises to redefine the future strategic significance of the maritime region around Greece.

The oil from the Gulf states directed through pipelines to Mediterranean ports or tankers in the Red Sea (and from there via the Suez Canal to the Mediterranean

Sea) requires a trouble-free route to its European destination. This new imperative for the eastern Mediterranean to become a sea of cooperation (at least among NATO allies) may be added to the already existing list of reasons that require the lessening of tensions between Greece and Turkey and the eventual establishment of a modus vivendi in the Aegean and Cyprus.

The Socialist government of Prime Minister Andreas Papandreou has pursued the concept of a nuclear-free Balkan zone, which was first championed by Romania in the 1960s. Romania and Bulgaria have expounded the idea of a collective pact that would abolish nuclear weapons from the territory of Balkan states. A conference of experts met in Athens in 1984 to discuss the prospects of cooperation on questions of commerce, environment, transportation, exploitation of natural resources, nuclear energy, and finally security. Although the issue of the nuclear-free zone was at the center of the discussions on security, it failed to make significant headway, which is hardly surprising since Albania refuses to participate, Yugoslavia appears to be more interested in the reduction of conventional weapons, and Turkey refuses to acknowledge the value of a regional denuclearization. The prospects of such an undertaking ultimately depend on both a positive consensus among Balkan states and the endorsement of the powers that possess nuclear forces.

Official Greek attitudes toward the reactivation of the Western European Union (WEU) have been patently cool. Greece's own security concerns require the kind of meditation that European states are unable or unwilling to provide. Greek policymakers therefore still consider the United States to be the only power that could intervene in a regional conflict between NATO allies. This line of reasoning, however, fails to anticipate the long-run isolation of Greece from the rest of the EC members, should the WEU (or some other scheme for Europeanization of defense) go into full force.

If the present state of international affairs persists, Greece will maintain its double vigilance to the north and east. No doubt, the pending problems with Turkey make it difficult even for the more Western-oriented among the politicians to accept a full-fledged commitment to NATO. If, on the other hand, international tension dramatically increases, Greece will be obliged to intensify its commitment to the Alliance. Such a development, however, would require wide consensus, which would be difficult to muster if public images of Turkey's policy remain as they are today in Greece. In either case the coherence of the southern flank will be put into question.

Both Greece and Turkey have a vital mission on the southern flank. Turkey is a buffer to the Soviet Union, a springboard for U.S. operations in the Middle East, and probably a future outlet of Middle East oil into the Mediterranean. Greece shares a common border with Bulgaria, provides strategic depth in the Aegean, is a main avenue of support for Yugoslavia, and controls the sea lanes in the eastern Mediterranean. Furthermore, Greece and Turkey complement each other and together form a unique strategic domain. Greece is the link that connects Turkey with the West. If the link is broken, the Turkish outpost will be isolated from its allies. For all these reasons, there are significant areas for future cooperation between these two countries.

16 Turkey: Uneasy Borders

Ersin Onulduran

The underlying basic themes of Turkish foreign and security policy are influenced by both the geopolitical situation of the country and the threat perception of its political leaders.

Geography is, of course, an important determinant of any country's security policies. This factor seems to take on a special significance in Turkey because, due to very different historical and strategic considerations, two of its neighbors, Greece and the Soviet Union, create an uneasiness that pervades all Turkish policy decisions.

The threat perception of the political leaders as well as the military forces coincides. Inevitably, past experiences as a nation and historical traditions and events find their reflection in current security considerations.

The behavior of Russia toward the Ottoman Empire as well as Russian designs over the Ottoman territories paired these two nations in conflict situations on countless occasions in recent history. The Republic of Turkey and the Soviet Union, on the other hand, began their relationship along much more peaceful lines. An atmosphere of mutual understanding, even friendliness, prevailed during the first two decades of the life of the Turkish Republic. However, due to the ever harsher policies of Stalin and possibly because the Soviet Union completed the process of securing the allegiance of its national components by the 1940s, the Soviets demanded military bases, as well as large territorial concessions in eastern Turkey. These demands were largely outlined in a conversation on June 7, 1945, between the Soviet Foreign Minister Molotov and Selim Sarper, the Turkish ambassador in Moscow.

These demands were taken by the Turkish leaders of the time as a rekindling of the historical designs of Russia. Their gist is the desire of the Russians to control the access to the Aegean and the Mediterranean. This access, of course, passes through the Turkish Straits, the Bosphorus, and the Dardanelles.

These developments, above all else, prompted the Turkish leaders to seek their security through alliance with powers that opposed Soviet expansionism. The accession of Turkey to NATO in 1952 was the result of continuous Turkish efforts to win support against the Soviet threat.

Although the Soviet Union formally rescinded its demands on May 30, 1953, it would be fair to say that there is always a sense of watchfulness on the part of the Turkish policymakers regarding their relations with the Soviet Union. This is natural enough, given the fact that Turkey is a strong ally of NATO, and the Soviet Union heads its arch-opponent, the Warsaw Pact.

At this point a short discussion might be useful for understanding why another neighbor, Greece, is also perceived in Turkey as an irritant, if not a full-fledged threat.

Turkish-Greek relations have had their ups and downs ever since Greece, a former Ottoman territory, gained its independence in 1830. The relations between Turkey and Greece began to be normalized soon after the Turkish War of Independence, which was fought mainly against the invading Greeks in 1920-23. The Treaty of Lausanne of 1923 resolved the conflict to the satisfaction of both Greece and Turkey, and relations between Turkey and Greece became friendly in the 1930s.

The emergence of the Cyprus question in the international scene followed the 1963 attacks on the Turkish Cypriots by the Greek Cypriots. These attacks brought Turkey, which supported the Turkish minority, and Greece, which supported the Greek majority, into conflict. It would be fair to say that the history of Turkish-Greek relations (especially following the 1974 intervention of Turkey in Cyprus, based on its treaty right to guarantee the independence of the island) is one of contention and often bothersome verbal conflict.

It seems very odd at first glance that two allied nations sharing the same waters of the Aegean Sea should constitute a security consideration, or to paraphrase the Greek Prime Minister Andreas Papandreou, a "threat" to each other.

This most regrettable situation arises from the assessment of various prevailing conditions as security risks in both Greece and Turkey. Turkey finds the militarization of the Aegean Greek islands lying in close proximity to the Turkish coastline to be in contravention of various treaties (such as the 1923 Lausanne Straits Convention). This creates a security hazard for Turkey and is therefore unacceptable. Another issue of conflict between the two countries is the Greek threat that they might increase the limit of their territorial waters to twelve mile. Because this would severely limit the free access of Turkish ships through the Aegean Sea, and put under Greek sovereignty some 71.53 percent of the Aegean, Turkey has decided that it would consider such an act a casus belli.

If one is to make a generalization based on an evaluation of the overall military strength and potential of both countries, it is obvious that Turkey should not consider Greece a serious security threat. On the other hand, the Greek government routinely refers to a Turkish threat and claims that there are Turkish designs on Greek territory. For example, it considers the presence of Turkish troops along the Aegean coast (the Fourth Army) to be a provocation. The Turkish premier has repeatedly stated that all of the existing problems may be resolved through negotiation, and that Turkey would be ready for talks without preconditions. Turkey also lifted visa requirements for Greek nationals who wish to visit Turkey for tourist purposes, to support its claims of goodwill.

One last point needs to be made concerning the threat perceptions of the Turkish leaders. There are three foci of potential hazard to Turkey's security in the Middle East. The first trouble spot that worries the Turks is the continuing struggle between the Arabs and the Israelis. While this struggle is relatively far from the Turkish borders, the tension and the volatility of the situation in itself carries with it the constant possibility of erupting into at least a regional, even a global conflict. The Turkish government has kept out of this conflict and continues to be one of the two countries in the area (the other being Egypt) that have diplomatic ties with Israel. In spite of this, in recent years the Turkish position has been one of support for the rights of the Palestinians, including their right to establish their own state. In addition, Turkey would like to see Israel pull out of the occupied Arab territories. However, the right of the state of Israel to exist in the region is also accepted and is included in all official Turkish statements.

The next focus of attention is the unfortunate war between Iran and Iraq. Here the conflict is closer to home, because both countries share long borders with Turkey and have been traditional friends and very significant trade partners. In addition, the Islamic revolution in Iran and the occasional utterances attributed to Iranian leaders of disapproval of the strictly secular Turkish political system causes displeasure in Turkey. It is also likely that Turkish strategists feel the need to be prepared for an admittedly remote possibility that a communist group, such as the Tudeh party might fill a power vacuum arising from future upheaval in Iran. During the course of seven years of this war, the Turkish government has been meticulously impartial. In spite of this, a "hot" conflict so close to home makes Turkey uneasy, and Turkish officials have tried to do their best to bring about a quick and acceptable solution to this conflict.

The final point of anxiety is the campaign of Kurdish separatist terrorists in Turkish territory. While this activity remains on a very small scale and often groups no larger than three to five people are involved, the fact that these people have bases beyond Turkish borders classifies them as agents of external threat. Reports in the Turkish press often finger Syria as providing training bases to these terrorists. Turkey's relations with Syria are not antagonistic. However, the fact that Syria is a close ally of the Soviet Union and Turkey of the United States makes for strange bedfellow. In the last year or so, there have been a number of high-level state visits between the two countries, and promises have been made by Syria to uproot the terrorists. The actual result of these promises remains meager to this date.

Let us now address the government policies designed to meet these potential threats :

1. The Soviet threat was countered by an alliance between Turkey and the West. Almost immediately after the establishment of the North Atlantic Treaty Organization in 1949, Turkey sought to find a way to join this new collective security system. In fact, the significant Turkish contribution to the UN forces in defense of South Korea is attributed by many analysts to an effort by the Turkish government to show to the Western nations that it possessed a strong fighting army that could fulfill any future Alliance defense responsibility.

In 1952 Turkey joined the North Atlantic Treaty Organization. The basic policy of seeking security in a collective defense arrangement remains the mainstay of Turkish defense strategy. In addition, Turkish officials tried to have harmonious, even cordial relations with non-NATO countries. In recent years Turkey has developed strong trade relations with various Arab countries. Furthermore, Turkish leaders have been careful not to provoke the Soviets. While it is clearly understood that the Republic of Turkey is in an opposing camp, Turkey and the Soviet Union have had civil day-to-day relations and a significant economic intercourse.

2. On the domestic front, Turkey has had a long-standing tradition of maintaining a strong army to counter potential or actual threats to its independence and territorial integrity. At the moment, it has the second largest standing army (after the United States) in NATO. In any given year, approximately 800,000 men and officers make up the land forces, the air force, the navy and the gendarmerie. This last group, numbering some 125,000, is in fact a part of the land forces, but is charged with keeping the peace in rural areas.

While the manpower and the training of the Turkish forces are up to par, the material strength and modernity of equipment leave a lot to be desired. There are constant efforts to modernize the equipment, but the necessary aid, especially from the United States is not as sizable or as speedy as the Turkish officials would like.

In 1980 Turkey and the United States signed a five-year Defense and Economic Cooperation Agreement (DECA). Under this agreement, the United States is committed to making its best efforts to provide defense equipment, services and training to Turkey. In 1985 foreign military sales (FMS) credit and grants have totaled $878.1 million. In 1986 this figure is $738 million. The DECA ran out in 1985, but it has been renegotiated in the spring of 1987 (although the amount of aid remains a source of friction). Another snag in the U.S. military assistance program has been the insistence of the U.S. Congress on a seven-to-ten ratio between Greece and Turkey in the magnitude of the aid to be provided to the two countries. Turkey feels that this is an artificial and unnecessary limitation and should be abandoned.

Throughout the history of the Turkish Republic, and especially following World War II, there has been a wide public support of national security policies. The national consensus, as represented by the various political parties, has been nearly unanimous on the broad issues, such as continued membership in NATO, increased efforts for economic integration with the EEC, and continued military alliance and cooperation with the United States. This is not to say, of course, that splinter groups have not existed that challenged this basis consensus.

In the period between 1965 and 1980, various small parties, sometimes represented in the Parliament and sometimes not, as well as various illegal organizations (either Marxist or ultraconservative religious) have advocated severing ties with NATO and the Western countries. However, these never amounted to any significant force when measured by the number of their followers or the percentage of votes received in general elections. For example, in the 1965 elections, the Marxist-oriented Turkish Labor party won fourteen seats in a parliament of 450 members and their representation fell to two seats in the 1969 elections.

Conversely, the political parties that advocated continued support of Western-oriented policy, whether they were in power or in opposition, whether center-right or left of center, always received over 85 percent of the votes. In short, while it is unrealistic to claim that the general public is very knowledgeable or even interested in the intricacies of security policy in a developing country such as Turkey, there is a clear-cut definition of the "good guys" and the "bad guys" in the collective mind. Needless to say, in this connection, the Soviet Union and its supporters do not fare very well at all.

Looking into the future, the fundamental security policies of Turkey will probably remain the same for several decades to come. One should not expect a pendulum effect such as we saw in Egypt between Nasser and Sadat to happen in Turkey. Both Kemal Ataturk, the founder of Turkey, and his close associate associate, Ismet

Inönü, who formulated the basic tenets of Turkish foreign policy, sincerely believed in a self-reliant, Western-oriented foreign policy. In recent years, as Turkey realized that there were certain cleavages emerging between the United States and Europe, it also began to appreciate the importance of a balanced relationship within NATO.

It appears to be a certainty that within the next 15 to 20 years, perhaps sooner, Turkey will become a full member of the European Economic Community. This will not only integrate Turkey into the European economic system, but it will also provide a counterbalance for Turkey's U.S. relations. While it is true that European and U.S. interests are not basically divergent, it would nevertheless provide an alternative to a single-focus (U.S.) security policy.

The minority opinion of the extremist groups of the religious right and the Marxist left are, of course, in conflict with the overwhelming majority opinion in the country. The Marxists are loath to propose that Turkey change sides and become a member of the Warsaw Pact. What they dare to propose is that Turkey sever all its ties with NATO, proclaim itself a nuclear-free zone, and join the nonaligned movement. It would take little imagination to guess what the next step would be for the Marxists to demand of Turkey.

The extreme religious right also advises that Turkey should pull out of NATO, but it goes further and recommends that Turkey become a theocratic state, follow the Koranic laws, and abandon its six decades of secular domestic policies. The religious right would probably like to see Turkey ally itself with either the conservative Arab states or Iran, depending on the particular persuasion of the splinter group one is talking about.

It is obvious from consistent election results that even watered-down versions of the scenarios briefly described above do not find followers. This is not to say that the Turkish state can lower its guard and let things take their own course. During the ten years between 1970 and 1980, the country suffered from a terror-ridden, chaotic period on the streets of larger cities, and on university campuses, and even in certain rural areas, as extremists of the right and left battled each other. In fact, when the army intervened on September 12, 1980, the average daily death toll had risen to some 30 people. This situation, of course, did little to increase the external security perceptions of the country. There were even proven links between drug traffickers and gun smugglers who helped arm the extremist groups without discrimination. Fortunately for Turkey and its allies who wish it well, those days are long gone. The domestic tranquillity of the country has been reestablished. In addition, democratic processes have returned; there is a freely elected government in power and almost a dozen political parties competing for the voters' favor.

In sum, the public and the political decision-makers in Turkey are aware of the security needs of the country. In the medium-range future of the next three decades, the security priorities of the country will remain much the same as they are today. The public support of the government's policies is solid. Among both the majority opinion of the elites and the population, seeking Turkey's security in a collective arrangement is widely supported.

The Neutrals

17 Finland: No Enemies

Unto Vesa

STABLE SECURITY

The countries of Northern Europe, including Finland, have enjoyed considerable stability and tranquillity since the end of the 1940s. Each country has contributed to this peaceful situation through its foreign and defense policy decisions : Sweden through its traditional policy of neutrality, Finland through its policy of neutrality and its relations with the Soviet Union, and Denmark and Norway through their unilateral limitations on Alliance bases and nuclear weapons. These countries have also traditionally learned to take each other's views and concerns into consideration in the formulation of their policies. Another Nordic element, contributing very much to their security, has been the steadily growing civilian interaction, (economic and social cooperation) that long ago established this subregion as a "security community" in the sense introduced by Karl W. Deutsch. Mutual responsiveness and a sense of togetherness are vital integrative processes in the Nordic region.

From the Finnish side, it has been emphasized that the peacefulness of the Nordic region, resulting from the established pattern of disengagement, has been in the interest not only of the Nordic countries but also of those outside. From the Finnish perspective, therefore, it should not be in anyone's interest to introduce changes into this state of affairs.

The premises of Finnish security policies have remained essentially unchanged since the end of the 1940s, when the country oriented itself to a new foreign policy course in its relationship with its eastern neighbor, the Soviet Union. The starting point for the new approach (later called the Paasikivi-Kekkonen line) was the recognition of the legitimate security interests of the Soviet Union in the direction of its northwestern border. These interests were considered to be of a defensive nature, and consequently they were also considered compatible with the Finnish desire to remain outside the conflicting interests of the superpowers. Both of these elements are therefore present in the Finnish-Soviet Treaty of Friendship, Cooperation and Mutual Assistance (FCMA) of 1948. The military clauses of the treaty are so formulated that they satisfy both demands.

The Finnish authorities have consistently underlined that the FCMA Treaty is not a military alliance proper. Thus the Third Parliamentary Committee argued :

> The FCMA Treaty differs from a military alliance treaty, above all in the sense that military cooperation is confined to the territory of Finland and does not take effect automatically. Also, according to the FCMA Treaty, Finland has the primary responsibility for the defense of her territory. If our capabilities are insufficient for repelling an attack of the kind defined in the Treaty, the FCMA offers alternatives of varying degrees to strengthen our defense.

An essential feature of Finnish security doctrine is the predominance of foreign policy over defense policy. The primacy of foreign policy means that Finland attempts to influence its security environment mainly by political means and; although the defense component of the doctrine was activated in the 1960s, its role is clearly a subordinate one, supporting the foreign policy.

The foreign policy line, defined as an "active, peace-pursuing policy of neutrality," consists of positive confidential relations with the Soviet Union, of the desire to stay outside the superpowers' conflicts of interest, and of the wish to maintain good relations with all countries. Finnish decision-makers have sought to stress that, for Finland, neutrality does not imply passivity, but an active search for peaceful solutions, for which the neutrality policy creates the necessary credibility. It is thus "neutrality for the benefit of international peace and security," as defined in Finnish-Soviet communiques since the beginning of the 1970s. Vital for the success of that policy are the trust and confidence of other countries, of neighbors and especially of the superpowers.

The principle of neutrality and good relations with the Soviet Union are interdependent in Finnish policy, as was pointed out by former President Urho Kekkonen : "The more we can gain the trust of the Soviet Union in Finland as a peaceful neighbor, the better our opportunities for close cooperation with Western countries."

Although the general situation in northern Europe has been satisfactory from the Finnish point of view, it has not been without critical moments. In 1961 the Soviet Union, on the basis of the FCMA Treaty, demanded military consultations, referring to the tense international situation and to the unsolved German problem. President Kekkonen argued successfully with the Soviet leaders that such consultations would, in fact, increase tension in the arena and therefore be counterproductive. Such consultations would also have decreased the credibility of Finnish neutrality, which had been acknowledged by the major powers. In 1965 President Kekkonen reacted against the multilateral nuclear force (MLF) plan, through which the FRG would have acquired access to nuclear weapons. Such a reaction was considered to be in accordance with the policy of neutrality and to reflect basic national interests, because, as Kekkonen stated, "we can only maintain our neutrality on the condition that peace is preserved in Europe."

THREAT PERCEPTIONS

The military articles of the FCMA Treaty read as follows :

Article 1

In the eventuality of Finland, or the Soviet Union through Finnish territory, becoming the object of an armed attack by Germany or any state allied with the latter, Finland will, true to its obligations as an independent State, fight to repel the attack. Finland will in such cases use all its available forces for defending its territorial integrity by land, sea and air, and will do so within the frontiers of Finland in accordance with obligations defined in the present Treaty and, if necessary, with the assistance of, or jointly with the Soviet Union.
In the cases aforementioned, the Soviet Union will give Finland the help required, the giving of which will be subject to mutual agreement between the Contracting Parties.

Article 2

The High Contracting Parties shall confer with each other if it is established that the threat of an armed attack as described in Article 1 is present.

The treaty has been extended three times, most recently in 1983 for a period of twenty years, each time unchanged, so it may well be said to reflect permanent interests and policies. But of course the interpretations of the treaty may change over time. As Finland pursues a policy of neutrality, it is in the Finnish interest to try to prevent circumstances where the application of the military articles of the treaty would become relevant, not only because it would imply the loss of neutrality but because such circumstances per se would be a threat to stability and peace in northern Europe.

Although the treaty transmits a kind of threat perception, and although the periods of Soviet-German tension and their projections to the north have implied critical moments in Finnish-Soviet relations, it would not be accurate to say that there is a Finnish threat perception, expressed at any official level and aimed at a certain state or group of states. Rather, it is characteristic of Finnish threat perceptions that they are concerned with general political and military tendencies, nuclear weapons in particular. Finnish authorities have observed with particular concern and commented on any trends that might jeopardize the established pattern of disengagement in Northern Europe.

Official threat perceptions can be found in many statements by Finnish presidents, foreign ministers, and other government figures, and wider security analyses are included in the reports of three Parliamentary Defense committees (1971, 1976, and 1981).

The present "uppermost" concern was first expressed in 1978 by the then President Kekkonen. He outlined overall trends as follows :

> Military alliances which were originally set up with defensive purposes have over the decades undergone dynamic changes. Being so rapid, technological development has influenced strategic thinking and strategic scenarios. Generally speaking the rapidity of technological advance has overtaken the process of political detente which, for natural reasons, tends to progress at a slower pace. We have in Europe entered a period of growing military-technological risks. The development of military technology in conjunction with continuing mistrust of the other side has accelerated the qualitative arms race in a frightening way.

And as for the impact of such developments on the situation in northern Europe, Kekkonen went on to say :

> Nuclear weapons--both warheads and means for their delivery--as well as the accuracy and maneuverability of weapons systems have been developed with the possibility in mind that one could actually wage a limited nuclear war instead of the dreaded general war. With regard to military technology, I content myself with referring to "mini-nukes," precision-guided munitions, the neutron bomb, and cruise missiles. I consider theories of limited nuclear war lunatic; they are mere stepping stones to general holocaust. But it is important to recognize the political trend behind them. A limited nuclear war would in plain language mean Europeanization of nuclear war. And Northern Europe is by no means immune to the effects of such strategies.
> A glance at the map shows why this is so. In the event of a conflict situation in Europe, what would it mean to the small Nordic countries if, for example, great-power missiles equipped with nuclear warheads flew over their air-space at the altitudes of a few hundred meters on their way to targets on the other side? From the political point of view, what does the mere existence of such a possibility mean to the two Nordic countries which pursue a policy of neutrality? Neutral countries are, as everyone knows, under an obligation to prevent violation of their air space.

These are still prevailing threat perceptions and they are bound to remain until a basic change in the international political and military situation takes place. As is evident, there are different levels in the threat perception : the fear of a nuclear war, the anxiety caused by the development of nuclear arms and technology, the concern about its impact on the closest security environment (Northern Europe), and the specific problem created, in particular, by the introduction of Cruise missiles. As President Kekkonen noted and as the present president of Finland, Dr. Mauno Koivisto, has underlined, Cruise missiles create a problem for the neutral countries by their mere presence, and this problem will be accentuated if such weapons (as seems probable) are deployed in still greater quantities, and by the navies in the North Atlantic.

In their more comprehensive security analysis, the Parliamentary Defense committees have taken such military developments into account, and they have expressed concern about the increasing interest of the superpowers in the northern maritime areas. Yet the Third Committee, in 1981, after analyzing Soviet and U.S. motives, interests, and deployments, concluded : "The strategic significance of Northern Europe has in the past few years increased and the military arrangements in the area have attracted greater attention than before. However, the structural focus of military tension continues to be in Central Europe and the situation in Northern Europe can still be considered relatively stable."

The threat scenarios envisaged in the reports of the Parliamentary Defense committees and perceived to be "more probable than a sudden outbreak of war is a gradually worsening situation which may last for a long time without erupting into an open war." The committee in 1981 outlined the Finnish response in the following terms:

> In such a situation, we will try, pursuing our policy of neutrality, to remain outside the conflicts, to convincingly demonstrate our determination and ability to maintain our territorial integrity, and to search for political means to alleviate the crisis. In case the situation deteriorates into a military conflict, our chances of remaining outside the scope of military operations will depend, apart from foreign policy measures, on our ability to answer for the defense of our territory and to make its use against a third party sufficiently costly. Should our own efforts prove insufficient, the FCMA Treaty offers political and military measures to support our activities. Resorting to these measures depends on the kinds of activities we consider necessary in the situation for our security.

As for the general population, the fear of nuclear war seems to be rather widespread and probably has grown during the early 1980s. In a survey conducted in 1984 by the Tampere Peace Research Institute, the short-term and long-term expectations of the population with regard to war, armament, and disarmament are demonstrated in Table 17.1.

Table 17.1 "Thinking about war, armament and disarmament, what do you believe the world situation will be like in five years?/twenty years?"

Answer	5 years (%)	20 years (%)
World war	1	7
More armament	42	19
About as now	28	5
Partial disarmament	13	24
Complete disarmement	1	6
Do not know	15	38
Total	100	100
N	1,061	1,061

Source : Tampere Peace Research Institute poll (1984).

We see that, in the short-term future, the world situation is predominantly expected to get worse, but that, in the longer perspective, a turn for the better is widely assumed to take place, although the number of those fearing a world war increases, too. When comparing these results with earlier data, one notes that pessimism in general has increased as well as the degree of uncertainty.

A notable feature in Finnish public images of other countries is the lack of any significant enemy. There are suspicions, stereotypes, and prejudices, but not strong hostile attitudes toward any nation. On the contrary, in some polls it has been found that the Finns regard these countries as Finland's "best friends" : Sweden, the Soviet Union, Norway, Denmark, the United States, that is, the Nordic neighbors and the superpowers. Thus we could argue that in Finland the threat perceptions and "friendship" images of the government and of public opinion seem to coincide and reinforce each other, which undoubtedly is of great value for the foreign policy leadership.

FINNISH POLICIES

The primacy of foreign policy over defense policy in the Finnish security concept will no doubt prevail in the future as well. This means that whatever threat perceptions there may be, the government will try to find and design political responses to counter such threats.

The foreign policy focus has traditionally been on the local environment and on neighborhood relationships, but since Finnish activities have grown in widening circles and have come to include efforts to promote European security and cooperation as well as global security in the UN context, all such efforts have undoubtedly served the double purpose of advancing short-term national interests and "common" security interests of the international community in such a way that would remove potential threats and risks. It is natural, therefore, that initiatives aimed at arms control and disarmament have assumed a vital role in Finnish foreign policy. In its disarmament policy, Finland has placed special emphasis on regional measures, such as nuclear-weapon-free zones, and on measures designed to promote nuclear disarmament. In the idea of a Nordic nuclear-weapon-free zone, first proposed by President Kekkonen in 1963, both of these elements are combined. Through this proposal, Finland aims to guarantee the stability and de facto nuclear-free status of the region and thereby to suppress the negative trends caused by the developments of strategy, doctrines and weapons technology.

It is, of course, the Finnish hope that such a zonal arrangement could be reached in the 1980s (and preferably in the near future) but regardless of whether this will succeed or not, the goal will remain the same. It is important to note that the government of Finland has been unwilling to go into details, but instead has sought to underline the flexibility and openness of its position by stating that a solution that is acceptable to all other parties would be acceptable to Finland as well. Thus Finland would undoubtedly welcome arrangements removing nuclear weapons from the Baltic Sea and from the vicinity of the Nordic zone, as suggested by the Swedish government.

The Nordic nuclear-weapon-free zone as such would, according to Finnish conception, promote stability in the north, but it might also be conceived as an element in a more profound process of advancing European nuclear disarmament and arms control, or in the near future, the removal of tactical nuclear weapons from the continent. As for the threat posed by Cruise missiles, a threat considered to grow with their introduction and deployment in the north Atlantic, Finland has tried to approach this problem with the same methodology by stressing political means, but also taking military countermeasures into account. Thus Finland has appealed to the superpowers to prohibit or introduce essential limitations on Cruise missiles, for example, by prohibiting long-range Cruise missiles. Such an appeal was made by President Kekkonen in 1978, and President Koivisto has reiterated it. Moreover, Finland has, in the Stockholm Conference, emphasized the need for negative security assurances in the following terms:

> The security assurances should be as comprehensive as possible in order to account for the new and developing nuclear-weapon technology and the threat thereof to the security of non-nuclear-weapon states. Thus, in addition to the need of general non-use assurances, the nuclear-weapon states are obligated to respect the sovereignty of non-nuclear-weapon states. Consequently, their territories including the air-space must not be violated in delivering nuclear weapons to their targets.

Even if such assurances were provided--and they are welcome--these alone would not suffice. President Kekkonen underlined in his New Year's statement in 1985 : "Anyway, we have to be prepared to repel the violations of our territory and air-space." This current issue is a pertinent reminder of the fact that there is an essential defense policy element in the security concept. It is readily admitted that in a nuclear war there is not much to be done except to seek protection by civil defense. However, in the reports of the Parliamentary Defense committees, a nuclear war is not regarded as a probable alternative; the most dangerous projected scenario is "a gradually worsening situation which may last for a long time without erupting into an open war." In such a crisis situation, a well-equipped national army has, according to the prevailing conception, a vital preventive role to play. Moreover, "an isolated attack against Finland is considered unlikely"; the Third Parliamentary Defense committee concluded, "If, on the basis of our resources and various threat scenarios, the practical possibilities to defend the country are realistically assessed, it is obvious that the primary task of the Defense Forces will have to be to repel a limited conventional attack against our country or through her territory."

And this is considered feasible. The Finnish defense policy, as outlined by the committees, has sought to develop and modernize all branches, the army, air force, and navy, in a balanced way. Finland can mobilize within a short time close to 700,000 men in reserve. In addition, its materiel preparedness is considered relatively good, although it is admitted that the rapid development of modern arms technology caused problems by rendering existing systems obsolete and by increasing the costs of procuring new ones.

A notable feature in Finnish defense policy has been that the level of defense spending has remained rather consistently below 1.5 percent of GNP.

Finnish society is characterized by a high degree of consensus, especially concerning foreign policy. There are no significant disagreements on its essence or orientation at the political level; the government parties and the opposition agree on the basic tenets of the Paasikivi-Kekkonen line. Moreover, the support of public opinion for foreign policy is strong and has steadily increased. In the surveys conducted annually by the Planning Commission for Information on National Defense, there have been a few standard questions measuring atitudes toward foreign policy and defense. The level of satisfaction with the conduct of foreign policy--measured with the question, "How good or bad do you consider the conduct of Finnish foreign policy in recent years?"--has been high : the share of positive assessments has varied between 84 and 95 percent from 1964 to the present; in the most recent poll, it was above 90 percent. The share of negative ratings has varied between 2 and 9 percent.

Another standard question has concerned the evaluation of the FCMA Treaty : "In your opinion, has the FCMA Treaty ... had a positive or a negative effect, or no efect at all with respect to Finland's international status?" The share of those giving a positive assessment has increased from 57 percent in 1964 to about 85 percent in 1984.

For many years the surveys asked the respondents to assess Finland's chances of securing its position through foreign policy, for example by international conferences and initiatives. More than three-quarters of the respondents considered the chances good.

As for the other element of security policy, namely defense policy, it has been traditionally much more controversial at the levels of both decision-making and public opinion. However, in this field, too, consensus seems to increase on some basic issues, such as the very need for national defense, but there are still notable disagreements, such as on the appropriate level of defense spending. In the Parliamentary Defense committees, which have no doubt contributed to the emerging consensus, compromises have been found even on the latter aspect, but these compromises have not always been accepted within the political parties concerned and have found still less acceptance among the general public. These facts can again be illustrated by some figures from the above-mentioned polls.

In 1984 about 90 percent of the Finns considered that the Defense Forces are needed, and 83 percent gave a positive answer to the question whether "the Finns should make armed resistance in all situations if the country is attacked." A critical attitude seems to be a bit more widespread among the younger age groups and, for the political groupings, among the supporters of the People's Democrats and the Greens. Measured by this question, the will to defend Finland has considerably increased during the past fifteen years. One should note, however, that the will to defend seems to be clearly dependent on the envisaged threat scenarios, and in particular on whether or not nuclear weapons are introduced into threat scenarios. In a poll in 1984, four different threat scenarios were given to respondents, and after the response an additional question was put forward : "and if nuclear weapons were used by the aggressor...?" (Table 17.2).

Table 17.2 : The perceived need of defense in different threat situations
A: "Let us assume that Finland would be drawn into a large-scale military conflict ..."
B: "And if nuclear weapons were used in such an aggression ..."

Question (%)	Finland should defend itself
A "... the Capital with its surroundings would be attacked"	87
B "... and if nuclear weapons were used"	42
A "... Finland's air space would be attacked"	81
B "... and if nuclear weapons were used"	47
A "... Finland's Lapland would be attacked"	87
B "... and if nuclear weapons were used"	45
A "... through Finland's Lapland an attack against another state is attempted"	79
B "... and if nuclear weapons were used	44

Source : Tampere Peace Research Institute poll (1984).

With regard to the level of defense spending, the public opinion has developed as indicated by Table 17.3.

Table 17.3 : Opinion polls about defense budget in 1964-85 : "Should we increase the defense budget, decrease it, or maintain the present level?" (in percentages)

Answer	1964	'69	'70	'71	'72	'73	'74	'75
Increase	17	46	56	46	36	42	42	41
Maintain	55	38	33	42	48	44	41	41
Decrease	16	9	8	8	8	9	9	11
Cannot say	12	7	3	4	8	5	8	7

	1978	'79	'80	'81	'82	'83	'84	'85
Increase	38	37	41	32	33	33	33	36
Maintain	38	43	42	48	49	48	51	48
Decrease	12	10	12	13	14	14	12	12
Cannot say	12	10	5	7	5	5	3	3

Source : Planning Commission for Information on National Defense poll (1985).

WHICH WAY FORWARD ?

Finnish security policy and foreign policy as its main component have been characterized by a considerable continuity. The satisfaction with its achievements is widespread and there are no major forces demanding essential changes. Inevitably, there are groups lobbying for additional funds for defense and others with opposite motivations, but support for the established policy is strong, and this factor alone would make deviations from the established line difficult. Furthermore, such demands lack the required credibility, as their supporters have not been able to point out how such changes would improve the present situation.

However, one should note that there are also seems to be a widespread feeling that Finland should assume a still more active role in its foreign policy, and that such an activity could have concrete results. The successful experiences of Finland with the CSCE initiative have undoubtedly encouraged this opinion. The foreign policy leadership seems to have a basically positive attitude toward this expectation, but at the same time reflects doubts about the possibilities of activating the foreign policy in a tense international atmosphere.

To sum up, from the Finnish perspective, it is not changes in Finnish policies that could enhance its security situation, and such changes are not likely to appear. Instead, Finland would welcome changes in the external security environment, although it has been fairly satisfied with the stable, strategic environment and has sought to act against tendencies that from the Finnish point of view appear negative.

The changes Finland would like to see in its security environment can be grouped subregionally, regionally, and globally. In each case, there are both political and arms control objectives on the agenda.

First, as for subregional objectives, the promotion of stability in Northern Europe through measures of disengagement, through arrangements guaranteeing the status of a nuclear-weapon-free zone, through intensified economic, social and political cooperation, has a high priority in Finnish policy. It has sometimes been stated that, from the Finnish perspective, the best possible state of affairs would be a common Nordic neutrality, but this cannot be regarded as a policy goal. On the contrary, it has been emphasized in recent years that each country can best judge its own security requirements, and that a nuclear-weapon-free zone can be established within the present national security arrangements. It would also be in the Finnish interest to remove any potential sources of tension and instability related to the Baltic Sea, which could be negotiated either in connection with the nuclear-weapon-free zone or as a separate understanding.

As for regional objectives, Finland has outlined its views mainly in the CSCE context. It is in this context, too, that Finland has underlined the need and fruitfulness of a wider concept of security (that is, an associative peace concept) where cooperation is seen as the best guarantee of peace, instead of arms, deterrence, or fear. President Kekkonen crystallized this belief eloquently in his CSCE statement in 1975 :

> Therefore it is imperative that we devote, to an increasing extent, our faith in the future and our activities to consideration of disarmament. We believe that the contribution paid even by the present Conference to the promotion of detente has brought us nearer the day when the idea of far-reaching international disarmament is not a remote prospect but an integral part of our cooperation. This belief is not just a wishful dream of a small country not belonging to any bloc. It is based on the consciousness that, rather than any system relying on the use of force, the cooperation initiated by us is the best guarantee of security.

The CSCE process has, of course, brought subsequent disappointments, but these have hardly shaken the fundamental view expressed above. Therefore, with regard to European security, Finland pursues the twin objectives of advancing cooperation and promoting European disarmament. It is recognized that European armament and disarmament problems are highly complex and sensitive, but what Finland has proposed is that all countries responsible for European security should strive together for a complete reassessment of problems involved in disarmament in Europe. All states have an interest and a legitimate right to express their views on this issue.

Of course, the same fundamental views find their expression in Finnish global policy. Finland has consistently supported the strengthening of the UN capacity to maintain international peace and security, and, in particular, the central roles of the Secretary-General and the Security Council. Finland has also provided contingents to the UN peacekeeping forces and is, in proportion to its population, the leading contributor to these forces. And within the United Nations framework, Finland has been actively involved in disarmament negotiations, concentrating its efforts on such aspects of nuclear disarmament as the nonproliferation of nuclear weapons and a comprehensive test ban and on other measures aimed at the prohibition of weapons of mass destruction. Although limited by nature and often technical in appearance, Finnish contributions to disarmament negotiations have in some cases been instrumental. Finland will undoubtedly try to retain a similar role in the future, if possible.

The policy directions briefly outlined above command wide popular support in Finland. In fact, in a recent poll, associative peace strategies such as the strengthening of the UN, increasing economic and social cooperation between states, general and complete disarmament, abolishing the gap between the rich and poor countries, were found to be the most widely supported proposals on a list of close to 30 different peace strategies. So the inhibiting factors for the realization of the measures and objectives Finland pursues are not internal, but are clearly external, and outside Finland's direct influence. Whether such changes will take place will depend not only on the policies of Finland, but on those of many other countries. And of course, Finland is not alone in its efforts; in the CSCE, the neutral and nonaligned countries have developed fruitful cooperation patterns. In the United Nations the Nordic group is quite influential when acting together; and on many issues regarding peace and security, the group of "like-minded" nations comprises most or even all states of the world, in principle.

The perennial question in the study of international politics is what the small states can do. The traditional answer has been : not very much. The Finnish response, first, has been at least in their own policy they can try to dissociate themselves from trends having adverse effects; second, they can appeal to the superpowers and remind them of their special responsibilities; and finally, the strengthening of multilateral institutions and arrangements best serves the interests of small states. Undoubtedly we can expect Finnish policies to remain on this course in the future.

REFERENCES

The basic sources for "official" threat perceptions and security policy are the reports of the three Parliamentary Defense committees, published in 1971, 1976 and 1981. Of these, the first was published only in Finnish and Swedish, but the last two are available in English as well : Report of the Second Parliamentary Defense Committee, Committee Report (Helsinki, 1976) and Report of the Third Parliamentary Defense Committee Report (Helsinki, 1981).

Many of the key statements by President Kekkonen on Finland's foreign policy are to be found in Neutrality : The Finnish Position : Speeches by Dr. Urho Kekkonen, President of Finland (London : Heinemann, 1972) and in Urho Kekkonen, A President's View (London : Heinemann, 1982). The Yearbook of Finnish Foreign Policy, published annually by the Finnish Institute of International Affairs, Helsinki, provides both short articles on current foreign policy and some of the most important foreign policy documents. The most useful source of documents on Finland's activities for disarmament is Finnish Disarmament Policy (Helsinki: Ministry for Foreign Affairs, 1983).

The data on surveys concerning attitudes towards defense originate with the Planning Commission for Information on National Defense, in particular from Markku Haranne, "Opinion Polls on Security and Foreign Policy and the Related Debate," Yearbook of Finnish Foreign Policy (Helsinki, 1980) : 48-52, and Markku Haranne, Finnish Opinions of Security Policy, 1985, mimeo, and a related paper by Haranne in Finnish on the same data, February 18, 1985, mimeo.

The data on Finnish expectations concerning the future as well as conceptions about various peace strategies are from a survey conducted by the Tampere Peace Research Institute and the University of Tampere in 1984. The first report by Pertti Suhonen, Unto Vesa and Hannu Virtanen providing all basic data is forthcoming.

A useful exposé and analysis of the Finnish security doctrine can be found in Kari Möttölä, "The Politics of Neutrality and Defense : Finnish Security Policy Since the Early 1970s," Cooperation and Conflict, 17, no. 4 (December 1982) : 287-313. Finland's views and policies with regard to international crisis have been analyzed in Unto Vesa, "Determining Finland's Position in International Crisis," in Yearbook of Finnish Foreign Policy 1979 (Helsinki : The Finnish Institute of International Affairs, 1980), pp. 2-19.

18 Sweden: Total Security

Bo Huldt

In the most recent Swedish Defense committee report (1985), it is stated that the aim of Sweden's security policy is " in all situations and by the means of our own choice, to ensure national freedom of action in order that within our own borders we may preserve and develop our society in political, economic, social, cultural, and all other respects, according to our own values, and in conjunction with this to promote international detente and peaceful development." The report also underlines the aim " of contributing to the maintenance of calm and stability in the Nordic area and reducing the risk of Sweden becoming involved in wars and conflicts."

The means through which these aims are to be realized are defined within the framework of a total security policy, the elements of which were explicitly defined already in the 1960s. The report refers to "interaction" between our foreign and defense policies and declares Sweden's policy of neutrality ("nonparticipation in alliances in peacetime with a view to neutrality in war") as the cornerstone of Swedish security policy.

In the public debate, the Social Democratic administration that took over in 1982 under Prime Minister Olof Palme made repeated statements to the effect that nonaligned policy must always be regarded as the first line of Swedish defense. In what was to be his last major foreign policy speech, at the Swedish Institute of International Affairs in Stockholm on December 12, 1985, Mr. Palme observed "Swedish neutrality should carry the imprint of irrevocability. The world around us must have confidence in Sweden's policy of nonalignment. It is important that this policy is supported by a strong defense, when considering our circumstances. However strong the defense, it would not avail us if the world around us were to start having doubts about our policy of nonalignment."

While there is little disagreement that foreign policy must always be the first line of Swedish defense, it is clear from recent debates in Sweden that a substantial portion of public opinion would be prepared to turn the Palme perspective around; should the "world around us"--in a crisis situation--see no deterrent effect in our defense efforts, then our policy of nonalignment would not by itself help us very much. Much of the foreign and security policy debate in Sweden during the years of the second Palme administration from 1982 to 1986 has focused on presupposed problems of priority between, on the one hand, a policy of neutrality with active peace and disarmament initiatives and, on the other, a strong defense posture. The political left has put emphasis on the former element, the right on the latter. Ultimately, however, it appears that in the minds of the vast majority of Swedes (making up those 80 percent of the population who have in repeated polls declared themselves prepared to resist armed aggression "even when the outcome may appear in doubt") Sweden's security rests on two pillars :

- an active policy of neutrality (or nonalignment) that includes subpolicies dealing with trade issues, foreign aid, disarmament and arms control, international organizations, environmental issues, etc.
- a defense policy that includes military, civil, economic, and psychological defense.

If the first pillar might also be referred to as the "first line of defense," the second would appear to constitute the "last line of defense." Swedish neutrality has deep roots (traced by some to the 1830s) but so have national defense concepts.

Much of the fireworks of the political debate during the second Palme administration (the first was between 1968 and 1976) has tended to mask a fundamental national consensus, fortified rather than weakened under the impact of international pressure in the 1980s, with roots far back in the 1930s. The present picture may contain contradictory elements (and we shall return to these) but the transition from the Palme administration, after the tragic murder of the prime minister, to the new Carlsson administration has shown a remarkable amount of harmony on the specifics of security and foreign policy.

HISTORY

History and continuity are important in understanding the Swedish security context today. Since the early 1700s Sweden has experienced a rather dramatic transition from great power status to small statehood, from imperial ambitions to "satisfaction" within "natural" boundaries. The European situation in 1945 did, through "accident," one might say, propel Sweden into a role of some strategic significance--a role that Sweden still today tries to fulfill, although the character of the strategic pattern in the north has changed substantially between 1945 and 1986.

Before pursuing the analysis further, let us first return to the beginning of the contemporary age. Swedish security policy has run through several phases since Sweden entered the League of Nations. the period from 1919 to 1933 (from joining the League till the collapse of the Disarmament Conference) was characterized by unequivocal commitment to disarmament. "Collective security" was essentially understood in such terms, not as a guarantee system with economic or military sanctions. The Swedish position was without compromise, and in 1925 a unilateral Swedish disarmament program was launched.

After the failure of the Disarmament Conference, Swedish security policy in the 1930s evolved along different roads : collective security with sanctions (against Italy over Ethiopia), Nordic cooperation (pursued very halfheartedly), and finally, with the new defense plan in 1936, rearmament. With the outbreak of World War II, the course was set according to a new formula, strong national defense, with which Sweden has really lived ever since. In 1939 Swedish defense was certainly far from strong but when the war ended, the Swedish found themselves in a unique position. Having been able to remain on the sidelines, profiting from trade with Germany and other belligerents, and having diligently built its military resources and defense industry, Sweden in 1945 was in a position of remarkable strength in a continent in ruins. During the first postwar decades, Sweden also had a military "weight" of its own that had a real impact on the European balance.

In 1948-49, facing an imminent division of Europe between hostile blocs, the Swedes tried to establish some form of Nordic defense cooperation with Denmark and Norway, an unaligned alliance that would keep the North out of harm's way and out of the alliance confrontation in Europe. The Swedish efforts failed, Norway and Denmark joined NATO (although on "minimal" conditions) while Finland rearranged its relations with the Soviet Union through a treaty of friendship and mutual cooperation. Sweden remained the armed neutral of the North. This pattern of security arrangements has been referred to as the "Nordic Balance," a system to the mutual advantage of both superpowers--and, of course, to the Nordic countries. This arrangement thus created a Nordic barrier between East and West, a buffer zone with several layers--to some of the more enthusiastic proponents of the Nordic balance concept, a self-regulating and self-perpetuating system. In this system, Sweden has a special role as the military "backbone" of the balance--the only "real" military power in the north, with its strong air force, its threshold nuclear capabilities, its large army and navy.

From Nordic Balance to Strategic North

By 1945 the Soviet Union has established itself as the dominant continental power--but it remained a landlocked power with very limited naval resources and no long-range aircraft. Given the correlation of forces at the time, the Nordic buffer, functioning as a flank protection in the north, should have appeared as the optimal solution to the Soviet leadership.

By the mid-1980s, however, the situation had changed rather drastically. The Soviet Union now commands naval and air force resources on a totally different scale. In a global sense, the Soviet Union is now the real rival and contender to the United States that it could only pretend to be during the first three decades of the postwar period.

The military buildup on the Kola peninsula, the Soviet northern fleet with a substantial portion of Soviet second-strike nuclear capabilities as well as resources for interdiction against NATO transatlantic communications (SLOC) : and new capabilities of conducting landing and airborne operations are factors that have changed the security milieu in the north. With an arms race now going on between NATO and the Soviet Union in the north Atlantic, Norwegian, and Barents Seas, the Nordic countries are increasingly concerned with Cruise missiles, inadvertent nuclear war through (strategic) anti-submarine warfare, and territorial violations (submarines and aircraft). What used to be described as NATO's "northern flank," and essentially a sideshow to the central front, now looms as a possible opening stage in a major East-West war, however unlikely such a war may seem.

In describing the strategic situation there still remains every reason to avoid alarmism. Military capabilities are not available in endless supply even to the superpowers. For the East, for example, it must still appear most doubtful whether it would be possible, in a major European war, to maintain, at one and the same time, the initiative on the central front <u>and</u> to engage in major operations on the flanks. Western estimates suggest that sufficient air and naval components will <u>not</u> be available for this. And if the initiative is lost on the central front, because of major engagements (for example in the north) and NATO is given time to mobilize, deploy, fortify, and reinforce from across the ocean, <u>then</u> the situation for the Warsaw Pact would look bleak indeed on the decisive front. With such a situation arising, we would seem, instead, to be heading for either protracted conventional war or for rapid nuclear escalation.

However, the very fact that military resources are scarce will force the superpowers to emphasize surprise, early moves and preemption, which for the Swedes (and their Nordic neighbors) introduces new elements of risk.

From the Soviet perspective, given a defensive strategy, the Nordic barrier may no longer appear protection enough in a world of Cruise missiles, strategic antisubmarine warfare, and a global (as distinct from previously regional) confrontation with the United States. In a conflict or war situation, there may thus arise a need for "strengthening" the barrier or pushing the defensive perimeter outward. That such moves would be seen as nonoffensive from a Soviet point of view will not make them less threatening to the Nordic countries. A more sinister interpretation of Soviet crisis and war strategies would underline the offensive elements--the thrust outward into the Atlantic, aiming for the sea lanes of communication and isolating Europe from North America.

While the pattern of security relations has remained unchanged in the north since the late 1940s, the environment has thus changed and the "Strategic North" of today poses new challenges to all Nordic countries, but above all to the Norwegians, who feel the immediate presence of the new Soviet naval might, and to the Swedes, who now have the misfortune of finding themselves in a more exposed position than before and with greater demands on their own military resources. These very resources (relative to the world around us) have diminished in number and have become increasingly difficult to maintain in terms of quality.

Sweden, like her Nordic neighbors, here finds itself caught in a squeeze between rising Soviet power and NATO (above all U.S.) countermoves, especially the new forward maritime strategy. At the same time, there is a resource squeeze, what Harold Sprout already in the 1960s saw as the crucial dilemma between increasing demands and insufficient resources for the advanced industrial (and welfare) societies.

The Nordic countries have responded to the challenges in two ways. Norway, Sweden, and Finland have strengthened their military resources in the northern parts of their respective territories. Norway has also entered into pre-positioning agreements with its NATO allies, improving its capacity to receive reinforcements, above all in terms of aircraft. The Swedes have taken the costly decision to develop a new generation of Swedish-made fighter aircraft (the JAS project). The Finns have improved their airdefense components and their ground forces structure in Finnish Lappland.

Military buildup has been one form of response. The other has focused on various ways to promote detente and confidence-building and to lower tension and superpower presence in the region. The various nuclear-free-zone proposals are elements of this type of response. From the Swedish perspective, the zone issue reflects an old concern that was apparent in the efforts of the 1930s to isolate the north from rising European storm (Foreign Minister Sandler and the Aland plan in 1938) and in the Nordic "alliance" negotiations in 1948-49--of keeping the superpowers as far away from the region as possible. Geography (the fact that the Soviet Union is a neighboring superpower) causes difficulties. The Swedish proposal of denuclearization of the Baltic, possibly a sine qua non of the official Swedish zone position, was established in 1981 by then opposition leader Olof Palme in connection with the "Whiskey on the rocks" (the U-137 incident) and may be seen as an effort to improve on geography.

The issue now discussed in Norway about increasing NATO naval presence in the Norwegian Sea is probably viewed with a certain hesitation in Sweden. Increased presence is contrary to the standard and unspoken rule of keeping the superpowers out of the region and is thus likely to provoke demands for negotiations and arms control rather than a buildup. Generally, the Swedes tend to focus on the Baltic rather than on the Atlantic, and there has undoubtedly been a certain lack of Swedish understanding of Norwegian problems. However, Swedish considerations of the security situation in the postwar period have been rather consistently influenced by a "realist" understanding of the need for a "balance"; such a "balanced" and "nonprovocative" NATO naval presence, both in the Baltic and in the northern seas, ought to be a Swedish desideratum, underlining the fact that these are international waters and not the closed preserves of any great power. Here the Nordic countries as a group steer the difficult middle way between "deterrence" and "reassurance" in relationship to the conflicting strategic interests in the north.

SWEDISH SECURITY POLICY AT THE CROSSROADS ?

In 1959, and by the signing of the Non-Proliferation Treaty in 1968, Sweden turned away from the nuclear option which untill then had been a logical continuation of the doctrine of a strong national defense. (Plans to make Sweden a nuclear power were at the time well advanced.) Instead, Sweden chose to stake its military security on a continued conventional buildup that would force any decision for escalation upon prospective aggressors. The fact that the two alliances in Europe tied down the bulk of the forces of the respective opponents was thought to present Sweden with a relatively favorable situation in which only marginal forces could be deployed against Sweden's armed might. A combination of a functioning balance of power and substantial Swedish resources supporting a policy of nonalignment would thus provide effective security.

This assumption has been challenged by the costs and the technological explosion in armaments, and by a continuing transfer of resources from the external security sector and defense to internal security--the welfare society. In the 1950s some 5 percent of GNP went into defense budgets. Today total GNP has grown considerably since the 1950s, but the defense share is now barely 3 percent. There is today a growing concern among the military (and the civilian experts) that the situation may become untenable if additional resources cannot be found. (The Commander-in Chief, General Bengt Gustafsson, has also made a plea for a return to the high levels of the 1950s. Parallel demands have been made by his colleague in Norway, General F.V. Bull-Hansen.)

The requirements for defense here collide head-on with demands for a continuing buildup (and the increasingly costly maintenance) of the welfare system, necessitating a fundamental reassessment of what our priorities ought to be. This is quite clearly not only a question of military expenditures but one of government spending and intervention in general. One may currently discern the beginnings of such a debate, but all the hard choices are stil ahead of us. The 1987 Defense Plan is likely to require considerable efforts on the part of the political leadership of the major parties to find common ground, and consensus is obviously the desired aim for a policy that is acceptable both politically and militarily.

Growing economic and technological problems in military upkeep have encouraged a search for "other means" by which to bolster security : through re-launching detente, promoting confidence- and security-building in Europe, and submission of specific peace and arms control proposals (i.e., the nonnuclear corridor in Central Europe proposed by the Palme Commission). Echoes from Swedish initiatives of the 1920s and 1930s may be heard here, but it is also important to underline the continuity of the Swedish antinuclear posture in disarmament negotiations since the early 1960s, when Sweden first joined the disarmament talks in Geneva.

While these proposals for improving confidence and security in Europe will undoubtedly remain elements of an active peace and disarmament policy, there now seems to be a tendency in the direction of more "realism" in security policy debates in Sweden. Requests made in the late 1970s and early 1980s within the Social Democratic party for unilateral Swedish disarmament have now been forgotten. There also seems to be a wider recognition of Sweden's role in maintaining stability in the north and of the demands made on our ability to hold our "position" between the two blocs. In this context, one should also underline the fact that, after all, stability remains the fundamental characteristic of the Nordic security pattern.

The Swedish reaction to the submarine incidents since 1981 has also been relatively balanced and restrained. Strong protests were issued to the Soviet Union in 1981 and 1982, but there has been no major shift in defense policy away from a balanced defense structure in the direction of a massive anti-submarine warfare buildup. NATO planners have expressed concern that the Swedes would squander limited resources that could be better used for air force modernization (i.e. the JAS program). Such worries seem unfounded. However, priorities will have to be set, not because of submarines but because of the cost squeeze. The establishment of such priorities will involve controversies over different defense concepts, essentially the air force and high technology versus the army and conscription.

Currently, as repeatedly stated here, consensus on defense issues seems refortified. Public opinion has also withstood the onslaught of the submarine shock quite well; as shown in polls, there is still a very strong belief in armed resistance against aggression even when the outcome may be in doubt. Swedish political leaders also feel the need to seek a wide consensus on these issues; this was not the case in the 1970s.

Competition over "insufficient" resources will be painful. There have also been indications of a reappearance of the old rift between left and right that existed in the interwar period prior to the forging of consensus in the late 1930s. The threat of "nuclear winter" and disaster in Europe may still promote disarmament at any price movements although the peace movements in the democratic West today generally seem to be in retreat. Nuclear awareness appears to recur in ten-year cycles and new waves will undoubtedly arise during coming decades. At the same time, there might be some ground for arguing that a qualitatively different situation has arisen since the late 1970s; awareness has now acquired a measure of permanence (Chernobyl may, or may not, contribute to this.).

The JAS-decision has been taken but other decisions still lie ahead of us : the modernization of the field army with armor and air defense components, civil defense and countermeasures against chemical warfare, the continuing modernization of the navy with its anti-submarine elements as well as new Swedish submarines.

When Sweden chose, in 1945, to continue the military buildup rather than relaunch the unilateral disarmament policy of the 1920s, this was no doubt a decision seen as temporary--some time in the future, it would be possible to improve the international climate and to reduce defense burdens. Sweden was buying time. Since then, however, time horizons have been repeatedly revised. Much hope was attached to detente in the 1970s and despite the deterioration in the overall climate of East-West relations and the specific difficulties in bilateral relations with the Soviet Union during the 1980s (Swedish public opinion now is as anti-Soviet as it was in the 1950s), the Swedes, much like their fellow Europeans in general, have refused to accept that detente may have passed away. Swedish views of European security will thus continue to be colored by expectations of detente and fundamental convictions about the anomalous and unacceptable character of a permanent confrontation between the two halves of Europe.

A HOST OF SECURITY ISSUES

Sweden's position rests on a total security policy. This implies two things : on one hand, that "threats" may be diverse, originate from various directions, and have to be met with various means; on the other, that all these various threats may "interact," from interconnected parts of a total security milieu and thus have to be countered through integrated defense strategies.

Traditionally, thinking about security has been all but dominated by military threat perceptions. Today, the military issue may still occupy center stage but a wide variety of "security" problems now compete for our attention. The recent nuclear disaster at Chernobyl in the Ukraine with apparent repercussions for Soviet neighbors (including Sweden) has underlined the importance of environmental issues as problems of international security.

International dependence, the integration of the Swedish economy into a global division of labor, Swedish reliance on imported technologies and components for its own export products (and for arms production)--these and other aspects of an ongoing process of internationalization are problems that have only relatively recently dawned on us. Economic security in the 1940s, 1950s, and 1960s was still largely seen in terms of the blockade and isolation Sweden had experienced in two world wars, an emergency that had to be met by storing supplies and reserves in Sweden. Today, it would seem difficult to maintain such a "limited" perspective. Economic threats are now seen as much more diverse and encompass "peace crises," such as the cutoff of certain key raw materials (or advanced products), even in the absence of a major war; economic warfare between the blocs (technology transfers, etc.); and the very transformation of the world economic system, with protectionism, " managed trade," regionalization, and trade blocs now threatening Sweden's position as a free trade country.

These diverse economic threats create security problems that for our every day lives are certainly no less serious than those posed by a changing strategic environment. One might even argue that these issues are rather _more_ urgent than Cruise missiles and the Soviet northern fleet. The same thing might actually be said about unemployment which, in a recent poll conducted by the Atlantic Institute, was declared to be _the_ threat as seen by citizens of the democratic West.

In 1945 there were those in Sweden who underlined the paramount importance of good relations with the Soviet Union and who saw these relations in economic terms. Despite substantial credits granted to the Soviet Union in the 1940s, very little came out of this effort to establish economic relations. Instead, Sweden in the postwar period became integrated within the Western economic system, and to an extent that has been seen by some analysts as a threat to the credibility of Swedish neutrality. To maintain a modern military organization, it has been necessary to import advanced military equipment. This, however, has created a measure of international dependence that the improved military capabilities can hardly counterbalance by themselves. Security has become a much more complex issue than in the 1940s. For reasons of neutrality, Sweden chose to stay out of the European Community, establishing instead a special agreement. Efforts in the 1970s to find, through relations with Third World countries, alternatives to the dependence on Western markets and imports have not been very fruitful. There is simply no alternative, and the 1980s generally signify a Swedish return to Europe in terms of both security concerns and economic relations.

Generally, there seems today to be a growing awareness about a "dwarfing of Sweden" with horizons shrinking and possibilities for acting "freely" diminishing both because of constraints imposed by a strategic situation and by our dependence on international economic processes and structures, trade regimes, Western markets, and technologies. This calls for adaptation to new conditions, but today there still seems to be little public awareness of these problems. Illusions still seem to exist that Sweden should be able to continue to enjoy freely the best of all worlds, while at the same time being able to isolate itself from disturbances and turbulence within the international system. Three successive shocks may have made us better prepared, however, for a more perilous road ahead : the oil crisis of the 1970s, the submarine incidents, and the tragic demise of Olof Palme.

As for the international scene and the surrounding security environment, short of a great (nuclear or conventional) war, the major challenges to Sweden will be posed by changes in the correlation of forces in Europe and adjacent waters and by political changes in the present European structure. In the 1960s much attention was paid by the Swedes to possible futures of Europe, various scenarios that would in different ways change the basic assumptions about the political structure in Europe. Not much of this has materialized, but among experts and analysts there now seems to be a realization that a new Europe is emerging, although opinions differ as to how fast the Europe of the Yalta inheritance will evolve into a new Europe of the Europeans (and which Europeans will be included).

As for Sweden itself, much will depend on how social consensus can be maintained over the long term. The Swedes have been spectacularly successful in this respect over the last 50 years. Today, the country still appears homogeneous (and this despite a large inflow of immigrants and guest workers from all over Europe and from overseas), fundamentally democratic, and characterized by a Swedish brand of equality that to the outside observer may appear excessive.

Antiestablishment movements, challenging the orthodox opinion on nuclear energy and high technology, have emerged in the 1970s, and various peace groups have voiced opposition not only to nuclear weapons, of which Sweden has none, but also to Swedish armaments and arms exports. An increasing measure of economic and class conflict has been detected by some analysts of a Marxist persuasion. Historically speaking, the greater danger for revolution and social unrest may be that arising from the counteroffensive of an entrenched elite that sees its interests threatened. Today, with Sweden transformed into a service sector economy and an information society, that threat may be coming less from traditional elites than from the ranks of the labor unions, which in a changing environment frequently appear to be a force of conservatism, defending captured territory (i.e., their hold on the political process through the Social Democratic party and the present version of the welfare state). Ironically enough, one might be tempted to say that should Sweden fail to solve some or all of its security problems over the coming decades, this may to no small extent be due to the fact that we have been so dramatically successful in providing both butter and guns, welfare and security for the past four decades.

19 Switzerland: Reinforcing General Defense

Daniel Frei

THE SWISS ASSESSMENT OF THE PRESENT SECURITY SYSTEM

Internal and External Threat Perceptions

Switzerland, a small country without any noticeable resources of its own except for stones and water, is highly dependent on the outside world in both politico-strategic and economic terms. This implies that Swiss authorities as well as the common citizen are quite sensitive about external changes evolving from the international situation. They are all aware that the survival and welfare of Switzerland, notwithstanding their own efforts, depend on stability and peace in both Europe and the world as a whole. This attitude is conducive to an attentive stance of caution as far as the international environment is concerned. Thus, threats are hardly ever underestimated and they tend to be perceived very thoroughly and soberly.

According to official documents, the threat posed to Switzerland is characterized by two current developments : first, the growth in the number of international conflicts, which may spread surprisingly and swiftly into distant regions, and second, the increasing range and firepower of modern weapon systems.[1] As far as the first feature is concerned, Switzerland assumes a rapid shrinking of available warning time; this requires vigilance against strategic surprise and actions. In addition, strategies of subversion, sabotage, terrorism, commando actions, and a variety of covert and psychological warfare techniques are seen to have growing importance and may thus constitute a particularly grave threat to the country.[2] Switzerland feels highly vulnerable in this respect owing to its nature as an open society, its complex and sensitive infrastructure, and its high degree of interdependence on the outside world.

Although Swiss military planners in principle do not expect a full-scale military conflict to happen in Europe in the foreseeable future, they are basing their threat assessment on the premise of a largely uncertain international situation that may generate incalculable risks and sudden escalation affecting Europe and Switzerland.

Even in case of a direct military confrontation between NATO and Warsaw Pact forces, the probability of a direct attack on Switzerland seems to be low, and Swiss planners do not believe Switzerland to be a primary target. The main thrust of a hypothetical Soviet attack against the West is not thought to pass through Swiss territory which, for geographical reasons, offers an invader no opportunity for a swift, smooth campaign. However, Switzerland is aware of the danger that might arise in any such situation sooner or later by becoming the target of secondary operations and/or political-military blackmail. Furthermore, there is also a growing concern about the potential use of nuclear weapons in Europe, which would inevitably affect Swiss territory even if no such weapons were used against Switzerland.

This overall assessment leads Swiss authorities to a systematic threat assessment envisaging four types or levels of threats :

1. Threats in the situation of relative peace. Even in the absence of armed violence, the present situation is characterized by political power rivalries. The collective security system of the United Nations is unable to cope with the danger originating in this situation. Therefore, peace is presently maintained by the balance of terror only, a delicate balance prone to destabilization by technological breakthroughs, the arms race, and irrational actions. The present situation of relative peace is also characterized by efforts undertaken by some powers to enlarge their spheres of influence by means of political, economic, and propagandistic pressure. Furthermore, the fluid state of raw materials markets and concentration or restructuring processes taking place in the world economy may also have serious repercussions for Switzerland.

2. Indirect warfare. Increasingly, priority is being given to political, psychological, and terrorist warfare short of military warfare. Indirect warfare exploits the vulnerability of modern society and plays on domestic contradictions with the conscious intention of destroying law and order. Swiss authorities are concerned about the growing number of actions of this sort taken against Switzerland.

3. Conventional warfare. Although it does not represent an acute threat at the present moment, Swiss authorities are aware that the risk of conventional war is omnipresent and may materialize within a surprisingly short span of time.

4. An attack by means of mass destruction. Although deemed to be highly improbable, it is clear to Swiss authorities that this constitutes the ultimate threat.[3]

On all four threat levels, evolutions are thinkable where threats are used for blackmail. This is held to be particularly dangerous if one side's threat against neutral Switzerland were countered by the other side employing counter-threats. Such threat-counter-threat scenarios can be dangerous to Switzerland even if Switzerland is not the principal target of any power; yet it may be indirectly affected, as is the case already in the field of economic sanctions and boycotts. Any such situation can lead Switzerland into a state of painful isolation.

Policies to Meet These Threats

The basic idea underlying Swiss policies to meet present and future threats is the concept of general defense (<u>Gesamtverteidigung</u>, or <u>Défense générale</u>).[4] This term covers a comprehensive system of policies, planning, and institutions aimed at coping with any situations dangerous to Switzerland in a coherent and flexible way. It basically comprises five elements :

1. <u>Foreign policy</u> serves security policy by a kind of "double-track diplomacy":[5] on one hand, it has to practice permanent neutrality and reinforce it by keeping it credible in the eyes of potential belligerents. This implies "dissuasive communication," that is, demonstrating Switzerland's intention and capability to defend its permanent neutrality in any circumstances.[6] On the other hand, there is also an active component inasmuch as Switzerland tries to contribute to the stabilization of the international environment, mainly by offering Switzerland's good offices in international disputes, by humanitarian activities, and by participating in multilateral conferences for disarmament and confidence-building.

2. <u>The Swiss army</u> is remarkably strong in comparison with the population and territory it has to defend.[7] In normal circumstances, it is meant to be an unmistakable reminder to a potential aggressor that a military invasion of Switzerland would involve heavy losses in men and materiel, that he would have to count on much destruction and a lengthy campaign, thus being obliged to pay a "high admission price." In a small country, this strategy of dissuasion is, in effect, the equivalent of a strategy of deterrence among great powers. In the event of invasion, the Swiss army would engage the aggressor at the frontier. In other words, the strategy is based on the conception of in-depth defensive action in several staggered zones. Frontier brigades, backed by mobile reserves of frontier divisions, would prevent an invader from achieving a rapid breakthrough in the frontier region. Infantry divisions and mechanized divisions would fight a defensive battle in the operationally important regions of the Swiss central plateau, deploying armored units to launch counter-attacks against troops who had already penetrated the area by ground and air attack. By exploiting the Alps as a natural tank barrier and relying on an extensive network of secret fortifications, the role of an army mountain corps would be to hold a large area of the Alps for a long period.

The Swiss army is equipped with the weapons it needs to carry out its task. Its operational equipment currently consists of 300 fighter aircraft (Tiger, Mirage, and Hunter), 800 battle tanks, 1,250 armored personnel carriers, 1,000 mobile artillery guns, 260 self-propelled howitzers, 2,800 antitank guided weapons, 1,000 antiaircraft guns as well as ground-to-air guided missiles (Bloodhound and Rapier). A long-term reequipment program ensures that armament is continually being updated. A large part of the army's equipment, as in the case of tanks, antiaircraft guns and antiaircraft missiles, is developed and produced inside Switzerland or, as in the case of aircraft, manufactured under licence or assembled within the country.

The character of the Swiss army can best be exemplified by referring to a simple sentence in Article 18 of the Federal Constitution : "Every Swiss is liable to military service." Switzerland thus has a citizen army based on universal conscription. Every male Swiss who is fit for military service is called up after his nineteenth birthday for 17 weeks of basic military training followed by annual refresher courses and reservist training until the age of 42. Switzerland has neither a professional army nor a standing army. This militia system has proved worthwhile in various ways. Establishing a close link between the people and the army, even to the extent of identifying one with the other, precludes the possibility of the army becoming a pawn in domestic politics. It is also relatively inexpensive and quite efficient since civilian expertise and skills can be turned to optimum account in the country's defense. In a comparative perspective, therefore, the Swiss system seems to be quite cost-efficient. Swiss defense expenditure accounts for a mere 2 percent of the gross national product (as compared with the 6 percent global average and 5.1 percent in NATO and 12.3 percent in Warsaw Pact countries). The 625,000 Swiss males who are conscripted for military service keep their personal weapons and personal equipment at home. In the event of mobilization, an individual can be called to the colors within hours, to take charge of his gun, tank, aircraft, or jeep and, proceeding to his fortification, signals unit, or field hospital, fulfill his "second function" of being a citizen in uniform. The only full-time soldiers are the training staff of 1,500 officers and men, the technicians in workshops and stores, and the senior officers of the rank of divisional commander and above.

   3. A civil defense system has been built up in view of the devastating effects both conventional and nuclear warfare could have for Switzerland, a densely populated country. Since there is no space available to evacuate the population to safe, remote areas, the idea has arisen of "vertical evacuation" into shelters. The Swiss have set about this task very systematically since the 1960s. Protective shelters, which are now available for some 85 percent of the population, are located under houses or have been constructed as communal shelters and are used in peacetime as underground garages or store-rooms. The construction of these shelters is expected to be completed by the year 2000 under the slogan of "Room in a shelter for every inhabitant." Every shelter has been constructed to afford protection against the effect of weapons exploding with a pressure range of 1 to 3 bars, and are equipped with filters against chemical warfare and radioactive dust. Water tanks, food stocks, and, sometimes, emergency generators enable the occupants of shelters to survive for at least 14 days, which is regarded as the critical period of exposure to contamination from radioactive fallout from atomic weapons. Every discharged soldier or male Swiss not called up for military service is liable to serve in civil defense and take part in annual exercises organized by the communes, doing duty in shelters, in the ambulance, supply, engineering, tranport, and communication services. There are also several thousand women volunteers serving in civil defense.

   The Swiss have no illusions about civil defense. They know that even the best civil defense organization cannot protect them from a direct hit by an atomic bomb. The efforts made in civil defense stem from the realistic assumption that they might mitigate the consequences and side effects of individual uses of tactical atomic weapons on Swiss or neighboring territory, and preparations might also give the population some protection from the increasingly frightful effects of the latest conventional weapons such as fragmentation bombs and "smart bombs."[8] By taking such measures, Switzerland is also less sensitive and vulnerable to blackmail in peacetime crises.

   4. Ensuring economic supplies. Switzerland imports almost 100 percent of its industrial raw materials, 80 percent of its energy, and 50 percent of its food supplies. As a result it is in an extremely vulnerable position. It tries to reduce the vulnerability through international cooperation and internal measures. It has joined the International Energy Agency (IEA), which was founded after the 1973 oil crisis, and participates in its stockpiling and emergency distribution programs. To ensure supplies of nuclear fuels, it is also active in the "London Club." It also maintains an oceangoing fleet of more than a

dozen merchant vessels, which sail under the Swiss flag.

The mainstays of Switzerland's economic supplies in crisis and war are its organized compulsory stocks. Firms of a certain size must lay in stocks of raw materials and fuel, storing the equivalent of their peacetime consumption over a period of six to twelve months. Basic foodstuffs are subject to similar regulations. The government guarantees favorable loans to help finance compulsory stocking. A food plan for use in emergency and war provides for increased production of home-grown food, a switch from a meat diet to a vegetarian diet, and a drop in calorie consumption, all based on an elaborate rationing scheme.

5. Information, psychological defense, internal security. In view of the crucial importance of the psychological and organizational factors in both covert and overt war situations, particular care is taken of communication flows between the authorities and the population. It is understood that good information is the basis of trust in the government and thus a preequisite for successful resistance against foreign threats. Institutions and activities in this field are highly decentralized, and are even more so in the field of internal security. The maintenance of law and order, counterintelligence, the protection of the infrastructure are largely the duties of the cantonal and communal police corps, while the federal police serves as hardly more than a clearing station for the 26 cantonal police corps, with practically no intervention capacity of its own. At first glance, the decentralized nature of internal security provisions seems to constitute a fatal weakness and makes Switzerland an ideal victim of all kinds of subversion and sabotage. Yet one must not disregard the advantages and obvious strength of this approach; by operating in small units, a high degree of flexibility can be attained, taking into account the varying local circumstances. More importantly, in a democratic country, political and public control of the police apparatus very much contributes to strengthening the legitimacy of the political system; it goes without saying that this type of control is much easier to achieve in a small-scale system than in the anonymity of centralization. In general, decentralization creates a particular kind of closeness and cohesiveness that a foreigner may find difficult to penetrate. It is a feature that is salient in Swiss political culture and it is the psychological climate prevailing in this country.

Public Opinion and Security Policy

The present Swiss concept of general defense is solidly and broadly supported by what can almost be called a universal consensus. As a matter of fact, given the obviously defensive nature of Swiss security policy, potential antimilitarists and pacifists have a hard time finding any reasonable argument against Swiss defense efforts. As a foreign observer noted, bumperstickers on Swiss cars say : "Everybody talks about peace--our army protects it!"[9] Public opinion polls indicate a continuing approval of both the government's threat assessments and the policies adopted to meet them.

There are only a few, clearly nonrepresentative groups basically rejecting the present concept. Not surprisingly, the Communists (voting turnout: 0.9 percent) reject any defense efforts by ridiculing them as unnecessary, given the definitely peace-loving attitude of the Soviet Union and hence the complete absence of any threat whatsoever. A small group of left-wing intellectuals recently started collecting signatures for initiating a "referendum for the abolishment of the Swiss army;" however, they found it extremely difficult to collect the necessary number of signatures (100,000), let alone to win the vote on the referendum. But for the rest, even those who participate in peace demonstrations overwhelmingly tend to approve Swiss defense efforts.[10]

Nevertheless, there is some discussion, heated at times, about Swiss security policy, but it is not a discussion in principle. Usually it concerns the question of which of the five elements deserves more emphasis. While the traditional mainstream is convinced that the army, flanked by civil defense, constitutes the backbone of Swiss security, others contend that a more active foreign policy ought to be adopted for the sake of international peace, which would make military defense less necessary. Yet, when it comes to discussing such proposals more specifically, there is little left to do beyond what is already done, simply because of the limited clout available to such a small country as Switzerland which can hardly play the role of an international peace broker and mediator.

Some also argue that the value of civil defense protection may be rather low once modern weapons are actually employed. Finally and not surprisingly, there is also a constant argument about the amount of money to be spent for defense on one hand and social security on the other. So far, none of these alternative views has been able to rally any significant support. Up to the present, and very probably also in the foreseeable future, the bills concerning defense appropriations have passed (and will pass) parliamentary procedures with comfortable majorities.

POLICY CHANGES ?

Switzerland's position in the international system is characterized by a high degree of stability. Provided the international environment, especially the European balance, does not change dramatically, Switzerland will find it hard to see any reason to change its present principles of security policy, in particular the policy of armed neutrality. Whatever may have been the historical reason for adopting neutrality, Switzerland today simply has no other alternative. Even those challenging the Swiss political system in a most radical way, as a rule, never criticize neutrality; paradoxically, all they do is accuse the government of not sticking strictly enough to neutrality.[11]

Free from commitments to military alliances, neutral Switzerland (with neutral Austria) constitutes a kind of "locking device" across the center of Europe. Situated between NATO and the Warsaw Pact, this locking device is important in the context of the tension between the two power blocs. The freedom of Austria and Switzerland from alliances is, for NATO, an obstacle in the direct link between NATO forces in Northern Europe (Federal Republic of Germany, Benelux countries, Denmark, and Norway) and its forces in Southern Europe (Italy and other Mediterranean countries). On the other hand, the Swiss-Austrian locking device could be useful to the Warsaw Pact countries by securing their flank in operations in Germany or Yugoslavia/northern Italy or as a corridor for a blitz push to the West.

In the event of tension or open conflict, both alliances would in principle be tempted to invade Swiss or Austrian territory, either by NATO forces moving in a north-south direction or by Warsaw Pact troops moving in an east-west direction. As these interests can thus be seen to cancel each other, the neutral locking device can be eliminated as a factor in the tension between the two power blocs in Europe, provided the two states remain neutral. As a matter of fact, permanent neutrality is perfectly in line with the strategic situation reflected in the locking device resulting from the rivalry between East and West. Equally important to both blocs but military accessible to neither, this "bolt" is a stabilizing factor in the strategic balance of power in Europe. Because the territory of a neutral country is not a vacuum, its contribution to stabilizing the international situation is so much greater. This is why Switzerland follows the principle of armed neutrality, and this is also why, short of a fundamental renversement des alliances in Europe, an alternative security policy for Switzerland is neither available nor conceivable.

Hence, there will be no changes, yet there will be evolution, especially with regard to the Swiss army and its operative missions. One of the questions facing Switzerland has to do with the exponential growth of arms procurement costs. So far, Switzerland has still been able to catch up and to finance the acquisition of sophisticated military hardware such as fighter aircraft, helicopters, self-propelled howitzers, electronic warfare equipment, tanks (such as the recently commissioned Leopard) and modern antitank weapons. But will it be able to do so 30 years from now? Some experts doubt this and blame the military planners for trying to keep up what will eventually become a mere "pocket-sized big-power army" (eine Grossmachtarmee im Taschenformat). They suggest putting more emphasis on infantry, making full use of natural obstacles (mountains, rivers, creeks, lakes) so abundantly available on Swiss territory, rather than spending so much on aircraft, tanks, and artillery.[12] Still, this view is met with strong reservations by those who are afraid of the modern location techniques which would simply wipe out infantry forces not combined with other weapon systems.

Therefore, the major changes likely to occur in the years to come will largely be oriented toward an organic evolution and adaptation of the present model. Among other things, this implies the following measures :

● organizing military training activities in a way to ensure some military cover all the year round in order to be ready to meet surprise attacks;[13]
● shortening the time required for the mobilization of the army (presently up to 48 hours);
● upgrading the capability for mobile operations;
● upgrading the preparations for guerilla-type resistance;
● upgrading antitank defense by introducing precision-guided ammunitions;
● completing the civil defense system.

These and other evolutionary changes are part of the official "Army Guidelines," serving as the basis for long-term defense planning.[14] They are backed by a broad political consensus. This also means that they will hardly be subject to alterations nor will they be affected by unforeseeable internal or external factors.

NOTES

1. Richtlinien der Regierungspolitik 1983-1987 (Bern: 1984) pp. 27ff.

2. "Armeeleitbild und Ausbauschritt 1984-87," Informationen zur Gesamtverteidigung, no. 18 (Zürich 1983), pp. 7ff.

3. Bericht des Bundesrats und die Bundesversammlung über die Sicherheitspolitik der Schweiz, June 27, 1973. Zwischenbericht zur Sicherheitspolitik, December 3, 1979.

4. Einführung in die Gesamtverteidigung (Bern, 1984); Hans Senn, Friede in Unabhängigkeit (Frauenfeld, 1983).

5. Edouard Brunner, "Neutral Countries and Arms Control," Documenta, no. 4 (1984), 28-32.

6. Gustav Däniker, "Dissuasive Kommunikation," Schweizer Monatshefte 64 (1984) : 405-12.

7. Ernst Wetter, Schweitzer Militär-Lexikon, (Frauenfeld, 1984); Gustav Däniker, "The Swiss Model of Conventional Defense," Armed Forces Journal, July 1984; Erich A. Kägi, Wie hoch ist der Eintrittspreis? Schweitzer Landesverteidigung heute und morgen (Zürich, 1985), pp. 47ff.

8. Cf. Freeman Dyson, Weapons and Hope (New York, 1984), Chap. 8.

9. John McPhee, La Place de la Concorde Suisse (New York, 1983), p. 27.

10. Année politique suisse 1983 (Bern, 1984), p. 57.

11. Margret Sieber, Die Abhängigkeit der Schweiz von ihrer internationalen Umwelt (Frauenfeld, 1981), p. 104.

12. Alfred Stutz, Raumverteidigung - Utopie oder Alternative? (Zürich, 1982).

13. Gustav Däniker, "Vom Zwang zu rascherer Einsatz-bereitschaft," Neue Zürcher Zeitung, weekend edition, September 7-8, 1985, p. 37.

14. Cf. "Armeeleitbild und Ausbauschritt, 1984-87," 1983, p. 7.

20 Austria: The Activist Imperative

Heinz Gärtner

Austrian security policy is founded on two objectives : first, the protection of the people and their basic peaceful values against all threats and, second, maintaining and defending the country's permanent neutrality. In this context, the recent National Defense Plan emphasizes strengthening peace "in a regional and global framework." At the same time, Austria seeks to ensure a capacity of deterrence, but also the fulfillment of its duties resulting from the status of permanent neutrality. The Austrian army always refers to Article 1 of the Constitution Act of October 26, 1955 which deals with Austrian neutrality :

1. For the purpose of the lasting maintenance of her independence externally, and for the purpose of the inviolability of her territory, Austria of her own free will declares her perpetual neutrality. Austria will maintain and defend this with all means at her disposal.
2. For the securing of this purpose, in all future times, Austria will not join any military alliances and will not permit the establishment of any foreign military bases on her territory.

Furthermore, Austria agreed to prohibit the possession, manufacture, or testing of nuclear weapons, weapons of mass destruction, chemical and biological warfare agents, self-propelled rockets and missiles, and artillery with ranges exceeding 30 kilometers.

In the National Defense Plan, which was publicly introduced early in March 1985 by the office of the Federal Chancellor, Austrian security policy is defined as "the sum of all measures, especially in the area of foreign policy, of a domestic policy to maintain stability and of a defense policy to protect the population and the fundamental values of this nation against all threats."[1]

The threat perceptions that are presented in the Plan take into account only one source : external military aggression and (mentioned marginally) political blackmail-- extortion, subversion and the like--derived from the threat of such an aggression. These images are mostly founded on selective perception. That is, elements of the general situation that seem to coincide with the established scheme of interpretation are perceived more intensely; others are ruled out when they divert from it.

A possible threat to Austria would be imaginable on five levels, which will be mentioned here in escalating order:[2]

1. A relative peace. This condition, which may be called a "precarious balance of power between the two alliance systems," is characterized by a coexistence of elements of conflict and détente.

2. A subversive-revolutionary war. At this level we are talking about changing, that is destroying society by means of so-called indirect aggression. Possible ways to achieve this aim are psychological warfare, sabotage, subversion, and attempts on the lives of prominent citizens.

3. A conventional war. According to Austrian analysis, a conventional conflict in Europe remains a small possibility as long as there exists the danger of a nuclear escalation. Still, two specific dangers for Austria have been noted : on one hand, the country could be turned into the object of a test case; on the other, the strategic importance of communication lines could tempt one of the two sides to attack Austria.

4. A limited nuclear war. Austrian experts do not think it likely that a nuclear war between the two alliance systems will break out, nor do they reckon with the possibility of Austria being attacked with these weapons, especially because of the danger of escalation to a nuclear conflict on a much larger scale. At this level, Austria should pay particular attention to the danger of forces in neighboring countries employing short-range tactical nuclear weapons against Austrian territory.

5. A massive employment of strategic nuclear weapons. This level of conflict seems quite unlikely. However, three possible dangers are being considered: (1) one side could attain a sufficient first-strike capacity; (2) a small step in the process of escalation could expand into a massive nuclear conflict; (3) last, there still exists the danger of an accidental war.

Historically, Austria has suffered from an identity crisis, and many leaders of the First Republic (1918-38) thought that the country was not a viable entity. The influence of pan-Germanist ideologies reinforced this belief and laid the foundations for the Anschluss. There is no doubt, however, that the development of a national identity has made a great deal of progress since World War II.

The threat perception of "the Russians" has been omnipresent in Austria after 1945. Some of the elements contributing to this perception were :

- the lingering effect of Nazi propaganda, which warned of punishment of Austria by the Soviets because of Austrian participation in the war;
- the abusive behavior of Soviet occupation forces and the removal of industrial machinery to the Soviet Union;
- the necessity for the social democratic and bourgeois leadership to consolidate its power by focusing on an external threat;
- the Communist seizure of power in neighboring countries of Central Europe (1947-48).

Austrian defense policy has been largely oriented toward this threat perception. Only in 1982 were army maneuvers (in the Kufstein area) directed against a potential attack from the West. In May 1984 the Austrian Federal Army held maneuvers, code-named

<u>Januskopf</u>, which symbolized the readiness to defend against the East <u>and</u> the West.

Austria also has to take into account economic threats as a small, dependent country. In 1980 it exported goods and services at a level of 37.2 percent of GNP and imported them at a level of 42.3 percent of GNP. The energy situation is characterized by a high degree of dependence on foreign sources (about 70 percent). Similarly, Austria is to a large extent dependent for other basic mineral and raw materials. A high economic vulnerability increases the possibility of coercing a country like Austria and decreases its chances of survival in times of crisis. An economic policy that is strongly oriented toward exports requires a continuous restructuring toward the newest technologies, another point of vulnerability. At the very least, in the areas of vital importance (food, energy, health), a country should have the highest level of self-support.

The National Defense Plan has deduced three concrete scenarios for the overall Austrian defense system :

● preventing an international crisis from spreading to Austria (case of crisis);
● maintaining neutrality in the case of a war in the region (case of neutrality); and
● defending against a direct military attack on Austria (case of defense).

The Austrian doctrine of national defense is keyed to these three scenarios (first defined by the government in 1965). Yet the Federal Army has always occupied an ambivalent position. Established in 1955 after the conclusion of the State Treaty, the army recruited its staff from the police (B-Gendarmerie) and depended on materiel left over from the Allied occupation forces. Its organizational structure strongly resembled that of the German <u>Wehrmacht</u>, thereby producing a good deal of criticism and calls for military reform. Some Austrians even questioned the existence of the Federal Army on constitutional grounds and sought its abolition.

The crisis of identity of the army in the 1960s, the success of the Socialist party (SPO) in the 1970 elections, and Socialist suspicion of a traditional army were the reasons for the general reorganization toward a militia system during the 1970s. In 1970 a reform committee, consisting of 55 representatives from all social groupings, was instructed to discuss and prepare necessary modifications of the armed forces. Four years later, a special department for coordinating overall defense was created within the Federal Chancellor's office. The structural change was accompanied by a constitutional law that mandated a defense system similar to the Swiss army, but with a smaller section of reservists. The law put forth the doctrine of "comprehensive defense" (<u>Umfassende Landesverteidigung</u>). Besides the military sector, the comprehensive defense system includes civilian, economic, and psychological aspects, with the goal of increasing internal solidarity, in the face of a potential aggression (again based on the Swiss model).

In 1986 the armed forces were composed of 55,000 regular soldiers and 170,000 reservists. There is universal military service for a period of six months, with supplemental militia training. The prevailing military doctrine is one of area (or territorial) defense. Taking advantage of the terrain, Austrian units are concentrated in specific, heavily fortified "key zones" where their objective is to inflict maximum losses and delays on an aggressor. The rest of the country is divided into "area security zones," where militia units are to apply obstructive tactics (ambushes, raids, sabotage, surveillance). In this plan, Austria is particularly handicapped by the State Treaty's prohibition of rockets and missiles which limits the effectiveness of its antitank and air defense missions.

In other areas, Austria suffers from a state of relative military unpreparedness (compared with Switzerland), and much of the equipment is outdated. The defense budget has amounted to only about 1.2 percent of the gross domestic product over the past several years (the lowest level in Europe after Luxembourg).

The few critics of Austrian defense organization deplore that the militia system, although now official doctrine, is far from being realized.[3] The main elements of the territorial defense concept are those conventional forces that should protect and defend in a flexible and mobile way the "key zones" against transit or occupation. Internal critics say that this concept requires a reinforcement of the shield by active participation of the population similar to the Swiss model. This new concept is different from guerilla warfare, since civilians and soldiers are clearly separated by uniforms and functions, and the army bears the primary burden of defense.[4] One far-reaching idea is the concept of social defense which is influenced by the teaching of Gandhi, the examples in Norway and Denmark during World War II, and the occupation of Czechoslovakia. Some supporters of this posture see social defense as a supplement of military defense, while others see it as a substitute for the military.

But the major problem of all these concepts is that the main military threat perceptions have not changed. These are based on the assumption of a major European conflict between the two alliance systems. The principal aim of the Austrian army in this conflict is to deter and delay an aggressor so that he is convinced that a transit attack is too risky, costly, and time-consuming. But this scenario is very unlikely. The political and military occupation of Austria without a full-scale East-West conflict or as a prelude to such a conflict is more likely. Empirical analyses show that border wars are not the dominant type of war, but rather that the political and military destruction of enemies is the objective in a conflict. For this type of threat perception, the Austrian army is not yet sufficiently prepared. In all likelihood the prevailing threat perception was constructed according to those tasks that the army is able to fulfill.

In principle, all political parties consider Austrian neutrality to be something positive. Minor differences did appear in the 1970s at the time of the one-party Socialist government. When considering the relationship between an active foreign policy and a national defense, the SPO attached greater importance to an active foreign policy than did the main opposition People's party (OVP). Declarations from the superpowers guaranteeing Austrian neutrality have been rejected as a matter of principle by all political formations.

Interestingly enough, it is always the OVP that has pointed out that Austrian security cannot be ensured by the superpowers or by systems of collective security. Differences of opinion, however, stem from the interpretation of how this security can best be guaranteed. The OVP has traditionally put more emphasis on developing a regional and Western European policy, whereas the SPO defines its policy within a more global context. In past years, the now dissolved SPO-FPO (Freedom Party) coalition had, however, put more weight on regional security and emphasized the need for reduction of tensions in <u>Mitteleuropa</u>. Socialists have always regarded the detente process as a positive development, while the OVP tends to refer to the illusions that had been connected with the policy of detente. All parties readily admit that Austria lies at the intersection of two heavily armed military alliances and that therefore it has a vital interest in disarmament and in a regional and global balance of power. The concept of a balance of power itself is not generally questioned, nor is the "action-reaction" element in the arms race.

The activist Austrian foreign policy outside Europe is largely associated with former Chancellor Bruno Kreisky (and with concerns about energy supplies). Kreisky defended his interest in the Middle East and Persian Gulf by stressing the danger of a military conflict outside Europe spreading to the continent. The OVP, for its part, has criticized this policy since it allegedly neglects closer (i.e., regional) interests. Kreisky also called for a new Marshall Plan providing a long-term aid program to Third World countries and sought to give Austria a larger role in international conferences and organizations (particularly the United Nations). Austrian troops now serve with the UN peacekeeping forces in Cyprus and on the Golan Heights.

No serious differences exist between official Austrian security policy and public opinion, as measured by polls. Only one percent of the population sees a real, immediate threat of war; unemployment, economic recession, crime, and environmental catastrophes present much stronger threats. About 25 percent of the sample foresee the possibility of a nuclear war within the next 20 years, although 80 percent believe that Austria would be struck in event of a nuclear conflict. There is strong support for the formulation of an active foreign policy to guarantee Austria's security. Still, about 85 percent of the respondents think that a domestic army is indispensable. The general opinion is that the military national defense would be effective only in the case of border clashes or threats at the border. In the case of a full-scale armed attack by a neighboring state, the army would be considered to be of limited usefulness. This means that Austrian defense doctrine in the cases of crisis or of neutrality (i.e., international tension or regional conflict) is considered effective, but in the case of defense (i.e., a direct attack on Austria) there is much less faith in a national defense.

Should a military bloc attack Austria directly, or should it want to use the country as a "transit" territory, the majority of Austrian would pin their hopes on the international reputation of the country. This optimism has been derived from the high prestige that Austria is supposed to have in the world; 74 percent of the Austrians believe that today Austria has more prestige than in the period between the two world wars. In this way, neutrality and an active foreign policy, in the eyes of the Austrians, have contributed substantially to the reinforcement of its international links. And yet there is doubt and skepticism to be observed among a strong minority which believes that, even today, Austria could be occupied by a major power in the world without much international resistance. Whether these prestige elements would be of any use in a "serious case" has been called into question and probably justly so (in light of political power realities). This is the problematic and ambivalent nature of the Austrians' attitude toward future policies of neutrality and detente.[5]

The reinforcement of the peace movement in many states of Europe has led to a sharp public polarization over matters of security. This tendency cannot be observed in Austria; whereas more than half the Austrian population has a positive attitude toward the peace movement, a large part of this group accepts an armed defense at the same time. The growing public interest in recent years for political questions like peace and security, together with the ongoing arms race spiral, have caused a critical attitude toward the policy of the two superpowers among Austrians. By this, we do not mean an ideological distance of equality, but rather a dwindling faith in the goodwill of the superpowers to start a real peace-promoting dialogue.

Generally, it is possible for smaller countries with an intelligent foreign policy to lead a safe and autonomous life next to great powers with a military superiority. The military force of a small country does not have the means, in any case, to ensure its existence in the face of the great powers. Only an active foreign policy can achieve this objective and should receive priority in policymaking.

According to the author's empirical and comparative survey about the causes of war, great powers intervene directly in smaller nations, when a special relationship (ranging from indirect political influence to control over a puppet government) has existed with a regional government and this relationship has been fundamentally disturbed, either through a change of attitude by the regional government or through the inherent weakness of the linkage itself.

This finding contradicts the "vacuum theory," according to which the very existence of an independent state leads to this intervention by one of the great powers. On the contrary, the situation becomes dangerous when a government has engaged itself in a close relationship with a great power. It is not independence, but dependence that enhances the danger of intervention.

The dangers of dependency, the need for internal cohesion, and the potential for outside intervention must be taken into account in formulating future Austrian security policy. Countries closely related to great powers are exposed to a double danger. Conceivably, they could be treated as an outpost or as a military "launching platform." In times of war, the danger exists that they could become involved in a conflict that breaks out at a remote spot in the world. In another context, the danger could be that of an increasing influence by the friendly power that could lead to intervention, should political relations change. Strict, unconditional independence is the best strategy for security.

Instead of increasing the costs by threatening countermeasures in case of an attack (i.e., deterrence), Austria should seek to increase the advantages of a "nonattack," in other words, to engage in a foreign policy that would underline the political utility of the country (as a "bridge" between the blocs) and the advantages in maintaining its right to a peaceful existence. The basis for this is a foreign policy that is founded on the national and cultural identity of a country.

Ambassador Hans Thalberg offers some examples of what such a policy typical of neutral countries might contain :

> There exists a wide spectrum of practical services that European neutrals are prepared to offer to antagonists in areas of conflict as well as to the community of nations at large. Good offices, mediation and arbitration are valuable instruments of neutral activity. The exchange of prisoners, caring for the sick, the right of asylum and the resulting provisions for refugees have become indispensable services provided by the European neutrals. The preservation of human rights and of human dignity, briefly the protection of humanitarian interests as well as peacekeeping operations in a divided world, are the cornerstone of neutral policies. Meeting places for international conferences, for peacemeaking as well as for discreet diplomatic activities, are offered by the European neutrals. Neutral states have become headquarters of international organizations.[6]

This does not amount to "neutralism" in the sense of withdrawal, but to an active policy of neutrality, economic development, and human rights in the context of an overall strategy for peace.

The Austrian defense system should not threaten anyone. Weapon systems ought to be characterized as unambigiously defensive, and their employment must be confined to a country's territory. Another future step to diminish any offensive threat perception might be to create bilateral demilitarized zones, refraining from keeping military installations or troops in particular parts of the border territory.

Austria can assert itself as a "symbol against the logic of the blocs" through other policy contributions. First, it could declare its territory (already <u>de facto</u> denuclearized) as a nuclear-weapon-free zone and work to extend this zone and to reduce the conventional military potential at its borders. Second, Austria could refrain from engaging in the international arms race and take exemplary steps toward weapon industry conversion and disarmament. Third, Austria can actively support a more equitable and thus more stabilizing global economic system. Fourth, Austria can increase cooperation with other European neutrals in the security field and can expand relations with Third World nonaligned countries who also seek independence from the two other blocs. One concrete measure might be to build a medical center for the treatment of victims of chemical warfare. Nevertheless, small states (like Austria) should not overestimate their role as professional "do-gooders" and should beware of playing superpowers off against each other.

The question of whether smaller states take the position of "free riders" in the nuclear deterrence system makes the problem obvious. One can imagine a hypothetical example : Austria being attacked or occupied by the Soviet Union. What would be the outcome of such a military conflict, and how would the United States react? Would it react with nuclear or heavy conventional weapons that carry the danger of self-destruction? Does Austria, in this example, represent a vital interest so that the United States would risk the danger of escalation to general war? There is consequently a great deal of uncertainty about whether the security of smaller states can rely on the nuclear deterrence of the two superpowers.

Despite its Western political culture and close links with the United States, Austria cannot rely on the U.S. nuclear capacity. It is impossible to determine whether nuclear weapons have kept the peace between the United States and the Soviet Union and thus it is unclear whether smaller states are really protected by nuclear weapons from an attack that may have otherwise occurred.

Since neither the superpower balance nor the Austrian army will be able to prevent an aggressor from an attack, the best guarantee for Austrian security will be stable political relations in Central Europe for the coming decades. This network of relations can be achieved only through an active and committed Austrian foreign policy.

NOTES

1. Bundeskanzleramt, <u>Landsverteidigungsplan</u> (Vienna, 1985), p. 3.

2. Ibid. pp. 32-34. See also Hanspeter Neuhold, "Grundlagen österreichischer Sicherheitspolitik," in <u>Wie sicher ist Österreich?</u>, edited by Heinrich Neisser and Fritz Windhager (Vienna, 1982), pp. 250ff.

3. See E. Entacher and L. Specht, "Ammerkungen zum Konzept der militärischen Landesverteidigung in Österreich," in <u>Dialog-Beiträge zur Friedensforschung</u>, edited by Österreichisches Institut für Friedensforschung (Stadt-Schlaining, 1984).

4. A. Skuhra, "Austrian Approaches to War and Peace Studies," <u>Coexistence</u>, October 1982, p. 187.

5. F. Trauttmannsdorf, "Österreichs Außenpolitik als Sicherheitspolitik," in <u>Außenpolitik und Demokratie in Österreich</u> (Salzburg, 1983) pp. 245ff. It is too early to assess the impact of the Waldheim controversy on these perceptions.

6. Hans Thalberg, "The European Neutrals and Regional Stability," in <u>The European Neutrals in International Affairs</u>, edited by Hanspeter Neuhold and Hans Thalberg (Vienna: Österreichisches Institut für Internationale Politik, 1984), p. 128.

21 Ireland: Looking North

Patrick Keatinge

THE PRESENT SECURITY SITUATION

Threat Perceptions

In Ireland it often seems that the term "security" is employed primarily, and at times almost exclusively, to refer to what in other Western European states would be categorized as internal concerns. Yet a closer examination of the focus of attention, the conflict in Northern Ireland, reveals the blurring, in this case, of the conventional dichotomy between "internal" and "external" security. In a formal sense, Northern Ireland is an external difficulty for the Dublin government in that it lies outside the government's jurisdiction, a situation which in itself is at the core of an intergovernmental dispute with Britain. In practice, however, the position is more complex, involving security cooperation with the British government against a transnational threat posed by extremist nationalists such as the Provisional Irish Republican Army (PIRA). This threat is seen as transcending Northern Ireland as such; terrorist groups are characterized as "subversives" who pose a direct challenge to the existing Irish state. The very duration of the threat is an indication of the seriousness with which it is viewed. Apparent since 1969, it has become marked since the early 1970s. Official estimates of the extra security costs arising out of violence over Northern Ireland claim it has accounted for about 25 percent of total security expenditure over the last ten years.[1]

By contrast, perceptions of external threat (in the sense in which "external" is usually employed, to refer to the context of East-West relations) are muted and diffuse. In part, this may be explained by the particular experience of the state since its foundation in 1921-22. The strong emphasis on bilateral relations with Britain did not preclude Ireland from pursuing a policy of neutrality throughout World War II, and when the postwar structures of East-West competition were being formed, the retention of this stance proved to be both possible and popular.[2] An important factor has been the relatively insulated geostrategic position of the state, for neither the imperatives of technological change nor diplomatic pressures have as yet combined to produce specific challenges to existing policies. Unlike Austria, Finland, Sweden or even Switzerland, Ireland is not a "front-line" neutral in terms of military threaters.[3] Indeed if external threat does have meaning in the Irish context, it is more likely to be seen in terms of economic insecurity rather than military consequence of East-West antagonism. Ireland has always been a very small and very open economy, not well developed by West European standards, and it may even be that a feeling of economic insecurity is so pervasive and deep-rooted in Irish culture that it overrides what seem to be much more remote threats of interstate war.

Government Policies

The principal security threat arising out of the Northern Ireland conflict has been met by a relatively high level of internal security measures. This includes special legislation for non-jury judicial proceedings and the involvement of the military (the Defense Forces) in a significant aid-to-the-civil-power mission. Border patrols and the provision of security for a wide range of internal installations and cash transfers represent the single most important type of operation for the army, and often appear in a prime position in official statements of defense policy.[4]

Underlying these operational activities is the search for a political settlement, or at least amelioration, in the form of intensive bilateral diplomacy between Dublin and London, most recently in the November 1985 agreement. This involves several persistent difficulties. The legitimacy of Dublin's role and its access to the highest level in the British government has often been uncertain, and aspirations and expectations may differ widely on either side. The tentative participation of third parties, particularly the United States but also the other members of the European Community, adds to this aspect of Ireland's "internal" security.[5]

The conventional focus of security policy, external defense, is officially designated as the "primary role" of the Defense Forces, but in practice this is an empty formula. A standing army of less than 1,500 men, with the sketchiest of naval and air elements, hardly provides an adequate capability either to deter or defend against a determined military intervention.[6] Occasionally this is admitted in rather cryptic terms; thus the Minister for Defense, Mr. Cooney, conceded in 1984 that "should there come a big bold aggressor from the East. . .our good friends in the West will defend us . . .," and in the following year he maintained that a defense posture comparable to those of Switzerland or Sweden would require a significant increase in expenditure.[7]

Given this manifest military weakness, it is not surprising that Irish governments prefer to emphasize the role of foreign policy in influencing international security. To some extent, Ireland's military policy has more credibility in this respect than with regard to national defense as such, for a considerable tradition of Irish participation in United Nations peacekeeping operations has developed over the last 25 years.[8]

The greater part of the government's policy, however, is executed within the framework of European Political Cooperation (EPC); on the main lines of policy toward East-West relations, Ireland does not diverge markedly from the general consensus, but an increasing sensitivity about neutrality has led to a refusal to include the direct military dimension of security in this network of diplomatic consultation.[9]

Irish participation in EPC is of course a corollary of the strong imperative to obtain a minimum of economic security (and hopefully a maximum of economic development) within the European Community. This broad strategy, decided in 1961 and realized since 1972, may not have succeeded in matching original expectations but it is still accepted as the best available position to adopt. Although the European Community as yet possesses no military dimension, it nevertheless has impinged on specific military aspects of Irish security policy as well as on the much broader context of economic security. Thus the establishment of an EC fisheries regime, in conjunction with the adoption of extended maritime economic zones, has made the question of naval capabilities to deal with fisheries protection a major concern of the last ten years.

Public Support

Over the last fifteen years, general support for government policies against "subversion" has been the norm, particularly when the personnel or institutions of the state have been challenged directly. Nevertheless, undercurrents of criticism can be discerned from time to time. On one hand, as in any liberal democracy faced with violence, there is concern that the state's countervailing action stays within accountable and controllable limits, and the problem of legitimacy becomes all the more pressing as emergency legislation and procedures tend to become the rule rather than the expectation.

Another source of doubt arises from an ambivalent attitude toward the stated central purpose of the subversives' challenge--a united Ireland. This aspiration is enshrined in the state's constitution as well as in the goals of the IRA; the latter may be seen as misguided only in the means it employs, and cooperation with the British government to suppress nationalist extremism can all too readily be represented as "collaboration" in the pejorative sense of the word. Similarly, when intergovernmental relations seem to be ineffective, the temptation to score short-term political points off the government of the day may arise. Since 1981, bipartisan consensus on policy toward Northern Ireland has worn increasingly thin, and, in the autumn of 1984, opposition rhetoric even included the suggestion of "withdrawing our troops from the border," a move that could only weaken the position of the state within its own jurisdiction.

So far as external security in the conventional sense is concerned, the lack of military capabilities arouses no significant public disquiet. Partly this is because the local orientation of Irish party politics leaves little space for this type of issue, and partly it may be explained by the weakness of threat perceptions, noted above. It may also be true that neutrality, however defined, has had a talisman effect over the years. It is certainly popular. A poll in 1984 showed that in the event of a superpower conflict, 77 percent preferred neutrality, and the following year, in response to a more broadly formulated question, 64 percent maintained Ireland should never join any military alliance.[10]

Indeed, among the most vocal critics of existing policies relating to external security are the advocates of a more "active" neutrality, placing even further emphasis on foreign policy positions which, for some, might be inconsistent with participation in European Political Cooperation. It is rare to find such critics accepting the implications of defending neutrality militarily.[11] Rather, the focus of attention is on what has been called "the affinity paradox"--that neutrality tends to be more irritating to friendly governments than to potential hostile powers.[12] Hence the perceived threat is as likely as not to be a threat to the country's neutrality rather than to its security, and the source of threat is friendly rather than hostile. Recent Irish experience does indeed show this phenomenon to exist among the attentive minority.[13] The net effect of public concern about neutrality has been to deflect attention away from either operational security issues or even more fundamental questions as to whether the state must be defended in the first place.

FUTURE POLICIES

Future Threats

Before discussing possible policy changes to enhance security in the long term, it is necessary to speculate briefly on future threats and threat perceptions. The Northern Ireland issue is likely to continue to be at the top of the agenda because of its entrenched and inherently complex nature. Even a "benign" outcome of attempted political settlement would imply continued vigilance against the residue of paramilitary extremism and continued oversight of political implementation; a "malignant scenario" possibly involving British withdrawal and the escalation of "tribal" conflict in Northern Ireland to a more general Irish civil war cannot be ruled out.[14]

Given the relative stability of the East-West security system over the last 30 years, in conjunction with its accommodation of Irish neutrality as noted above, future external threats may seem more remote, but over a 30-year time span cannot be discounted. In particular, any serious disengagement by Britain from the Western Alliance would have the effect of bringing Ireland into a much more central position in British strategic calculations, representing the sort of change in the country's security environment that might call for a fundamental policy reappraisal.

Policy Changes

A first policy change that can be prescribed, therefore, is the basic one (taken for granted in most Western European states) of creating a viable "policy framework" for security. In form this would mean establishing policymaking procedures at the parliamentary and administrative levels that would make the appraisal of security policy a normal, periodic task of government. There is still no parliamentary committee or mixed political-administrative commission dealing with either foreign policy or defense; nor is there an explicit concept of national security, covering economic, civil, and military aspects. Such a "policy vacuum" at the overarching political level of policymaking may be compensated to some extent by pragmatic adaptation at the operational levels of the government and military machines, but it nevertheless ensures that the future is bound to be "surprising."

Against this background, it would be presumptuous to make very specific prescriptions for future security policy. It is possible, however, to indicate some of the issues that are likely to arise. The state's position in the international system as a whole, but especially in the context of Western European integration, suggests that at the very least it would be prudent to develop a concept of national security that did not rely solely on the one-dimensional rhetoric about neutrality that has sufficed up to the present. In particular, it might be wise to explore more fully the nature and extent of Britain's strategic interest in the only state with which it shares a land border. Given both the political sensitivities involved on the Irish side and the relative neglect of attentions to "home defense" on the British side, such a task might in the first instance be undertaken at a nongovernment level.

The roles and structures of the Defense Forces provide a second set of questions. The continuing need for aid to the civil power internally highlights the problems of finding an appropriate balance between the Army and the civilian police force, any overemphasis on the military leading to difficulties both in regard to military professionalism and civil-military relations. Within the Defense Forces, the balance between their separate components may also change. The increasing demands for maritime protection (potentially covering oil extraction as well as fisheries) suggest that questions of inter-service rivalry, hitherto very muted in the Irish case, may prove to be contentious. With regard to external defense, the costs of providing a credible posture remain to be systematically assessed, and it is possible that such an evaluation would provoke searching questions about the desirability and feasibility of the Defense Forces' "primary role."

The nonmilitary aspects of security policy may also emerge more clearly. Civil defense appears to be minimal, partly because it is assumed that the state is not targeted by nuclear weapons, but doubts may be raised, for example, about the capacity to deal with refugees. With regard to economic stockpiling, European Community norms may be adhered to nominally on some items (e.g., oil), but it is not at all clear that a comprehensive policy either exists or is implemented. Here, as with the diplomatic and military aspects of security trends, the questions have hardly been posed, let alone answered in terms of policy.

Opportunities and Constraints

To date, Irish political culture has encouraged a bureaucratic tradition characterized by pragmatic adaption at best and ineertia at worst, and a political indifference toward many of the security issues that are contested in other Western European countries. A first prerequisite for the development of a comprehensive debate on security is the continuation of tentative moves to reform parliamentary procedures and the public service, started in 1982 but as yet not impinging on security policy as a distinctive area of public policy. A second internal factor might be the restoration of bipartisan consensus, which was eroded in the volatile electoral struggles of the early 1980s, although it must be admitted that, in the past, bipartisanship has encouraged inertia as much as innovation.

The most pressing external factor influencing the future evolution of Irish security is the situation in Northern Ireland. Amelioration there would not only represent a substantive improvement in security; it would reduce the distorting effect of compelling a standing army to act as a <u>gendarmerie,</u> and could clear the ground for a rational consideration of other security issues. An escalation of the conflict, on the other hand, would impose very serious strains on the Irish government's approach.

In the final analysis, however, the overriding external determinant is the state of the international economic system and its influence on national economic development. This may be a truism with general application, yet it is particularly acute in one of Western Europe's more dependent economies. The inclination to neglect security may be explained by underlying historical and geographical factors, but the financial implications of remedying neglect may also be a powerful incentive not to ask too many searching questions.

NOTES

1. See "The Cost of Violence Arising from the Northern Ireland Crisis since 1969," New Ireland Forum (1984), Table 6.

2. For the evolution of Irish neutrality, see Patrick Keatinge, A Singular Stance: Irish Neutrality in the 1980s (Dublin: Institute of Public Administration, 1984), Chap. 2.

3. For a comparative analysis of the European neutrals, see Bengt Sundelius, ed., The Neutral Democracies and the New Cold War (Boulder: CO: Westview, 1986).

4. See, for example, the speech of the Minister for Defense on the annual parliamentary estimates debate July 10, 1985 (Dail Debates: 360, 1324-39).

5. For the diplomacy of the Northern Ireland conflict, see the contributions of Paul Arthur, Ronan Fanning, and Eamon Gallagher in Irish Studies in International Affairs, 2, no. 1 (1985); Patrick Keatinge, "An Odd Couple? Obstacles and Opportunities in Inter-State Political Cooperation between the Republic of Ireland and the United Kingdom" in Political Cooperation in Divided Societies: A Series of Papers Relevant to the Conflict in Northern Ireland, edited by Desmond Rea (Dublin: Gill and Macmillan, 1982).

6. For military capabilities, see Keatinge, A Singular Stance, pp. 65-72.

7. See The Irish Times, October 25, 1984; Dail Debates: 360, 1389 (July 10, 1985).

8. See Lieutenant General Gerald O'Sullivan, "Ireland's Participation in United Nations Peacekeeping Missions," unpublished paper presented at a symposium on "The Peacekeeping Operations of the United Nations: the Contribution of the Neutral States of Europe," Salzburg, September 9-10, 1985.

9. See Patrick Keatinge, "Ireland: Neutrality in EPC," in National Foreign Policies and European Political Cooperation, edited by Christopher Hill (London: Allen and Unwin, 1983).

10. See the Irish Marketing Surveys poll published in The Irish Independent, May 8, 1984; Market Research Bureau of Ireland poll, published in The Irish Times, April 29, 1985 (author's emphasis).

11. An exception is Bill McSweeney, "The Case for Active Irish Neutrality," in Ireland and the Threat of Nuclear War, edited by Bill McSweeney (Dublin: Dominican Publications, 1985).

12. See Gerald Stourzh, "Some Reflections on Permanent Neutrality" in Small States in International Relations, edited by A. Schou and A.O. Brundtland (Stockholm: Abingvist and Wiksell, 1971).

13. See Keatinge, A Singular Stance, Chap. 6.

14. The concise formulation of "benign" and "malignant" scenarios made by Conor Cruise O'Brien. States of Ireland (London: Hutchinson, 1972), Chap. 12, merits the attention of would-be security analysts.

Conclusion

Conclusion: Transforming Western European Security

Luc Reychler

Western Europe is brimming over with new security concepts. Most of them promise a more cost-effective, less risky, and increased European security. Despite this conceptual creativity, few publications or research groups have developed a long-term perspective. Most of the long-term future studies are concerned with "low politics", that is, with economic, demographic, ecological and technological forecasts. Security-related studies tend to be of a short-term nature. In addition, most of them are partial analyses, not treating security as a whole. This approach is reflected by the present political leadership. Europe has no political movers, only caretakers. It also lacks a common grand strategy, or a shared vision that communicates a realistic, credible and attractive security future for Western Europe, a condition that is better in some important ways than what now exists. While waiting for a new vision, we can, however, discern some trends that will affect its development. And as in John Naisbitt's <u>Megatrends,</u> we can assume that they are like horses--easier to ride in the direction they are already going.[1] The following trends are the result of an effort to synthesize and to provide an overview. We risk displeasing the experts and specialists who can argue that daring to describe Western European security links in terms of ten shifting categories is too simplistic an undertaking. In their way, they are probably right. But we think it is worth the risk to bring some order out of the present muddle.

I. AN INCREASING DEMAND FOR "NEW REALISM"

Over the last ten years, pressure has mounted for a major reappraisal of the traditional security approach. The old consensus has decreased considerably and the debate has been polarized and dominated by the doves and the hawks. The peace movement is one extreme in the polarized discussion. Paradoxically, there seem to be more similarities than differences between the thinking of doves and hawks.[2] Both claim to be striving for peace and to have a better understanding of the changed international realities. Not accepting the first claim, the peace organizations contrast their positive peace with the negative peace pursued by the hawks. But despite those differences, the thinking of both schools contains many more similarities, such as : (1) their preference for worst-case analyses, as both hawks and doves like to "scare the hell" out of people; (2) their propensity to simplify reality; (3) their one-sided approach; (4) their preference for normative and prescriptive analyses; (5) their strong conformity pressures; (6) their self-righteousness; and (7) their lack of a sense of humor. One hour of listening to them frequently gives you the impression of having come 60 minutes closer to your death. Consequently, we notice an increased "peace fatigue." Many people are getting tired of the end of the world. Instead one notices a growing and healthy skepticism about the security prescriptions from the left and the right and from the traditional security establishment. More people are less inclined to endorse the blank check of an undefined peace policy or movement. The stronger the request for an operational definition of peace, the quicker peace movements and their pluralistic character tend to evaporate and leave their alternative elites exposed. Skepticism is not only reserved for the left and right, but also for the "aloofness" of the established security communities. The decline of the legitimacy of the defense policy in most Western countries is one clear indicator of this. The new realism distinguishes itself not only by a greater insistence on clarity of purpose, but also by a replacement of sentiment by pragmatism. The peace movement could, to a great extent, be explained by an aspiration gap between the rising expectations cultivated during the period of affluence and detente and the harsh confrontation with the economic recession and post-detente realities. A reluctant but gradual recognition of the constraints and complexities of international relations has forced hard questions and softened many happy assumptions. This new sense of realism was echoed in Helmut Schmidt's farewell speech. "Young people must have ideas," he said, "but idealism cannot be romantic, but must be rooted in <u>vernunft</u> (rationality)." He called for "an ethos of political pragmatism with moral intent."[5] The growing recognition of the complexity and scale of problems has given prudence a new appeal. For those younger Europeans who still support NATO, the Alliance is less an object of sentiment than of practicality. To the extent it reinforces real national and European interests (and only to that extent) it receives their support. A third characteristic of the new realism is the demand to promote rather than to react. People are getting dissatisfied with the muddling through, inertia, and short-term thinking of their governments. Most politicians' time horizons usually extends no further than the next election; they do not seem to care much about consequences that are going to affect their successors. They should be asked to develop a more anticipatory security policy. Parties and governments will have to create thinktanks to help them to anticipate the next "hot" issues and to develop visions of better security futures. Election campaigns will be less about missiles and guns but more about alternative security futures 20 to 30 years from now. Finally, the new realism distinguishes itself by a growing appreciation that a new consensus is a <u>sine qua non</u> for a better security future. Neither the extreme left, nor the extreme right, nor any other ideological pressure group appears to attract a majority of the successor generation. The term "successor generation," implying a cohesive political group with consistent views, is misleading for its members do not constitute a political monolith. They are not overwhelmingly wedded to any political party and do not wish to be political successors. A large number of them are looking for new syntheses--combinations of participation and flexibility, defense and arms control, human rights and security--that are alien to the textbooks of traditional political parties.

II. A RELUCTANT BUT GROWING AWARENESS THAT EUROPE IS AT A TURNING POINT

The European peace movements may be seen as a pole in a polarized discussion but also as an indicator of a reluctant but increasing consciousness that Europe is at a turning point. Strategic, economic, and political pressures will oblige the Western Europeans to take a greater security responsibility and speed up the integration process. The first set of perceived pressures comes from the United States. There have always been problems with respect to the security interdependence of the United States and its European allies, but in recent years they have become more acute. First of all, this is due to the continuing hegemonic recession of the United States. Although defiant under Reagan, the eagle remains entangled. At the military level, the United States' share of world military spending and personnel between 1960 and 1980 decreased from 51 percent to 28 percent. In the East-West context, at the strategic level, one can speak of parity; at the regional level, however, there is not only a perceived conventional but also a Euro-strategic imbalance. The effect has been twofold: it has undermined the credibility in Europe of the U.S. military guarantee, contributing to a latent fear of "decoupling"; second, it has raised the fear of nuclear war. Several measures intended to uphold the credibility of extended deterrence did everything but reassure a great part of the public opinion. This anxiety was further enhanced by a lack of results in arms control. Another aspect of the hegemonic recession is the United States' share in the Gross Planetary Product (GPP). In 1950, the war-ravaged Western European economies accounted for 17.3 percent of the GPP, while the United States produced 33.9 percent. By 1980 Europe's share had risen to 28.6 percent, while that of the United States had fallen to 23.3 percent.[4] This shift has contributed to a growing feeling of dissonance. The U.S. public finds it more difficult to understand that they have spent 6 percent of the GNP on security, the Europeans 3.8 percent, and the Japanese 1 percent. Concerns about equitable burden-sharing or "free riding" are increasingly becoming common ground for liberals and conservatives. Senators Sam Nunn and Ted Stevens have publicized the burden-sharing issue, and the Gramm-Rudman act may add to its impact. Another matter of concern has been the U.S. frustration about the "cocoon mentality" they find in European capitals in the face of expanded Western security problems touching all corners of the world; this has encouraged U.S. unilateralism which "has been on the rise in recent years, partly reflecting nostalgia for past American strength, but also reflecting impatience with friends and allies."[5]

The second factor that will force the Western Europeans to increase European security integration is the range of Soviet force improvements that put pressure on NATO's nuclear dilemma and cast doubt on the credibility of NATO's strategy : from the continuing improvement of Soviet forces in Eastern Europe, to the deployment of the new short-range nuclear systems, to the new intermediate range systems like the SS-20, and this despite the fact that there was no longer any need to keep Western Europe "hostage."[6] Equally disturbing are the continuous Soviet efforts to drive a wedge between the United States and its European allies and between the nonnuclear and nuclear member states of NATO. The Soviet Union offered, for example, not to aim its missiles at the Netherlands if the Dutch abstained from the installation of Cruise missiles--an incredible offer but not without some impact. This "divide and rule" approach, together with the still important gap between Soviet peace rhetoric and political-military realities, will continue to pressure the Europeans into further integration of their defense policies. A third factor that will enhance the security integration process is the realization that France and Britain are coming to terms with the limits of their power and that Western Europe as a whole is becoming conscious of its status as a "hard-pressed minority" in a rapidly changing world. The Western Europeans live in a relatively small peninsula of the vast Eurasian continent and comprise today 6 to 7 percent of the world population (and by the year 2000 only 5 percent). Europe faces growing economic competition and the international spread of technology; the diffusion of power and Third World instability; possibly closer cooperation between the Soviet Union and China; and the anti-Western nationalism of some Third World countries. To cope more efficiently with its high interdependence, sensitivity, and vulnerability, Europe will have to do something about the gap between its potential and real power. In Luigi Barzini's words, "A unified Europe could prepare itself in time for the dangerous, turbulent, and violent decades ahead, possibly the most treacherous times since the fall of the Roman empire."[7]

A last factor that has stimulated renewed interest at government and nongovernment levels in the development of an integrated European security policy is a widespread feeling among the public of political inefficacy, of being a dependent variable in the NATO decision-making process. A more integrated European approach to defense would permit a more faithful articulation of European interests and increase the identification of the population with the security of Europe, and thereby, it is felt, strengthen popular commitment to defense. In this context, it is interesting to note that the French nuclear defense policy is supported by a great majority of the French people; in Britain, a majority expressed itself against U.S. Cruise missiles, but another majority was for its own nuclear arsenal.

III. AN ADMISSION THAT EUROPEANIZATION IS NO LONGER AN ASPIRATION BUT A NECESSITY

Despite frequent flare-ups of new nationalisms and Atlanticism, there is a growing appreciation of the European level of security. The change is visible at intergovernment, and transnational levels and among public opinion. The forces for cooperation are the Eurogroup, the Independent European Program Group (IEPG), the European Community, and the Western European Union (WEU). Over the last few years, security and defense have become part of the agenda of European Political Cooperation (EPC). The political revitalization of the WEU could not have happened without a Franco-German rapprochement, and the reactivation of the IEPG would not have occurred in the absence of British and Dutch encouragement stimulated by Franco-German cohesion. Of all those forces, the EPC is expected to become the central forum for the coordination of West European foreign and security policies. In the meantime, however, the Western European Union plays the role of an active center for reflection and cooperation on security matters. Moreover, on the transnational level, one notices a significant increase in consulation and cooperation. Much of the inspiration of the Flemish Socialist party in recent years has come from "Scandilux" --a forum for discussion on security between the Social Democratic parties in Norway, Denmark and the three Benelux countries, in which the British Labour party, the French Socialist party and the German Social Democrats participate as observers. And, at the academic level, there are significantly more collaborative efforts. Recently in the Low Countries a colloquium was organized about defense integration beginning with the Benelux. At the industrial level, one notices an increase of consortia--for example, between the British Rolls Royce, the German WTU, the Italian Fiat, and the Spanish Sener to produce the engine for a future European fighter aircraft. The growing European cooperation in security matters is positively endorsed by the Eurobarometer. Comparing the answers of polls taken in 1976 and 1984, we notice an increase in support for the joint European response from 48 percent to 64 percent.[8] A strong habit of cooperation is developing. This habit does not, however, mean agreement, let alone binding decisions, but it does mean an increasing community of substance. Although Europe will continue for a long time to speak with several tongues, it is necessary to listen to the similarities in what those tongues are saying. In Atlanticist circles, the term "Europeanization" tends to provoke some apprehension, especially when it is associated with images of neutralism and independence. Of course, on the left and the right, one finds proponents of the latter policies, but these are still in the minority. There is little basis in reality or in public sentiment for speculation about a self-contained European defense separate from the United States. Total Europeanization of defense is out of the question for several reasons. First, one of the superpowers is close to Europe; in fact it is part of Europe. Insofar as it presents a threat, Europe is one of the theaters where this threat becomes effective. It is therefore crucial that the other great power should also maintain a presence there. Furthermore, the alliance is still the most cost-effective way to secure Europe's vital interests. The Atlantic Community has all the characteristics of a pluralistic security community : an awareness of common values, a shared belief in human rights as well as in social choices, and a shared commitment to the open society in which conflicts can be managed without bloodshed or threats of violence. These values and their importance in holding the Alliance together are a strong argument why the Alliance must be seen to be more than a geopolitical necessity. Its deterioration could be considered a historical regression. In most NATO countries public opinion shows little support for the neutrality/nonalignment option. In 1975, 36 percent of the German people favored neutrality versus 48 for staying in NATO. In 1982, however, given a direct choice between neutrality and NATO, 70 percent chose NATO and only 13 percent neutrality.[9] On the whole, Europeanization is not directed against the United States, but it does mean that one of its motives is the assertion of a difference, of a European way forward.[10] The logic of greater European security cooperation is compelling: it would convince the Soviet Union that there will be no opportunity either to split or to dominate Western Europe; it could lead to a greater equity in the distribution of responsibilities and costs in the Alliance and reduce the possibilities for friction between the United States and its European partners; it would mean more cost-effective defense expenditures, rationalization and procurement practices, and improvement of training and supply structures; it would discourage the temptation to shove the costs of security onto another country; it would give the Western Europeans a more influential role in international relations; and finally it might attract and hold public support among Western European peoples by demonstrating that their government's security policy stems primarily from Western European concerns and assessments.[11] Trend-reinforcing actions could be :

<u>Strengthening the institutional machinery to sustain European defense and security cooperation by</u> :

- building up the responsibility of the EC Council of Ministers of Foreign Affairs; establishing a European Community Security Council;
- giving real power to the European Parliament (the only body with legitimacy based on popular universal suffrage);
- ultimately instituting a European Cabinet responsible to the European Parliament;
- developing a yearly European security assessment, which would identify the threats to European interests, including those associated with instability and conflict outside of Europe;[12]
- inaugurating a European Arms Control and Disarmament Agency;
- Europeanizing those arms control negotiations that deal with weapons stationed on European soil (INF and MBFR);[13]

<u>Enhancing military integration by</u> :

- creating a new balance in NATO by bringing France back into the European system;
- initiating a more efficient division of labor and integration of the conventional forces;
- assuming the major responsibility for conventional ground forces and preparing for a gradual withdrawal of U.S. conventional forces (leaving a residual force of 50,000 to 100,000, as a symbol of commitment);
- creating a European Nuclear Planning Group;
- establishing European control over nuclear forces; first, in a negative sense, over U.S. nuclear forces deployed in Europe; second, European control, in a positive sense, over European nuclear forces serving the objectives of the European peoples themselves;[14]
- appointing a European to the office of Supreme Allied Commander Europe (SACEUR);
- and why not : a European defense budget?

<u>Encouraging European defense industrial cooperative ventures by</u> :

- creating an economically competitive European-scale market;
- expanding Eureka, Esprit, Hermes, and weapon cooperation through IEPG and Eurogroup;
- transferring functions and procedures from the Eurogroup to the IEPG; and extending the IEPG's functions from the limited aspect of production and procurement of equipment to the more important and fundamental questions of how much equipment to choose and to produce, that is, the search for agreement on operational doctrine.[15]

<u>Assuming the principal responsibility for resolving intra-European disputes</u> :

- Greece-Turkey
- Northern Ireland
- Gibraltar
- others (including terrorism)

IV. AN EVOLUTION FROM A LIMITED INTEREST IN SECURITY TO THE DEVELOPMENT OF A EUROPEAN STRATEGIC CULTURE

Ten years ago, with the exception of France and Britain, international security studies were not in the curriculum of universities; and only a few think tanks were concerned with strategic issues. In several countries, not even a minimal research infrastructure existed; the same was true at the European level. With respect to security and defense research, there was no European brain trust; but rather a "scatterbrained" Europe.[16] In the meantime, we have noted a near exponential growth of think tanks and publications and a slowly evolving transnational network for security and defense discussion. All of this reflects an increasing demand for more European-initiated strategic concepts. For Europeans, burden-sharing refers not only to financial and material contributions, or to the division of risks, but also to conceptual contributions. The increasing amount and variety of ideas in the European strategic marketplace is having a considerable impact on public opinion and the opinion leaders. The peace élan has given way to a greater skepticism and appreciation of political, strategic, and economic constraints.

At question is the credibility of not only establishment-type research centers but also of the products of peace research institutions. People do not want more information and analyses but more objective and credible information and analyses. These pressures are, for example, being felt in the peace research community, where we observe a split between Peace Research I and Peace Research II. Peace Research I centers saw it as their task to support the peace movement and became similar to the traditional political party study bureaus. On the other hand, Peace Research II centers insist on their political independence and the scientific character of their research products.[17] The growing strategic culture is having a positive impact on the thinking about international security; it has, for example, created a greater appreciation of the fact that any asymmetry between objective and subjective security enhances risks and that exhortations to look at the Soviet Union as a friend or as an enemy are quite irrelevant, that what counts is to attain an accurate perception of the other side; that empathy is useful but that sympathy or antipathy could be quite counterproductive. It also is having an impact on thinking about detente and deterrence. More people are conscious of the possibilities, but also of the limits of deterrence. Deterrence is seen as an arms-control measure that does not solve conflicts but prevents the use of military force. It could contribute to detente, if parallel efforts are undertaken to identify mutual military, economic, commercial, and cultural interests and to manage conflicts in a constructive way, for example, by having serious arms control negotiations; by developing mutually beneficial economic relations; and by desisting from mutual invective. Parallel to M(B)FR, one could start "Mutual Propaganda Reduction" negotiations. The growing strategic culture is not only enhancing a better appreciation of the limits of deterrence, but also of the traditional approach to detente. Opinion leaders are more conscious of the complex relationship between external and internal detente, and of the fact that authoritarian governments frequently use external insecurity as a way to legitimize their repressive regimes, and that without changes within Eastern European countries, external detente efforts can go only so far. Another aspect of the strategic culture is the realization of the difficulty in developing a widely acceptable substitute for current defense arrangements. A debate, recognizing that real strategic challenges exist, must take place in order to formulate new security policies before present policies are abandoned. This would be a decidedly preferable alternative to the recent alternation of ill-informed acquiescence and sensational hysteria, leading many opposition groups in Europe to threaten to tear down the present security structure without having evolved a credible alternative.[18]

Part of the evolving strategic culture is also a greater willingness of individual defense experts and political leaders to treat their population as adults and to try to earn support for their own policy views by stating clearly and sincerely what assumptions and intelligence have brought them to hold those views and what tradeoffs were involved in their preferred security policy. Such an approach will diminish the still strong polarization of the present debate and turn the debate into a joint search for objective criteria by which to evaluate security policies.

V. A SHIFT TO A MORE REASSURING DEFENSE APPROACH

Reassurance has become one of the key words in the European security debate. The public is demanding reassurance--that Western policies designed to provide security are not also a primary source of insecurity.[19] The term became current since Michael Howard's article in Foreign Affairs, "Reassurance and Deterrence: Western Defense in the 1980s."[20] Reassurance is not meant to be the result of political rhetoric, but the product of a given defense policy and strategic situation; in other words, it is not emphasizing peace of mind over real security. In the present debate, this concept seems to refer to (1) reassuring one's own people through bolstering their confidence in the security policy; and (2) reassuring the opponent by the development of a deterring but nonprovocative defense policy. Proposals concerning defensive defense, self-imposed restraints, the coordination of force posture and strategy changes with likely Soviet reactions, and so on are dealing with the second aim of reassurance. A great deal of the discussion focuses on the "iatrogenic" aspects of the present security policy and researches ways to escape the security dilemma. The most favored remedies are the transfer to a no (early) first-use strategy; the creation of nuclear-free zones; the reliance on a minimal (European) nuclear deterrent at sea; the development of a more defensive defense; and the energetic pursuit of arms control and confidence building.

No (Early) First Use

There is a strong consensus among some authors on raising the nuclear threshold by strengthening NATO's conventional posture. Over the years, there has been no shortage of suggestions from U.S. and European authors. The conventional menu includes, for example, the Rogers Plan, including Follow-on-Forces Attack (FOFA); William Kaufmann's nonnuclear deterrence; Steven Canby's more efficient and price-wise reorganization of NATO forces; and the European Security Study proposals to strengthen conventional deterrence. From France, we have proposals from Guy Brossolet and François Heisbourg; from Britain, David Greenwood and a series of suggestions from the British Atlantic Commission; and finally a great variety of German proposals, ranging from Horst Afheldt's chessboard to Norbert Hannig's fire barrier.[21] These proposals differ in terms of price, in their employment of emerging technologies, and in their use of offensive or defensive means of defense. But all these conventionalization plans aim at raising the nuclear threshold and the realization of a no (early) first-use strategy.

Nuclear-Free Zones

Sharing the same aim as conventionalization are the proposals for moving away from the reliance on short-range nuclear weapons. There is no consensus about their total elimination. Some argue that NATO should maintain a residual tactical and battlefield nuclear capability as a deterrent to the use of comparable Soviet systems. To make Europe not only nuclear-free, but also more nuclear-secure, several experts proposed strengthening the air defense barrier and exploring the possibility of developing effective nonnuclear antitactical missiles--a European Defense Initiative.[22]

The Reliance on a Minimal (European) Nuclear Deterrent at Sea

Nuclear weapons are not liked but seem to be accepted as a necessary evil by majorities of populations in most European countries. But the public will have to be convinced that everything is being done to minimize the likelihood of the failure of deterrence.[23] There are strong arguments for sea-basing : mobility, relative invulnerability to preemptive destruction, and lack of obvious retaliatory options against European territory inherent in land-based systems. There is also a growing demand for European control over U.S. nuclear forces. This could be achieved through providing the host governments with negative controls (double-key arrangements). The European desire for greater participation in all parts of nuclear decision-making, including U.S. strategic and arms-control policy, will increase. The growing assertive role of the Europeans marks a period during which expanding Soviet capabilities have exacerbated intra-Alliance tensions, especially regarding the chronic problem of extended deterrence. Over the longer term, those problems can only be addressed--if they are ever to be addressed--through a further integration of the Alliance or a dramatic increase of European nuclear cooperation, or even the creation of a European nuclear force. Although still somewhat taboo, the last option is receiving more attention. The French and British have occasionally floated ideas regarding nuclear cost-sharing, reflecting a certain insight into the long-term economic wisdom of continuing on an independent path. Hedley Bull suggested the establishment of a European Nuclear Planning Committee, analogous to that of NATO, to which Britain and France would report on their nuclear weapons policies, and to which other European governments could make known their concerns. The creation of a European political authority controlling nuclear forces of its own would be a further step. The purpose of a European nuclear force would not be to enable Europe to dispute world primacy with the superpowers, but rather to provide a minimum deterrent against the Soviet nuclear threat.[24] Of course, the viability of a European deterrent will, to a great extent, be a function of the compliance of the other nuclear powers with the Non-Proliferation Treaty and of the progress in strategic defense of both superpowers.

The Development of a More Defensive Defense

A favored remedy for the security dilemma is the development of a nonprovocative defense, which would not be perceived as a threat and could be elaborated in such a way that its exclusively defensive purpose becomes absolutely clear.[25] Here one finds a panoply of proposals : in Germany, we have proposals from Jochen Löser, from Horst Afheldt, and from the Social Democratic party, in Britain we have Adam Roberts and the report of the Alternative Defense Commission.[26]

Although providing a solution for part of the security problem, many of these proposals lack a conceptual grand design. In many cases, they forget the "geopolitics of peace"; they tend to be nationalistic, to overlook sea, air, and space dimensions and to neglect indirect and "out-of-area" threats, such as the possibility of blockades, the interruption of sea lanes, and so on. A second weakness of several defensive defense proposals is their unilateralist approach. None of the authors suggests a mutual and balanced transarmament between East and West, and some concede that one should not expect the Soviet Union to transarm in Eastern Europe, because that would give the latter countries a greater potential for resistance to Soviet interference.[27] A third concern is the cost factor--some of the alternatives might not be dramatically cheaper.

Energetic Pursuit of Arms Control and Confidence-Building

The last strand of a more reassuring defense policy is the energetic pursuit of arms control. Henry Kissinger's proposals in his March 1984 essay on NATO that "Europe should take over those arms control negotiations that deal with weapons stationed on European soil" (the INF and MBFR negotiations) could be considered more seriously.[28] Europeans, however, will press for more tangible arms-control and confidence-building measures. The Soviets can be expected to accept the principle of parity for Europeans as they did for SALT. Declaratory confidence-building measures will be accepted on condition that they are reinforced by procedural and constraining measures, such as the "mutual and balanced reduction of offensive defense systems."[29]

VI. AN IMPERATIVE FOR WESTERN EUROPE TO PLAY A GREATER ROLE IN A MORE COMPREHENSIVE ARMS CONTROL PROCESS

Perceptions of the Soviet system no longer appear to be the primary determinant of support for Western policy toward the Soviet Union. Rather, it appears that the attitudes toward military power, Soviet or Western, are the key factors. The growth of military power is often considered to be the primary threat to security.[30] Inevitably, the Europeans will play a more vigorous role in arms-control negotiations. While trying not to inflate the political expectations about the role of arms control, we can expect a greater demand for serious negotiations, or a narrowing of the gap between rhetoric and results and between the rationale for a given program and its justifications as a bargaining chip. Political leaders will have to justify military preparations less as a spur toward multilateral disarmament and more in terms of their intrinsic security value. Arms-control proposals should flow directly from this security rationale of identifying which capabilities would no longer be required if certain Soviet programs were discontinued. If particular systems become obsolete without such a deal, they should be withdrawn unilaterally rather than retained as a possible bargaining chip (as was the case with many battlefield nuclear weapons). This more honest approach to the arms-control problem might provide greater long-term benefits than would rhetoric about disarmament.[31] Trend-reinforcing actions could include merging of the negotiations, a search for objective criteria for evaluating arms control behavior,[32] and the creation of a Permanent Council of European Neutral States, which could mediate conflicts, provide arms-control initiatives, and facilitate arms-control agreements. Correlated with the strong interest in arms-control, is a gradual shift from a narrow (let's call it Arms Control I) to a broader definition (Arms Control II).[33] In the narrow definition, one focuses predominantly on the direct control of the military instrument, military decision-making, and military doctrine. Compared with Arms Control I, Arms Control II distinguishes itself through, first, a shift from a direct to an indirect approach to arms control. Rather than trying to directly control the military instrument, one tries to shape political and economic incentives at both international and domestic levels to reduce its usefulness. The second shift is from the East-West conflict to regional and domestic conflicts. Those conflicts are considered to differ radically from the U.S.-Soviet strategic conflicts from which Arms Control I emerged. One should not only have specialists in international relations or in area studies, but also in country studies. The third shift, very much related to the second, is the claim that domestic political aspects of international security and economic arrangements are ultimately central to shaping more profound and more effective security for the future. African, Asian, and Latin American (and European) security systems have to be shaped around domestic factors. The fourth shift characterizing Arms Control II is the focus on economic and technological factors. Attention is given to the impact of future technological advances, to the increased blurring between peaceful and military uses of science and technology, and to technology transfer. The equally great stress on the indirect and nonmilitary dimension of arms control should not be considered as a "European cop-out." Instead, it is part and parcel of a more comprehensive European security concept. Arms Control II is considered to be complementary to Arms Control I. There is a strong belief that both, if successfully pursued, could considerably increase European security.

VII. A REALIZATION THAT EUROPEANS NO LONGER HAVE THE LUXURY OF IGNORING ECONOMICS

The distinction between "high" and "low" politics is rapidly becoming academic. Security and economics will become mixed in ways unheard of two decades ago. The antinuclear movement of recent years was motivated as much by economic as by nuclear insecurity. The banners were very outspoken about it. They demanded "Disarmament for development" and "Jobs instead of arms." The economic recession guarantees an Argus-eyed defense budget. Under such difficult economic circumstances, the opportunity costs of any military spending increase will be high.[34] Economic concerns frequently lead to unsatisfactory security decisions. The INF issue would have been easier if the shared control of the missiles, once deployed, had been more explicit. The "dual-key" system would have accomplished this. For some Europeans, the overriding consideration in favor of a single-key arrangement was money. The decision against sea-basing was also driven mostly by costs. Money, in this way, was obscuring the possibility of better security arrangements.[35] Some political parties and pressure groups even have the propensity to evaluate the armed forces not so much in terms of their ability to deter and defend, but according to their capacity to perform socio-economic functions.

Another factor that reinforces the military-economic connection is the growing costs of new weapons. The cost of advanced weapons is escalating. According to Jacques Gansler, "the generation-to-generation increase in the cost of weapon systems has been consistently rising by 5 to 6 percent every year, after adjusting for inflation and annual variations in the number of weapons purchased."[36] Economics has also intruded into security as a consequence of the increased economic and trade relations with the Eastern bloc. The different approaches to economic security on the two sides of the Atlantic are a serious and growing source of conflict in the Alliance; Europe's greater dependence on trade for its economic growth and development has led to an economic security policy different from that of the United States. According to Boyce Greer, "trends in trade patterns, raw materials availability, business practices, and worldwide economic interdependence require Europeans to take a much broader view of security." As a result, they have adopted a portfolio strategy in their trade relations, spreading uncertainties over a large number of producers, including those of the Eastern bloc. This approach conflicts with U.S. restrictive tradepractices.[37]

Another example of an enduring link between economics and security is the Alliance's (minus Iceland and Japan) procedure for controlling the export of sensitive technologies to the Soviet Union and other Warsaw Pact countries. One of the most controversial areas of COCOM control concerns "dual technology" items with both civilian and military uses, some of which are also available from non-COCOM members. In making a strong case for greater protection of technology protection, the United States quantified the costs and leakages to potential adversaries. A Department of Defense publication estimated that Warsaw Pact exploitation of Western technology could have cost the Alliance between 4.6 and 7.3 billion dollars.[38] In addition, the discovery by French intelligence at the beginning of the 1980s of the cost-efficiency calculations drawn up by the Soviet military mission on Western technology transfers came as a major shock.[39]

All the above-mentioned military-economic correlations will pressure the European allies to provide more cost-effective security, to regain their position in "high-tech" research and production, to control technology transfers as effectively as possible, and to continue their portfolio trade policy. A more cost-effective security policy will be provided through increased intergovernmental and transnational cooperation in the three areas : (a) military-strategic and tactical concepts, (b) development of force structures, and (c) arms cooperation. With respect to the first area of cooperation, we can expect a gradual reduction of the differences; the Franco-German defense consultations are exemplary.[40] In the area of force structures, there will be pressures toward a new division of labor and specialization between the NATO allies. According to Ken Booth, "one will have to choose between missions, services and equipment, or alternatively have 'equal misery.'" Two analysts of NATO defense problems, Steven Canby and Ingemar Dorfer, for example, suggested that NATO allies in the central region reduce their air forces and use the money saved to strengthen their ground forces. The United States would assume the air mission dropped by the Europeans, using some of the U.S. Air Force inventory currently not programmed for European missions.[41] The third area where much efficient cooperation can be expected concerns the weapon acquisition and modernization process. Internal financial and economic pressures will make this kind of cooperation a high priority. Stronger efforts will be made for further standardization, interoperability and rationalization of weapon procurement and production. The recent upgrading of the Independent European Program Group (IEPG) and the extension of its scope to advanced technological cooperation are especially noteworthy. Planning among Britain, Germany, Italy, and Spain for a European Fighter Aircraft (EFA) is one of the 30 projects being launched or studied by European nations and European companies. For the first time, according to the New York Times, all-European objectives have replaced national designs.[42]

This trend could be reinforced considerably if the Europeans would take away the last barriers to developing a real European industrial base. Until now, the Europeans have been unable to realize any sort of European defense market. Competitive bidding frequently is still not open to foreign European firms in any given European country (at least when there is an indigenous producer in the running).[43] But here again, necessity can be expected to be the mother of invention.

VIII. AN UNDERSTANDING THAT ATTITUDES TOWARD THE EASTERN EUROPEANS MUST BE MORE DIFFERENTIATED

The growing interest in improving East-West relations has created a gradual and slow learning process about Eastern Europe. The consequences are a more nuanced picture of the Eastern Europeans and a more differentiated threat perception and approach to them. Despite the propensity of some leftist parties and pressure groups to treat the two superpowers as similar, the larger public does not yet consider both to be cut from the same cloth. The Soviet Union is perceived as an adversary and not as a benign opponent, and trust in Soviet goodwill is minimal.[44] However, Gorbachev's style of speaking softly while carrying a big stick has encouraged wider differences of interpretation--from the notion of a sinister Soviet attempt to bully the Western European allies into strategic helplessness, to the notion of the Soviet Union as a defensive, status quo power forced to compete in a perilously accelerating arms race.[45] These two images recommend very different security approaches and explain the absence of a strong consensus behind the Alliance security posture. Only in France, where the nouveaux philosophes have sensitized public opinion about the horrors of the gulag, does one find a profound anti-totalitarianism and a strong consensus on the dangers posed by Soviet power.[46]

But despite the Soviet efforts to depict themselves as just another European country, the Europeans tend to make a clear distinction between the Soviet Union and the other Eastern Europeans. For the Western Europeans, the Soviet Union is not a normal power, but a superpower with Eurasian dimensions--and the only European country that fights a war (in Afghanistan) and uses military force to keep its allies in line. The Soviet Union does not belong to the notion of Europe relevant for the majority of opinion leaders. "The reason is that Europe is perceived as consisting of small and medium-sized countries. It does not include a superpower, nor does it aspire to be one. Whatever Russia's role in the history and culture of Europe may be, the Soviet Union represents ambitions and instruments of domination that are alien to Europe today."[47] Romania, Hungary, Czechoslovakia, Poland, and East Germany are all European; but they are at least as different in culture and society as any five West European countries.

They tend to be perceived not as enemies but as hapless victims and even tacit allies. As Josef Joffe has observed, "with the Federal Republic in the vanguard, the West Europeans will fight tooth and nail against a doctrine that would seek to deter the Soviets by threatening the East Europeans and hence the ethos of Ostpolitik and detente."[48] The strongest version of the changing attitudes toward the other Eastern Europeans is expressed in the Deutschlandpolitik of the FRG. Deutschlandpolitik includes not only "low politics" (i.e., trade, transportation, energy, and environmental concerns) but also security issues. The importance of security issues within the conduct of German Ostpolitik is clearly evident in the way both German states seek to ensure the security of Germany as a whole : West German officials tend to oppose changes in military doctrine, especially when these entail increased offensive capabilities. With respect to the French nuclear weapon targeting strategy, one West German official said : "We want some sort of nuclear guarantee whereby France regards German territory, East and West, as its [Bonn's] own security area."[49]

With respect to Eastern Europe, one can expect the Western Europeans to continue an active Ostpolitik, characterized by an acceptance of territorial status quo, even if Europe will never accept total division. In the words of West German president Richard von Weizäcker, the German question wil remain open as long as a wall blocks the Brandenburg Gate. Bonds between the two Europes (and in particular between the two Germanies) will continue to grow, regardless of fluctuations in U.S.-Soviet relations, and perhaps even in spite of them.

IX. A PROGRESSION FROM A NARROW EURO-CENTRIC TO A MORE GLOBAL SECURITY AWARENESS

Another trend transforming the European security approach is a shift from inward-to outward-looking tendencies. This concern with issues outside Europe was very strong in the 1950s and 1960s, then became less outspoken. But since the end of the 1970s, the European countries gradually became aware of their interdependence, and vulnerability. A deep feeling of vulnerability is responsible for a widespread threat perception that may arise in the Western European public because of disturbances in economic-political West-South relations.[50] The false hope of isolating Europe from conflicts within and between societies outside the NATO area is disappearing. The numerous crises and wars that have erupted in the Third World since the late 1970s have raised again the problem of the link between European security and Third World contingencies, particularly when they involve energy and vital strategic minerals. In 1979 oil imports accounted for 100 percent of the total oil consumption for the Federal Republic and 80.7 percent for France, and 62 percent of the European oil imports come from the Persian Gulf. The Iran-Iraq War is a good example of such a danger. If this war had started a few years earlier, it would have strained the world oil market and the world economy much more seriously. Political terrorism has strongly reinforced the feeling of vulnerability. Middle Eastern terrorism occurs in the region itself as well as outside and often in the heart of Europe. Western European countries have been hit by the bulk of this terrorist aggression, and public opinion ranks this as a serious threat. Of all the terrorist attacks in 1984, 40.5 percent happened in Western Europe, 20.6 percent in the Middle East, 16.5 percent in Africa, 13.6 percent in South America, 2.9 percent in Central America, 1.5 percent in North America and 0.2 percent in Eastern Europe.[51]

Another factor increasing out-of-area concern is the greater involvement of the Soviet Union in the Third World. Finally, the United States feels that Europe, although dependent on other regions is leaving the job of military policing of the world to the United States, another example of U.S. perceptions of European "free-riding."[52] Increasing awareness of these pressures is making West-South relations a vital dimension in European thinking. The next decade will certainly be marked by a much more active engagement, and support of friendly regimes with political, economic, and military aid. According to Yves Berthelot, a European Südpolitik is also something desired by many Third World leaders : "They expect from Europe an openness and an acceptance which the turn-key models of neither the United States nor the Soviet Union can offer them."[53]

At the moment, Europe has its preferential system of trade with the Lomé countries. Aid from several European countries is of a financial and political nature. There is also a military dimension. The British in the early 1980s had several thousand military and civilian providing training and other defense services in Saudi Arabia, Kuwait, Oman, and other countries of the region. Oman's forces, which patrol the Straits of Hormuz, still depend on seconded British officers. France has 3,000 troops in Djibouti, 1,000 in the Central African Republic, 1,200 in Senegal, 900 in Ivory Coast, and 450 in Gabon, as well as peacekeeping troops in Lebanon and its support mission in Chad. Recently, West Germany has extended its Südpolitik from financial and economic aid to arms export. Contracts for delivery of German weapons have been signed with several Arab and African countries. Despite the more strongly felt need for unity, the European Community is still lacking the conceptual and practical instruments needed to deal coherently with emerging circumstances. There is a great need for close cooperation.[54]

Maurizio Cremasco offers an agenda for a different approach, including (a) intensification of intelligence collection in out-of-area regions and sharing it with the most concerned and involved allies; (b) a greater show of determination in addressing out-of-area crises (European solidarity is important as a political deterrent and, even though indirect, as a diplomatic aid for the country that will decide to act autonomously in an out-of-area contingency); (c) the coordination of the European rapid intervention forces; (d) a better coordination of the European crisis management centers; and (e) the coordination, for example, of European arms transfers to the Middle East, the Gulf, and North African countries in such a way that they could be utilized as an instrument to consolidate regional stability. In other words, Europe will have to consider not only the economic, but also the political impact of its arms transfer policy in any future out-of-area crises.

There will be a greater sharing of the out-of-area responsibilities with the United States. An example of such cooperation is the Western Contact Group (the United States, Britain, France, the Federal Republic, and Canada) seeking a negotiated solution to the Namibian conflict. Europeans could also contribute by allowing the United States more flexibility in the use of its forces stationed in Europe to meet threats beyond Europe.

Finally, there could be some division of responsibility. Why not transform the Mediterranean into a "sea of cooperation" among the littoral countries and Europe; negotiate superpower naval disengagement; give littoral states responsibility for Mediterranean security; formulate economic development plans (expanded to other African and Middle Eastern states); and create a Council for Mediterranean Security and Cooperation to reduce tensions and mediate conflicts (Arab-Israeli, Greek-Turkish, Lebanon)? This could serve as a model for regional cooperation in security and development. All those possible developments will, however, not change the European preference for the United Nations as an organizational framework within which to act in case of out-of-area crises. The participation of European military contingents in multilateral forces would be more likely if those forces are formed under the UN auspices and if their task is clearly one of peacekeeping or peace-building.[55]

X. A REDISCOVERY OF DEMOCRACY AS A NECESSARY FOUNDATION OF INTERNATIONAL SECURITY

Over the last few years we have observed a greater awareness of the domestic structure of security. This was brought about by a rise in the saliency of security issues and an accompanying feeling of discomfort. The many marches since the end of the 1970s reflected a decreasing public confidence in the way governments handled security. The legitimacy status of the defense policy has dropped considerably. The initial reaction of many governments was one of aloofness: this attitude, however, turned somewhat belatedly into a strong reappraisal of the social and psychological dimension of security. The whole experience strengthened the belief that a peacetime alliance of democracies is ultimately dependent for its success and survival upon widespread support and understanding by the public. Another factor leading to the reappraisal of the social and psychological dimensions of security has been the vulnerability of democracies to terrorism. The increasing number of terrorist acts increased the awareness of the need of the entire population to remain vigilant and united in the defense of democratic traditions. Finally, the importance of the domestic structure of security also became apparent in the pursuit of detente. The frustration with the results of traditional detente policy led to a more profound appreciation of the correlation of detentes--of the fact that external detente efforts (such as arms control, an improvement of trade relations, communications, etc.) cannot achieve real detente if they are not accompanied by internal detente efforts (an opening up and democratization of detente-seeking countries).

In most West European countries, the domestic scene has changed dramatically. For over three decades after World War II, the power structure for foreign policymaking in many Western European countries was a steep pyramid. At the top were the prime minister and the ministers of Foreign Affairs and Defense. Beneath them was a tiny handful of other executive branch officials and sometimes a few key legislative leaders. Not far from the top was a small, largely homogeneous "establishment" or elite of private opinion leaders, including a few academics, columnists, editorial writers, and radio/TV commentators. At the bottom of the pyramid was the general public, empowered to vote but largely inattentive to and uninformed about most foreign policy and security issues except in times of crisis. This has been changed by widescale information campaigns organized by an increased number of political pressure groups (particularly by peace organizations) and the overriding impact of media (especially television). These and other factors have made the security decision-making process more open, accountable, and responsive to the public view. Extending participation in security policy decision-making to those at the bottom of the pyramid is undoubtedly democratic, but whether it results in wise and constructive decision-making depends on the adequacy and accuracy of the information provided. It is clear that there has been a greater awareness of security issues, but it is not so evident that the quality of information or the competence to judge these matters has improved.[56]

This is partially the result of the propensity of pressure groups, of the left and right, giving a one-sided presentation of security issues, and of the passively aloof attitude of governments. But, to a great extent, radio and especially television tend to make oversimplified presentations of multifaceted problems; to omit less dramatic but important developments; to amplify "eye-catching" minority protests; to show a disproportional amount of negative news from open countries where such information is free and, for the sake of a good picture, to exaggerate the role of force in the world by focusing on colorful, violent and dramatic conflicts. Last year, for example, it was exceptional to have a day go by without a European TV channel depicting a war of yesterday, today, or the day after.

Such an informed public may be easy game for leftist or rightist demagoguery, and may urge undeservedly nasty or deceptively painless decisions on their governments. To cope with this, leaders are expected to change their passively aloof or narrow managerial approach to security issues. To create a new domestic consensus, governments will have to discuss their present and future policies more openly and within a broader political setting; and they will be expected to be clear about the assumptions and tradeoffs underlying them. In Lawrence Freedman's words, they will have to trust and tell the people.[57]

Of course, campaigns to "educate" the public at large, while worthy, will be less successful without efforts to re-create a minimum consensus among the experts and the attentive public. If one has a rough consensus, the public mood will moderate, and the rival elites will be less able to mobilize public opinion.[58] This new approach could be reinforced by creating a better infrastructure for providing security information and research services and for training security analysts. There is certainly no need for more information, but rather a great demand for credible information.

The awareness of the domestic dimension is caused not only by a concern about the diminished legitimacy of Western defense; it is also caused by a concern about detente. More opinion leaders realize that arms control and trade relations can produce only "relative" detente, and that "real" detente will never be achieved, if no changes are made at the domestic level. There is a feeling that the West is ready for a "real" detente, but that Eastern Europe is not. The achievement of "real" detente or of a security community requires a greater openness and pluralism between and within the Eastern European countries, or in Vaclav Havel's words: "Without free, self-respecting, and autonomous citizens, there can be no free and independent nations. Without internal peace, that is peace between the citizens and the state among the citizens, there can be no guarantee of external peace: a state that ignores the will and the rights of its citizens can offer no guarantee that it will respect the will and the rights of other peoples, nations and states."[59]

Consequently, one can expect a more active detente policy from Western Europe, aimed at carefully encouraging the peaceful evolution of a more open and pluralistic Eastern Europe. Negatively, that could mean a request to stop the jamming of radio and TV broadcasts, the restriction of telephone calls, limited access to Western newspapers and magazines, and the control of social contacts between Western and Eastern (including Soviet) citizens. It could also mean a Mutual and Balanced Propaganda Reduction (MBPR).

More positively, it could mean an increase in transactions. Active detente is transaction: about emigration, travel, and tourism, about scientific and cultural cooperation, and in the end, even about the common adherence to some values, such as basic human rights. The active detente approach is difficult because it touches the sensitive nerves of detente. But there is no good reason whatsoever why clear language should not be used in mutual relations, so that there is not even a hint of appeasement in the intention of detente.[60] Besides, more Europeans (including several peace organizations) are leaving behind the view that the introduction of human rights into discussions of detente complicates its realization. Democracy and detente, in the end, are mutually reinforcing.

NOTES

1. John Naisbitt, Megatrends (New York: Warner Books, 1982).

2. Luc Reychler, "The European Peace Movement: Appearance and Reality," Studia Diplomatica 34, no. 3 (1986) : 285-304.

3. "Schmidt Bows Out, Style Showing," International Herald Tribune, September 11, 1986, p. 1.

4. Herbert Block, The Planetary Product in 1980, (Washington, D.C.: U.S. Department of State, 1981).

5. Gregory Treverton, Making the Alliance Work, (London: Macmillan, 1985).

6. Wolf Graf von Baudissin, "How to Maintain Europe as One of the Safest Regions of the Globe," in West European Pacifism and the Strategy for Peace (London: Macmillan, 1985), pp. 184-192.

7. Luigi Barzini, The Europeans, (Middlesex: Penguin Books, 1983), p. 21.

8. Eurobarometer, December 23, 1984.

9. Hans Rattinger, "The Federal Republic of Germany. Much Ado about (Almost) Nothing," in The Public and the Atlantic Alliances, edited by Gregory Flynn and Hans Rattinger, (London: Rowland and Allanheld, 1985), p. 101-174.

10. Ralf Dahrendorf, "The Europeanization of Europe," in A Widening Atlantic? Domestic Changes and Foreign Policy, edited by Andrew Pierre (New York: Council on Foreign Relations, 1986), pp. 5-56.

11. See Pieter Dankert, "Europe Together, America Apart," Foreign Policy, no. 53 (Winter 1983-84): 18-33.

12. See Stanley R. Sloan, NATO's Future: Toward a New Transatlantic Bargain (Washington, D.C.: National Defense University Press, 1985).

13. Henry Kissinger, "A Plan to Restore NATO," Time, March 5, 1984, pp. 20-24.

14. See Hedley Bull, "European Self-Reliance and the Reform of NATO," in Foreign Affairs, no. 53 (Spring 1983) : 874-892.

15. See Bernard Burrows and Geoffrey Edwards The Defense of Western Europe, (London: Butterworth Scientific, 1982).

16. See Luc Reychler and Robert Rudney, "Towards a more Efficient Organization of European Security and Defense thinking," Studia Diplomatica, no. 3 (1983) : 289-310; Robert Rudney and Luc Reychler, In Search of European Security: An Assessment of the European Security and Defense Sector (Leuven: Leuven University Press, 1986).

17. Luc Reychler, "Querela Pacis: Vredesonderzoek op een keerpunt," in De Soviet-Unie en de Europese Veiligheid, Liber Amicorum V. Werck, (Leuven: Leuven University Press, 1987).

18. Philip A. G. Sabin, "Reassurance, Consensus and Controversy: The Domestic Dilemmas of European Defense," in Securing Europe's Future, edited by Stephen Flanagan and Fen Hampson (London: Croom Helm, 1986).

19. See Gregory Flynn and Hans Rattinger, eds., The Public and Atlantic Defense, (Totowa, NJ: Rowland and Allanheld, 1985).

20. Foreign Affairs, 61, no. 2 (Winter 1982-83) : 309-324.

21. Bernard Rogers, "Follow-on-Forces Attack (FOFA): Mythe en Werkelijkheid," NAVO Kroniek, no. 6 (December 1984) : 1-9; Steven Canby, "The Alliance and Europe, Part IV: Military Doctrine and Technology," in Adelphi Papers (London: IISS, 1974); "Military Reform and the Act of War," Survival, (May-June 1983) : 120-127; William Kaufmann, "Non-Nuclear Deterrences," in Alliance Security: NATO and the No-First Use Question, edited by John Steinbruner and Leon V. Segal (Washington, D.C.: Brookings Institution, 1983), pp. 43-91; ESECS, Strengthening Conventional Deterrence in Europe (New York: St. Martin's Press, 1983); Guy Brossolet and Emil Spannochi, Verteidigung ohne Schlacht, (Munich: Deutsche Taschenbuch Verlag, 1976); François Heisbourg, "Conventional Defense: Europe's Constraints and Opportunities," in The Conventional Defense of Europe: New Technologies and New Strategies edited by Andrew Pierre (New York: Council on Foreign Relations, 1986), pp. 71-111; David Greenwood, "Reshaping NATO's Defenses," Defense Minister and Chief of Staff, no. 5, (1984); The British Atlantic Commission, Diminishing the Nuclear Threat : NATO's Defense and New Technology (London, 1984); Horst Afheldt, Defensive Verteidigung (Reinbeck, 1983); Norbert Hannig, Abschreckung durch konventionelle Waffen (Berlin: Berlin Verlag, 1984); Carl F. von Weizäcker ed., Die Praxis der Defensiven Verteidigung (Hameln: Sponholtz Verlag, 1984); Andreas von Bülow, "Defensive Entanglement: An Alternative Strategy for NATO," in Pierre The Conventional Defense of Europe, pp. 112-151.

22. A. Knoth, "E.D.I.: a European Defense Initiative," Military Technology, no. 12, (1985): 18-26.

D. S. Sorensen, "Ballistic Missile Defense for Europe," Comparative Strategy 5, no. 2 (1985) : 159-78.

23. Flynn and Rattinger, The Public and Atlantic Defense, pp. 371-88.

24. Bull, "European Self-Reliance," p. 885.

25. This idea has been popularized by Johan Galtung, "Transarmament: from Offensive to Defensive Defense," Journal of Peace Research, 21, no. 2, (1984) : 127-139.

26. Jochen Löser, Weder rot noch tot, (Munich: Olzog, 1981); Socialdemokratischer Informationsdienst, "Argumente für eine alternatieve Verteidigungspolitik," Frau und Gesellschaft, (September 1982); Adam Roberts, "The Alternative Non-nuclear Way to Defend Ourselves," New Society 59, no. 1003 (February 4, 1982) : 175-177; Alternative Defense Commission, Defense Without the Bomb, (London and New York: Taylor & Francis, 1983).

27. Egbert Boeker, Europese veiligheid: alternatieven van de huidige veiligheidspolitiek (Amsterdam: VU Uitgeverij, 1986), pp. 87-95.

28. Henry Kissinger, "Plan to Restore NATO," pp. 20-24.

29. Luc Reychler, "I-CBM's, YOU-CBM's and WE-CBM's," Cahiers of the Center for Peace Research (University of Leuven), no.9 (March, 1985).

30. Flynn and & Hans Rattinger, The Public and Atlantic Defense, pp. 370-72.

31. Philip Sabin, "Reassurance, Consensus and Controversy: The Domestic Dilemmas of European Defense," in Flanagan and Hampson, Securing Europe's Future, p. 153.

32. Luc Reychler, Arms Control Evaluation: A Joint Search for Objective Criteria, unpublished paper delivered at the UN International Year of Peace Seminar, May 16-17, 1986, Kyung Hee University, Seoul, Korea.

33. See John Barton and Ryuckicki, eds., Arms Control II: A New Approach to International Security (Cambridge, MA : Oelgeschlager, Gunn & Hain Publishers, Inc., 1981).

34. Phil Williams and William Wallace, "Emerging Technologies and European Security," Survival (March-April 1984) : 70-78.

35. Treverton, Making the Alliance Work, pp. 48-49.

36. Jacques Gansler, "We Can Afford Security," Foreign Policy (Summer 1983) : p. 7.

37. Boyce Greer, "European Economic Security," in Flanagan and Hampson, Securing Europe's Future, pp. 221-241.

38. U.S. Department of Defense, "Soviet Asquistion of Militarily Significant Western Technology," (Washington, D.C. : GPO, September 1985).

39. Henri Regnard, "L'URSS et le renseignement scientifique, technique et technologique," Defense nationale (December 1983) : 107-121.

40. See Heisbourg, "Conventional Defense" pp. 71-111.

41. Sloan, NATO's Future: Toward a New Transatlantic Bargain, pp. 144-145.

42. Michael Moodie, "Managing Technological Change: An Alliance Imperative," NATO Review (August 1986) : 21-27.

43. See Heisbourg, "Conventional Defense", p. 369.

44. Flynn and Rattinger, The Public and Atlantic Defense, p. 369.

45. Philip Sabin, "Reassurance, Consensus, and Controversy,", p. 139.

46. See Pierre Hassner, "Western European Perceptions of the USSR," Daedalus 108, no. 1 (1979) : 113-150; André Glucksmann, Les maîtres penseurs (Paris: Grasset, 1977); Bernard-Henry Levy, La Barbarie à visage humain (Paris: Grasset, 1977).

47. Dahrendorf, "The Europeanization of Europe," pp. 37-38.

48. Josef Joffe, "Stability and Its Discontent: Should NATO Go Conventional?" Washington Quarterly (Fall 1984) : 136.

49. "Bonn Seeks More Influence on French Nuclear Targeting," Washington Post, April 20, 1984.

50. Gianni Bonvicini, "Security Outside NATO," unpublished paper delivered at the International Conference on the Atlantic Alliance and Its Borders Exposed to Crises, Trans-European Policy Studies Association, Brussels, July 2-3, 1986.

51. Gerd Langguth, "Origin and Goals of Terrorism in Europe," Aussenpolitik: German Foreign Affairs Review, no. 2 (1986): 162-174.

52. Gregory Treverton, Making the Alliance Work, p. 101.

53. Yves Berthelot, "The Need for a 'Südpolitik,'" Center for European Policy Studies Newsletter (Summer 1986): 5.

54. See Maurizio Cremasco, "The Do-It-Ourself Syndrome : The European Approach to the Out-of-Area Question," unpublished paper delivered at the International Conference on the Atlantic Alliance and Its Borders Exposed to Crises, Trans-European Studies Association, Brussels, July 2-3, 1986.

55. Ibid, p. 15. See also Robert Rudney, "On the Southern Flank: A Reassessment of NATO's Mediterranean Strategy," SAIS Review (Summer-Fall 1986) : 163-75.

56. See Luc Reychler, "Belgische defensie in de peiling," Cahiers of the Center of Peace Research, no. 11, (May 1985); Flynn and Rattinger, The Public and Atlantic Defense, p. 376.

57. L. Freedman, "Tell and Trust the People," in <u>Challenges to the Western Alliance</u>, edited by Joseph Godson (London: Time Books, 1984), pp. 110-113.

58. See Hans Rattinger, "The Federal Republic of Germany: Much Ado About (Almost) Nothing," <u>The Public and the Atlantic Alliance</u>, pp. 101-174.

59. Vaclav Havel, "Peace: The View from Prague," <u>New York Review of Books</u>, November 21, 1985, p. 30.

60. Dahrendorf, "The Europeanization of Europe," in <u>A Widening Atlantic</u>, p. 39-40.

INDEX

ACX Rafale Combat Aircraft 46
Aegan Sea 7, 219, 220-222, 224, 226
Afghanistan 4, 12, 50-51, 55, 75, 105, 146, 147, 217, 296
Afheldt, Eckhart 90, 100, 101
Afheldt, Horst 87, 89, 90, 93, 290, 292
Africa 36, 53-54, 58, 201-203, 204, 217, 293, 297-298
Air Forces (posture and mission) 29, 37, 45, 46-47, 55, 65, 86, 94, 95, 96, 108, 196-197, 204, 209, 220-221, 229, 240, 252-253, 261, 264, 276, 289
Airland Battle Plan 15, 24, 28, 68, 81, 83-84, 89, 94, 108 (see also Conventional Force Improvements)
Aland Plan 251
Albania 224
Algeria 192, 197, 204, 208, 212
Alliance (UK Liberals / SDP) 29, 36, 38-41
Alternative Defense Strategies 36, 83, 87, 90-92, 284, 292
Andreotti, Giulio 212, 216
Angola 51, 201-202, 204-205
Anti-Submarine Warfare (ASW) 180, 181, 201, 203, 204, 253
Anti-Tactical Ballistic Missile (ATBM) Defense 16, 41, 58, 81-82, 85, 86, 87, 94-95, 96, 108, 214-215, 291 (see also European Defense Initiative, EDI)
Apel, Hans 81
Area Defense, 84, 85-87, 90-91, 93
Area Covering Defense 87
Ariane Rocket 54
Armaments Cooperation (European) 43, 45, 47, 57, 58, 69, 84, 92, 108, 292
Arms Control 3, 11, 17, 24, 27, 39-40, 43, 47, 67, 69-73, 80, 85, 106, 118, 112, 116, 123, 126, 130, 149-152, 157, 167, 169, 172, 238, 242, 248, 252, 284, 288, 289, 290-293, 299-300
Army Forces (Posture and Mission) 25, 36, 37, 44, 46, 54-55, 57, 80, 81, 83-84, 85-86, 87-88, 91, 1 8, 168-169, 177, 196-197, 205, 228, 239, 250, 259
Atlanticists 3, 4-5, 29, 43, 83, 116-118, 120-121, 123, 129-130, 145, 151-152, 153, 155, 207, 209, 210, 286
Austria 5, 6, 8, 11, 13, 16, 17, 85, 87, 93, 147, 209, 263, 265-272, 274
Austrian State Treaty 266-267
AWACS Reconnaissance Aircraft 46, 58, 181
Azores 9, 201, 203-204

Backfire Bomber 224
Balkans 220, 223, 224
Baltic Sea 50, 138, 165, 169, 238, 242, 251
Baltrap 169, 177
Barents Sea 144, 180, 250
Bases (U.S. Military) 6, 24, 31, 35, 182, 196, 203, 212, 219
Basque Separatism 9, 33, 192, 195
Bebermeyer, Hartmut 81-82
Belgium 3, 6, 8, 13, 115-133, 176, 263, 286
Berlin 63, 71, 72, 192, 201
Booth, Ken 6, 8, 15, 17, 294
Bornholm 165, 169
British Army of the Rhine (BAOR) 6, 34, 36, 37
Brauch, Hans Günter 8, 9, 11, 14, 15, 79, 83, 85
Brossolet, Guy 57, 87, 90, 290
Brugsma, W. L. 107
Bulgaria 220, 224
Bundestag 51, 69-70, 79, 95
Bundeswehr 47, 64, 66, 68, 72, 81-83, 86, 87, 91-92, 93, 95-96

Camp David Agreements 52
Canada 84, 145, 298
Canary Islands 9, 192, 196-197, 205, 207
Carlucci, Frank 203
Cataluna 9, 192, 194-195
Center Party (Norway) 151
Central America 199, 293, 297
Central Command (U.S. Centcom) 217
Ceuta and Melilla 9, 192, 198
Chad 53-54, 55, 298
Chemical Warfare 56, 66, 80, 104, 111, 253, 260
Chemical Weapon Free Zones 71, 123, 124
Chernobyl Accident 8, 254-255
Chirac, Jacques 49-50, 55
Christian Democratic Parties 68, 94, 108,

About the Editors and Contributors

Prof. L. Reychler teaches in the Division of International Relations, Catholic University of Leuven. He is the author of <u>Patterns of Diplomatic Thinking</u> (1979) and co-author of the Atlantic Institute study, <u>NATO's Northern Allies</u> (1985), and of <u>Supermachten: USA</u> (1985). He is also directing the first comprehensive study of Belgian defense policy (to appear as a book in Dutch in 1987) and is doing research on methodology for developing objevtive criteria in arms control evaluation.

Dr. Robert Rudney is Research Associate in the Division of International Relations at Leuven. He has published a number of articles on European security issues in journals such as <u>The Washington Quarterly</u>, <u>SAIS Review</u>, <u>Orbis</u>, and <u>Strategic Review</u>. He is presently engaged in a reassessment of NATO Mediterranean strategy and an analysis of long-range French strategic thinking.
Both editors have previously collaborated on the <u>Directory Guide of European Security and Defense Research</u> (1985) and <u>In Search of European Security : An Assessment of the European Security and Defense Research Sector</u> (1986).

Dr. Ken Booth is Reader in the Department of International Politics, University College of Wales (Aberystwyth). His most recent book is <u>Law, Force and Diplomacy at Sea</u> (1985).

Dr. Hans Günter Brauch is Lecturer in the Institute for Political Science, University of Stuttgart, and Director of the Institute's Study Group on Peace Research and European Security Policy. Among many other works, he has most recently edited <u>From 'Star Wars' to Strategic Defense Initiative : European Perceptions and Assessments</u> (1986).

Dr. Christopher Coker is Lecturer in the Department of International Relations, London School of Economics, and the author of, among other works, <u>NATO, the Warsaw Pact and Africa</u> (1985) and <u>A Nation in Retreat? Britain's Defence Commitment</u> (1986).

Steven Dierckx, until recently Research Assistant in the Division of International Relations in Leuven, is now at the Georgetown School of Foreign Service.

Dr. Ib Faurby, previously at the University of Aarhus, is now Foreign Editor of <u>Politiken,</u> the largest daily morning newspaper in Denmark.

Prof. Daniel Frei teaches at the Institute of Political Science, University of Zurich, and is Director of the Swiss Institute of International Studies. He is also a member of the Council of the International Institute of Strategic Studies (IISS). Among other works, he has published <u>Risks of Unintentional Nuclear War</u> (1983) and <u>Assumptions and Perceptions in Disarmament</u> (1984).

Dr. Heinz Gärtner is Research Fellow at the Austrian Institute of International Affairs, Laxenburg. He most recently published <u>Handbuch zur Rustungskontrolle</u> (1986).

Nicole Gnesotto is Research Associate at the French Institute of International Relations, Paris, where she collaborated on numerous projects regarding European security and defense.

Gunnar Gunnarsson is the Director of the Icelandic Commission on Security and International Affairs, Reykjavik, where he recently published The Keflavik Base: Plans and Projects (1986).

Dr. Bo Huldt is Deputy Director of the Swedish Institute of International Affairs, Stockholm, and a member of the IISS Council. He has co-edited European Neutrals and the Soviet Union (1985) and Security in the North: Nordic and Superpower Perceptions (1984).

Prof. Virgilio Ilari teaches in the Faculty of Law, University of Macerata, Rome. He has recently co-authored Il pensiero militare italiano dal primo al secondo dopoguerra (1919-1949) (1985).

Prof. Patrick Keatinge is a member of the Department of Political Science, Trinity College, Dublin. He is the author of A Singular Stance: Irish Neutrality in the 1980s (1984).

Prof. Baard Bredrup Knudsen teaches in the Institute of Politcal Science, University of Oslo, and is the author of the Atlantic Institute study, Europe Versus America: Foreign Policy in the 1980s (1984).

Michel Makinsky is Secretary-General of the Study Group on International Problems and Defense, Paris. He has published widely in French defense and foreign policy jounals.

Prof. Ersin Onulduran teaches in the Department of Politcal Science, University of Ankara, and is Executive Director of the Turkish Fulbright Commission.

Antonio Sanchez-Gijon is Director of the Spanish Institute of International Questions, Madrid, and a member of the IISS Council.

Prof. Reimund Seidelmann teaches at the Institute of Political Science, University of Gissen. In 1985-86, he was Konrad Adenauer Visiting Professor in the Georgetown School of Foreign Service.

Dr. Jan G. Siccama is Research Associate in the Netherlands Institute of International Relations, The Hague. He is the author of Call-Sign AirLand Battle (1984) and Dutch contributor to NATO's Northern Allies (1985).

Alvaro Vasconcelos is Director of the Portuguese Institute for Strategic and International Studies, Lisbon, and contributor to the Atlantic Institute study of NATO's southern flank.

Prof. Thanos Veremis teaches in the Department of Political Science, University of Athens, and is one of the founders of the Hellenic Institute for Defense Studies. He is the author of the IISS <u>Adelphi Paper</u>, "Greek Security: Issues and Politics" (1982), and contributor to The Atlantic Institute study of NATO's southern flank.

Unto Vesa is Research Fellow at the Tampere Peace Research Institute and has co-edited <u>Peace Research in Finnish and Soviet Scientific Literature</u> (1983).